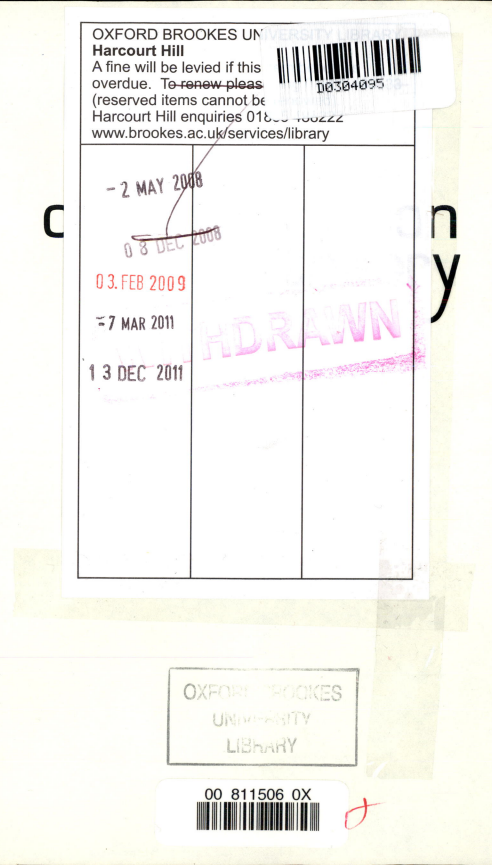

communication
theory
SECOND EDITION

edited by
C. David Mortensen

with a new introduction and
postscript by the editor

Transaction Publishers
New Brunswick (U.S.A.) and London (U.K.)

Library of Congress Catalog Number: 2007039150
ISBN: 978-1-4128-0679-4
Printed in the United States of America

Library of Congress Cataloging-in-Publication Data

Mortensen, C. David, comp.
    Basic readings in communication theory.

    Includes index.
        1. Communication—Addresses, essays, lectures.
            I. Title.

P91.25.M6   1979   301.14   2007039150
ISBN 0-06-044633-1

Contents

CONTENTS

CONTENTS

Introduction to the Transaction Edition

Few academic concepts stand the test of time. Initial hunches, assumptions, inferences, implications, statements, claims, propositions, models, theories and alternative world-views must be subject to scrutiny, criticism, and rigorous reality-testing exercises. Competing truth claims are judged against the total magnitude of measurement error. What counts in the larger equation are observable outcomes that are subject to confirmatory standards that rise above the level of chance, randomness, accident, and fortuity.

The subject of communication theory qualifies are an emergent paradigm of social inquiry. It is a relatively late entry on the academic scene. The fields of psychology, communication, and sociology are responsible for multiple contributions of applied social knowledge. Comparative theories of individuals, relations, and collective affiliations coalesce into a great triangle. Psychology provides basic knowledge derived from careful study of the individual as the basic unit of analysis. Central concerns include broad measures of genetic inheritance combined with critical interest in how early socialization promotes an acquired baseline (or set point) of physical activation, temperament, trait, mood, state, emotion, and cognition across the life span.

Psychological theory, however valuable, leaves too much out of the larger equation. Human beings are subject to powerful "individualistic" forces but not in isolation from extensive contact with other individuals across a broad spectrum of daily activities.

Communication theory may be described as a "transactional" paradigm. The interplay of speaking subjects and topical subjects remains an object of focus. Much emphasis is placed on shared conditions of mutual influence. Strategic connections between messenger and message occur insofar as the conduct of A influences the responses of (A<—>B) and as the conduct of

B influences the responses of (A<—>B). Striving subjects may produce a wide array of synchronous (concurrent) and dyachronic (successive) patterns of collective outcome. At issue is what it means for speaking subjects to initially become communicatively competent and eventually prove to be relationally compatible. High standards of communicative competence do not guarantee that optimal conditions of relational compatibility will be achieved. It is necessary, therefore, to promote better understanding of how striving individuals establish strong connections with one another.

Sociological theory provides the third dimension of the great triangle. After all, individuals do not come into direct or mediated contact with each other in a social or cultural vacuum. To the contrary, human encounters occur within a matrix of embedded communication networks and diverse communal affiliations. In effect, what participants feel, think, say, and do is subject to direct/indirect influence from their wider contracts with second and third parties who are located within or beyond the scope or province of the local community. It is also necessary to factor in the wider influence of social interaction that occur within the hierarchical ranks of diverse institutional affiliations. It does not matter whether the current context happens to be the family, education, organizations, political alliances, religious rituals, ethnic gatherings, or the use of media, technology, and conventional language across cultural/global boundaries. The important point is to approach the study of communication theory not as a self-contained enterprise but as an intersection of what human beings bring with them to a broad spectrum of social settings in the shared pursuit of desirable ends.

The subject of communication theory qualifies as an emerging paradigm. The critical analysis of human performance is both theoretical and practical. It is theoretical in the sense that all literate adults, as a consequence of their biological inheritance and early socialization, acquire the necessary and sufficient resources (capacities), abilities (knowledge), and skills (activity) to participate in collective endeavors (goal-directed behavior). At stake is the pursuit of desirable end states (optimal outcomes) and the avoidance of aversive effects (undesirable outcomes). The subject is also practical as a source of applied social knowledge. Engaged participants incorporate their own abstract theories of social interaction into a collective sense of what works out well or badly.

Public performance may give rise to unconscious modes of adaptation, accommodation, and adjustment as well to more fully conscious awareness of what transpires along the way. Stated simply, preparation and performance produce implicit and explicit standards of evaluation, appraisal, and judgment. It takes two or more separate entities to make one strong connection. Communication occurs when speaking subjects engage in multiple acts of reciprocal adaptation to their current surroundings (inter-action) and thereby are able to promote facilitating conditions of mutual influence (communication) designed to culminate in shared conditions of common ground, working agreement, and mutual understanding.

The distinction between "interaction" (a constant) and "communication" (a variable) requires labor-intensive effort to change, adapt, or respond to any external constraints and to an open confluence of opportunities. Suc-cessful interaction may produce optimal, supportive conditions of mutual adaptation. Conversely, unsuccessful interaction may promote suboptimal, subversive conditions of nonadaptation (lack of responsiveness) or acts of maladaptation (adverse reactions). In general, the possibility of effective communication (a high order achievement) is predicated on individual adaptions and reciprocal adjustments to other people, places, and things.

The study of strategic communication is directed toward the careful examination of the critical resources, abilities, and skills that make it possible for engaged participants to make sense of each other's actions. Three distinctive standards of performance assume greatest priority. It is necessary for striving subjects to be able to express themselves clearly (a coherence standard). It is also necessary for striving subjects to adapt multiple perspectives (an interpretive standard). Finally, it is also neces-sary for striving subjects to respond accuracy (a relevance standard). What qualifies as coherent, interpretive, and relevant aspects of shared inquiry all contribute to whether the participants are able to make sense of the syntacti-cal, semantic, and pragmatic dimensions of goal-directed behavior.

The conceptual framework of communication theory is grounded in utilitarian standards of efficacy, effectiveness, and progressive outcome. Five broad performance considerations provide tentative starting points for sutained inquiry. Part I examines conditions of translation, interpretation, and perspective taking from a utility standard of accuracy motivation and the corresponding risk of bias. Part II describes protracted controversy over the symbolic significance of interpersonal behavior based on internal modes of self-regulation or attributed appeals to external constraints on cognitive appraisals. Part III explains how form (structure) is imposed on content (reference). The structural features of face-to-face interaction work together to control, shape, and alter the context, content, or topics that emerge over time.

It turns out that the way participants talk to each other matters just as much as what gets talked about from one act or episode to another. Part IV examines strategic aspirations aimed toward the wider potential to establish foundational considerations of common ground, working agreement, and mutual understanding. The promise of achieving a state of genuine human understanding cannot be separated from a corresponding risk or threat of promoting a state of disagreement, misunderstanding, or problematic talk. Part V expands the range of social exchange to include broad interest in mediated, disembedded, or diffuse associations with communication networks, institutional affiliations, media effects, technological innovations, and pervasive cultural/global factors. At all levels of definition, classification, and explanation, human beings are shown to engage in protracted struggle, strife, and strain to make sense of their own distinctive position and place in the dynamic public sphere, the wider scheme of things, and the human world conceived in global, universal, and integrated terms.

Efficacious standards of goal-directed behavior are not self-evident, readily apparent, or simply obvious. Much of what transpires may register well below current thresholds of conscious awareness. Studies of sensation, perception, and conception demonstrate how difficult it can be for striving subjects to achieve facilitative conditions of working agreement, mutual understanding, and collective realization. The promise of individual achievement and social accomplishment emerges alongside the perils of perpetuating insufficient outcomes based on subversive conditions of disagreement, misunderstanding, and failure of realization.

What stands out as a routine transaction often yields to problematic conditions of maladaptation, misinterpretation, miscommunication, and misunderstanding. Sometimes faulty communication is the *source* or the *object* of problematic circumstance. Three decades of theory construction have contributed a great deal to our collective understanding of how tacit, covert, or unstated inferences and implications work together to produce the assumptive foundations on which so much personal observation and social participation is based. Faulty implications, cognitive distortions, interpersonal disruptions, and linguistic confusions are leading indicators of protracted communicative difficulties that are not effortless to recognize, deal with, or resolve one way or another. Process sensitive models show how changing contexts of communication may lead to greater appreciation of the dialectical integration of constraint and opportunity, promise and threat, praise and blame.

Personal disclosures and shared meanings unfold alongside the need to protect against the risk and threat of coercive or invasive activities aimed at extracting manipulative or calculative gains from resistant subjects. Classic references to biased perception may now, in hindsight, appear naive, in light of more refined contemporary conceptions. Nonetheless, the early work under the nominal headings of translation, interpretation, and reconstruction provide critical terminology that has been instrumental in directing theory construction toward problematic issues rather than self-evident considerations. Classic observations under the headings of context, change, feedback, transaction, social perception, appraisal, and axiom work together to reinforce the credibility and currency of foundational principles that have stood the test of time.

There is a broad need to make sense of what transpires around us. Early formulations in communication theory help to explain in what sense human beings qualify as active participants, not passive recipients, of what takes a life span to acquire. Communicative activities are fabricated, arbitrary, and capricious. The difference between success and failure is a matter of what registers more in terms of more-or-less influence rather than all-or-nothing effects. On matters of personal interpretation, there are no perfect replicates. All social constructions are fallible. The pursuit of meaning is a constant. The discovery of meaninglessness is intolerable. If everyone could somehow view the world in a singular, transparent manner, there would be no compelling reason to talk to each other at all. Dialectical tensions based of the discovery of difference, disagreement, and discrimination work to encapsulate the universal need to appreciate what makes each human being so unique and yet still so common at the same time.

The formal study of message production and message reception constitutes a vital enterprise. The compelling metaphor of "conversational detours around painful topics" is responsible for opening up an entirely new domain of applied social knowledge. One could easily trace the echo of such an astute generalization to the subsequent discovery of a wide array of substantive issues: avoidance motivations, insecure attachments, risky family bonds, communicative apprehension, reticence, shyness, defense, or desire to escape from unpleasant, unwelcome, entrapping, ot coercive modes of social exchange. Nonetheless, sufficient faith is allowed for the resolute capacity of literate human beings to overcome stress, strain, and strife in genuine, authentic ways that work to dissolve the impact of risk, threat, danger, cynicism, and bargaining in bad faith in a massively unpredictable world.

Mathematical models of information transmission have lead to greater understanding of how social interactions may be constrained by toxic or adverse environmental conditions. Early studies of channel interference (noise) eventually paved the way for more sophisticated theoretical conceptions of the common struggle to reduce uncertainly, minimize ambiguity, and reconcile differences between message sent and message received. Similarly, early studies of feedback slowly gave way to greater appreciation of the utility of positive affect as a source of stability, consistency, and predictability in what an speaking subjects in affectionate relationships may feel, think, say, or do to preserve favorable or optimal conditions that can prove to be so difficult to achieve or sustain. Conversely, the corrective significance of negative affect can be also difficult to identify, deal with, or resolve. Negative feedback, nonetheless, provides cautionary information that can lead to corrective measures designed to shift shared focus away from aversive exchanges that are predictive of escalating spirals of conflict, confusion, and relational deterioration.

No viable conception of human communication would be complete without sufficient recognition of certain critical limitations. Human conceptions are ultimately bounded by operative thresholds of sensory activation, selective attention, perspective taking, and what Simmons and McCall describe as a workable admixture of truth and error. Initial study of pragmatic conditions produced tentative axioms that are themselves a curious admixture of truth and error. The once fashionable notion that "you cannot not communicate" is no longer taken seriously. It is, in effect, one of those confusing notions that is not linguistically defensible. No one has yet devised a coherent way of saying precisely what it is that you cannot communicate. The specious argument that "behavior has no opposite" could not possibly apply to people who are inattentive, ignored, excluded, missing, forgotten or dead. More importantly, we know that a great deal of public activity occurs well outside the multiple perspectives of the respective parties themselves. Similarly, because human attention is strategic, tactical, and selective, we know that striving individuals do not pay total attention to all of the people all of the time. Attention must precede recognition. Hence, behavior that is ignored, missed, or has no impact does not and cannot, as a matter of principle, convey any information value.

So some tentative theoretical conceptions can be proven wrong. Scientific observers are no more immune from standards of falsification than persons who are not so well academically informed. Nonetheless, it is important to recognize that the classic volume, *Pragmatics of Human Communication*, was once widely regarded as the most influential and significant contribution to a field that still exists in a state of infancy. The most enduring idea can be stated in a formal proposition. Every direct human encounter produces content (subject matter) and relational definition (personal identity). It follows that the unfolding sequence of change produces emergent modes of organization, structure, and pattern but also content, referent, and objects of inquiry that extend well beyond the immediate social context. What social interaction makes manifest is by definition embedded in a more inclusive framework of the creative enterprise. Conventional language provides speaking subjects with an abstract tool to make multiple references to what may exist well beyond the horizons of the immediate social context.

The limits of human communication are bounded only by the outer limits of imagination, creativity, innovation, and discovery. Thus, human communication always occurs in an open, contingent, tentative, and provisional setting. Equally important, what registers on the surface of cognitive awareness, volition, and deliberate choice also signifies a depth dimension of metacommunication. Communication about communication equals metacommunication. The process of communication may be the subject or the object of consideration. Sometimes faulty communication is worse that no communication at all. Decades later, we know that the ability of speaking subjects to communicate well must implicate, by definition, the implicit resources, abilities, and skills to metacommunicate just as well. This means that it is necessary to make implicit or unspoken message elements both the source and object of overt and explicit modes of shared inquiry. Pathological modes of communication occur insofar as the communicative defects or incompetence of the respective parties makes it difficult, arduous, or virtually impossible to metacommunicate (effectively) about communicative difficulties (ineffectiveness). As a rule, what registers as faulty communication is also symptomatic of the inability or unwillingness to make the conditions of faulty metacommunication worthy of explicit deliberation.

The symbolic significance of human behavior also complicates matters. Protracted academic turf wars have been fought over the critical issue of what acts or episodes of shared behavior may produce at the level of signal, sign, and symbol. Broad theories of symbolic interaction are at odds with narrowly defined themes of observable behavior. On one side are abstract claims that what transpires is *representational* in definition. The other side counters that what transpires is *constitutive* in definition. The former tends to privilege the *internal* impact of message production, whereas the later tends to emphasize the *external* impact of message reception. There may be a wide degree of latitude in social exchanges that are subject to internalizing influence as against those that are subject to externalizing influences. Unsettled controversy arises because small units of social interaction can have a large impact on short-term outcomes while large units of social interaction can have a small impact on long-term consequences. In other words, the basic subunits of human behavior are not created equally. A great deal of what transpires may make no difference in the end. Conversely, a small scale act may matter most, at least when measured by social outcomes rather than individual intentions. Competing theories, classic and contemporary, are left to parcel out the magnitudes of what transpires and the cumulative impact of what matters most or least in short-term effect or long-term consequence.

One thing is certain. The significance of social interaction depends largely on what is subject to translation, interpretation, and reflection along the way. Some (weak) effects may last no longer than the duration of face-to-face interaction itself. Other (strong) effects may linger well after a given act or episode of face-to-face interaction is complete. Out of sight does not necessarily mean out of mind. Moreover, tacit, covert outcomes may prevail over explicit, overt effects and vice versa. There is, in effect, no standard yardstick or uniform measure of what makes a difference to any given participant or observer of collaborative endeavors.

The notion that reality is socially constructed is subject to alternative, even contradictory interpretation. After all, it is individuals conceived as separate, distinctive entities who generate the very conditions of what may be seen, said, touched, or moved within a distinctive social context. Moreover, human beings are biologically constructed at the moment of conception well before they can be later subject to the socialization process. Creation precedes construction. Preparation precedes performance. So whatever qualifies as socially constructed must be derived from what already has been biologically constituted. To place exclusive emphasis on nature at the expense of nurture is just as one-sided as to place exclusive emphasis on nurture at the expense of nature. We know, more clearly than before, that the nature-nurture debate is bogus. Human genes interact in dual patterns with pervasive environmental influences just as complex environmental influences work to alter genetic factors. It is for each striving subject to reconcile what is unique and distinctive with what is shared or constructed in common.

The constructive aspects of human reality are most vivid in the massively compelling realm of the public sphere. We depend on the reactions of others to tell us what we do not know or cannot observe about our own distinctive participation in salient social settings. Every specific aspects of observed behavior is subject to alternative conceptions construed at a distance and from a remote vantage point. Sensation, perception, and conception work together as an assemblage of patterns, typifications, and abstractions that recede from the immediate foreground—the here-and-how—into the remote background of communal affiliation with contemporaries, predecessors, and successors across the life span. What appears as merely subjective, internal, or individualistic is not bounded or fixed in the manner of a bottle or bucket but rather as permeated with invasive sources of objectivity that exist prior to and well after our conscious awareness of their hold over us.

Perhaps the subjective-objective split has outlived any usefulness for the same reasons that the binary distinction between nature-nurture may be dismissed out of hand. From a communicative standpoint, any serious discussion of horizon, boundary, or parameter must not be allowed to harden or rigidify into separate compartments of what is falsely located in either-or constructions: inside/outside, subjective/objective, self/other, or any other pernicious dualism. To qualify as a communicative subject or object of shared inquiry is to be open and vulnerable to the wider impact of the hidden order of things.

Personal knowledge is designed to function as an integrated set of steering mechanisms required to move, navigate, and travel across a diverse landscape of immense proportions. What qualifies as symbolic significance transcends the pull and tug of pain and pleasure, the passage of time, or movement through space. Signals (stimuli) give rise to signs (association) which cluster into symbols (concepts) which resonate and register in what matters more or less in all that matters at all. Studies of symbolic interaction are based on critical distinctions between what actually transpires and what we make of what transpires by assigning priorities to possibilities as not yet fully formulated. The most completely developed person is one who can most successfully integrate past, present, and future horizons into a coherent personal biography of a life well lived before others.

Whatever is transmitted from one source to another may be located as close, far, up, down, rapidly approaching, or slowly receding. Whatever rises above current thresholds of attention or recognition may be transposed or reclassified based on scaled comparison, rank, or scope of importance, relevance, or use to one speaking subject or another. What qualifies as salient is whatever acquires meaning, significance, or importance. These nominal definitions help to explain why little things mean a lot and why big things may make little or no difference at all. What counts are (small scale) differences that make a cumulative (large scale) difference in effect, result, or outcome. Stated differently, we see in ways the conform to the way we want, need, or desire to see the way things work out. We listen to what we are prepared to hear and disregard or ignore the rest as noise, chatter, or din. Likewise, we speak as a vivid expression of the way we strive to speak in a style that is worthy of being taken seriously.

To discover what it means to be a human being is to act upon what has taken place and thereby to invest the social world with explanation, justification, and verification. Collective engagements act upon each participant just as every individual participates in the larger collective endeavor. Strategic communication is a vivid expression of intention, interpretation, explanation, and planning directed toward the fulfillment of desirable individual achievements and distinctive social accomplishments. What registers as conscious awareness is infiltrated with inference, implication, ambiguity, rule, and multiple styles of articulation, responsiveness, and legitimacy. Social performance consists of acting in a way that leads others to suspend disbelief just long enough to be taken seriously as a credible source.

Small talk, gossip, and idle chatter provide temporal relief from concerted, strategic striving and thereby replace extrinsic motivations for intrinsic appreciation of the opportunity for speaking subjects to grow older together, alongside one another, in shared movements conceived as collective inquiry into a domain of infinite possibilities. Recorded transmission of information would be nondescript, boring, or robotic without enhanced investment in drama, magic, myth, confusion, and metacommunication. The immediacy of specific language use is infiltrated with unspoken, tacit, covert markers of solidarity and cohesion or subtle indicators of alienation and estrangement. No wonder that speaking subjects arrive at embedded social situations with prefabricated defenses to adapt, cope, or avoid what subverts rather than supports the (re)production of the larger process. The lofty promise of establishing democratic and egalitarian relations with kindred spirits is also subject to the corrosive implications of calculation and manipulation of others treated as objects.

Much depends on the delicate interaction between *what* is disclosed and the *way* it is revealed. Communicative structures may be examined on a global, macro-level of order and organization. In classic terms borrowed from transmission models, one may discover who speaks to whom about what for how long and with what effect. The dialectic tension between who speaks can only occur if others are willing to remain silent. On a small, micro-level scale, the sequential punctuation of shared events depends on turn-taking transitions in multiple ways that extend or expand the continuity of what transpires or, conversely, introduces entropy, disorder and interference. Any cross-talking, interruption, topic shift, break, or lapse of inattention may interfere or disrupt the larger process.

Sensitive communicative boundaries are permeable rather than fixed. What opens up one matter may be constrained by what closes down another matter. Nonverbal cues acts as regulatory devices and provide unspoken indicators of reservation, hesitation, and qualification. What qualifies as observed behavior may serve to illustrate, accentuate, accommodate, or dramatize what is heard, touched, or moved. Communicative silences are shown to perform multiple forms and functions that expand and enrich the pursuit of desirable valuations.

Perhaps the most important consideration is whether the resources, abilities, and skills of engaged subjects enable or disable the larger quest for greater human understanding. Personal knowledge is grounded in tacit, covert, and unspoken recognition of what registers on the surface as coherent, relevant, and useful. Pioneering studies of dyadic communication underscore the promise of socially constructed modes of working agreement, mutual understanding, and collective realization. Strong ties between striving subjects are predicated on negotiated ability and mutual willingness to place as much value on the shared recognition of relational commitments as they do to substantive matters of personal achievement and social accomplishment.

Attributed factors of credibility, support, and legitimation are also subject to the countervailing impact of discredit, devaluation, and denigration. A condition of mutual understanding promotes common recognition of strength, affection, and involvement. Conversely, a state of reciprocal misunderstanding produces shared recognition of weakness, disaffection, and disengagement. Genuine dialogue, an old-fashion term, is made possible by being fully present, by overcoming the temptation to treat others as objects for the mere sake of appearance, and to fulfill an unspecified potential for mutual affirmation.

All socially constructed theories are fallible. Communication theory is no exception. Both classic and contemporary versions may be justly faulted for the wider tendency to place greatest emphasis on participation and performance dimensions taken as self-evident. The impact of environmental constraints (affordable contingencies) on personal conduct are often described in a limp or lifeless reference to situation, setting, or context. As a consequence, critical questions of how human subjects adjust their personal styles in conjoint methods of accommodation and reciprocity are prone to leave out deeper problems of individual adaptation to pervasive environmental influences. After all, human beings do not just take into active consideration the direct or mediated presence of other human beings in situated actions. The material circumstance of what transpires need not be taken for granted or described as an inactive, inert background or backstage of foreground activity. How effectively or ineffectively engaged individuals are able to adapt to their shared surroundings may be decisive in how well or badly they respond to the personal conduct of one another.

The environment of communication is decisive. Embedded actions are not simply acted out but also acted upon. Physical conditions exert both active and passive influences on use of information, control of behavior, and relevance of meaning. Complex environmental settings that are rich in material resource may help to sustain the generative features of the transactional process. In contrast, when human environments have depleted or insufficient resources, the participants may be more adversely influenced by their common surroundings than anything else that they may feel, think, say, or do in response to one another.

Much of what transpires is situation specific. However, a larger question pertains to what is transacted when the confluence of people, places, and things leads to cross-situational outcomes that are applicable across a broad array of personal relationships, and institutional affiliations. Speaking subjects must also take into account what has taken place before their actual meeting (of minds) and what will transpire afterward. Participant and observer may also make reference to second and third parties as sources of indirect or mediated influence.

Institutional affiliations operate against standards of inclusion, exclusion, rule, and resource distribution. Face-to-face interaction that takes place in productive work settings may be enabled or disabled by the promise of recognition and reward or the threat of punishment and sanction. The ratio of constraint and opportunity is widely applicable to matters of inclusive participation or exclusive elimination of active participation. Moreover, the medium or channel of communication may impose a host of additional assumptions on message construction. What occurs within a given culture may also provide multiple pathways and passages to unexplored matters or unchartered territory. Intercultural resources may also enlarge the scope of cultural connections, adumbrations, and discoveries that enable speaking subjects to steer a smooth course through the life span. Intercultural contact may also yield to more informed participation in disparate ways of living that do not easily reveal their secrets from afar.

In the final analysis, everyone and everything is grist for the construction of communication theory. There is no inexorable reason for human beings to be at the utter mercy of language. The theories that matter most need not hold us captive to any singular, monothetic, or infallible conception of what is at stake. The value of communication theory that must not be compromised or sacrificed at any cost turns out to be the one personality trait that is precious and beyond measure—openness to disclosure and to the world at large. Human beings have, by necessity, a lifetime investment in devising viable conceptions of what transpires in a constantly changing landscape. What matters most is for literate persons to remain open, disclosive, and sufficiently courageous to share and compare a diverse range of biographical theories in a spirit of world openness. The life lessons of every participant must remain as accessible as possible to every other one in a spirit of inquiry where no one gets in the last word.

Preface

The book is designed for any introductory course that seeks to acquaint students with a basic understanding of the process of human communication. The breadth and scope of subject matter is adaptable to a number of approaches to the first course in communication, whether theoretical, practical, contemporary, or traditional in orientation. Students in performance courses will find the material useful in assessing their own participation in communicative situations; those enrolled in courses built around the insights of communication theory will find much to enrich lectures and discussions on the subject.

The readings do not presuppose any prior background or technical competence. The framework of this book provides an introduction to five topics of central interest to the field of communication theory. Part I describes the process of communication as it unfolds in face-to-face environments. Part II considers the symbolic significance of interpersonal behavior. Part III examines the organization of communicative acts and shows why human interactions tend to become more synchronous over time. Part IV explores the complex problem of understanding other people, demonstrating the tendency of understanding to become intersubjective. Part V accounts for the communicative significance of several basic human environments—communities, organizations, media, institutions, and culture.

Appreciation is due many authors, publishers, and professional associations for making this book possible and for contributing to the larger interests of a field increasingly aware of an embarrassment of riches.

C. DAVID MORTENSEN

Introduction

In seeking to understand the nature of human communication, the most complex and ennobling personal achievement of human beings, one is hardly at a loss for important subject material. Most of us spend up to 70 percent of our waking hours engaged in some form of communication. Listening and responding to the messages of others occupies much of this time; the rest is taken up by talking, reading, and writing. An additional consideration is the rich assortment of nonverbal cues. All together, the stream of verbal and nonverbal information that bombards our senses is composed of as many as 2000 distinguishable units of interaction in a single day. The kinds of interaction change constantly: morning greetings, cereal labels, bus signs, charts, traffic lights, hate stares, graffiti, coffee shop banter, gestures, laughter, and head nods. The themes are endless.

We approach the study of communication in the spirit of a search—a deeply personal and rewarding search—of ways to examine and understand various modes of communicative experience. Our objective is a broad one: It requires a working knowledge of the communication process and an understanding of the underlying forces at work in given social settings. It also requires a certain familiarity with alternative explanations for the outcomes of communication.

When one sifts through the fascinating complexities of human conduct, it is generally advisable to examine a number of possible interpretations. Something as complex and elusive as human communication does not lend itself to neat and tidy theories. Hence, it is too much to expect a study of basic theory to yield a single, unified perspective on the subject. The concept of communication theory should be taken as an umbrella term for a host of general principles and orienting statements designed to specify key relationships among given facets of communicative behavior. Underlying this vast range of theoretical ideas is a diverse assortment of concepts, insights, and research findings. Some discoveries emerge from investigations of the psychological factors involved in the production and reception of messages. Others focus on the social influences in communication, particularly the roles and crosscurrents of tension and conflict in face-to-face settings. Still others relate to the impact of the physical environment and the larger role of culture in communication.

Given the complex nature of our subject, it will be useful to approach the study of communication from a number of perspectives. The first part concerns the critical issue of how it is even possible for communication between people to occur at all. The central theme is that communication is sustained by our willingness to translate the presence of others into our own unique interpretive frame of reference. The second part builds on the foundation of Part I by focusing on the problem of human symbolism. We know that other people are vividly experienced in the "here and now"; yet as soon as information registers in our memories and activates our expectations, the reality of the present begins to point to or represent a significance that transcends the immediate moment. The task of symbolism is to show how the world of appearance is transformed into a world of personal symbols. The third part explores the tendency of face-to-face interaction to become more orderly and more organized without a corresponding loss in spontaneity. Part IV describes factors that determine the ability of persons to come to know and understand one another at an intersubjective level. A final part places the process of communication within the context of basic human environments—communities, organizations, media, institutions, and cultures. The five parts present a view of human beings becoming bound together by the reality of the messages they create for themselves and others.

Part I
THE TRANSLATION OF HUMAN EVENTS

Human language translation is often associated with the ability to understand the essential links between one language or code and another. We speak of a translator as someone who can identify a word or message in relation to a corresponding set of terms in a different linguistic system, establishing connections from say English into Spanish or from German into French. What is less widely recognized, however, is that translational activity also occurs in the ordinary use of conventional language. In fact, any person who uses language may be viewed as a translator simply because everyone uses language in unique ways. To translate means to transform, to impose one's own interpretive slant on the way things are perceived. Translation occurs, therefore, whenever people attempt to place their own unique frame of reference on some form of human experience. Such a performance need not require an exhange of words nor even any direct acknowledgment of another's presence. The concept of translation refers rather to a host of subtle and intricate acts sustained by the sheer willingness of a person to assign significance to human events.

Translation must be sustained for human communication to occur. In face-to-face environments, a communicative act involves a *source* which transmits a *message* through a *channel* to a *receiver* the responses of which provide *feedback* to the initial source of information. This definition of communication may seem self-evident, but it is also potentially misleading unless interpreted with caution. It is important to recognize that translational activity occurs within a unified and integrated field of experience. Persons ordinarily interact without making sharp distinctions between source and receiver. Such distinctions are often tentative and provisional depending upon the shifting perspectives of the participants. This same elusiveness characterizes a definition of "message."

It would be misleading to think of the exchange of a message as you would think of an exchange of some physical object. A message is not an entity or object that has an existence independent of the experiences of the people involved with it; nor is it something that is literally passed back and forth between interactants. In a strict sense, a message has no significance until some form of translation takes place. If you blink your eyes but no one notices, the movement occurred, of course, but not—and this is the crucial point—within the perspective of any other participant. From a communicative viewpoint, a message may be defined as any unit of information that functions as a link between persons who exist in a state of interaction. Informational linkages should be examined in the context of emotive or affective consequences. For instance, when the rate of information exchange is slow, the subjective feeling is often passive; when the rate is rapid, the subjective feeling is usually one of interest and excitement. The degree of change in the state of a message is directly related to the accumulative force of the translation process.

The distinction between what is available for translation and what is actually translated is quite critical. Communication is not continuously and automatically sustained just because people happen to be in each others presence. We cannot assume that everything that occurs between people in a face-to-face environment has actual communicative significance. Nor can we assume that translation occurs without breaks and disruptions. It is well documented that the human nervous system can handle only a limited amount of information and that one's field of awareness is rarely an objective sample of the information potentially available. Moreover, just because you are in the presence of someone does not mean that you are necessarily present for that other person. Attention spans and involvement levels naturally fluctuate from one moment of conversation to another. There are also inevitable "blank spots" in meaning and momentary lapses in concentration which result in the presence of one person ceasing, however momentarily, to have any informational value for another. It is at such moments that the continuity of translation may become severely strained or disrupted altogether.

The continuity of translation depends on the maintenance of two distinct but interrelated modes of interpretive activity. One is known as *decoding*, the other as *encoding*. Decoding refers to the logic or procedures used to interpret the behavior of another person, and encoding refers to the standards used to create one's own performance. We decode while listening or watching someone talk, and we encode while actively conveying information to another. Both decoding and encoding involve personal logics that help regulate and monitor performance. In formal systems of communication such as telegraphy or Morse code, the logic of translation is governed by a formal set of rules. In informal systems of expression, such as laughter or play, the logic of performance tends to be regulated more by intensity of feeling and subjective involvement.

Problems in understanding coding logic arise not only because of the complexity of factors involved in understanding other persons, but also because complex configurations of forces operate at the same time. Communication may well qualify as the most elaborate and intricate form of human experience. Everything is in a state of flux—the participants, their messages and codes, and the variations of information in their immediate surroundings. This quality of elusiveness makes the study of communication interesting, but it also creates problems. With so much going on at once, it is often difficult to know exactly what to look for and what to ignore. Since we cannot possibly consider all of the subtleties of a given act of communication, we need guidelines—basic reference points—to help us locate what is most apt to be significant. The essays in this section are designed to serve as road maps for our inquiry; each one specifies in broad terms some fundamental determinant of communicative experience. Communication occurs in a context of change, and people react differently to the forces of change. Change is threatening to some, while others find it necessary for growth. In "Communication: the Context of Change," Dean C. Barnlund examines the strategies people use in their attempts to cope with change. Among the defensive reactions are avoidance, silence, psychic withdrawal, noncommittal replies, verbal cocoons, detours, formulas, doubletalk, and isolation. Barnlund considers ways to escape these selfimposed defenses and discusses the need for communication based on mutual involvement and responsible selfdisclosure.

The problem of change is also related to the amount of information that can be processed within a given segment of time. Decoding and encoding both require the selection of certain units of information from a larger set of alternatives.To be fully intelligible, these basic units must appear in a proper sequence or pattern. We perceive change as shifting patterns of organization. In "The Mathematics of Communication," Warren Weaver examines a host of factors that determine the *potential* for accurate transfer of information from source to receiver. Historically, this essay is important in clarifying the impact of channels, noise, signals, uncertainty, and redundancy on the detection of information.

When viewed in a broader context, the concept of a channel refers to the medium used to transmit messages from source to destination. We tend to associate channels with technical apparatus —telephone switchboards, microphones, bull horns, radio transmitters, and teletype machines. Yet there are many other types of channels. Blackboards and writing paper may serve as channels of information. Seating arrangements and architecture are also channels that influence the flow of information from person to person. Channels of communication operate at all levels of society; access to a channel facilitates interaction between individuals, machines, groups, organizations, and mass audiences. From a simple morning greeting to the activities of decision-making groups and larger intercultural affiliations, channels are necessary to assure continuous access and response. In their essay "Feedback," Theodore Clevenger, Jr., and Jack Matthews analyze the web of personal contacts from the standpoint of feedback. The concept of feedback underscores the dynamic and evolving aspects of the communication process. Whether it is positive, negative, or indifferent, feedback has a profound impact on the flow of information. In ways that differ as widely as individual personalities, feedback alters the fabric of human information and the streams of reactions that are attributed to it.

The concept of human translation may be understood as a complex transaction between people and their environments. A transactional perspective emphasizes the wholistic and unifying nature of the interchange, with no sharp divisions in regard to the particulars that make the event possible. The key assumption is that everything is ultimately connected with everything else; changes tend to be dynamic and interdependent. In "A Transactional Model of Communication," Dean C. Barnlund describes the evolution of meaning that takes place in face-to-face environments. Meaning is not fixed or given; rather, it is a creative act that Barnlund describes in a model of the general forces at work in the definition of a given situation. Models are like road maps; they provide orientation and direction but not detail. Remember, too, that models—like road maps—should not be confused with the reality they represent.

Translation depends, above all else, on the ability to perceive other persons accurately. Our perceptions are not merely a passive recording of objects and events; they are an elaborate and defiant creation of meaning. As George J. Simmons and J. L. McCall demonstrate, every phase of "Social Perception and Appraisal" actively involves the perceiver in the flow of sensory data. Only a small fraction of the human environment is ever recognized, and only a selective portion of awareness ever acquires personal significance. Sensory data are constantly sorted, classified, transformed, and recorded into patterns of unique interpretation and importance. Sensory thresholds, personal perspective, and expectation all help to shape what is salient in the experience of an individual person. Ultimately, what we experience as a message is nothing less than a transformation of data, complete with a margin of error that involves estimation, misinformation, and other reflections of the peculiarities of anyone who participates in the definition of the event.

It is often said that we can stop talking but we cannot stop behaving. As Paul Watzlawick, Janet Beavivn, and Don Jackson demonstrate in "Some Tentative Axioms of Communication," it becomes impossible not to communicate to the degree that our behavior influences the perceptions of other people. These authors consider the complex interplay between message content and human relationship and show how the impact of messages depends on the nature of the relationships in which they occur. Finally, they indicate how individual viewpoints give rise to unexpected ways of defining ongoing streams of communicative experience. This essay contains many exciting, if difficult, ideas, and you may find that a careful reading will lead to important self-discoveries.

1

COMMUNICATION: THE CONTEXT OF CHANGE

Dean C. Barnlund

Among the few universals that apply to man is this: That all men—no matter of what time or place, of what talent or temperament, of what race or rank—are continually engaged in making sense out of the world about them. Man, according to Nicholas Hobbs, "has to build defenses against the absurd in the human condition and at the same time find a scheme that will make possible reasonably accurate predictions of his own behavior and of the behavior of his wife, his boss, his professor, his physician, his neighbor, and of the policeman on the corner."[1] Although men may tolerate doubt, few can tolerate meaninglessness.

To survive psychically, man must conceive a world that is fairly stable, relatively free of ambiguity, and reasonably predict-

Reprinted by permission from *Perspectives on Communication*, edited by C. E. Larson and F. E. X. Dance (Madison, Wisc.: Helix Press, 1968), pp. 24–40.

able. Some structure must be placed on the flow of impressions; events must be viewed from some perspective. Incoming sensations will be categorized, organized around some theme. Some facts will be noted and others neglected; some features will be emphasized and others minimized; certain relationships will appear reasonable, others unlikely or impossible. Meaning does not arise until experience is placed in some context.

Man is not a passive receptor, but an active agent in giving sense to sensation. The significance that any situation acquires is as much a result of what the perceiver brings to it as it is of the raw materials he finds there. Terms such as "personal constructs," "social schema," or "perceptual sets" have been used to identify the cognitive processes by which men render experience intelligible. As George Kelly notes, "Man looks at this world through transparent patterns or templets which he created and then attempted to fit over the realities of which the world is composed. The fit is not always good. But without such patterns the world appears to be such an undifferentiated homogeneity that man is unable to make any sense out of it. Even a poor fit is more helpful to him than nothing at all."[2]

As the infant matures into adulthood he gradually acquires a picture of the world he inhabits and his place within it. Pervasive orientations—of trust or suspicion, of affection or hostility—are learned early, often at considerable pain, and through communication with significant other people. Every success or failure contributes in some way to his accumulating assumptions about the world and how it operates. Such cognitive predispositions are learned unconsciously, and most people are only vaguely aware of their profound effects. Yet they are, in the view of Roger Harrison, "the most important survival equipment we have."[3] Thus it is not events themselves, but how men construe events, that determines what they will see, how they will feel, what they will think, and how they will respond.

Such perceptual biases, taken together, constitute what has been called the assumptive world of the individual. The world men get inside their heads is the only world they know. It is this symbolic world, not the real world, that they talk about, fight about, argue about, laugh about. It is this world that drives them to cooperate or compete, to love or hate. Unless this symbolic world is kept open and responsive to continuing experience, men are forced to live out their lives imprisoned within the constructs of their own invention.

The worlds men create for themselves are distinctive worlds, not the same world. Out of similar raw materials each fabricates meanings according to the dictates of his own perceptual priorities. It is not surprising that nurtured in different families, inforced by different sources, frightened by different dreams, inspired by different teachers, rewarded for different virtues, men should view the world so differently. The way men project private significance into the world can be readily illustrated. Here is a group of people asked to respond to an ordinary photograph showing adults of various ages, standing together, and looking up at a distant object. The experimenter asks, "What do you see?" "What does it mean?" Some of the viewers comment on the mood of the figures, reporting "grief," "hope," "inspiration," or "despair." Others notice the identity of the persons, describing them as "peasants," "members of a minority," "Mexicans," or "Russians." Still others see the "ages of man," a "worshipping family," or "three generations." Even at the objective level there is disagreement, some report three persons, some four, some five. When shown before lunch "hunger" is one of the first interpretations; after lunch this meaning is never assigned. A similar process of projection would seem to fit the varying reactions people have to a peace demonstration, Charles de Gaulle, a labor contract, the Hippies, or the Pill.

Two behavioral scientists, Hastorf and Cantril, studied the conflicting reactions of Princeton and Dartmouth students to a hotly contested game between their football teams. The students seemed not to have attended the same game, their perceptions were subservient to their personal loyalties. The investigators conclude: "It is inaccurate and misleading to say that different people have different attitudes toward the same 'thing.' For the 'thing' is *not* the same for different people whether the 'thing' is a football game a presidential candidate, Communism, or spinach. . . . We behave according to what we bring to the occasion, and what each of us brings to the occasion is more or less unique. And except for these significances which we bring to the occasion, the happenings around us would be meaningless occurrences, would be 'inconsequential.' "[4]

While we are continually engaged in an effort after meaning, every perception is necessarily a private and incomplete one. No one ever sees all, for each abstracts in accordance with his past experience and emerging needs. Where men construe events similarly, they can expect to understand and agree readily; where they construe events differently, agreement is more difficult. In exploring the impact of cognitive styles upon communication, Triandis found that pairs of subjects who categorized objects similarly communicated more effectively than those who categorized them differently.[5]

Paradoxically, it is these differences in perception that make communication inevitable. If men saw the same facts in the same way, there would be no reason to talk at all. Certain rituals of recognition or flattery might interrupt the silence, but there would be no experiences to share, no occasion for serious talk. There would be no experiences to share, no conflicts to negotiate. A simple experiment will demonstrate this idea. At the next conversational opportunity, agree completely, both in fact and feeling, with the person who has just expressed an opinion. (This is more difficult than many people imagine). In a matter of seconds following this restatement, the conversation will grind to a halt, or someone will change the subject. The reason is clear: Where men see and feel alike there is nothing to share. Talk is primarily a means of confronting and exploring differences. Conversation moves from disagreement to disagreement, interrupted only occasionally to note areas of momentary concurrence.

It is not only inevitable that men communicate, but fortunate that they do so. The exposure to differences through communication, painful as it sometimes is, provides the only opportunity to test our private perceptions, to construct a total picture out of our separate visions, and to find new ways of negotiating unresolved problems.

Research on decision-making illustrates how important communication is in improving human performance. Subjects in one of these studies solved a set of problems working alone, then through majority vote, and finally by discussing them in small groups.[6] The problems resembled those in everyday life; that is, they were difficult, emotionally involving, and presented a range of possible solutions. The results indicated that voting did not improve the quality of solutions reached by solitary effort, but group decisions were clearly superior to individual decisions. In some instances, groups of the least competent subjects were, through discussion, able to surpass the decisions made by the most talented person working alone. Subsequent research using executives in labor, government, education, and business confirmed these findings. Even groups composed of persons who were unable to solve *any* of the problems by themselves, made better group decisions than the most effective person working alone. That is, administrators with no ability to solve the test problems by themselves, showed superior judgment when allowed to confer. Maximizing communicative opportunity produced superior judgments.

How can we account for these results? Careful study of the recorded conversations revealed a number of contributing factors: Groups had a wider range of information so that each person benefited from the knowledge of others. Every person had his own view of the problem, and sharing these perspectives enlarged the number of possible approaches. More solutions were proposed in the groups, supplying more alternatives from which to choose. The different biases of participants prevented any subject from suffering the consequences of his own prejudices. Finally, sharing opinions led to more critical examination of proposals. Where persons worked alone they could remain blind to their own errors, but groups quickly identified mistakes that would lead to wrong decisions.

After finishing the analysis, one further question arose: Why were the groups not infallible? Although this smacked of asking why men are not perfect, the question led to new findings. Two conditions accounted for most of the group errors. In some cases the groups lacked conflict, and, assuming that unanimity proved they were correct, did not discuss the problem. In others, despite the occurrence of conflict, the subjects lacked the patience or skill to resolve it, and compromised to avoid interpersonal antagonism. The absence of conflict or the inability to explore it prevented communication and thereby diminished the quality of decisions. In the vocabulary of science, communication among mature persons may be a necessary if not a sufficient condition for personal growth and social progress.

What, then, prevents men from transforming their differences into agreements? Why are facts so often distorted and disputed? What inhibits the flow of new ideas? What produces friction? Why is there so often an undercurrent of resistance when men talk? It is, I believe, because communication nearly always implies change. Aside from common social rituals, *men nearly always talk in a context of change*. What prompts communication is the desire for someone else to see our facts, appreciate our values, share our feelings, accept our decisions. Communication is initiated, consciously or unconsciously, to change the other person. If difference is the raw material of conversation, influence is its intent.

For most people, change is threatening. It is the old and familiar that is trusted; the novel and unknown that arouses alarm. "No one," John Dewey once wrote, "discovers a new world without forsaking an old one."[7] To change is to give up cherished values, to be left defenseless and forced to assume responsibility for a new organization of experience. The degree to which fear is aroused is usually proportional to the extent to which core values are placed in question. In some cases the fears may be quite specific, and can be articulated. More commonly, the threatened person is unable to identify the reason for his anxiety. Ordinarily threat arises from the source, the content, or the manner of communicating.

The mere presence of some people produces tension. Persons who are superior in age, power, wealth, appearance, esteem may create apprehension. Secretaries and lathe operators, medical interns and practice teachers are often incapable of accurate work while supervisors are observing their performance. There is evidence that people who control the destiny of others, such as parents, teachers, supervisors, provoke ego defensive reactions, quite apart from what they may say. The same seems to be the case for those who interrupt or reverse the direction of self-growth.[8] Threatening people, Landfield found, are those who perceive us as we once were, or now are and no longer wish to be.[9] Even status signs—the policeman's uniform, the judge's gavel, the executive's desk, the physician's stethoscope, the psychologist's tests—can arouse fear before or during interpersonal encounters. The presence of threat, of course, affects the depth and accuracy of communication. A number of studies demonstrate that where superiors are feared, information is withheld or distorted.[10] Thus where human institutions proliferate status differences or personal habits aggravate them, communication may be more difficult because of the repressive context in which it occurs.

The substance of communication, that is, the subject being discussed, may also trigger defenses. A new fact tests an old fact; a new attitude challenges an existing one. New proposals may provoke fear of an unknown future, fear of possible failure, fear of loss of power or prestige. No matter how frustrating the present, its dangers are palable and familiar. Time has permitted some adjustment to them. But to turn in new directions is to face a host of uncertainties. Even consideration of a new program implies an attack on those who created or support an existing program. "We tend to maintain our cognitive structures in relatively stable form," writes Joseph Precker, "and select and interact with those who do not attack these structures." When encounters were unavoidable he found they aroused defensiveness or rejection of the attacker.[11] Any new or unassimilated thought challenges the assumptions on which behavior is based, and no one is so secure that he cannot be aroused at the thought of revising favored values. Thus, even where people are not initially hostile and try to avoid unnecessary friction, the topic, because of its emotional significance, may trigger resistance.

Beyond the source and content lies the manner in which men talk. One cannot separate who is speaking and what is talked about from the way differences are expressed. Matter and manner interact to produce meaning. Although all men have their own rhetoric, preferring some interpersonal strategies to others, a number of techniques that complicate communication can be identified.[12] Since interpersonal attitudes are conveyed both by verbal and nonverbal codes, any discrepancy in these codes may be regarded as a warning signal. Warm words are spoken in a cold voice. Frank statements are offset by calculating glances. Expressions of respect are contradicted with every interruption. Against the deceit that is evident in a confusion of codes, men become apprehensive and guarded in their own messages.

An attitude of infallibility discourges communication. The dogmatic assertion of difference leaves no opportunity for influence to move in both directions. Where men claim, "There is only one conclusion," "It all boils down to," "The only course of action is," there will be neglible exploration of differences. The person who is impervious to the words of others while demanding sympathetic consideration of his own denies his associates any significant role in communication. They are forced to disregard their experience, deny their feelings, censor their thoughts. Since unquestioned statements are untested statements, the dogmatic person appears to be more interested in triumph than in truth.

Messages that convey a manipulative purpose also subvert communication. A calculated use of argument, a carefully phrased idea, a solicitous manner, a restrained reaction, all indicate that someone is being maneuvered into a predetermined position. Sooner or later the manipulated recognizes his manipulator. He begins to feel regarded as an object, not as a person. He becomes suspicious, emotionally tense, and verbally devious himself. That the manipulator is sometimes unaware of his own desires to control others, does not reduce the threat he poses for them.

Information normally flows between communicants in both directions: The man who speaks also listens. But often, through deliberate design or personal preference, interaction is blocked so that one person sends all the messages, the other only receives them. The captain commands, the soldier obeys; the teacher lectures, the student takes notes. A letter from a friend who is an educational consultant in India illustrates how far it is possible to carry this kind of communicative irresponsibility. His daughter, raised in one of the great cattle provinces of Western Canada, is attending school in India.

> Thora came home the other day doggedly repeating to herself, "A cow is a big animal with four legs and two horns. It is the most useful of all animals. The feet of the cow are called hoofs." I asked what she was doing, repeating this over and over again, and she replied that this was nature study and she had to memorize the cow. The teacher will not tolerate improvised replies, but the

students must jump up smartly beside their desks and repeat exactly what was copied from the blackboard the day before. It sounds fantastic, but the end of the system is to stifle initiative, destroy creativity and engender a violent dislike for learning.[13]

One-way communication implies, of course, that meanings in the nervous system of one person can be deposited in the nervous system of another. Unfortunately communication is not this simple. Men differ not only in experience, but in their habits of speech as well. The only way to arrive at common meanings is through mutual accommmodation. Each must share some responsibility for calibrating his words and intentions with the other.

Limiting communication to the sending of messages impoverishes the process and renders at least one participant impotent. Studies by Leavitt and Mueller illustrate some of the difficulties that attend one-way communication.[14] Persons attempting to give even the simplest instructions found their orders were inaccurately executed, that errors of interpretation could not be corrected, and that this condition produced extremely low morale. It is not difficult to estimate the cause of the low morale: For someone to receive confusing or complicated information and to be unable to clarify it, especially when it affects his performance or status, can be unnerving. Since all messages are ambiguous in some respect, cutting off efforts to confirm their meaning leaves the receiver without protection in a potentially punishing situation.

A threatening atmosphere is probable, also, in encounters in which one of the communicants maintains considerable emotional distance. The person who is coldly objective or who refuses to disclose his own feelings is likely to be viewed with suspicion. To be treated as a set of facts or as a problem to be solved, rather than as a human being, seldom contributes to interpersonal rapport. Such emotional distancing creates, to use a phrase of Martin Buber's, an I-It rather than I-Thou relation. One is not likely to approach or expose himself to an unresponsive facade. It is safer to remain on guard in the company of those who are themselves guarded. Any verbal indiscretion or spontaneous revelation may give an advantage or be used against one. As interaction continues, participants draw farther and farther apart from any real confrontation with their differences.

The most familiar form of threat is found in a highly evaluative communication context. There is continual appraisal. Remarks are judged rather than understood. Conversation becomes cross-examination. Criticism may be given directly through attack, or indirectly through sarcasm or innuendo. (The latter, because of its ambiguity, is far harder to handle.) Compliments seem only slightly less corrupting than insults, for in one case the receiver modifies his behavior to gain further rewards and in the other to avoid further punishments. In either case he is encouraged to distort his judgment. It becomes hazardous to be honest, to be open, to be original. Ideas are suppressed and remarks tailored to fit the expectations of others. The result is to diminish honest contribution to the conversation, and to isolate men from their own experience.

A more subtle form of threat occurs when conversation is converted into a struggle over identity. At one level, talk flows around a common interest or problem; at another, communication becomes a competition for status. Participants present their credentials and challenge those of others. In organizational life these claims relate to the respective power, intelligence, skill, or rank of the communicants. But even in ordinary encounters, men verbally compete to determine who is in better physical condition, who has the more talented children, who can consume more alcohol, or who is more attractive to the opposite sex. Communication becomes an occasion for asserting and validating personal identity rather than for testing what we know. Status-reminding phrases, such as "I've devoted years to this matter," "I've had much more experience," or "You wouldn't be able to appreciate," are likely to invite reaction in kind. "Once the 'proving' syndrome is present," according to Paul Goodman, "the boys are quite out of touch with the simplest realities."[15] People who constantly remind us of who they are and of who we are—especially when who they are is superior, and who we are is inferior—threaten the concept we have of ourselves. When identity is challenged, few have enough insight or strength to resist. What might have become a productive conversation turns into an interaction of roles and of facades. Even the expression of affection can turn into a competitive affair:

> "I love you," she said.
> "I adore you," he said.
> "Love you more," she said.
> "More than what?" he said.
> "Than you love me," she said.
> "Impossible," he said.
> "Don't argue," she said.
> "I was only . . ." he said.
> "Shut up," she said.[16]

In short, the prospect of communication may threaten people for a number of reasons: Because such interactions occur with persons endowed with considerable power and status; because the underlying purpose is to change perceptions that have personal significance; because the communicative approach prevents a full and sympathetic exploration of differences. Any of these factors alone can produce an undercurrent of tension in human affairs; but in many instances all three combine to arouse deeper anxiety.

Through all there runs a common theme. Though manifested differently, there is always a challenge to the personal integrity and self-respect of the person in communication. To talk to some people is dangerous because they control what it is possible for us to be and do. To talk about some topics is hazardous for it exposes one to differences in attitude and feeling. To talk in some ways is disturbing for one must guard continually against being exposed and attacked. But it is at the intersection of all three that men are most vulnerable: Where a sensitive topic must be discussed with a powerful person in an emotionally charged atmosphere.

During a lifetime of painful encounters people acquire an extensive repertoire of defensive strategies.[17] At low levels of stress men tend to remain open to new facts, flexible in interpretation, creative in response. As the perceived threat increases, they narrow their vision, resist certain kinds of information, distort details to fit their own biases, even manufacture evidence to bolster their preconceptions. The old, whether appropriate or not, is favored over the new. Anxiety is aroused when a person, in encounters with others, confronts perceptions that are beyond his capacity to assimilate. As Gregory Bateson has suggested, "This is a terrifying moment . . . , you've been climbing up a ladder, you know it was an unsound ladder and now you're asked to step off it and you don't really know there's going to be another ladder—even if the ladder you were on was a rather unsound one. This is terror."[18] Defenses protect the individual against facts that might otherwise undermine the system of assumptions that give stability and significance to his experience.

Not all defending behavior, of course, is defensive. Most men hold tentative conclusions about many issues. We believe that certain ways of looking at the world and at ourselves have some credibility. At any time we may voice these opinions. If, when confronted with opinions that differ from our own, we can explore these differences quietly, comfortably, thoroughly, and with the aim of testing the validity of our own beliefs, then we are only defending an opinion to reach more reliable conclusions, However, if when confronted with disagreement, we find it difficult to examine that thought or feeling, find the opposing view arousing us emotionally, find our hearts racing and our minds frantically seizing upon arguments, find we cannot reply calmly and without antagonism, the reaction is probably defensive. Words are being used to protect rather than to test private judgment.

Some defensive techniques are conscious; most of them are unconscious. Each person has his own hierarchy of tactics to which he retreats when faced with inadmissible perceptions. These defenses, provoked in a context of change, constitute the major barriers to communication among men. When attacked, as Paul Tournier notes, "Each of us does his best to hide behind a shield."

> For one it is a mysterious silence which constitutes an impenetrable retreat. For another it is facile chit-chat so that we never seem to get near him. Or else, it is erudition, quotations, abstractions, theories, academic argument, technical jargon; or ready-made answers, trivialities, or sententious and patronizing advice. One hides behind his timidity, so that we cannot find anything to say to him; another behind a fine self-assurance which renders him less vulnerable. At one moment we have recourse to our intelligence, to help us to juggle with words. Later on we pretend to be stupid so that we cannot reply. . . . It is possible to hide behind one's advanced years, or behind one's university degree, one's political office, or the necessity of nursing one's reputation. A woman can hide behind her startling beauty, or behind her husband's notoriety; just as, indeed, a husband can hide behind his wife.[19]

One of the principal forms of defense is to avoid communicative contact altogether. It is unlikely that anyone reading these words has not, on some occasion, deliberately avoided certain persons. It may have been a teacher, a parent, a supervisor, or, depending on circumstances, anyone with the ability to contradict, to embarrass, to attack us. Selective communication—Whites talking with Whites, Republicans with Republicans, Generation with Generation, Physicians with Physicians—greatly reduces the prospect of having to cope with discrepant or damaging points of view.

Even when contact cannot be avoided, it is possible to resist exposure by remaining silent. If a person does not speak he cannot expose himself or his judgments to public scrutiny. By retreating into his own private world he can remain untouched by the worlds of others. Theodore Newcomb has identified the process of communicative avoidance, whether of persons or topics, as "autistic hostility."[20] Confrontation is avoided to protect prevailing attitudes. In talking together people run the risk of understanding one another, hence of having to alter existing prejudices. Fraternizing with the enemy or socializing with competitors is traditionally avoided lest one become incapable of manipulating and mistreating them on other occasions.

A kind of psychic withdrawal is also possible. In this case the person never really presents himself as he is. According to Ronald Laing. "He never quite says what he means or means what he says. The part he plays is always not quite himself."[21] Where this withdrawal occurs, there is often an undercurrent of nonverbal signs that express defensive feelings. Recent research shows that people who wish to avoid communication choose to sit at a greater distance from others than those who wish to interact.[22] Tension-reducing body movements and gestures which serve no instrumental purpose increase.[23] Any act, from smoking a cigarette to doodling on a note pad, may reflect developing resistance. Research on mutual glances shows that eye contact is reduced when persons are in competitive, embarrassing, or critical encounters with others.[24] Thus many nonverbal indicators may convey the defensive attitudes of another person.

Just short of the verbal forms of resistance lies the noncommittal reply. Such phrases as "Uh-huh," "I guess so," "Maybe," and "Oh yeah" fill the void left by a preceding question, but reveal little of the thought or feeling of the respondent. They provide an escape route, for at the moment of utterance they convey only an ambiguous neutrality; later, according to the shifting intent of the speaker, they may be given a variety of meanings.

Yet men also talk to protect themselves from confronting differences. Words become a substitute for, rather than a means to, understanding. People spin verbal cocoons around themselves that disquieting ideas cannot penetrate. One person describes it this way: "If, for example, I can talk at such an abstract level that few can determine what I am saying, then I must have high intelligence. This is especially true if no one can understand me. The reason I could not communicate was that I did not want to."[25] Men often talk compulsively, and through long and frequent repetitions leave others no chance to reflect on what was said, to explore their own reactions, or to answer objections. Opponents are overwhelmed and defeated in a rush of words. Sometimes this takes the form of counter-attacks, with the defensive person placing the burden of proof upon the opposition. By turning attention to others and exposing their weakness he hopes to hide his own vulnerability.

Conversational detours around painful topics are not uncommon. This may be done consciously, as in the case of the hostess who steers talk away from religious or political topics. More commonly it is done unconsciously by people who are unaware of the threat they seek to avoid. The essential point of a remark is disregarded, and some tangential or entirely new thought is introduced. Parents who fear discussing sex with their

children, or supervisors who prefer not to know about critical
failures of their subordinates, often rely upon topical control to
neutralize communication. Each time a threatening or sensitive
comment is made talk is turned abruptly in a new direction. Men
have become so skillful at defensively diverting conversation into
painless channels that some are able to avoid meaningful interaction
on nearly every vital issue that touches their lives.

Men also hide from each other through communicating by
formula. Talk is prompted not by inner necessity, but by social
convention. Everyone is familiar with the meaningless phrases used
in social greetings. But this same verbal game may be extended to
cover more serious encounters. Phrases are uttered and repeated,
but when examined turn out to be empty. Flattery substitutes for
frankness. There is much moralizing and sloganizing. Instead of
examining differences, communicants obscure them in large
abstractions that permit a multitude of interpretations. A kind of
double-talk preserves the illusion of confrontation while preventing
it from ever occurring. There is often an interaction of roles rather
than of persons. When people speak as parents, professors, as
physicians, or as political candidates, listeners are likely to discount
or mistrust much of what is said. Their remarks are seen as a
consequence of their position, not of their personal experience. Of
all the defenses, this currently seems most disruptive of efforts to
reach across races and generations.

There is also the use of indirection. Instead of speaking frankly,
men speak in double meanings. At the explicit level, one idea is
transmitted; at the implicit level another idea, often the opposite.
The most familiar forms include kidding and sarcasm. Humor,
despite its high reputation as a form of recreational communication,
often serves defensive and destructive ends. Verbal indirection is
almost an unassailable strategem, for anyone who takes the
implied meaning seriously may be accused of projecting false
interpretations of it. With a few oblique comments, efforts to
openly explore differences may be totally blocked.

Defensive behavior is characteristic of some men all of the
time. Everyone must build the house of his own consciousness to
interpret events around him. It is this "personal cosmology" that
stands between us and the unknown and unacceptable. With such
a guidance system events become recognizable and comprehensible.
Those who perceive reality in different terms—as everyone does—
alarm us because they shake the stability of our system. Defenses,
note Kahn and Cannell, "are designed in large part to help us to
protect ourselves against making some undesirable revelation or
against putting ourselves in an unfavorable light. They are man's

methods of defending himself against the possibility of being made to look ridiculous or inadequate. And in most cases we are not content merely to avoid looking inadequate, we also want to appear intelligent, thoughtful, or in possession of whatever other virtues are relevant to the situation from our point of view."[26] Confronted with difference, men may deny it, obscure it, confuse it, or evade it in order to protect their own assumptive world against the meanings of others.

Unfortunately, to the extent that men insulate themselves from the worlds that others know, they are imprisoned within their own defenses. They become blind to the limits of their own knowledge, and incapable of incorporating new experience. They are forced to repeat the same old ways of thinking because they result from the same old ways of seeing. Interaction loses the significance it might have. "This shutup self, being isolated," writes Ronald Laing, "is unable to be enriched by outer experience, and so the whole inner world comes to be more and more impoverished, until the individual may come to feel he is merely a vacuum."[27] Without access to the experience and perceptions of others, the individual deprives himself of the raw material of growth. Defenses corrupt the only process by which we might extend and deepen our experience. Until we can hear what others say, we cannot grow wiser ourselves.

To appreciate the full significance of incomplete communication in organizational life, another factor must be added. It is this: The higher men rise, the fewer the problems with which they have direct contact, and the more they must rely on the words of others. Unfortunately, as men assume greater power their higher status increases the difficulty in obtaining reliable accounts from others, and increases their own capacity to shield themselves from unpleasant information. Given a superior who prefers reassurance and a subordinate who fears to speak out, there is every reason to expect censored and distorted reports. Yet is it imperative that those in high places cope with realities rather than defensive fantasies.

What, then, can be done to create conditions in which men are not afraid to communicate? How can the destructive cycle of threat and defense be broken? Are there conditions that encourage men to respond to each other more creatively, so that differences can widen and deepen human experience? Can self-protective encounters be converted into self-enriching ones?

To reduce defenses, threat must be reduced. Such threats, as suggested earlier, spring from the source, the content, or the manner of communicating. Where it is the person who threatens, it is usually because differences in status exist, are introduced, or accentuated. For this reason groups and organizations ought regularly to review their internal structure to see if differences in authority are essential to or destructive of effective performance. Differences in rank are often multiplied or emphasized without regard for their inhibiting and distorting effects on the flow of information and ideas. Studies of organizational behavior suggest that those marked by severe competition for status often have serious problems of communication.[28] Status barriers, however, may dissolve in the face of facilitating interpersonal attitudes.

Where the threat arises from different perceptions of problems and policies there are ways of rendering these differences less disruptive. Proposals can be made as specific as possible to counteract fears of an uncertain future; they can be introduced gradually to reduce the amount of risk involved; they can be initiated experimentally so that failure can be remedied; they can include guarantees against the loss of personal prestige and power. Every new idea, since it is an implicit criticism of an old idea, may disturb those responsible for the prevailing view; but it is possible to innovate without attacking unnecessarily those associated with former policies.

Neither the source nor the subject, however, is as critical as the climate in which interaction occurs. Communication as a physical fact produces no magic: Words can lead toward destructive or productive outcomes depending on the attitudes that surround them. Where the object is to secure as complete, as frank, as creative an interaction of experience as possible, the following attitudes would seem to promote communication in a context of change.

Human understanding is facilitated where there is a willingness to become involved with the other person. It means to treat him as a person, not as an object; to see him as a man, not as a number, a vote, or a factor in production. It is to regard him as a value in himself, rather than a means to some other value. It is to prize his experience and his needs. Most of all, it is to consider and explore his feelings. In practical terms it means one is willing to take time, to avoid interruptions, to be communicatively accessible. Dozens of superficial and fragmentary conversations do not encourage a meeting of minds. There must be as much respect for his experience as we expect for our own. Since it is the loss of self-esteem that men fear most, such respect can do much to reduce the motivation for defensive interaction.

Communication is facilitated when there is a frank and full exposure of self. It is when men interact in role, speaking as they feel, that communication is often corrupted. In the words of Sidney Jourard, "We say that we feel things we do not feel. We say that we did things we did not do. We say that we believe things we do not believe."[29] We present, in short, persons that we are not. As one person retreats behind his false self—performing his lines, weighing his words, calculating his movements—the danger signs are recognized. Rarely does the other person fail to detect them. In an atmosphere of deceit, his suspicion is aroused and defenses go up. He begins to edit his thoughts, censor his feelings, manipulate his responses, and assume the rituals and mask of his office. Not only does communication stop, but mistrust lingers on to corrupt future encounters. Afterwards each says to himself, "I don't believe him," "I don't trust him," "I will avoid him in the future." This pattern accounts for much of the communicative isolation of parent and child, teacher and student, Black and White. It may also be the reason why interaction is so often accompanied by an undercurrent of strain, for it takes considerable energy to sustain both a false and a real self.

In contrast, defenses tend to disintegrate in an atmosphere of honesty. There are no inconsistent messages. What is said is what is known, what is felt, what is thought. Pretenses are dropped and contrivance ceases. Instead the effort is to express, as spontaneously and accurately as possible, the flow of thought and feeling. In the absence of deceit, there is less reason to distort or deny in reply. A genuine interaction of experience can occur. Much of the tension goes out of personal relationships. Communication becomes something to seek rather than something to avoid. Through talk it becomes possible to learn more about ourselves and more about the issues we face as men.

The willingness to be transparent leads to a further condition that promotes healthy interaction. In social encounters men see their purposes in many ways: Some as manipulative, some as dominating, some as competitive, some as impressive, some as protective. People seldom talk for more than a few moments without exposing their underlying communicative strategy. Most of our defenses are designed to prevent damage to the symbolic self that occurs in the face of these depreciating motives. But an attitude of mutuality can also be heard, and heard loud and clear. This attitude is manifest in many ways: Whenever there is patience rather than impatience, whenever there is a tentative rather than dogmatic assertion of opinion, whenever there is curiosity rather than indifference for alternative views, whenever there is a creative rather than inflexible approach to arguments. Where there is a feeling of mutual involvement among communicative equals, defenses are unlikely to interfere with the pursuit of new meanings.

Understanding is also promoted when people assume their full communicative responsibilities. Now what does that mean? Simply that one will listen as well as speak, that he will try to understand as well as try to be understood. There is little doubt among specialists that listening is by far the harder communicative task. Then why is it so often assigned to the younger, the weaker, the less competent? Usually it is the student who must understand the teacher, the employee who must understand the supervisor, the patient who must understand the doctor, the young who must understand the old. In response to an essay "On Being an American Parent," one college student wrote the following lines as part of a "Letter to the Editor."

> Your paragraph under "Listen" very well sums up what I'm trying to say. I could never tell my parents anything, it was always "I'm too busy . . . too tired . . . that's not important . . . that's stupid . . . can't you think of better things. . . ." As a result, I stopped telling my parents anything. All communication ceased.
>
> I have only one important plea to parents . . . *Listen, listen,* and *listen again.* Please, I know the consequences and I'm in hell.[30]

In instance after instance the heavier communicative burden is forced upon the weaker, and the easier load is assumed by the stronger. It is not surprising that such exploitation should occasionally arouse defensive reactions.

Research in the behavioral sciences gives consistent support to the principle that two-way, as compared with one-way, communication produces more accurate understanding, stimulates a greater flow of ideas, corrects misunderstandings more efficiently, and yields a higher level of morale. Why, then, do men so often block feedback? Partly out of habit. In many interpersonal encounters listening means no more than a passive monitoring of the conversation, a time in which men prepare their next remarks. Partly we prevent feedback because of fear. It is upsetting to find how confusing our instructions have been, how inconsistent our words and deeds, how irritating our actions sometimes are. Where receivers have been given a chance to talk back after long periods of following orders, they usually respond at first with hostility. Yet the easing of communicative restrictions, in most instances, quickly restores a constructive and cooperative relationship.

On the national scene these days we hear much about the need for more dialogue. Many are skeptical of this demand. Has there not always been the right of free speech, free access to the platform for every advocate? True, but freedom to speak is not freedom to influence. For genuine dialogue there must be someone to

talk, but also someone to listen. To speak is an empty freedom—
as racial clashes and political demonstrations should remind us—
unless there is someone willing to hear. And to reply in ways that
prove that what was said has made a difference.

Within the intimacy of the therapeutic relationship—where
communicative principles are tested at every moment—this premise
seems equally valid. Again, it is not the talking that appears to
accomplish the cure but association with someone capable of
hearing. To be with someone who is truly willing to listen, who
concentrates sensitively on all that is said, is no longer to need
defenses. Such listening, of course, involves the risk of change. No
one can leave the safety and comfort of his own assumptive world
and enter that of another without running the risk of having his
own commitments questioned. Not only questioned, but perhaps
altered. To communicate fully with another human being, since it
entails the risk of being changed oneself, is to perform what may
be the most courageous of all human acts.

Communication is facilitated when there is a capacity to
create a non-evaluative atmosphere. Defenses are provoked not so
much by the expectation of difference, as by the expectation of
criticism. "The major barrier to interpersonal communication," Carl
Rogers has suggested, "is our very natural tendency to judge, to
evaluate, to approve, or disapprove the statement of the other
person or group." Under the surface of many, if not most,
conversations there runs an undercurrent of censure. If we differ,
one of us, usually the other fellow, must be wrong, must be stupid,
must be incompetent, must be malicious. In so polarized a setting,
where conversation becomes cross-examination, it is not surprising
that men speak cautiously, incompletely, ambiguously; it is not
surprising that with such critical preoccupations they listen
suspiciously, partially, vaguely, to what is actually said. "The
stronger our feelings," continues Rogers, "the more likely it is
there will be no mutual element in the communication. There will
be just two ideas, two feelings, two judgments, missing each other
in psychological space."[31] When people recognize that they will not
be forced beyond their own limits, when they see that their
meanings will be respected and understood, when they feel that
others will help in exploring difficult or dangerous experiences,
they can begin to drop their defenses.

As the atmosphere becomes less evaluative, men are more
likely to express and examine a wider range of differences without
distortion. Where the intent is to comprehend rather than to
attack, communication becomes a source of benefit rather than
harm. In a permissive climate people feel comfortable, feel

respected, feel secure enough to talk openly. "Conveying assurance
of understanding," writes Anatol Rapoport, "is the first step in the
removal of threat."[32] Research done on the attributes of helpful
people indicates that they are easy to talk with, maximize areas
open to discussion, minimize embarrassment, and seldom
disapprove.[33]

In such trusting relationships men can develop empathy. They
can participate in each other's experience, sharing the assumptions,
and the meanings that events hold for them. This is not to insist
that evaluation always be avoided, for decisions must be made
about facts, theories, policies, even people. It is only to argue that
mutual understanding should precede mutual evaluation. Problems
cannot be solved until they are understood, and highly critical
attitudes inhibit the communication of problems.

It appears that whether communication promotes
understanding and affection, or blocks understanding and builds
defenses, depends more on the assumptions than on the techniques
of the communicator.[34] Or, rather, it is to say that technique cannot
be divorced from assumption: As men assume, so will they
communicate. Where men presume their knowledge to be complete
or infallible, there is no communication or only a manipulative
concern for others. Where men presume—as we know to be the
case—that their knowledge is fragmentary and uncertain, genuine
communication can occur. To recognize the limits of one's own
facts and feelings is to become curious about the facts and feelings
of others. At such moments men are likely to be open, honest,
trusting, empathic, not because of some altruistic motive, but
because it is the only way to correct and to extend their own
perceptions of the world. Each stands to gain: The speaker
because he can test what he believes and because it is rewarding
to be understood; the listener because he can broaden his
experience and because it is stimulating to understand.

Every significant human crisis begins or ends in a
communicative encounter of one kind or another. It is here that
differences are voiced. It is here that differences threaten. It is
here that words may be heard. It is here that understanding may
be reached, that men may cross the distance that divides them.
"In my civilization," wrote Antoine de Saint-Exupèry, "he who is
different from me does not impoverish me—he enriches me."[35]

Notes

1. Hobbs, Nicholas, "Sources of Gain in Psychotherapy," *American
   Psychologist* 17, (1962):74.
2. Kelly, George A., *The Psychology of Personal Constructs* (New
   York: Norton, 1955), pp. 8–9.

3. Harrison, Roger, "Defenses and the Need to Know," in Paul Lawrence and George V. Seiler (eds.), *Organizational Behavior and Administration* (Homewood, Ill.: Irwin and Dorsey) pp. 267.

4. Hastorf, Albert, and Cantril, Hadley, "They Saw a Game: A Case Study," *Journal of Abnormal and Social Psychology* 49, (1954):129–134.

5. Triandis, Harry, "Cognitive Similarity and Communication in a Dyad," *Human Relations* 13, (1960):175–183.

6. Barnlund, Dean C., "A Comparative Study of Individual, Majority and Group Judgment," *Journal of Abnormal and Social Psychology* 58, (1959):55–60.

7. Dewey, John, *Experience and Nature* (Chicago: Open Court, 1925), p. 246.

8. Hurwitz, Jacob, Zander, Alvin, and Hymovitch, Bernard, Some Effects of Power on the Relations among Group Members," in D. Cartwright and A. Zander (eds.), *Group Dynamics: Research and Theory* (New York: Harper & Row, 1960).

9. Landfield, A., "A Movement Interpretation of Threat," *Journal of Abnormal and Social Psychology* 49, (1954):529–532.

10. See, for example, John Thibaut and Henry Riecken, "Authoritarianism, Status, and the Communication of Aggression," *Human Relations* 8, (1955):113–133; Arthur Cohen, "Upward Communication in Experimentally Created Hierarchies," *Human Relations* 11, (1958):41–53; William Read, "Upward Communication in Industrial Hierarchies," *Human Relations* 15, (1962):3–16.

11. Precker, Joseph, "The Automorphic Process and the Attribution of Values," *Journal of Personality* 21, (1953): 356–363.

12. Efforts to identify nonfacilitating techniques may be found in Jack Gibb, "Defensive Communication," *Journal of Communication* 11, (1961):141–148; in Frank Miyamoto, Laura Crowell, and Allan Katcher, "Communicant Behavior in Small Groups," *Journal of Communication* 7, (1957):151–160; and in Philip Lichtenberg, "Emotional Maturity as Manifest in Ideational Interaction," *Journal of Abnormal and Social Psychology* 51, (1955): 298–301.

13. Personal correspondence.

14. Leavitt, Harold, and Mueller, Ronald, "Some Effects of Feedback on Communication," *Human Relations* 4, (1951): 401–410.

15. Goodman, Paul, *Growing Up Absurd* (New York: Random House, 1960), p. 206.

16. Ciardi, John, "Manner of Speaking," *Saturday Review*, 23 December, 1967.
17. Men defend themselves intrapersonally as well as interpersonally. The principal forms of such inner defense—introjection, identification, repression, denial, regression, reaction-formation, displacement—will not be treated here. It is the character of defensive behavior in interpersonal relationships that is our major concern.
18. Bateson, Gregory, lecture at San Francisco State College, 1959.
19. Tournier, Paul, *The Meaning of Persons* (New York: Harper & Row, 1957), p. 219.
20. Newcomb, Theodore, "Autistic Hostility and Social Reality," *Human Relations* 1, (1947):69–86.
21. Laing, Ronald, *The Divided Self* (Chicago: Quadrangle,1960).
22. Rosenfeld, Howard, "Effect of Approval-Seeking Induction on Interpersonal Proximity," *Psychological Reports* 17, (1965): 120–122.
23. Krout, Maurice, "An Experimental Attempt to Determine the Significance of Unconscious Manual Symbolic Movements," *Journal of General Psychology* 51, (1954):121–152.
24. Exline, Ralph, and Winters, Lewis, "Affective Relations and Mutual Glances in Dyads," in S. Tomkins and C. Izard (eds.), *Affect, Cognition, and Personality* (New York: Springer, 1965).
25. Personal correspondence.
26. Kahn, Robert, and Cannell, Charles, *The Dynamics of Interviewing* (New York: Wiley, 1967), p. 6.
27. Laing, *Divided Self*, p. 75.
28. Read, "Upward Communication."
29. Jourard, Sidney, *The Transparent Self* (New York: Van Nostrand Reinhold, 1964).
30. *Time*, 22 December, 1967, p. 7.
31. Rogers, Carl, *On Becoming a Person* (Boston: Houghton Mifflin, 1961), p. 54.
32. Rapoport, Anatol, *Fights, Games and Debates* (Ann Arbor: University of Michigan Press, 1960).
33. Thomas, Edwin, Polansky, Norman, and Kounin, Jacob, "The Expected Behavior of a Potentially Helpful Person," *Human Relations* 8, (1955):165–174.
34. Barnlund, Dean C., *Interpersonal Communication* (Boston: Houghton Mifflin, 1968), pp. 613–641.
35. Saint Exupéry, Antoine de, *Airman's Odyssey* (New York: Reynal, 1939), p. 420.

2

THE MATHEMATICS OF COMMUNICATION

Warren Weaver

How do men communicate, one with another? The spoken word, either direct or by telephone or radio; the written or printed word, transmitted by hand, by post, by telegraph, or in any other way—these are obvious and common forms of communication. But there are many others. A nod or a wink, a drumbeat in the jungle, a gesture pictured on a television screen, the blinking of a signal light, a bit of music that reminds one of an event in the past, puffs of smoke in the desert air, the movements and posturing in a ballet—all of these are means men use to convey ideas.

The word communication, in fact, will be used here in a very broad sense to include all of the procedures by which one mind can affect another. Although the language used will often refer specifically to the communication of speech, practically everything said applies equally to music, pictures, to a variety of other methods of conveying information.

In communication there seem to be problems at three levels: 1) technical, 2) semantic, and 3) influential .

The technical problems are concerned with the accuracy of transference of information from sender to receiver. They are inherent in all forms of communication, whether by sets of discrete symbols (written speech), or by a varying signal (telephone or radio transmission of voice or music), or by a varying two-dimensional pattern (television).

The semantic problems are concerned with the interpretation of meaning by the receiver, as compared with the intended meaning of the sender. This is a very deep and involved situation, even when one deals only with the relatively simple problems of communicating through speech. For example, if Mr. X is suspected not to understand what Mr. Y says, then it is not possible, by having Mr. Y do nothing but talk further with Mr. X, completely to clarify this situation in any finite time. If Mr. Y says "Do you now understand me?" and Mr. X says "Certainly I do," this is not necessarily a certification that understanding has been achieved. It may just be that Mr. X did not understand the question. If this sounds silly, try it again as "Czy pan mnie rozumie?" with the answer "Hai wakkate imasu." In the restricted field of speech communication, the difficulty may be reduced to a tolerable size, but never completely eliminated, by "explanations." They are presumably never more than approximations to the ideas being explained, but are understandable when phrased in language that has previously been made reasonably clear by usage. For example, it does not take long to make the symbol for "yes" in any language understandable.

The problems of influence or effectiveness are concerned with the success with which the meaning conveyed to the receiver leads to the desired conduct on his part. It may seem at first glance undesirably narrow to imply that the purpose of all communication is to influence the conduct of the receiver. But with any reasonably broad definition of conduct, it is clear that communication either affects conduct or is without any discernible and provable effect at all.

One might be inclined to think that the technical problems involve only the engineering details of good design of a communication system, while the semantic and the effectiveness problems contain most if not all of the philosophical content of the general problem of communication. To see that this is not the case, we must now examine some important recent work in the mathematical theory of communication.

This is by no means a wholly new theory. As the mathematician John von Neumann has pointed out, the 19th-century Austrian physicist Ludwig Boltzmann suggested that some concepts of statistical mechanics were applicable to the concept of information. Other scientists, notably Norbert Wiener of the Massachusetts Institute of Technology, have made profound contributions. The work which will be here reported is that of Claude Shannon of the Bell Telephone Laboratories, which was preceded by that of H. Nyquist and R. V. L. Hartley in the same organization. This work applies in the first instance only to the technical problem, but the theory has broader significance. To begin with, meaning and effectiveness are inevitably restricted by the theoretical limits of accuracy in symbol transmission. Even more significant, a theoretical analysis of the technical problem reveals that it overlaps the semantic and the effectiveness problems more than one might suspect.

A communication system is symbolically represented in the drawing that follows. The information source selects a desired message out of a set of possible messages. (As will be shown, this is a particularly important function.) The transmitter changes this message into a signal which is sent over the communication channel to the receiver.

The receiver is a sort of inverse transmitter, changing the transmitted signal back into a message, and handing this message on to the destination. When I talk to you, my brain is the information source, yours the destination; my vocal system is the transmitter, and your ear with the eighth nerve is the receiver.

In the process of transmitting the signal, it is unfortunately characteristic that certain things not intended by the information source are added to the signal. These unwanted additions may be distortions of sound (in telephony, for example), or static (in

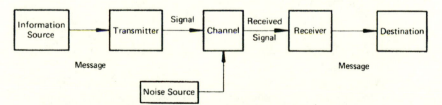

A communication system may be reduced to these fundamental elements. In telephony the signal is a varying electric current, and the channel is a wire. In speech the signal is varying sound pressure, and the channel the ear. Frequently things not intended by the information source are impressed on the signal. The static of radio is one example: distortion in telephony is another. All these additions may be called noise.

radio), or distortions in the shape or shading of a picture
(television), or errors in transmission (telegraphy or facsimile).
All these changes in the signal may be called noise.

The questions to be studied in a communication system have
to do with the amount of information, the capacity of the
communication channel, the coding process that may be used to
change a message into a signal and the effects of noise.

First off, we have to be clear about the rather strange way in
which, in this theory, the word "information" is used; for it has a
special sense which, among other things, must not be confused at
all with meaning. It is surprising but true that, from the present
viewpoint, two messages, one heavily loaded with meaning and
the other pure nonsense, can be equivalent as regards information.

In fact, in this new theory the word information relates not
so much to what you *do* say, as to what you *could* say. That is,
information is a measure of your freedom of choice when you select
a message. If you are confronted with a very elementary situation
where you have to choose one of two alternative messages, then it
is arbitrarily said that the information associated with this situation
is unity. The concept of information applies not to the individual
messages, as the concept of meaning would, but rather to the
situation as a whole, the unit information indicating that in this
situation one has an amount of freedom of choice, in selecting a
message, which it is convenient to regard as a standard or unit
amount. The two messages between which one must choose in such
a selection can be anything one likes. One might be the King
James version of the Bible, and the other might be "Yes."

The remarks thus far relate to artificially simple situations
where the information source is free to choose only among several
definite messages—like a man picking out one of a set of standard
birthday-greeting telegrams. A more natural and more important
situation is that in which the information source makes a sequence
of choices from some set of elementary symbols, the selected
sequence then forming the message. Thus a man may pick out
one word after another, these individually selected words then
adding up to the message.

Obviously probability plays a major role in the generation of
the message, and the choices of the successive symbols depend
upon the preceding choices. Thus, if we are concerned with
English speech, and if the last symbol chosen is "the," then the
probability that the next word will be an article, or a verb form
other than a verbal, is very small. After the three words "in the
event," the probability for "that" as the next word is fairly high,
and for "elephant" as the next word is very low. Similarly, the

probability is low for such a sequence of words as "Constantinople fishing nasty pink." Incidentally, it is low, but not zero, for it is perfectly possible to think of a passage in which one sentence closes with "Constantinople fishing," and the next begins with "Nasty pink." (We might observe in passing that the sequence under discussion *has* occurred in a single good English sentence, namely the one second preceding.)

As a matter of fact, Shannon has shown that when letters or words chosen at random are set down in sequences dictated by probability considerations alone, they tend to arrange themselves in meaningful words and phrases (see illustration on page 38).

Now let us return to the idea of information. The quantity which uniquely meets the natural requirements that one sets up for a measure of information turns out to be exactly that which is known in thermodynamics as entropy, or the degree of randomness, or of "shuffledness" if you will, in a situation. It is expressed in terms of the various probabilities involved.

To those who have studied the physical sciences, it is most significant that an entrophy-like expression appears in communication theory as a measure of information. The concept of entropy, introduced by the German physicist Rudolph Clausius nearly 100 years ago, closely associated with the name of Boltzmann, and given deep meaning by Willard Gibbs of Yale in his classic work on statistical mechanics, has become so basic and pervasive a concept that Sir Arthur Eddington remarked: "The law that entropy always increases—the second law of thermodynamics—holds, I think, the supreme position among the laws of Nature."

Thus when one meets the concept of entropy in communication theory, he has a right to be rather excited. That information should be measured by entropy is, after all, natural when we remember that information is associated with the amount of freedom of choice we have in constructing messages. Thus one can say of a communication source, just as he would also say of a thermodynamic ensemble: "This situation is highly organized: it is not characterized by a large degree of randomness or of choice—that is to say, the information, or the entropy, is low."

We must keep in mind that in the mathematical theory of communication we are concerned not with the meaning of individual messages but with the whole statistical nature of the information source. Thus one is not surprised that the capacity of a channel of communication is to be described in terms of the amount of information it can transmit, or better, in terms of its ability to transmit what is produced out of a source of a given information.

The transmitter may take a written message and use some code to encipher this message into, say, a sequence of numbers, these numbers then being sent over the channel as the signal. Thus one says, in general, that the function of the transmitter is to encode, and that of the receiver to decode, the message. The theory provides for very sophisticated transmitters and receivers— such, for example, as possess "memories," so that the way they encode a certain symbol of the message depends not only upon this one symbol but also upon previous symbols of the message and the way they have been encoded.

We are now in a position to state the fundamental theorem for a noiseless channel transmitting discrete symbols. This theorem relates to a communication channel which has a capacity of C units per second, accepting signals from an information source of H units per second. The theorem states that by devising proper coding procedures for the transmitter it is possible to tranmit symbols over the channel at an average rate which is nearly C/H, but which, no matter how clever the coding, can never be made to exceed C/H.

Viewed superficially, say in rough analogy to the use of transformers to match impedances in electrical circuits, it seems very natural, although certainly pretty neat, to have this theorem which says that efficient coding is that which matches the statistical characteristics of information source and channel. But when it is examined in detail for any one of the vast array of situations to which this result applies, one realizes how deep and powerful this theory is.

How does noise affect information? Information, we must steadily remember, is a measure of one's freedom of choice in selecting a message. The greater this freedom of choice, the greater is the uncertainty that the message actually selected is some particular one. Thus greater freedom of choice, greater uncertainty and greater information all go hand in hand.

If noise is introduced, then the received message contains certain distortions, certain errors, certain extraneous material, that would certainly lead to increased uncertainty. But if the uncertainty is increased, the information is increased, and this sounds as though the noise were beneficial.

It is true that when there is noise, the received signal is selected out of a more varied set of signals than was intended by the sender. This situation beautifully illustrates the semantic trap into which one can fall if he does not remember that "information" is used here with a special meaning that measures freedom of choice and hence uncertainty as to what choice has been made.

Uncertainty that arises by virtue of freedom of choice on the part of the sender is desirable uncertainty. Uncertainty that arises because of errors or because of the influence of noise is undesirable uncertainty. To get the useful information in the received signal we must subtract the spurious portion. This is accomplished, in the theory, by establishing, a quantity known as the "equivocation," meaning the amount of ambiguity introduced by noise. One then refines or extends the previous definition of the capacity of a noiseless channel, and states that the capacity of a noisy channel is defined to be equal to the maximum rate at which useful information (*i.e.*, total uncertainty minus noise uncertainty) can be transmitted over the channel.

Now, finally, we can state the great central theorem of this whole communication theory. Suppose a noisy channel of capacity C is accepting information from a source of entropy H, entropy corresponding to the number of possible messages from the source. If the channel capacity C is equal to or larger than H, then by devising appropriate coding systems the output of the source can be transmitted over the channel with as little error as one pleases. But if the channel capacity C is less than H, the entropy of the source, then it is impossible to devise codes which reduce the error frequency as low as one may please.

However clever one is with the coding process, it will always be true that after the signal is received there remains some undesirable uncertainty about what the message was; and this undesirable uncertainty—this noise or equivocation—will always be equal to or greater than H minus C. But there is always at least one code capable of reducing this undesirable uncertainty down to a value that exceeds H minus C by a small amount.

This powerful theorem gives a precise and almost startlingly simple description of the utmost dependability one can ever obtain from a communication channel which operates in the presence of noise. One must think a long time, and consider many applications, before he fully realizes how powerful and general this amazingly compact theorem really is. One single application can be indicated here, but in order to do so, we must go back for a moment to the idea of the information of a source.

Having calculated the entropy (or the information, or the freedom of choice) of a certain information source, one can compare it to the maximum value this entropy could have, subject only to the condition that the source continue to employ the same symbols. The ratio of the actual to the maximum entropy is called the relative entropy of the source. If the relative entropy of a certain source is, say, eight-tenths, this means roughly that this source is, in its choice of symbols to form a message, about 80 per cent as free as it could possibly be with these same symbols. One minus the relative entrophy is called the "redundancy." That is to say, this fraction of the message is unnecessary in the sense that if it were missing the message would still be essentially complete, or at least could be completed.

It is most interesting to note that the redundancy of English is just about 50 per cent. In other words, about half of the letters or words we choose in writing or speaking are under our free choice, and about half are really controlled by the statistical structure of the language, although we are not ordinarily aware of it. Incidentally, this is just about the minimum of freedom (or relative entrophy) in the choice of letters that one must have to be able to construct satisfactory crossword puzzles. In a language that had only 20 per cent of freedom, or 80 per cent redundancy, it would be impossible to construct crossword puzzles in sufficient complexity and number to make the game popular.

Now since English is about 50 per cent redundant, it would be possible to save about one-half the time of ordinary telegraphy by a proper encoding process, provided one transmitted over a noiseless channel. When there is noise on a channel, however, there is some real advantage in not using a coding process that eliminates all of the redundancy. For the remaining redundancy helps combat the noise. It is the high redundancy of English, for example, that makes it easy to correct errors in spelling that have arisen during transmission.

The communication systems dealt with so far involve the use of a discrete set of symbols—say letters—only moderately numerous. One might well expect that the theory would become almost infinitely more complicated when it seeks to deal with continuous messages such as those of the speaking voice, with its continuous variation of pitch and energy. As is often the case, however, a very interesting mathematical theorem comes to the rescue. As a practical matter, one is always interested in a continuous signal which is built up of simple harmonic constituents, not of all frequencies but only of those that lie wholly within a band from zero to, say, W cycles per second. Thus very satisfactory communication can be achieved over a telephone channel that handles frequencies up to about 4,000, although the human voice does contain higher frequencies. With frequencies up to 10,000 or 12,000, high-fidelity radio transmission of symphonic music is possible.

The theorem that helps us is one which states that a continuous signal, T seconds in duration and band-limited in frequency to the range from zero to W, can be completely specified by stating 2TW numbers. This is really a remarkable theorem. Ordinarily a continuous curve can be defined only approximately by a finite number of points. But if the curve is built up out of simple harmonic constituents of a limited number of frequencies, as a complex sound is built up out of a limited number of pure tones, then a finite number of quantities is all that is necessary to define the curve completely.

Thanks partly to this theorem, and partly to the essential nature of the situation, it turns out that the extended theory of continuous communication is somewhat more difficult and complicated mathematically, but not essentially different from the theory for discrete symbols. Many of the statements for the discrete case require no modification for the continuous case, and others require only minor change.

The mathematical theory of communication is so general that one does not need to say what kinds of symbols are being considered—whether written letters or words, or musical notes, or spoken words, or symphonic music, or pictures. The relationships it reveals apply to all these and to other forms of communication. The theory is so imaginatively motivated that it deals with the real inner core of the communication problem.

One evidence of its generality is that the theory contributes importantly to, and in fact is really the basic theory of, cryptography, which is of course a form of coding. In a similar way, the theory contributes to the problem of translation from one language to another, although the complete story here clearly requires consideration of meaning, as well as of information. Similarly, the ideas developed in this work connect so closely with the problem of the logical design of computing machines that it is no surprise that Shannon has written a paper on the design of a computer that would be capable of playing a skillfull game of chess. And it is of further pertinence to the present contention that his paper closes with the remark that either one must say that such a computer "thinks," or one must substantially modify the conventional implication of the verb "to think."

The theory goes further. Though ostensibly applicable only to problems at the technical level, it is helpful and suggestive at the levels of semantics and effectiveness as well. The formal diagram of a communication system on page 29 can, in all likelihood, be extended to include the central issues of meaning and effectiveness.

Thus when one moves to those levels it may prove to be essential to take account of the statistical characteristics of the destination. One can imagine, as an addition to the diagram, another box labeled "Semantic Receiver" interposed between the engineering receiver (which changes signals to messages) and the destination. This semantic receiver subjects the message to a second decoding, the demand on this one being that it must match the statistical semantic characteristics of the message to the statistical semantic capacities of the totality of receivers, or of that subset of receivers which constitutes the audience one wishes to affect.

Similarly one can imagine another box in the diagram which, inserted between the information source and the transmitter, would be labeled "Semantic Noise" (not to be confused with "engineering noise"). This would represent distortions of meaning introduced by the information source, such as a speaker, which are not intentional but nevertheless affect the destination, or listener. And the problem of semantic decoding must take this semantic noise into account. It is also possible to think of a treatment or adjustment of the original message that would make the sum of message meaning plus semantic noise equal to the desired total message meaning at the destination.

Another way in which the theory can be helpful in improving communication is suggested by the fact that error and confusion arise and fidelity decreases when, no matter how good the coding, one tries to crowd too much over a channel. A general theory at all levels will surely have to take into account not only the capacity of the channel but also (even the words are right!) the capacity of the audience. If you overcrowd the capacity of the audience, it is probably true, by direct analogy, that you do not fill the audience up and then waste only the remainder by spilling. More likely, and again by direct analogy, you force a general error and confusion.

The concept of information developed in this theory at first seems disappointing and bizarre—disappointing because it has nothing to do with meaning, and bizarre because it deals not with a single message but rather with the statistical character of a whole ensemble of messages, bizarre also because in these statistical terms the words information and uncertainty find themselves partners.

But we have seen upon further examination of the theory that this analysis has so penetratingly cleared the air that one is now perhaps for the first time ready for a real theory of meaning. An engineering communication theory is just like a very proper and discrete girl at the telegraph office accepting your telegram. She pays no attention to the meaning, whether it be sad or joyous or embarrassing. But she must be prepared to deal intelligently with all messages that come to her desk. This idea that a communication system ought to try to deal with all possible messages, and that the intelligent way to try is to base design on the statistical character of the source, is surely not without significance for communication in general. Language must be designed, or developed, with a view to the totality of things that man may wish to say; but not being able to accomplish everything, it should do as well as possible as often as possible. That is to say, it too should deal with its task statistically.

This study reveals facts about the statistical structure of the English language, as an example, which must seem significant to students of every phase of language and communication. It suggests, as a particularly promising lead, the application of probability theory to semantic studies. Especially pertinent is the powerful body of probability theory dealing with what mathematicians call the Markoff processes, whereby past events influence present probabilities, since this theory is specifically adapted to handle one of the most significant but difficult aspects of meaning, namely the influence of context. One has the vague feeling that information and meaning may prove to be something like a pair of canonically conjugate variables in quantum theory, that is, that information and meaning may be subject to some joint restriction that compels the sacrifice of one if you insist on having much of the other.

Or perhaps meaning may be shown to be analogous to one of the quantities on which the entropy of a thermodynamic ensemble depends. Here Eddington has another apt comment:

> Suppose that we were asked to arrange the following in two categories—*distance, mass, electric force, entropy, beauty, melody.*
> I think there are the strongest grounds for placing entropy alongside beauty and melody, and not with the first three. Entropy is only found when the parts are viewed in association, and it is by viewing or hearing the parts in association that beauty and melody are discerned. All three are features of arrangement. It is a pregnant thought that one of these three associates should be able to figure as a commonplace quantity of science. The reason why this stranger can pass itself off among the aborigines of the physical world is that it is able to speak their language, *viz.*, the language of arithmetic.

One feels sure that Eddington would have been willing to include the word meaning along with beauty and melody; and one suspects he would have been thrilled to see, in this theory, that entropy not only speaks the language of arithmetic; it also speaks the language of language.

---

1. Zero-Order Approximation

XFOML RXKHRJFFJUJ ZLPWCFWKCYJ
FFJEYVKCQSGXYD QPAAMKBZAACIBZLHJQD

---

2. First-Order Approximation

OCRO HLI RGWR NMIELWIS EU LL NBNESEBYA TH EEI
ALHENHTTPA OOBTTVA NAH BRL

---

3. Second-Order Approximation

ON IE ANTSOUTINYS ARE T INCTORE ST BE S DEAMY
ACHIN D ILONASIVE TUCOOWE AT TEASONARE FUSO
TIZIN ANDY TOBE SEACE CTISBE

---

4. Third-Order Approximation

IN NO IST LAT WHEY CRATICT FROURE BIRS GROCID
PONDENOME OF DEMONSTURES OF THE REPTAGIN IS
REGOACTIONA OF CRE

---

5. First-Order Word Approximation

REPRESENTING AND SPEEDILY IS AN GOOD APT OR
COME CAN DIFFERENT NATURAL HERE HE THE A IN
CAME THE TO OF TO EXPERT GRAY COME TO
FURNISHES THE LINE MESSAGE HAD BE THESE.

---

6. Second-Order Word Approximation

THE HEAD AND IN FRONTAL ATTACK ON AN ENGLISH
WRITER THAT THE CHARACTER OF THIS POINT IS
THEREFORE ANOTHER METHOD FOR THE LETTERS
THAT THE TIME OF WHO EVER TOLD THE PROBLEM
FOR AN UNEXPECTED

Artificial language results when letters or words are set down statistically. 1. Twenty-six letters and one space are chosen at random. 2. Letters are chosen according to their frequency in English. 3. Letters are chosen according to the frequency with which they follow other letters. 4. Letters are chosen according to frequency with which they follow two other letters. Remaining examples do the same with words instead of letters.

3

FEEDBACK

Theodore Clevenger, Jr., and Jack Matthews

INTERACTION WITH FEEDBACK

Whenever a speaker alters his speaking behavior by adapting in
some way to response from his listener, he may be said to be
responding to feedback. Neither the foregoing statement nor the
process to which it refers is nearly as simple as it seems, but the
feedback function is so important in human communication that it
is worth taking time to understand it.

The term *feedback* comes from cybernetics, the branch of
engineering science dealing with control systems.[1] Such systems
control operations by using information about effects. The now-
classic example of a simple cybernetic system is the thermostat on a

furnace. When the temperature in a room drops below a minimal level, the thermostat closes a switch, sending a signal that turns on the furnace. The themostat continuously monitors the room temperature; and when it reaches the desired maximum, the thermostat opens the switch, sending a signal that turns the furnace off. Engineers would refer to the signal that turns the furnace off as "negative feedback"; it causes the furnace to discontinue what it has been doing. Positive feedback has no place in a thermostat system because furnaces burn at a more or less constant temperature, and the effect of positive feedback would be to cause the furnace to burn hotter and hotter. In both cases, information about the effects of the operation (in this case, the effect upon room temperature of the firing of the furnace) is used to control the operation (turning it off or causing it to burn hotter). Positive feedback says, in effect, "Do even more of the same," while negative feedback says, "Stop what you have been doing."

Positive and Negative Feedback

Because people use information about the effects of their communication in controlling how they communicate, it is natural to extend the concept of feedback into human interaction. If, for example, one's initial greeting to a stranger meets with a pleasant response, one is likely to continue the conversation, often with a more extended message than the first. This is positive feedback at work. However, if the first message meets with indifference or grouchiness, one is likely to terminate the conversation at that point; here we see the operation of negative feedback. Now, because the words "positive" and "negative" have—in addition to their technical meanings in cybernetics—evaluative meanings for people, it is easy to confuse the two when talking about feedback. In the above example it is not the pleasantness of the listener's response that makes it negative feedback. It is simply a question of whether his response causes an increase or a decrease in some aspect of the speaker's behavior. In this case, the question is whether it causes the speaker to enlarge the conversation or terminate it.

As a matter of fact, favorable responses from the listener often signify negative feedback, and unfavorable responses may signify positive feedback. If I am explaining something to you and observe nonverbal cues that tell me you don't understand what I am saying, your response may be characterized as negative; but the feedback it gives to me is positive if it causes me to repeat or enlarge my explanation. On the other hand, if you show that you understand, your response can be said to be positive, but its effect on my behavior will be negative feedback if it signals that I should stop explaining.

Variable Influence of Feedback

From this, it should be clear that the term *feedback* refers not to any catalog of listener behavior, but to a *relationship* between the behavior of the speaker, the response of the listener, and the effect of that response on the further behavior of the speaker. Thus, a response of the listener is not feedback if it has no effect on the speaker's subsequent behavior. I may shake my head, frown, even speak out in an effort to generate feedback signals that will influence your communication behavior to me; but if you fail to note my response, or—noting it—refuse to adapt your message in light of it, then my behavior is not feedback. In a sense, then we may say that feedback, in order to *be* feedback, must be *used* as feedback.

Just as no listener behavior can automatically be classified as feedback if it does not influence the behavior of the speaker, there is no behavior that cannot serve as feedback if it does influence the further behavior of the speaker. In particular, we need to bear in mind that feedback messages need not be transmitted *deliberately* or consciously by the listener. Indeed, most people seeing a film or videotape of their listening behavior in a group discussion or an audience are appalled at the transparency of their reactions. They thought they were sitting in poker-faced inscrutability, but the tape shows many reactions that can be read clearly by an alert observer. They did not intentionally transmit feedback messages to the speaker, but those messages were there to be used as feedback if the speaker was willing and able to perceive and respond to them.

Using Feedback to Enrich Interaction

To introduce possibilities for feedback into human interaction is to enrich the quality of human contact enormously; for now each partner in the interaction can not only influence and be influenced by the other, but the behavior of each will be conditioned by the behavior of the other. In the alternating monologue we see two people talking in one another's presence. In the stimulus-response interaction pattern, at least one of the people is responding to what the other says. In interaction with feedback, the further behavior of the speaker is conditional upon the nature of the listener's response.

We should note that in order to make use of feedback, the speaker must retain some flexibility in his own behavior. At any given moment several options must be open to him; otherwise, the listener's response cannot influence his behavior, and thus cannot serve as feedback. For example, the public speaker who has written out a manuscript and attempts to present it orally is able to make very limited use of feedback from his audience. He can observe their reactions and adjust features of his delivery to comfortable levels by speaking loudly enough and at a rate that is comfortable for them to listen to. He can pause for laughs, applause, or jeers; he can repeat a passage that did not seem to sink in. But beyond these relatively mechanical matters he cannot adjust without scrapping or ignoring the manuscript. Sometimes it is more importance to be precise than to be flexible, and then a manuscript is useful. Most people, however, do not learn how to interact with an audience until they give up the practice of reading speeches from prepared texts.

INTERACTION WITH FEEDBACK AND FEEDFORWARD

Feedback, as we have seen, is the process whereby a system modified its operations so as to adjust to the known consequences of those operations. In the case of human communication, this refers to the process of adjusting one's communication behavior so as to take account of the observed influence of that behavior on the listener. But how does the speaker know what behaviors to use as feedback from his interaction partner, and how does he decide what alternatives to follow in the event of a particular listener response.

Some feedback adjustments amount to automatic social habits, such as adjusting one's loudness level when the listener displays signs of difficulty in hearing, or asking him a question when he seems bored. But other adjustments seem to result not from habit but from forethought. It is as if the speaker had anticipated certain listener behaviors at specific points in the interaction, and had laid out alternative courses of action depending on whether the expected reactions occurred or not. The setting up of such expectancies and contingencies is called *feedforward*.

Like feedback, feedforward is a term that originated in cybernetic theory. In the same sense that the operation of a thermostat is the simplest example of feedback, setting the thermostat to a desired temperature range, the operator may be said to "feed forward" the maximum and/or minimum temperature to the point in the heat cycle where these temperature values will be needed. A more interesting and representative example of feedforward would be an attachment to keep track of both the inside and the outside temperature and to pour into a storage tank ahead of time just the amount of fuel needed to bring the temperature back into the desired range. Such a device could be said to "anticipate" fuel needs. Although there are many significant differences between thermostats and human beings, there are also some intriguing analogies which, if not taken too literally, provide insights into the ways in which we as human beings react and interact.

In human interaction, feedforward most often takes one of three forms: (1) *Goal-setting*, (2) *establishing expectancies*, and (3) *planning contingencies*.

Goal-Setting

In some ways, setting a specific goal that we hope to achieve with a listener operates much like feedforward: When that goal is reached, our goal-seeking behavior will cease. If the goal is vague or ill-defined, our behavior will be as unreliable as a furnace without a thermostat, and somebody else will have to turn us off. If we are not sensitive to potential feedback signals that tell us the goal has been reached, we will operate like a furnace whose control circuit from the thermostat has been broken.

We should also note that goals are often revised during interaction, and such revision also qualifies as feedforward. Suppose, for example, that you are trying to sell a subscription to the college humor magazine to a student you have just met, and in the process you discover that he seems to know a good deal about magazine writing and publishing. You may now decide that you want more from him than a subscription. If, for example, you now want him to donate some time to the magazine, you will have fed forward a revised goal into the continuing interaction.

Establishing Expectancies

Marshall McLuhan,[2] along with many contemporary psychologists, would argue that except for the simplest reflex behaviors, human beings seldom communicate without some kind of expectancy. This form of feedforward may occur at many levels, from the linguistic to the social. You will recall, for example, that . . . we said that one of the most reasonable theories of language decoding (speech recognition) holds that we use a few clues to "synthesize" or "generate" a best guess as to what the speaker is saying, then check that guess against what we can hear of the utterance. The synthesis of the "best guess" is a kind of feedforward. If we are led to synthesize an estimate of what the speaker will say before he says it, then the synthesis represents the kind of feedforward we call *expectancy*.

As we move from the linguistic to the interactional level, we can find still more examples of feedforward. The "canned" sales pitch is a study in feedforward. Far from being the rigid "speech outlines" that they once were, such interaction plans are now adapted to a variety of listeners, moods, and circumstances. The planner who organizes the pitch will try to anticipate points in the presentation where a listener will ask questions or raise objections, and at each such point will construct appropriate answers. Thus, anticipation of the questions has been fed forward into the interaction plan.

Not all anticipatory feedforward is the result of preplanning. Indeed, much of it arises during the course of interaction with others. For example, suppose that your hobby is shortwave radio. In talking to me you discover very early in the conversation that I know none of the technical terminology. You may very well feed forward the anticipation that I would think it foolish of you to spend so much time and money on the hobby; for unless I know at least some of the terminology, I am not likely to have experienced the satisfactions arising from operating an amateur station, and I certainly will not have dreamed of the amount of money involved. Having encountered such novices in the past, you may predict that I would be amazed to find out how much your hobby costs. Consequently, you will be anticipating this response and will be either marshalling your arguments in defense of such spending or planning ways to dodge the issue.

Whenever anybody says something to us or reacts to something we have said to him in such a way as to increase our awareness of his attitudes or predispositions, we are likely to feed forward new anticipations regarding that person. Since new insights into others happen frequently in interaction, this type of feedforward is a very common occurrence.

Of course, the fact that such feedforward is common is no guarantee of its accuracy or dependability. In the foregoing example, for instance, your prediction about my reaction might become embarrassing, you may deprive both of us of a satisfying encounter. Or, if you were in a more aggressive mood, you might increase the likelihood of an interpersonal crisis between us. By anticipating negative reactions, you might behave in such a way as to increase the likelihood of obtaining one. Thus, you might perversely exaggerate the amount of time and money you spent on your ham station. To such exaggeration I might respond with genuine surprise, which you might interpret as mild disapproval, which might lead you to become defensive, which I might interpret as belligerence, which might lead me to respond coolly, which you might interpret as an escalation of the hostilities, and so on to an interpersonal breakdown—all of which started with your anticipating a negative response. This behavior leads to paranoia, which can be characterized as a condition of distorted feedforward.

Planning Contingencies

In an earlier example, we said that the prepared sales talk is a study in feedforward, and illustrated it with examples of anticipating the customer's questions and objections. A still more sophisticated approach to the prepared sales talk involves contingency planning. The person organizing the talk may go further than anticipating questions or objections from the customer; the sales strategist may, in fact, introduce questions into the talk that demand the customer give some response. By anticipating the different possible responses at each of these points in the talk, the sales person may plan a highly flexible program of information and persuasion capable of being adapted to a very great variety of different customers. The essence of such a plan is the feedforward of contingencies to the crucial choice-points in the discussion, and the preparation of appropriate plans for meeting each imagined contingency. Most experienced salesmen have in effect programmed themselves to such a contingency plan. Through long experience of success and failure in marketing a particular product, they have come to know the critical choice-points in a sales interaction, and have developed appropriate means of dealing with each.

Just as goals may be revised and expectancies changed during interaction, so may contingency plans arise or be modified during the course of interaction. Perhaps the most primitive, everyday example is the desperate thought: "If he says that again, I'm going to let him have it." This is a simple contingency plan arising during the course of interaction. More constructive examples occur also:

"Is she smiles, I'll ask her to the game."

"If he likes the IBM deal, I'll show him the entire portfolio; otherwise, I'll switch to the chemical stocks."

"If he seems friendly, I'll ask him to join today."

"The question of salary is bound to come up sooner or later. If he mentions a specific figure below $12,000, we'll agree to it immediately; but if he asks what we're offering, we'll mention $10,000."

"We escalate our demands until the president can no longer say 'yes.' Then, if he says 'no,' we occupy the administration building; if he refers it to the faculty senate, we move in and take over the senate meeting. Charlie, you start to work on the speeches and signs for the ad-building bash; Annette, you get the stuff ready for the senate."

"By this point, they ought to have a pretty good idea of what I'm talking about. If they seem to understand, I'll drop out the third example."

All of the foregoing are examples of feedforward of the type we call contingency planning. An ability to develop and execute plans of this sort is a necessary skill in effective social interaction, and most people develop at least some of this ability at an early age. It is obvious that the more one knows about people in general, about his listener in particular, and about the topic under discussion, the more effective can be his planning in this regard.

We have seen three kinds of feedforward in social interaction: (1) Goal setting, (2) expectancy, and (3) contingency planning. It should have occurred to you that these three levels of feedforward are not in fact strictly separable from each other. Where one leaves off and the other begins is often difficult to determine. But together the three terms describe a continuum of feedforward activities that clearly play a vital role in human communication. Without feedforward, feedback would be a static and sterile affair; and without flexible feedback, interaction could scarcely be human.

Notes

1. See Norbert Wiener, *Cybernetics* (Cambridge, Mass.: M.I.T. Press, 1948).
2. McLuhan, Marshall, *Understanding Media: The Extensions of Man* (New York: McGraw-Hill, 1964).

4

A TRANSACTIONAL MODEL OF COMMUNICATION

Dean C. Barnlund

A PILOT MODEL

A pilot study is an "experimental experiment" in which an
investigator attempts a gross manipulation of his variables to
determine the feasibility of his study, clarify his assumptions and
refine his measuring instruments. The drawings that follow are
"pilot models" in the same spirit, for they are preliminary
experiments in diagramming self-to-environment, self-to-self and
self-to-other communication.

INTRA-PERSONAL COMMUNICATION

It may help to explain the diagrams that follow if the abstract
elements and relations in the models are given concrete illustration

Reprinted by permission from *Language Behavior: A Book of Readings,*
Johnnye Akin, Alvin Goldber, Gail Myers, and Joseph Stewart, eds., The
Hague, The Netherlands: Mouton and Co., Publishers.

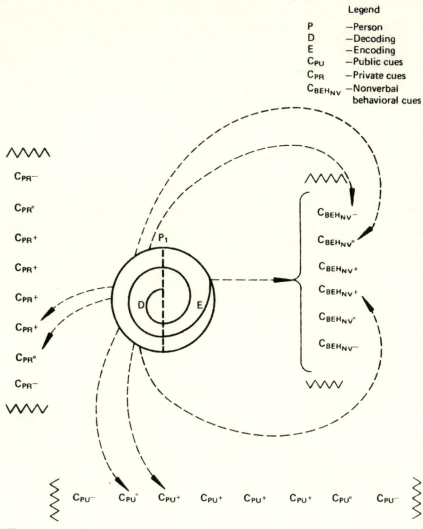

Figure 1

by using a hypothetical case. Let us assume a simple communicative setting. In Figure 1 a person (P_1), let us say a Mr. A, sits alone in the reception room of a clinic waiting to see his doctor. As a communication system Mr. A decodes (D), or assigns meaning to the various cues available in his perceptual field by transforming sensory discriminations into neuro-muscular sets (E) so that they are manifest to others in the form of verbal and nonverbal cues. Evidence is not available which will permit us to establish if encoding and decoding are separate functions of the organism, successive phases of a single on-going process, or the same operation viewed from opposite ends of the system, but it is reasonable to assume until we have solid proof that they are closely articulated and interdependent processes. The spiral line connecting encoding and decoding processes is used to give diagrammatic representation to the continuous, unrepeatable and irreversible nature of communication that was postulated earlier.

The meanings presented in Mr. A at any given moment will be a result of his alertness to, and detection of, objects and circumstances in his environment. The lines terminating in arrows on Figure 1 can be used to indicate either the different stimuli that come into focus as Mr. A's attention shifts from moment to moment, or that a single "experience" may be a mosaic of many simultaneous perceptions. The direction of the arrows illustrates the postulate that meaning will be assigned to, rather than received from, the objects admitted to perception.

There are at least three sets of signs—or cues—to which Mr. A may attribute meaning in this setting.[1] Any of them may trigger interpretations or reactions of one kind or another. One set of cues derives from the environment itself. These cues are identified in Figure 1 as public cues (C_{Pu}). To qualify as a public cue any object or sound or circumstance must fulfill two criteria. First, it must be a part of, or available to, the perceptual field of all potential communicants. Second, it must have been created prior to the event under analysis and must remain outside the control of the person under observation. Two types of public cues can be distinguished. Natural cues, those supplied by the physical world without the intervention of man, include atmospheric conditions of temperature and humidity, the visual and tactual properties of minerals, the color and forms of vegetable life and climatic crises such as hurricanes and rainstorms. Artificial cues, those resulting from man's modification and manipulation of his environment, include the effects created by the processing and arranging of wood, steel and glass, the weaving and patterning of clothing, the control of climate through air or sound conditioning.

As Mr. A glances about the office he may be aware of the arrangement of furniture, a worn carpet, a framed reproduction of a Miro painting, a slightly antiseptic odor, and end table covered with magazines. To any of them he may attach significance, altering his attitude toward his doctor or himself. In some instances the cues may be authored and edited by a number of persons. The painting, for example, is a message from Joan Miro, its framing a message from the decorator, its choice and location a message from the doctor. All these cues are available potentially to anyone who enters the reception room. The perception of any specific cue, or the meaning assigned to it, however, will be similar for various people only to the extent that they possess the same sensory acuity, overlapping fields of perception, parallel background experiences, and similar needs or purposes.

A second set of cues consists of those elements or events that are essentially private in nature, that come from sources not automatically available to any other person who enters a communicative field. Private cues might include the sounds heard through a pair of earphones, the sights visible through opera glasses, or the vast array of cues that have their origin in the taste buds or viscera of the interpreter. In the case of Mr. A, the private cues (C_{PR}) might include the words and pictures he finds as he riffles through a magazine, the potpourri of objects he finds in his pocket, or a sudden twitch of pain he notices in his chest. Public and private cues may be verbal or nonverbal in form, but the critical quality they share is that they were brought into existence and remain beyond the control of the communicants.

Although no one else has yet entered the communicative field, Mr. A has to contend with one additional set of cues. These, however, are generated by, and are substantially under the control of, Mr. A himself. They consist of the observations he makes of himself as he turns the pages of his magazine, sees himself reflected in the mirror, or changes position in his chair. The articulation and movement of his body are as much a part of his phenomenological field as any other cue provided by the environment.[2] Indeed if this were not true he would be incapable of coordinated acts. To turn a page requires the assessment of dozens of subtle muscular changes. These cues are identified in Figure 1 as behavioral, nonverbal cues ($C_{BEH_{NV}}$). They comprise the deliberate acts of Mr. A in straightening his tie or picking up a magazine as well as his unconscious mannerisms in holding a cigarette or slouching in his chair. They differ from public cues in that they are initiated or controlled by the communicant himself. When public or private cues are assigned meaning, Mr. A is free to interpret as he will, but his meanings are circumscribed to some extent by the environment around him. Where his own behavior is involved, he controls (consciously or unconsciously) *both* the cues that are supplied and their interpretations as well. Two sets of lines are required in Figure 1 to reflect the circularity of this communication process, one to indicate the encoding of meaning in the nonverbal behavior of Mr. A, the other to show interpretation of these acts by Mr. A.

The jagged lines ($\wedge\wedge\wedge\wedge$) at either end of the series of public, private and behavioral cues in Figure 1 simply illustrate that the number of cues to which meaning may be assigned is probably without limit. But, although unlimited in number, they can be ordered in terms of their attractiveness, or potency, for any viewer. Men do not occupy a neutral environment. The assumptive world of Mr. A, a product of his sensory-motor successes and failures in the past, combined with his current appetites and needs, will establish his set toward the environment so that all available cues do not have equal valence for him. Each will carry a value that depends upon its power to assist or defeat him in pursuit of adequate meanings. Tentative valences have been assigned to the public, private, and behavioral cues in Figure 1 through the addition of a plus, zero or minus sign (+, 0, −) following each of them.

The complexity of the process of abstracting can readily be illustrated through the diagram simply by specifying the precise objects which Mr. A includes or excludes from his perception. Research on dissonance and balance theory suggests the direction followed in the discrimination, organizing and interpreting of available cues.[3] Unless other factors intervene, individuals tend to draw toward the cues to which positive valences can be assigned, that is toward cues capable of reinforcing past or emerging interpretations, and away from cues to which negative valences are attached or those that contradict established opinions and behavior patterns.

> By a balanced state is meant a situation in which the relations among the entities fit together harmoniously; there is no stress towards change. A basic assumption is that sentiment relations and unit relations tend toward a balanced state. This means that sentiments are not entirely independent of the perceptions of unit connections between entities and that the latter, in turn, are not entirely independent of sentiments. Sentiments and unit relations are mutually interdependent. It also means that if a balanced state does not exist, then forces toward this state will arise. If a change is not possible, the state of imbalance will produce tension.[4]

Successive diagrams of a particular communicative event could be made to demonstrate in a cognitively dissonant setting how a person avoids negatively-loaded cues, maximizes or minimizes competing cues, or reassigns valences in order to produce consonance.

An illustration, even though oversimplified, will suggest the course of Mr. A's communication with himself. At the moment he is faintly aware of an antiseptic odor in the room, which reinforces his confidence in the doctor's ability to diagnose his illness ($C_{PU} +$).

As he glances through a magazine ($C_{PR}0$) he is conscious of how comfortable his chair feels after a long day on his feet ($C_{PR}+$). Looking up, he glances at the Miro reproduction on the wall, but is unable to decipher it ($C_{PU}0$). He decides to call the nurse. As he rises he clumsily drops his magazine ($C_{BEH_{NV}}-$) and stoops to pick it up, crosses the room ($C_{BEH_{NV}}0$), and rings the call bell firmly and with dignity ($C_{BEH_{NV}}+$).

INTERPERSONAL COMMUNICATION

The communication process is complicated still further in Figure 2 by the appearance of a second person (P_2), let us say Dr. B, who enters the reception room to look for his next patient. The perceptual field of Dr. B, as that of Mr. A, will include the public cues supplied by the environment (C_{PU}). These cues, however, will not be identical for both persons, nor will they carry the same valences, because of differences in their backgrounds and immediate purposes. Dr. B may notice the time on the wall clock

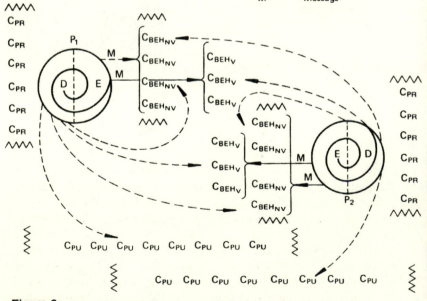

	Legend
P	—Person
D	—Decoding
E	—Encoding
C_{PU}	—Public cues
C_{PR}	—Private cues
$C_{BEH_{NV}}$	—Nonverbal behavioral cues
C_{BEH_V}	—Behavioral verbal cues
M	—Message

Figure 2

or the absence of other patients, and he may assign different valences to the disarray of magazines on the table or to the Miro print. In addition, Dr. B will be interpreting private cues (C_{PR}) that belong exclusively to his own phenomenological field, such as his own fatigue at the moment, and these may alter the interpretations he attaches to Mr. A's conduct. Finally, there are the behavioral cues ($C_{BEH_{NV}}$) that accompany his own movements to which he must be tuned in order to act with reasonable efficiency.

Even before any verbal exchange takes place, however, there will be a shift in communicative orientation of both individuals. As Mr. A and Dr. B become aware of the presence of the other (sometimes before), each will become more self-conscious, more acutely aware of his own acts, and more alert to the nonverbal cues of the other as an aid to defining their relationship. Each will bring his own actions under closer surveillance and greater control. The doctor, as he enters, may assume a professional air as a means of keeping the patient at the proper psychological distance; the patient, upon hearing the door open, may hastily straighten his tie to make a good impression. A heightened sensitivity and a shift from environmental to behavioral cues identifies the process of social facilitation. Men do not act—or communicate—in private as they do in the presence of others. While audiences represent a special case of social facilitation, and mobs an unusually powerful and dramatic one, the mere appearance of a second person in an elevator or office will change the character and content of self-to-self communication in both parties.[5]

At some point in their contact, and well before they have spoken, Mr. A and Dr. B will have become sufficiently aware of each other that it is possible to speak of behavioral cues as comprising a message (M). This is, each person will begin to regulate the cues he provides the other, each will recognize the possible meanings the other may attach to his actions, and each will begin to interpret his own acts as if he were the other. These two features, the deliberate choice and control of cues and the projection of interpretation, constitute what is criterial for identifying inter-personal messages.

Dr. B, crossing the room, may initiate the conversation. Extending his hand, he says, "Mr. A! So glad to see you. How are you?"[6] At this point, despite the seeming simplicity of the setting and prosaic content of the message, Mr. A must solve a riddle in meaning of considerable complexity. In a nonclinical environment where the public cues would be different, perhaps on a street corner (C_{PU}), Mr. A would regard this message (C_{BEH_V}) as no more than a social gesture, and he would respond in kind. This, on the other hand, is a clinic (C_{PU}). Is this remark, therefore, to be given the usual interpretation? Even here, the nonverbal cues ($CBEH_{NV}$) of Dr. B, the friendly facial expression and extended hand, may reinforce its usual meaning in spite of the special setting. On the other hand, these words ($CBEH_V$) may be interpreted only as showing the sympathetic interest of Dr. B in Mr. A. In this case, the message requires no answer at all but is a signal for Mr. A to come into the office. In spite of the clinical setting (C_{PU}) and the gracious gesture ($CBEH_{NV}$), however, the last phrase ($CBEH_V$), because of a momentary hesitation just before it ($CBEH_{NV}$), might be an invitation for Mr. A to begin giving an account of his symptoms. In deciphering the meaning, Mr. A will have to assign and reassign valences so that a coherent interpretation emerges. (No valences are assigned in Figure 2 because their positive, negative or neutral value would depend upon the interpretive decisions of Mr. A and Dr. B.) All three contexts, the environmental, behavioral and verbal, will have to be scanned, assigned meanings, and compared in order for Mr. A to determine a suitable response.

Meanwhile, Dr. B is involved in weaving some interpretation of his own out of the cues he detects and the valences he assigns to them. Mr. A smiles back and says, "Nice to see you again, too, I wish the circumstances were different." At this moment Dr. B turns his attention from the carpet which needs repairing (C_{PU}) to Mr. A. How should he interpret this message? Since they are in a clinic (C_{PU}) it is not surprising that Mr .A should speak of the "circumstances" of his visit. Yet, could this be a warning that the visit concerns a serious medical problem rather than a trivial one? Mr. A's relaxed posture ($CBEH_{NV}$) does not reinforce the former meaning, but his flushed face does ($CBEH_{NV}$). Or could this remark be no more than a semi-humorous reference to a past epsiode on the golf links (C_{PR})? In any case, Dr. B, like Mr. A, must reduce the ambiguity in the situation by experimentally assigning meanings to public, private, nonverbal and verbal cues, relating them to the surrounding conditions of time and place, and determining the extent of congruence or incongruence in the meanings given them. Not until further verbal and nonverbal cues are supplied will Dr. B be confident that he has sized up the message properly.

This analysis suggests that meanings are assigned to verbal cues according to the same principles that govern the interpretations of all other cues. Indeed, this seems to be the case.[7] Meaning is cumulative (or ambiguity reductive) and grows as each new cue, of whatever type, is detected and assigned some sort of valance. Verbal cues are distinctive only in the sense that they constitute a special form of behavior, are finite in number, and are presented in a linear sequence.

One further clarification must be added concerning the transferability of cues. A public cue can be transformed into a private cue by manipulating it so that it is no longer available to all communicants. Mr. A may refold his coat so that a worn cuff cannot be seen by Dr. B, or the doctor may turn over his medical chart so that Mr. A cannot read his entry. Private cues may be converted into public ones. Mr. A may want Dr. B to see a cartoon in the *New Yorker* he has been reading or Dr. B may choose to show Mr. A the latest photograph of his daughter. Sometimes an action on the part of a communicant involves manipulating or altering an environmental cue. Dr. B may unconsciously rearrange the magazines on the table while speaking to Mr. A and, in this case, environmental and behavioral cues merge.

The aim of communication is to reduce uncertainty. Each cue has potential value in carrying out this purpose. But it requires that the organism be open to all available cues and that it be willing to alter meanings until a coherent and adequate picture emerges. Conditionality becomes the criterion of functional communication which, according to Llewellyn Gross, "involves the attitude of thinking in terms of varying degrees and changing proportions; the habit of acting provisionally and instrumentally with a keen awareness of the qualifying influence of time, place, people, and circumstances upon aspirations and expectations; the emotional appreciation for varieties and nuances of feeling."[8]

What is regarded in various academic fields as an "error of judgment," or "a communication breakdown," or a "personality disturbance," appears to be a consequence of a sort of communicative negligence. The nature of this negligence is intimated in what a British psychiatrist has called "The Laws of the Total Situation."[9] To the extent that a person is unable to respond to the total situation—because he denies critical cues from the environment, distorts verbal or nonverbal cues from the opposite person, fails to revise inappropriate assumptions regarding time and place—to that extent will it be difficult, or impossible, for him to construct meanings that will allow him to function in productive and satisfying ways.

The observance and disregard of the Law of the Total Situation can be documented again and again in human affairs, at the most intimate interpersonal levels, and at the most serious public levels. Since communicative negligance is so omnipresent, it might be refreshing to consider an instance that illustrates a sensitive observance of the Law of the Total Situation.

Betty Smith, writing in *A Tree Grows in Brooklyn*, tells of a neighborhood custom. On the night before Christmas a child could win a tree if he stood without falling while it was thrown at him. When Francie was ten and Neeley nine, they went to the lot and asked the owner to throw the biggest tree at the two of them. The small children clasped each other to meet the force of the great tree. For just a moment the man agonized, wanting simply to give it to them, but knowing that if he did he would have to give away all his trees, and the next year no one would pay for a tree. Realizing he must do it, he threw the tree as hard as he could. Though the children almost fell, they were able to withstand the impact and claimed the tree. As they started to pick it up Francie heard the man shout after them. "And now get the hell out of here, you lousy bastards." There was no doubt about what he said. But Francie was able to hear beyond the rough words. She knew that this tone of voice, on Christmas Eve, from one who had no other language really meant, "Merry Christmas, God bless you." The man could not have said that, and Francie recognized it. He used the only words he had and she was able to understand him, not from his words alone, but from the totality of time, place, personality, and circumstance.

The complexities of human communication present an unbelievably difficult challenge to the student of human affairs. To build a satisfactory theory about so complex an event through sole reliance upon the resources of ordinary language seems less and less promising. Any conceptual device which might give order to the many and volatile forces at work when people communicate deserves attention. The value of any theoretical innovation, such as a symbolic model, may be measured by its capacity to withstand critical attack, its value in prompting new hypotheses and data, or finally, by its contribution to the improvement of human communication. The pilot models described here may not fulfill any of these criteria completely, but they will have served a useful purpose if they prompt the search for better ways of representing the inner dynamics of the communication process.[10]

Notes

1. The more generic term of cues has been adopted to avoid some of the difficulties that attend the sign-symbol distinction.
2. While this sort of intra-personal communication is usually identified as feedback, the connotation of this term may be unfortunate when applied loosely to human communication for it suggests a sender-receiver dualism where there may be

none, and implies that a person receives information about his performance from his environment. Actions, however, are incapable of sending meanings back to the source. The individual acts and as he acts observes *and* interprets his own behavior. As long as this is understood the term need not cause difficulty but this does not always seem to be the case in the literature on communication.

3. See Leon Festinger, *A Theory of Cognitive Dissonance* (New York: Harper & Row, 1957) and Fritz Heider, *The Psychology of Interpersonal Relations* (New York: Wiley, 1958).

4. Heider, ibid., p. 201.

5. See Erving Goffman, *The Presentation of Self in Everyday Life* (Garden City, N.Y.: Doubleday Anchor, 1959).

6. We do not have, as yet, in spite of the efforts of linguists and students of nonverbal behavior, an adequate typology for identifying message cues. In the case of this simple remark, is the unit of meaning the phoneme, morpheme, word or phrase? And, in the case of nonverbal cues, is it to be bodily position, gesture, or some smaller unit? Until we have better descriptive categories the careful analysis of communicative acts cannot proceed very far.

7. Richards, James M., "The Cue Addivity Principle in a Restricted Social Interaction Situation," *Journal of Experimental Psychology* (1952):452.

8. Gross, Llewellyn, "The Construction and Partial Standardization of a Scale for Measuring Self-Insight." *Journal of Social Psychology* **28**, (1948):219.

9. Harris, Henry, *The Group Approach to Leadership Testing* (Boston: Routledge & Kegan Paul, 1949), p. 258.

10. Only slight modifications are needed to adapt these models for use in representing the dynamics of mass communication.

5

SOCIAL PERCEPTION AND APPRAISAL

George J. Simmons and J. L. McCall

Through the process of "social perception" we appraise the things and people around us and strive to assess what meanings they may have for the fulfillment of our role-identities. This statement does not mean that social perception is always selfish, for we often define others as people we want to help or love or make sacrifices for, but in the broad sense social perception is always self-centered.

As other people and objects are perceived and interpreted in terms of their meanings for us, it follows that our definitions and classifications only in part reflect the "real nature" of things. We create, as much as we define, the meanings of things, and, as we

Reprinted with permission of Macmillan Publishing Co., Inc. from *Identities and Interactions* by George J. McCall and J. L. Simonns. Copyright © 1966 by The Free Press, a division of the Macmillan Company.

have seen, there is a large class of social objects that "exist" only as created and collectively understood meanings. No stolen base or flag can be found in nature.

The perception of other people and objects as opportunities, as threats, or as irrelevant—and the imputation of qualities to them more generally—is somewhat arbitrary from the standpoint of their "objective natures," and in many cases such meanings cannot be derived from knowledge of such objective qualities. Beauty—and many other qualities of objects—is in the mind of the beholder.

It is in this sense that we can be said to interact, not with individuals and objects, but with *our images* of them. We do not, after all, deal with them directly as physical "things" but as *objects* that we have clothed with identities and meanings. We act toward them on the basis of their meanings for us, the implications they have for our manifold plans of action.

The meanings of persons as objects are much more difficult to discern than are the meanings of less intractable objects like animals and simple machines, simply because people are *aware* that they have implications for other people. Human beings, as opposed to inanimate objects, continually attempt actively to influence the meanings attributed to them by their fellows, for they too have plans of action. Accordingly, they conduct themselves in ways calculated to gain their own ends as far as possible.

Interpersonal appraisal therefore has a number of unique features, as well as features common to social perception in general. In this article, the generic perceptual processes of identifying and interpreting objects will be taken up first, and then we shall turn to a detailed consideration of the more complex processes of interpersonal appraisal. And, as we go along, it should become ever more apparent that social perception is the two-way bridge between identities and interactions.

The process of perceiving objects, as we have repeatedly emphasized, is not a passive recording of external events. During each phase of the process, the perceiver actively intrudes upon the flow of data. Therefore, to understand what is "seen" we must understand the perceiver himself, as well as "what is really out there."

Only a small, selected fraction of the data emanating from the world around us is ever perceived in any sense by the individual. And of this fraction, only a selected portion is in turn "chosen" in some sense by the individual to be interpreted. The phase of interpretation, of assigning meaning to this fraction, is largely determined by the accumulated experiences and the role-identities of the individual, and it is creative in the sense that the meanings

assigned are compounds of the qualities of the objects perceived
and the qualities of the perceiver. Each of these phases is further
subject to biases, that is, to errors of omission and of commission.

These processes and their ramifications constitute the subject
of the present article.

DIRECT PERCEPTION

"Nobody really understands me" is a complaint that has rolled
down the ages, and it always contains some measure of truth. The
perceptions we have of others, which form the bases for our
interactions with them, are always incomplete and are also usually
somewhat less than accurate.

> Organisms have a highly limited span of attention and a highly
> limited span of immediate memory. . . . In the interest of
> ecomomizing effort we do three things . . . we narrow the selectivity
> of attention more or less to those things that are somehow essential
> to the enterprises in which we are engaged. Secondly, we "recode"
> into simpler form the diversity of events that we encounter. . . .
> Sometimes these recordings of information serve their economical
> function but lead to a serious loss of information. . . . *Not only is
> information lost, but misinformation is added.* Finally, we deal with
> the overload of information provided by the environment . . . by the
> use of technological aids.[1]

To understand the individual's appraisal of the people and
situations he encounters, we must examine in detail this process of
perception and recoding in which "not only is information lost, but
misinformation is added."

Sensory Limits

The physical sciences describe our universe as a continuous and
highly variegated kaleidoscope of particles in motion. The flux and
swirl of events occur all along the breadth of the electromagnetic
wave spectrum and involve all objects, from giant stars to the
internal mechanisms of the smallest molecules. Every situation we
step into contains a flood of these emanations. But the overwhelming
proportion of these data makes no impression upon us whatever.

In the first place, there are the sense limitations of the
individual as an animal. The physical characteristics of our sense
organs impose limitations on both the breadth and the acuity of
our perceptions. Even "normal" vision is sensitive to only a tiny

fraction of the total electromagnetic spectrum, and our other senses are similarly restricted. Sight, as well as our other senses, is further quite limited in terms of the distance at which events can be detected and in acuity of perceiving small objects.

"Normal" sensitivity is therefore a relative and human-centered yardstick, and, from the standpoint of the total wealth of data that could theoretically be perceived, the entire race of man is quite severely handicapped. It would be genocentric and pretentious to assume that nothing important happens that lies beyond our sense limits.

Science has, of course, developed technological devices that vastly extend the range, acuity, and breadth of our sensory abilities. But these devices still fall far short of total sensitivity, and, furthermore, they can be employed only under special conditions.

Perspective

Beyond these sense limits, one's perceptions are limited simply by the perspective or position from which he does the observing. His view is fundamentally colored by the position from which he looks, and it is therefore inevitably one-sided. While looking down the street, one, of necessity, misses what is going on up the street. Even a telescope, a microscope, or a television camera is bound by this same limitation of vantage point.

The bias of perspective that results from one's *social* positions is usually more extensive and more difficult to escape than are the effects of one's physical position in space. One's view of a university, for example, differs greatly, depending on whether he is a student, an administrator, or a naïve taxpayer.

Accuracy of perception quickly diminishes with increasing "social distance," just as it does with increasing physical distance, as a large number of studies has shown.[2] We tend to perceive only the gross outlines of people and events that lie any distance from our own positions in the social structure. Our appraisals of the very rich, the very poor, the Bohemian, and the priest tend to be exceedingly superficial. Just as buildings block our view of the next street, so the relative insulation of strata and subcultures from one another partly obstructs the visibility of even those social positions that are fairly close to us. And finally, just as people employ closed doors and window shades to screen themselves from their physical neighbors, so do they also employ polite conservation, etiquette, and "public relations" to screen themselves from their neighbors in the social structure.

Selective Perception

Even more important than sensory limitations and the limits
imposed by the position of the perceiver, perhaps, are the selective
attention and selective inattention of the perceiver. A man driving
a car through heavy traffic is selectively attuned to the movements
of other cars and the colors of traffic lights and does not even
"perceive" the movement of leaves on the trees along his path.
The native of a jungle, however, would be keenly aware of such
slight movements of leaves because they would signify the
movements of animals through the underbrush.

On the basis of our earlier discussion of social objects and plans
of action, we have seen that people tend to pay attention to those
social objects that they think most relevant to their plans of action
and tend to ignore those they judge irrelevant. ". . . [T]he
significance of objects for men and women is, in the final analysis,
what gives them the character of reality. For things are not real
because they exist, merely, but because they are important."[3] Of
course, the judgment of what perceptions are relevant and
irrelevant is not necessarily or automatically accurate; foreign
travelers have lost their lives because they ignored the twitching
of leaves, and primitives have been impaled on hood ornaments for
neglecting the significance of drivers' outstretched arms.

This example points up the fact that past training and
experience have a great deal to do with how one perceives situations
and other people. The learned cultural patterns, the perspectives
engendered by social position, and the individual's personal history
all enter into the determination of which subset of incoming stimuli
one perceives and which he ignores.

Much of the socializing of a child and also much of the
specialized training of youths and adults for skilled jobs involve
teaching specific ways of looking at and listening to the world.[4] And
a good deal of what we usually mean by "sophistication" is
the ability to "read the signs" that portend the circumstances
surrounding us.

Beyond all these considerations, the person's current hierarchy
of role-identities differentially affects his sensitivity to stimuli. He
selectively perceives those social objects that are most relevant to
his currently salient roles; as he drives down the street, a hungry
man is most likely to perceive an EAT or CAFE sign, and a man with
a headache is most likely to perceive a DRUGS sign. A burglar
appraises the same downtown street rather differently.

One's cultural belief system learned during socialization, the
sum of one's experiences, and one's currently salient roles all

contribute to the composition of what Bruner has called the individual's "expectancy set"; what he is set for perceiving in a situation and in other people.[5]

And the individual may sometimes be quite dogged in perceiving only those things congruent with his expectancy set. The force of external events can, however, break in upon one's expectancy set, and there are categories of stimuli—screams, explosions, shouts for help—that almost universally have this "breaking-in" property.

Less dramatically, the situation or the other people in it may present such an excellent opportunity for fulfilling a role-identity that is currently not salient that the individual's identity hierarchy and its corresponding expectancy set undergo change. One may come to complain about the noise of a party but stay to revel; an interruption becomes an encounter; the soldier joins the revolt.

The generalization . . . that the animal actively *seeks* those stimuli that will fulfill his current needs or desires must now be qualified. Just as the animal can actively choose situations, so do situations sometimes have the power to "change the animals mind."

INTERPRETATION

"Messages" from the outside world are even further altered as the individual *interprets* what he has perceived. He concentrates upon that subset of the incoming selected perceptions that seems most important to him and his current enterprises. This selective attention to some perceptions is in addition to the selective perception discussed before; that is, biased perception is further compounded by biased contemplation. One pays selective attention to one's selective perceptions. The common case of two people arguing over the "facts" of a situation that each feels should be obvious to anybody becomes more understandable in this perspective.

All these remarks on limitations and biases in perception per se apply to the process of interpretation as well. A human being has sense limitations, but he has even greater limitations of the number of things he can consciously entertain simultaneously. The person's currently salient roles influence how things are interpreted and defined as objects even more than they influence perception. Furthermore, the sum of one's post experiences affects both perception and the interpretation made of such perceptions.

Beyond these parallels, there is an additional factor involved in interpretations, that is, the "recoding" Bruner speaks of. *We simplify the waves of incoming perceptions by recording their contents into summary categories.* A flux of visual perceptions along a certain segment of the light band is registered as "red"; the nerve transmissions from several hundred taste buds are registered as "salty"; the inundation of sensory data as we pass a girl on the street is registered as "pretty," or perhaps "slim, pretty, and lost in thought."

These categories—usually made up of words or images—are rather high-level abstractions; that is, the chain of inference from the raw sense data is quite long in most cases. The less concrete and descriptive the words, the greater the abstraction involved. The abstraction "red," as a summary of a few thousand nerve excitations on the retina, is fairly simple and straightforward. But many other abstract categories, like "pretty," "well-meaning," "prosaic," are not. The greater the level of abstraction of the categories into which incoming preceptions are recorded, the more chance there is for such factors as selective attention, perspective resulting from the sum of one's experiences, and the current expectancy set (stemming from the currently salient identities) to influence and color how these perceptions will be interpreted by the individual.

It must be emphasized that this process of matching categories with sense data is neither simple nor automatically correct. We have seen that the inference is always based only on a biased subset of the total sense data available. We have also seen that the perceptions are often only signs for invented social objects like a "stolen base" or "freedom." In addition, that data are often ambiguous, and the interpretations are therefore fairly arbitrary. At best, the signs are merely elliptical hints. It is in this sense that we remarked earlier that reality is not given but is "fragile and adjudicated—a thing to be debated, compromised, and legislated."

Particularly with the more abstract social categories that have been invented by man rather than named by him (particularly that is, in the social realm), the organization and interpretation of incoming sense data are debatable. Most of what is commonly called description is actually interpretation, and people who think they are arguing over the facts are often actually arguing over how the facts should be interpreted.

These daily debates are engendered by the fact that people recode the sense data in different ways and into different categories. That is, people have divergent categories, and people also diverge on how they match data with categories. The pessimist sees that his glass is already half empty, and the optimist sees that his glass is still half full. The distinctive pattern of an individual's categories constitutes his belief system or world view, the perspective from which he tries to make sense of the world.

And it should be remembered that incompleteness, as well as twisting of facts, constitutes distortion. From a rather neutral conversation, one person selects those items that suggest positive reactions of others to him; another person selects those items that suggest rejection of that first person by the others. As the conversation includes both sets of items, each interpretation is based upon a true, but incomplete, perception and interpretation of the interaction.

Introduction of Misinformation

It is in the process of recoding sense data into symbolic categories that misinformation may be added. The process can be seen most clearly in identifying persons in terms of their *social* identities, the social categories to which they belong. Each major position (like "policeman"), as well as many important combinations of social positions (like "Irish policeman"), has attached to it in the popular culture a stereotype—a set of personal characteristics and behaviors that are expected of anyone who occupies that position. These stereotypes ordinarily contain certain amounts of statistical truth in them and thus are useful in orienting people toward those who occupy such positions.

Few individual members of any category, however, are truly typical in terms of the stereotype. Some of the characteristics one would expect to find in a member of the category are actually missing in most concrete instances, and the individual has additional characteristics that are not included in the stereotype. The stereotype only partially fits the individual.

Consequently, when we appraise a stranger by identifying his salient social positions and ringing in the corresponding stereotypes, our expectations toward him include things that do not apply to him, and they omit important things that *do* apply to him. In recoding the sense data on this person into symbolic categories (social positions and the attached stereotypes), we thus introduce two important kinds of misinformation into our appraisal of him: errors of commission and of omission.

Stereotyping

These notions lead to a somewhat different perspective on stereotyping and "prejudice" and suggest that the popular condemnation of all prejudgments and stereotyped thinking is facile and unrealistic. All living creatures, it seems, must employ stereotypes to categorize and deal with the kaleidoscopic flow of events around them. Nor can they wait contemplatively until all the facts are in; they must prejudge the meaning of the whole on the basis of a few signs and must act upon this jot of knowledge.[6]

In addition to errors of omission and commission, however, stereotypes often have two further inadequacies. The generalities employed by all living things tend to focus upon and to exaggerate those qualities of the objects that are most relevant to their own plans and lives. Such qualities often include only fractional and very biased subsets of the total properties of those objects. For example, a young man may think of females almost exclusively as objects possessing some degree of the multidimensional attribute "desirability." He is surprised to learn that they must also budget their money, defecate, and have dental checkups, as he himself does.

There is yet another way in which our imputations may lead us astray. We tend to impute to objects fixed qualities, when in reality the objects are characterized by variables that wax and wane. No one is smart or pretty all the time, and conversely, all of us have our moments. Nevertheless, our daily thoughts and conversations are filled with statements like "Jason's sure a bright fellow," "Gil's wife is very pretty," and "health food enthusiasts are out of it." These and a host of similar statements actually describe the statistical probabilities that objects will possess attributes at given moments, and we employ them because they are our best predictions of what we can expect from those objects in a series of encounters. But their validity is statistical rather than absolute.

In light of this perspective, stereotyping involves not merely the attitudes of rigid people discriminating against racial and ethnic outgroups. It is an inherent and inevitable aspect of every human appraisal of every person encountered.

It is therefore misleading to inquire about the presence or absence of stereotypes and prejudgments. Although all people employ these devices, the quality, objectivity, and validity of them vary tremendously, however. On one hand, there are the stereotypes of superstitions and prejudice, based upon emotion and faulty information and unamenable to change by contrary evidence. On the other, there are the stereotypes called "scientific generalizations and theories," which are arrived at by the most objective tchniques man has yet been able to develop and which are deliberately constructed to facilitate alteration or replacement by more accurate generalizations. It is true that many superstitions contain more than a little truth and that many scientific theories contain more than a little superstition and prejudice. But, despite this qualification, the contrast between the two types is basically the contrast between ignorance and knowledge. We must therefore inquire into the *quality*, not the existence, of stereotyping.[7]

Most individuals are aware, to some extent, that the stereotypes or categories they employ in coding incoming perceptions involve the hazarding of guesses. Consequently, people usually do not form instant judgments and hold them unalterably. Rather, they usually engage in a process of appraisal in which they seek further cues that will confirm, supplement, or refute their tentative first impressions. Often numbers of alternative judgments are simultaneously entertained, each of which is only tentatively held and each of which may be only tentatively discarded as further evidence accumulates. As evidence continues to accumulate, these alternatives are narrowed down, but often the process never reaches a final judgment. In this important sense, people are fundamentally ambivalent toward many of the people and objects around them. The individual acts toward the person or object in an equivocal way that takes some account of the various alternative evaluations he is entertaining; that is, he acts in such a way as to hedge his bets that any of the interpretations is actually valid, so that he is covered to some extent, whatever the outcome. And even though first impressions produce some selective perception and interpretation of the subsequent events, the person is still more or less prepared to change his mind.

In summary, then, the interpretation of incoming sensory perceptions by fitting them into abstract categories with attached stereotypes is altogether a gamble carried out by educated guesswork.

Nonetheless, it is often the best one can do, particularly in a first encounter. In mobile, pluralistic societies like our own, such stereotypes attached to social identities are typically our sole source of orientation toward the majority of people we encounter. From visible clues to social identity, we connect strangers with stereotypes, so that we may predict their behavior and characteristics.[8]

Personal Reputations

Another device very much like stereotypes is the *personal reputation*, indirect knowledge about another person that preconditions one's view of him. Unlike a stereotype, which has to do with a person's *social* identity, a personal reputation has to do with *personal* identity. Reputations, then, are unique, whereas stereotypes are applied to any and all occupants of a given position.

Despite this difference, however, both devices function similarly by providing us with "prepackaged" appraisals of the other person, so that we need not start from scratch in deciphering the potential meaning of that other. Both also share the curious mixture of truth and error that stems from the partial overlap of category with person. That is, both stereotype and reputation (1) are incomplete and (2) contain a certain freight of misinformation about the person.

In fact, the two devices are seldom independent. In most concrete instances, the symbolic molds into which we recode incoming data about another person represent some kind of synthesis of impersonal reputation (the stereotypes associated with his social positions) and personal reputation. The relative contribution of the two varies from case to case, of course, including the oft-encountered extreme in which only the impersonal reputation is known. This situation is more frequent in *Gesellschaft* societies like our own than in small *Gemeinschaft* communities but it must be remembered that even in our own society we move in highly limited circles: Very often we have heard at least some fragmentary information about a particular person before we actually come in contact with him.

In light of the importance of reputations, we should consider the manner in which they are formed and employed.

INDIRECT PERCEPTION

The reputations we associate with persons are fundamentally indirect perceptions of them. We hear anecdotes, epithets, and characterizations of people from third parties, and through them we form impressions of these people without ever having met them. Therein lies the economy of reputations and their liability.

Presumably the third parties have had direct contact with alter and are speaking from personal knowledge, at least in part. As we have seen, even direct appraisal of persons is a hazardous and inherently somewhat inaccurate process. A third party's direct knowledge of alter in itself represents a simplified, distorted, and selective distillate of those limited data about alter that he has managed to take in.

But, more important, what this third party in turn *tells* us about alter represents only a biased sample of his own limited knowledge. The things this third party decides to tell us are influenced by his own feelings, about alter, his perceptions of what our own goals toward alter might be, and the sort of feelings he wishes us to have toward alter.

Nor does distribution end there. We, in turn, selectively perceive and interpret this biased transmission of information. The message received is not the same as the message sent. What we make of it depends on its congruence with other information we may have about alter, on our estimates of the third party's reliability and allegiances, and so forth.

Consequently, personal reputations are thrice cursed from the point of view of dependable knowledge of alter. Yet reputational knowledge is priceless, for, despite its deficiencies, it does allow us to orient ourselves toward alter *before* we actually encounter him; it affords us "lead time" in dealing with him. It would ordinarily require a number of meetings to obtain the kind of information about alter, however incomplete and distorted, that is contained in his prepackaged reputation. Very often this utility of reputations, like that of stereotypes, outweighs the risks attendant upon their use.

PECULIARITIES OF PERSONS AS OBJECTS

As we have seen, perception is generically a most difficult enterprise and one that is rewarded with varyingly mediocre success. The perception of persons, as a particularly important special case of this process, is subject to certain unique difficulties that arise from some peculiarities of persons as objects.

In the first place, no other object can purposefully and differentially conceal or reveal certain of its characteristics. Being a self-conscious animal, man—like no other object—modifies his behavior in view of the fact that he is under observation. He hides certain facts about himself and advertises others, in an attempt to influence our appraisals of him. We are all engaged in public relations for ourselves. Furthermore, to another observer in a quite different relationship to him, the person adjusts this concealing and revealing behavior, hiding some things that have been previously revealed and advertising some that have been previously hidden.

Consequently, a person is never quite the same object to any two observers. Knowledge of a person is relative to the relationship in which one stands with him. What is truth from the perspective of an observer in one relationship to him is error from the perspective of another observer in a different relationship to him. In this pragmatic sense, his nature as an object is not determined by himself as an individual but rather in interaction with another.

Of course, this analysis is not the whole story. His tactics of concealment and revelation are not completely effective. Those data about himself that he purposely reveals or permits to be discovered (what Goffman calls "expressions given")[9] may not be the only data that the observer receives. The person's expressive control is never total; unconscious gestures, attitudes, habits, and slips reveal things without his conscious effort (which Goffman calls expressions "given off"). Furthermore, the observer may have learned from others certain facts about the person that the latter thought he had effectively concealed.

Beyond these problems of information control,[10] by which we mean control of expression of information, there is often a discrepancy between expressions transmitted and the impressions received. An act, gesture, or sentence is often amenable to more than one interpretation, so that the impression received by the observer may not be the one intended for him to receive.

The person as object has still another peculiar means of controlling appraisals of himself, however. Persons, unlike other objects, purposively reward the observer for making certain appraisals and punish him for making others. Through differential sanctions, the person thus helps to bring about the desired image of himself in the eyes of the observer, reinforcing the effects of concealment and revelation tactics.

THE ROLE OF PERCEPTION IN INTERACTION

Altogether, then, it appears that our appraisals of people are considerably less than completely accurate. But if identification of objects, especially persons, is so crucial to interaction, how can we proceed on the basis of such faulty appraisals? It is certainly true that we would do better in interaction if we had more or better information about the other persons, but we have seen that the pictures we receive of others necessarily contain mixtures of truth and error. These pictures bear only probabilistic correspondence to the other persons themselves.

In consequence, we must act always on the basis of incomplete evidence. We cannot wait for an illusory sense of certainty, for life moves too swiftly; we must continually gamble that our appraisals of others are fairly accurate.

There are two kinds of error that can befall us in these gambles: We may be overly cautious and reluctant to bet upon our appraisals, or we may too rashly assume that our superficial images of the others are essentially correct. Individuals no doubt differ rather characteristically in the types of error that they are prone to make, some being rashly bold in interaction and others being timidly overcautious in acting on their appraisals.

But even when we manage to avoid either of these gambling errors by taking only tentative action, on the basis of moderate evidence, our images of alter are still incomplete and somewhat misleading. Nevertheless these images are all we have; accordingly, we are really acting toward our images rather than toward the metaphysical realities that somehow lie behind them. We *impute* to the real him all those characteristics, goals, and motives that constitute our image of him, *and then we act toward him in terms of those imputed features.*

If our images are not minimally accurate, we cannot have successful social lives, yet there is a wide gap between this sort of minimum and complete accuracy. The relative worth of these images reflects the extent to which they contain that information most relevant to the particular interaction situations in which we encounter alter and the extent to which the freight of misinformation is either pragmatically irrelevant to those particular situations or is cleared up by alter in response to our actions toward him.

In general, the greater the breadth and the duration of our experiences with alter, the more accurate our images of him become. Yet this clarification process is not an automatic one, for, although accurate appraisal of persons is rewarding to the individual in that it helps him deal more effectively with the world, this reward factor motivates him only up to the point where he *thinks* he is getting along well with alter. It does not motivate him to strive for greater accuracy of perception beyond this point.

In fact, this reward factor may be counteracted by rewards for maintaining a particular inaccurate image of alter. Ego-defense needs, for example, may necessitate believing that alter thinks highly of one or denying that alter knows more about cabbages or kings than ego does.

By various mechanisms ego may thus actively strive to maintain his distorted view of alter.[11] He may selectively ignore data about alter that are at variance with his view of him, and, when this method fails, he may explain away the incongruous data as resulting from factors like temporary mood or unusual circumstances. For example, the informal gaiety of a "dull, bookish professor" may be explained away as the result of a break in the rainy weather or a publication acceptance, so that one's image of him remains intact. This sort of thing may be supported by others who share the same motives, reinforcing one's image of alter regardless of what alter may actually do.

Whether or not his initial inaccurate image of alter is functional for ego, he may actually cause it to become accurate, an instance of what is known as a "self-fulfilling prophecy."[12] That is, by proceeding as though his image of alter were true, the person may effectively force alter to behave in a fashion that supports the person's image of him. This process might be described by the following paradigm:

A. Ego makes an inference about alter.
B. Ego acts toward alter in terms of this inference.
C. Alter makes inferences about ego in terms of his action.
D. Alter tends to react toward ego in terms of his inference.
E. Thus ego's inferences tend to be confirmed by alter's actions.

. . . To choose an example among many possible ones, my informant rented a room for several days from a middle-aged woman. After seeing her only briefly, and before he had spoken with her, he "intuited" that she was a warm accepting person who was filled with psychic strength and goodness. When he first talked with her a couple hours later, his manner was far more friendly and patronizing than usual. He showed interest in her collection of antiques, asked about her children, and ended up by saying he felt she was a wonderful person and he wanted to rent from her, partly because they would have a chance to talk together. During the next few days, the writer had a chance to question other tenants and neighbors about the landlady. They described a fairly caustic gossiper who was unreasonably strict about the use of electricity, and of her property and grounds. Her attitude toward the writer was taciturn. But she responded graciously to my informant's open friendliness. She sought him out to talk with on several occasions, she inquired if there was enough light in his room for late reading and supplied him with a table lamp, etc. In her behavior toward him, my informant's intuition certainly seemed correct.[13]

The inevitable conclusion we must draw from our consideration of person perception, however foreign it may seem to common-sense realism, is that our images of people will always contain some admixture of truth and error but that this must be a *workable* admixture. That is to say, it must contain just enough of the relevant truth about alter to allow us to take minimally successful action toward him. Seldom are we truly *en rapport* with him, for we do not truly know him. Ordinarily, we understand him just well enough to work out a sort of fumbling, on-again, off-again accommodation in which we manage to get along with, and past, one another without serious conflict. Only rarely, and then most often in quite intimate relationships, do we truly communicate and interact in harmony.

Notes

1. Bruner, Jerome S., "Social Psychology and Perception," in E. E. Macoby, T. M. Newcomb, and E. L. Hartley (eds.), *Readings in Social Psychology* (3rd ed.), (New York: Holt, Rinehart and Winston, 1958), pp. 85–94. Quotations from p. 86.

2. See, for example, Allison Davis, B. B. Gardner, and M. R. Gardner, *Deep South* (University of Chicago Press, 1941), p. 65 and passim. Also, Milton Rokeach, *The Open and Closed Mind* (New York: Basic Books, 1960), pp. 166 ff.; and J. L. Simmons, "Tolerance of Divergent Attitudes," *Social Forces* **43**, (March 1965):347–352.

3. Park, Robert E., "Human Nature, Attitudes, and Mores," in Kimball Young (ed.) *Social Attitudes* (New York: Holt, Rinehart and Winston, 1931), pp. 17–54. Quotation from p. 35.

4. Strauss, Anselm L., *Mirrors and Masks* (New York: Free Press, 1959), pp. 91–93.

5. Bruner, "Social Psychology and Perception."

6. Hess, Eckhard H., "Ethology: An Approach Toward the Complete Analysis of Behavior," in Roger Brown, Eugene Galanter, and George Mandler, (eds.) *New Directions in Psychology* (New York: Holt, Rinehart and Winston, 1962), pp. 157–266, especially pp. 179–187.

7. Klapp, Orrin E., *Heroes, Villains, and Fools* (Englewood Cliffs, N.J.: Prentice-Hall, 1962), pp. 1–24; and Joshua A. Fishman, "An Examination of the Process and Function of Social Stereotyping," *Journal of Social Psychology* **43**, (February 1956):27–64.

8. Stone, Gregory P., "City Shoppers and Urban Identification: Observations on the Social Psychology of City Life," *American Journal of Sociology* **60**, (July 1954):36–45; William H. Form and Stone, "Urbanism, Anonymity, and Status Symbolism," *American Journal of Sociology* **62**, (March 1957):504–514; Erving Goffman, "Symbols of Class Status," *British Journal of Sociology* **2**, (December 1951):294–304.

9. Goffman, Erving, *The Presentation of Self in Everyday Life* (Garden City, N.Y.: Doubleday Anchor, 1959), pp. 2 ff.

10. Cf. Erving Goffman, *Stigma: Notes on the Management of Spoiled Identity* (Englewood Cliffs, N.J.: Prentice-Hall, 1963), especially Chapter 2 ("Information Control and Personal Identity").

11. Simmons, J. L., "On Maintaining Deviant Belief Systems: A Case Study," *Social Problems* **11**, (Winter 1964):250–256.

12. Merton, Robert K., "The Self-Fulfilling Prophecy," in Merton (ed.), *Social Theory and Social Structure* (rev. ed.) (New York: Free Press, 1957), pp. 421–438.

13. Simmons, "On Maintaining Deviant Belief Systems," p. 253.

6

SOME TENTATIVE AXIOMS OF COMMUNICATION

Paul Watzlawick, Janet Beavin, and Don Jackson

THE IMPOSSIBILITY OF NOT COMMUNICATING

First of all, there is a property of behavior that could hardly
be more basic and is, therefore, often overlooked: Behavior
has no opposite. In other words, there is no such thing as
nonbehavior or, to put it even more simply: One cannot *not*
behave. Now, if it is accepted that all behavior in an interactional
situation[1] has message value, i.e., is communication, it follows
that no matter how one may try, one cannot *not* communicate.
Activity or inactivity, words or silence all have message value:
They influence others and these others, in turn, cannot *not*

Reprinted from *Pragmatics of Human Communication* by Paul
Watzlawick, Janet Helmick Beavin, and Don D. Jackson, with permission
of W. W. Norton & Company, Inc. Copyright © 1967 by W. W. Norton
& Company, Inc.

respond to these communications and are thus themselves communicating. It should be clearly understood that the mere absence of talking or of taking notice of each other is no exception to what has just been asserted. The man at a crowded lunch counter who looks straight ahead, or the airplane passenger who sits with his eyes closed, are both communicating that they do not want to speak to anybody or be spoken to, and their neighbors usually "get the message" and respond appropriately by leaving them alone. This, obviously, is just as much an interchange of communication as an animated discussion.[2]

Neither can we say that "communication" only takes place when it is intentional, conscious, or successful, that is, when mutual understanding occurs. Whether message sent equals message received is an important but different order of analysis, as it must rest ultimately on evaluations of specific, introspective, subject-reported data, which we choose to neglect for the exposition of a behavioral theory of communiication. On the question of misunderstanding, our concern, given certain formal properties of communication, is with the development of related pathologies, aside from, indeed in spite of, the motivations or intentions of the communicants.

To summarize, a metacommunicational axiom of the pragmatics of communication can be postulated: *One cannot* not *communicate*.

THE CONTENT AND RELATIONSHIP LEVELS OF COMMUNICATION

Another axiom was hinted at in the foregoing when it was suggested that any communication implies a commitment and thereby defines the relationship. This is another way of saying that a communication not only conveys information, but that at the same time it imposes behavior. Following Bateson (2), these two operations have come to be known as the "report" and the "command" aspects, respectively, of any communication. Bateson exemplifies these two aspects by means of a physiological analogy: Let A, B, and C be a linear chain of neurons. Then the firing of neuron B is both a "report" that neuron A has fired and a "command" for neuron C to fire.

The report aspect of a message conveys information and is, therefore, synonymous in human communication with the *content* of the message. It may be about anything that is communicable regardless of whether the particular information is true or false, valid, invalid, or undecidable. The command aspect, on the

other hand, refers to what sort of a message it is to be taken as, and, therefore, ultimately to the *relationship* between the communicants. All such relationship statements are about one or several of the following assertions: "This is how I see myself . . . this is how I see you . . . this is how I see you seeing me . . ." and so forth in theoretically infinite regress. Thus, for instance, the messages "It is important to release the clutch gradually and smoothly" and "Just let the clutch go, it'll ruin the transmission in no time" have approximately the same information content (report aspect), but they obviously define very different relationships.
To avoid any misunderstanding about the foregoing, we want to make it clear that relationships are only rarely defined deliberately or with full awareness. In fact, it seems that the more spontaneous and "healthy" a relationship, the more the relationship aspect of communication recedes into the background. Conversely, "sick" relationships are characterized by a constant struggle about the nature of the relationship, with the content aspect of communication becoming less and less important.

For the time being let us merely summarize the foregoing into another axiom of our tentative calculus: *Every communication has a content and a relationship aspect such that the latter classifies the former and is therefore a metacommunication.*[3]

THE PUNCTUATION OF THE SEQUENCE OF EVENTS

The next basic characteristic of communication we wish to explore regards interaction—exchanges of messages—between communicants. To an outside observer, *a series of communications can be viewed as an uninterrupted sequence of interchanges.* However, the participants in the interaction always introduce what, following Whorf (3), Bateson and Jackson (1) have termed the "punctuation of the sequence of events." They state:

> The stimulus-response psychologist typically confines his attention to sequences of interchange so short that it is possible to label one item of input as "stimulus" and another item as "reinforcement" while labelling what the subject does between these two events as "response." Within the short sequence so excised, it is possible to talk about "psychology" of the subject. In contrast, the sequences of interchange which we are here discussing are very much longer and therefore have the characteristic that every item in the sequence is simultaneously stimulus, response and reinforcement. A given item of A's behavior is a stimulus insofar as it is followed by an item contributed by B and that by another item contributed

by A. But insofar as A's item is sandwiched between two items contributed by B, it is a response. Similarly A's item is a reinforcement insofar as it follows an item contributed by B. The ongoing interchanges, then, which we are here discussing, constitute a chain of overlapping triadic links, each of which is comparable to a stimulus-response-reinforcement sequence. We can take any triad of our interchange and see it as a single trial in a stimulus-response learning experiment.

If we look at the conventional learning experiments from this point of view, we observe at once that repeated trials amount to a differentiation of relationship between the two organisms concerned —the experimenter and his subject. The sequence of trials is so punctuated that it is always the experimenter who seems to provide the "stimuli" and the "reinforcements," while the subject provides the "responses." These words are here deliberately put in quotation marks because the role definitions are in fact only created by the willingness of the organisms to accept the system of punctuation. The "reality" of the role definitions is only of the same order as the reality of a bat on a Rorschach card—a more or less over-determined creation of the perceptive process. The rat who said "I have got my experimenter trained. Each time I press the lever he gives me food" was declining to accept the punctuation of the sequence which the experimenter was seeking to impose.

It is still true, however, that in a long sequence of interchange, the organisms concerned—especially if these be people—will in fact punctuate the sequence so that it will appear that one or the other has initiative, dominance, dependency or the like. That is, they will set up between them patterns of interchange (about which they may or may not be in agreement) and these patterns will in fact be rules of contingency regarding the exchange of reinforcement. While rats are too nice to re-label, some psychiatric patients are not, and provide psychological trauma for the therapist!

It is not the issue here whether punctuation of communicational sequence is, in general, good or bad, as it should be immediately obvious that punctuation *organizes* behavioral events and is therefore vital to ongoing interactions. Culturally, we share many conventions of punctuation which, while no more or less accurate than other views of the same events, serve to organize common and important interactional sequences. For example, we call a person in a group behaving in one way the "leader" and another the "follower," although on reflection it is difficult to say which comes first or where one would be without the other.

Disagreement about how to punctuate the sequence of events is at the root of countless relationship struggles. Suppose a couple have a marital problem to which he contributes passive withdrawal, while her 50 percent is nagging criticism. In explaining their frustrations, the husband will state that withdrawal is his only *defense against* her nagging, while she will label this explanation a gross and willful distortion of what "really" happens in their marriage: Namely, that she is critical of him *because of* his passivity. Stripped of all ephemeral and fortuitous elements, their fights consist of a monotonous exchange of the messages "I withdraw because you nag" and "I nag because you withdraw." Represented graphically, with an arbitrary beginning point, their interaction looks somewhat as shown below.

It can be seen that the husband only perceives triads 2—3—4, 4—5—6, 6—7—8, etc., where his behavior (solid arrows) is "merely" a response to her behavior (the broken arrows). With her it is exactly the other way around; she punctuates the sequence of events into the triads 1—2—3, 3—4—5, 5—6—7, etc., and sees herself as ony reacting to, but not determining, her husband's behavior. In conjoint psychotherapy with couples one is frequently struck by the

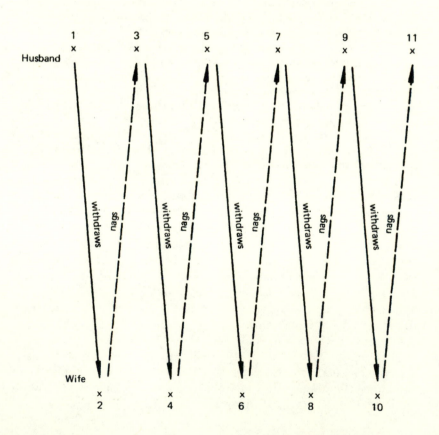

intensity of what in traditional psychotherapy would be referred to as "reality distortion" on the part of both parties. It is often hard to believe that two individuals could have such divergent views on many elements of joint experience. And yet the problem lies primarily in an area already frequently mentioned: their inability to metacommunicate about their respective patterning of their interaction. This interaction is of an oscillatory yes-no-yes-no-yes nature which theoretically can go on ad infinitum and almost invariably is accompanied . . . by the typical charges of badness or madness.

Thus we add a third metacommunicational axiom: *The nature of a relationship is contingent upon the punctuation of the communicational sequences between the communicants.*

Notes

[1] It might be added that, even alone, it is possible to have dialogues in fantasy, with one's hallucinations, or with life. Perhaps such internal "communication" follows some of the same rules which govern interpersonal communication; such unobservable phenomena, however, are outside the scope of our meaning of the term.

[2] Very interesting research in this field has been carried out by Luft, who studied what he calls "social stimulus deprivation." He brought two strangers together in a room, made them sit across from each other and instructed them "not to talk or communicate in any way." Subsequent interviews revealed the highly stressful nature of this situation. To quote the author:

> He has before him the other unique individual with his ongoing, though muted, behavior. At this point, it is postulated, that true interpersonal testing takes place, and only part of this testing may be done consciously. For example, how does the other subject respond to him and to the small nonverbal cues which he sends out? Is there an attempt at understanding his enquiring glance, or is it coldly ignored? Does the other subject display postural cues of tension, indicating some distress at confronting him? Does he grow increasingly comfortable, indicating some kind of acceptance, or will the other treat him as if he were a thing which did not exist? These and many other kinds of readily discernible behavior appear to take place.

[3] We have chosen, somewhat arbitrarily, to say that the relationship classifies, or subsumes, the content aspect, although it is equally accurate in logical analysis to say that the class is defined by its members and therefore the content aspect can be said to define the relationship aspect. Since our primary interest is not information exchange but the pragmatics of communication, we will use the former approach.

References

1. Bateson, Gregory, and Jackson, Don D. "Some Varieties of Pathogenic Organization," in David McRioch (ed.). *Disorders of Communication*, vol. 42 (Research Publications, Association for Research in Nervous and Mental Disease, 1964), pp. 270–283.
2. Ruesch, Jurgen, and Bateson, Gregory. *Communication: The Social Matrix of Psychiatry* (New York: W. W. Norton, 1951).
3. Whorf, Benjamin Lee. "Science and Linguistics," from *Language, Thought, and Reality*, in John B. Carroll (ed.). *Selected Writings of Benjamin Lee Whorf* (New York: Wiley, 1956), pp. 207–219.

Part II
THE SYMBOLIC SIGNIFICANCE OF BEHAVIOR

Human behavior is essentially symbolic in nature. The point is not that everything we do and say is symbolic by definition, but rather that our conduct acquires a certain abstract, symbolic quality that somehow conveys a distinctive personal significance that cannot be explained in purely physical terms—so many glances, movements, sounds, and so forth. Behavior is immediate and concrete but it is also abstract; that is, it tends to represent or point beyond itself. The characteristic and enduring devices that people use to express or represent experiences constitute what is meant by the "symbolic significance" of behavior. We express not only how we see ourselves, but also how we interpret others as they experience themselves within a given situation. Thus, as Author Burton says, "the symbol not only gathers to itself all of the individual energy but the collective aspects as well." It would not be an exaggeration to claim that a person who engages in communication is a living enactment of a uniquely constituted symbolic reality. Face-to-face interaction could hardly be sustained apart from the willingness of participants to seek through word and gesture to translate their own unique experience of the situation into symbolic configurations that have common, consensual value. It is largely through this process of identifying with certain symbols (and by ignoring others) that individuals come to know and understand one another. Since every human environment has its own distinct possibilities for personal exploration, the actual range of potentialities for symbolic interchange are virtually inexhaustible.

The essays in this part examine the pervasive impact of symbols on human identity and relation. In "Social Interaction in Everyday Life," Peter L. Berger and Thomas Luckmann examine the place of signs and symbols in daily experience. The prototype of all social interaction, they contend, is the face-to-face situation. In the vivd presence and concreteness of the "here-and-now," people create symbolic meaning through the very sequencing of reflective signs and reactions that "mirror" their personal orientations and response. Signs reveal subjective meaning and intent; and language, with its ability to transcend the immediate moment, gives order to these symbolic themes and integrates them into a meaningful whole. Thus, Berger and Luckmann conclude: "Symbolism and symbolic language become essential constituents of the reality of everyday life and of the common sense apprehension of this reality." Such a position assumes that an individual acts toward people and events on the basis of the meanings that are derived through personal interaction. As Herbert Blumer explains in "The Nature of Symbolic Interactionism," the meaning of an encounter cannot be separated from the personal interpretations that are attributed to the sequence of nonverbal and verbal activity. One does not experience the meanings of another person directly, but indirectly, by being willing and capable of stepping out of one's own immediate frame of reference and adopting the perspective or role assumed by the other. By addressing ourselves as both subject and object of others' responses, we gradually acquire the indications and signs required to form a "reflected" definition of self.

In a discussion of "Symbolic Strategies," Sol Worth and Larry Gross distinguish natural events from symbolic events by the type of interpretive strategy used to assign meaning. We recognize the existence of natural events such as leaves falling from a tree, but we employ no particular strategy of interpretation in such cases. There is a certain transparency associated with natural events, a correspondence between awareness and the

objects of awareness. We also recognize the existence of symbolic
events but add an expectation of *intentionality* that gives rise
to interpretive strategies. The concept of intent refers to the
sense of direction and purpose that is associated with a given
human act or event. Symbolic events convey an *assumption*
of intentional creation, a creation conceived and enacted for a
particular communicative purpose. The authors further distinguish
between strategies arising from the assumption of intent as
implied by the one who performs and the assumption of intent
as *inferred* by the one who is the object of the performance. A
communicative situation is described as one in which the various
interpretations of intention are verified through the words,
gestures, rules, conventions, and styles of performance.

The remaining essays in Part II examine particular sources of
symbolic identification. When judging the import of human
meaning, we naturally focus on the face and facial expression for
cues. The face is the primary expressor of emotional meaning.
There is evidence that the face conveys a primitive and
perhaps universal code of emotional meaning. The face is visible,
transparent, and accessible to inspection. In "Facial Engagements"
Erving Goffman explores the complex rules that govern the various
readings that human beings assign to certain basic facial
expressions. The themes vary from looks of nonrecognition,
indifference, and other modes of "civil inattention" to phases of
visual activity that change from opening moves and clearance signs
to later moments of focused visual interest. Goffman concludes with
an analysis of facial cues used in leave-taking and other signs of
impending separation from the implicit communicative contract.

Given the staggering complexity of language, there is no
limit to the number of ways of classifying and interpreting what
happens symbolically when persons interact through the spoken or
written word. Of importance is the fascination of sound itself, the
psychological significance of word meanings, syntax, and the effect
of speech on relationships. Also, one may cut through the particulars
and focus on the larger functional importance of what is said and
done. The term function refers to the use words play in human
affairs, particularly their impact on the respective notions of what
is occurring between the respective parties of communication. In
the essay "When People Talk with People" John Condon offers
an absorbing account of the functional uses of language and shows
how patterns of human talk reflect particular psychological wants,
emotions, inner defenses, and needs for information, magic, ritual,
and understanding of the subtext or "metacommunication" of
messages.

Symbols vary greatly in degree of immediacy. The immediacy of a given message is constrained by the sense of personal presence, proximity, and availability in the here-and-now. In "Language within Language" Albert Mehrabian examines evidence that behavior conveys immediacy to the degree that participants can sustain a positive and supportive orientation toward the physical presence of one another. Some cues to immediacy, such as word choice, tense, and pronoun usage, exist within the content of speech. Others emerge from style, mode of address, and signs of similarity or disaffiliation with another person. Also important are spatial-temporal terms ("these," "those," "here," "there") because of their impact on one's sense of psychological distance and remoteness. Mehrabian also considers specificity in symbolism, selective emphases, the interplay among "agents," "action," and "objects," modifers, and automatic phrasing. The data suggest that any decision involved in what to say or leave unsaid may define the immediacy of subjective involvements in symbolic activity.

In studying the dynamics of personal encounters, it is important to discover the sense in which the most powerful messages are conveyed in silence. Communication cannot be equated solely with the impact of spoken or written words. Feelings, emotions, moods, expectations, and biases do not necessarily lend themselves to verbal expression. In "Communication without Words," Albert Mehrabian discusses the communicative importance of facial expression, tone of voice, gesture, and other aspects of messages. He concludes with an engaging discussion of the complex interplay that goes on between verbal and nonverbal modes of interaction.

The information gained from symbolic interaction shapes our experience of ourselves and others. We participate in the symbolic reality of others as a means of obtaining personal identification and worth. At the same time we need protection against exposure to symbols that undermine our most privileged definitions of who we are. Thus, the symbolic environment serves two critical, life-sustaining functions: (1) to expand and deepen our basic sense of uniqueness and (2) to protect against unpleasant and unwanted information. Implicit in the notion of symbolic interaction is the idea of risk. Communication involves the risk of change, and sometimes the change is not pleasant. Hence, persons create inner defenses to ward off the potentially adverse exposure to unwanted information. In a discussion of "Defensive Communication" Jack Gibb examines the complex interplay between our inner feelings of threat and the process of communication. Defensive behavior diverts energy from common tasks to self-defense; it may also trigger defensive reactions in others or interfere with effective listening and accurate perception. If left unchecked, it may lead to severe losses of efficiency in communication. From data gathered from recordings of various conversations, Gibb offers an insightful view of defensive communication and the requirements necessary to establish a supportive social climate.

7

SOCIAL INTERACTION IN EVERYDAY LIFE

Peter L. Berger
Thomas Luckmann

The reality of everyday life is shared with others. But how are
these others themselves experienced in everyday life? Again, it is
possible to differentiate between several modes of such experience.

The most important experience of others takes place in the
face-to-face situation, which is the prototypical case of social
interaction. All other cases are derivatives of it.

In the face-to-face situation the other is appresented to me in
a vivid present shared by both of us. I know that in the same vivid
present I am appresented to him. My and his "here and now"
continuously impinge on each other as long as the face-to-face
situation continues. As a result, there is a continuous interchange of
my expressivity and his. I see him smile, then react to my frown by

Reprinted with permission from *The Social Construction of Reality* by
Peter L. Berger and Thomas Luckmann (Garden City, N.Y.: Doubleday
and Company, Inc., 1966).

stopping the smile, then smiling again as I smile, and so on. Every expression of mine is oriented toward him, and vice versa, and this continuous reciprocity of expressive acts is simultaneously available to both of us. This means that, in the face-to-face situation, the other's subjectivity is available to me through a maximum of symptoms. To be sure, I may misinterpret some of these symptoms. I may think that the other is smiling while in fact he is smirking. Nevertheless, no other form of social relating can reproduce the plenitude of symptoms of subjectivity present in the face-to-face situation. Only here is the other's subjectivity emphatically "close." All other forms of relating to the other are, in varying degrees, "remote."

In the face-to-face situation the other is fully real. This reality is part of the overall reality of everyday life, and as such massive and compelling. To be sure, another may be real to me without my having encountered him face to face—by reputation, say, or by having corresponded with him. Nevertheless, he becomes real to me in the fullest sense of the word only when I meet him face to face. Indeed, it may be argued that the other in the face-to-face situation is more real to me than I myself. Of course I "know myself better" than I can ever know him. My subjectivity is accessible to me in a way his can never be, no matter how "close" our relationship. My past is available to me in memory in a fullness with which I can never reconstruct his, however much he may tell me about it. But this "better knowledge" of myself requires reflection. It is not immediately appresented to me. The other, however, *is* so appresented in the face-to-face situation. "What he is," therefore, is ongoingly available to me. This availability is continuous and prereflective. On the other hand, "What I am" is *not* so available. To make it available requires that I stop, arrest the continuous spontaneity of my experience, and deliberately turn my attention back upon myself. What is more, such reflection about myself is typically occasioned by the attitude toward me that *the other* exhibits. It is typically a "mirror" response to attitudes of the other.

It follows that relations with others in the face-to-face situation are highly flexible. Put negatively, it is comparatively difficult to impose rigid patterns upon face-to-face interaction. Whatever patterns are introduced will be continuously modified through the exceedingly variegated and subtle interchange of subjective meanings that goes on. For instance, I may view the other as someone inherently unfriendly to me and act toward him within a pattern of "unfriendly relations" as understood by me. In the face-to-face situation, however, the other may confront me with attitudes and acts that contradict this pattern, perhaps up to a point where I am led to abandon the pattern as inapplicable and to view him as friendly. In other words, the pattern cannot sustain the massive evidence of the other's subjectivity that is available to me in the face-to-face situation. By contrast, it is much easier for me to ignore such evidence as long as I do not encounter the other face to face. Even in such a relatively "close" relation as may be maintained by correspondence I can more successfully dismiss the other's protestations of friendship as not actually representing his subjective attitude to me, simply because in correspondence I lack the immediate, continuous and massively real presence of his expressivity. It is, to be sure, possible for me to misinterpret the other's meanings even in the face-to-face situation, as it is possible for him "hypocritically" to hide his meanings. All the same, both misinterpretation and "hypocrisy" are more difficult to sustain in face-to-face interaction than in less "close" forms of social relations.

On the other hand, I apprehend the other by means of typificatory schemes even in the face-to-face situation, although these schemes are more "vulnerable" to his interference than in "remoter" forms of interaction. Put differently, while it is comparatively difficult to impose rigid patterns on face-to-face interaction, even it is patterned from the beginning if it takes place within the routines of everyday life. (We can leave aside for later consideration cases of interaction between complete strangers who have no common background of everyday life.) The reality of everyday life contains typificatory schemes in terms of which others are apprehended and "dealt with" in face-to-face encounters. Thus I apprehend the other as "a man," "a European," "a buyer," "a jovial type," and so on. All these typificatious ongoingly affect my interaction with him as, say, I decide to show him a good time on the town before trying to sell him my product. Our face-to-face interaction will be patterned by these typifications as long as they do not become problematic through interference on his part. Thus he may come up with evidence that, although "a man," "a European" and "a buyer," he is also a self-righteous moralist, and that what appeared first as joviality is actually an expression of contempt for Americans in general and American salesmen in particular. At this point, of course, my typificatory scheme will have to be modified, and the evening planned differently in accordance with this modification. Unless thus challenged, though, the typifications will hold until further notice and will determine my actions in the situation.

The typificatory schemes entering into face-to-face situations are, of course, reciprocal. The other also apprehends me in a typified way—as "a man," "an American," "a salesman," "an ingratiating fellow," and so on. The other's typifications are as susceptible to my interference as mine are to his. In other words, the two typificatory schemes enter into an ongoing "negotiation" in the face-to-face situation. In everyday life such "negotiation" is itself likely to be prearranged in a typical manner—as in the typical bargaining process between buyers and salesman. Thus, most of the time, my encounters with others in everyday life are typical in a double sense—I apprehend the other *as* a type and I interact with him in a situation that is it itself typical.

The typifications of social interaction become progressively anonymous the farther away they are from the face-to-face situation. Every typification, of course, entails incipient anonymity. If I typify my friend Henry as a member of category X (say as an Englishman), I *ipso facto* interpret at least certain aspects of his conduct as resulting from this typification—for instance, his tastes in food are typical of Englishmen, as are his manners, certain of his emotional reactions, and so on. This implies, though, that these characteristics and actions of my friend Henry appertain to *anyone* in the category of Englishman, that is, I apprehend these aspects of his being in anonymous terms. Nevertheless, as long as my friend Henry is available in the plenitude of expressivity of the face-to-face situation, he will constantly break through my type of anonymous Englishman and manifest himself as a unique and therefore atypical individual—to wit, as my friend Henry. The anonymity of the type is obviously less susceptible to this kind of individualization when face-to-face interaction is a matter of the past (my friend Henry, *the Englishman,* whom I knew when I was a college student), or is of a superficial and transient kind (the Englishman with whom I have a brief conversation on a train), or has never taken place (my business competitors in England).

An important aspect of the experience of others in everyday life is thus the directness or indirectness of such experience. At any given time it is possible to distinguish between consociates with whom I interact in face-to-face situations and others who are mere contemporaries, of whom I have only more or less detailed recollections, or of whom I know merely by hearsay. In face-to-face situations I have direct evidence of my fellowman, of his actions, his attributes, and so on. Not so in the case of contemporaries—of them I have more or less reliable knowledge. Furthermore, I must take account of my fellowmen in face-to-face situations, while I may, but need not, turn my thoughts to mere contemporaries. Anonymity increases as I go from the former to the latter, because the anonymity of the typifications by means of which I apprehend fellowmen in face-to-face situations is constantly "filled in" by the multiplicity of vivid symptoms referring to a concrete human being.

This, of course, is not the whole story. There are obvious differences in my experiences of mere contemporaries. Some I have experienced again and again in face-to-face situations and expect to meet again regularly (my friend Henry); others I *recollect* as concrete human beings from a past meeting (the blonde I passed on the street), but the meeting was brief and, most likely, will not be repeated. Still others I *know of* as concrete human beings, but I can apprehend them only by means of more or less anonymous intersecting typifications (my British business competitors, the Queen of England). Among the latter one could again distinguish between likely partners in face-to-face situations (my British business competitors), and potential but unlikely partners (the Queen of England).

The degree of anonymity characterizing the experience of others in everyday life depends, however, upon another factor too. I see the newspaper vendor on the street corner as regularly as I see my wife. But he is less important to me and I am not on intimate terms with him. He may remain relatively anonymous to me. The degree of interest and the degree of intimacy may combine to increase or decrease anonymity of experience. They may also influence it independently. I can be on fairly intimate terms with a number of the fellow-members of a tennis club and on very formal terms with my boss. Yet the former, while by no means completely anonymous, may merge into "that bunch at the courts" while the latter stands out as a unique individual. And finally, anonymity may become near-total with certain typifications that are not intended ever to become individualized—such as the "typical reader of the London *Times*." Finally, the "scope" of the typification —and thereby its anonymity—can be further increased by speaking of "British public opinion."

The social reality of everyday life is thus apprehended in a continuum of typifications, which are progressively anonymous as they are removed from the "here and now" of the face-to-face situation. At one pole of the continuum are those others with whom I frequently and intensively interact in face-to-face situations —my "inner circle," as it were. At the other pole are highly anonymous abstractions, which by their very nature can never be available in face-to-face interaction. Social structure is the sum total of these typifications and of the recurrent patterns of interaction established by means of them. As such, social structure is an essential element of the reality of everyday life.

One further point ought to be made here, though we cannot elaborate it. My relations with others are not limited to consociates and contemporaries. I also relate to predecessors and successors, to those others who have preceded and will follow me in the encompassing history of my society. Except for those who are past consociates (my dead friend Henry), I relate to my predecessors through highly anonymous typifications—"my immigrant great-grandparents," and even more, "the Founding Fathers." My successors, for understandable reasons, are typified in in an even more anonymous manner—"my children's children," or "future generations." These typifications are substantively empty projections, almost completely devoid of individualized content, whereas the typifications of predecessors have at least some such content, albeit of a highly mythical sort. The anonymity of both these sets of typifications, however, does not prevent their entering as elements into the reality of everyday life, sometimes in a very decisive way. After all, I may sacrifice my life in loyalty to the Founding Fathers—or, for that matter, on behalf of future generations.

Human expressivity is capable of objectivation, that is, it manifests itself in products of human activity that are available both to their producers and to other men as elements of a common world. Such objectivations serve as more or less enduring indices of the subjective processes of their producers, allowing their availability to extend beyond the face-to-face situation in which they can be directly apprehended. For instance, a subject attitude of anger is directly expressed in the face-to-face situation by a variety of bodily indices—facial mien, general stance of the body, specific movements of arms and feet, and so on. These indices are continuously available in the face-to-face situation, which is precisely why it affords me the optimal situation for gaining access to another's subjectivity. The same indices are incapable of surviving beyond the vivid present of the face-to-face situation. Anger, however, can be objectivated by means of a weapon. Say, I have had an altercation with another man, who has given me ample expressive evidence of his anger against me. That night I wake up with a knife embedded in the wall above my bed. The knife *qua* object expresses my adversary's anger. It affords me access to his subjectivity even though I was sleeping when he threw it and never saw him because he fled after his near-hit. Indeed, if I leave the object where it is, I can look at it again the following morning, and again it expresses to me the anger of the man who threw it. What is more, other men can come and look at it and arrive at the same conclusion. In other words, the knife in my wall has become an objectively available constituent of the reality I share with my adversary and with other men. Presumably, this knife was not produced for the exclusive purpose of being thrown *at me*. But it expresses a subjective intention of violence, whether motivated by anger or by utilitarian considerations, such as killing for food. The weapon *qua* object in the real world continues to express a general intention to commit violence that is recognizable by anyone who knows what a weapon is. The weapon, then, is both a human product and an objectivation of human subjectivity.

The reality of everyday life is not only filled with objectivations; it is only possible because of them. I am constantly surrounded by objects that "proclaim" the subjective intentions of my fellowmen, although I may sometimes have difficulty being quite sure just what is it that a particular object is "proclaiming," especially if it was produced by men whom I have not known well or at all in face-to-face situations. Every ethnologist or archaeologist will readily testify to such difficulties, but the very fact that he *can* overcome them and reconstruct from an artifact the subjective intentions of men whose society may have been extinct for millennia is eloquent proof of the enduring power of human objectivations.

A special but crucially important case of objectivation is signification, that is, the human production of signs. A sign may be distinguished from other objectivations by its explicit intention to serve as an index of subjective meanings. To be sure, all objectivations are susceptible of utilization as signs, even though they were not originally produced with this intention. For instance, a weapon may have been originally produced for the purpose of hunting animals, but may then (say, in ceremonial usage) become a sign for aggressiveness and violence in general. But there are certain objectivations originally and explicitly intended to serve as signs. For instance, instead of throwing a knife at me (an act that was presumably intended to kill me, but that might conceivably have been intended merely to signify this possibility), my adversary could have painted a black X-mark on my door, a sign, let us assume, that we are now officially in a state of enmity. Such a sign, which has no purpose beyond indicating the subjective meaning of the one who made it, is also objectively available in the common reality he and I share with other men. I recognize its meaning, as do other men, and indeed it is available to its producer as an objective "reminder" of his original intention in making it. It will be clear from the above that there is a good deal of fluidity between the instrumental and the significatory uses of certain objectivations. The special case of magic, in which there is a very interesting merging of these two uses, need not concern us here.

Signs are clustered in a number of systems. Thus there are systems of gesticulatory signs, of patterned bodily movements, of various sets of material artifacts, and so on. Signs and sign systems are objectivations in the sense of being objectively available beyond the expression of subjective intentions "here and now." This "detachability" from the immediate expressions of subjectivity also pertains to signs that require the mediating presence of the body. Thus performing a dance that signifies aggressive intent is an altogether different thing from snarling or clenching fists in an outburst of anger. The latter acts express my subjectivity "here and now," while the former can be quite detached from this subjectivity—I may not be angry or aggressive at all at this point but merely taking part in the dance because I am paid to do so on behalf of someone else who *is* angry. In other words, the dance can be detached from the subjectivity of the dancer in a way in which the snarling *cannot* from the snarler. Both dancing and snarling are manifestations of bodily expressivity, but only the former has the character of an objectively available sign. Signs and sign systems are all characterized by "detachability," but they can be differentiated in terms of the degree to which they may be detached from face-to-face situations. Thus a dance is evidently less detached than a material artifact signifying the same subjective meaning.

Language, which may be defined here as a system of vocal signs, is the most important sign system of human society. Its foundation is, of course, in the intrinsic capacity of the human organism for vocal expressivity, but we can begin to speak of language only when vocal expressions have become capable of detachment from the immediate "here and now" of subjective states. It is not yet language if I snarl, grunt, howl, or hiss, although these vocal expressions are capable of becoming linguistic insofar as they are integrated into an objectively available sign system. The common objectivations of everyday life are maintained primarily by linguistic signification. Everyday life is, above all, life with and by means of the language I share with my fellowmen. An understanding of language is thus essential for any understanding of the reality of everyday life.

Language has its origins in the face-to-face situation, but can be readily detached from it. This is not only because I can shout in the dark or across a distance, speak on the telephone or via the radio, or convey linguistic signification by means of writing (the

latter constituting, as it were, a sign system of the second degree).
The detachment of language lies much more basically in its
capacity to communicate meanings that are not direct expressions
of subjectivity "here and now." It shares this capacity with other
sign systems, but its immense variety and complexity make it much
more readily detachable from the face-to-face situation than any
other (for example, a system of gesticulations). I can speak about
innumerable matters that are not present at all in the face-to-face
situation, including matters I never have and never will experience
directly. In this way, language is capable of becoming the objective
repository of vast accumulations of meaning and experience, which
it can then preserve in time and transmit to following generations.

In the face-to-face situation language possesses an inherent
quality of reciprocity that distingiushes it from any other sign
system. The ongoing production of vocal signs in conversation can
be sensitively synchronized with the ongoing subjective intentions
of the conversants. I speak as I think; so does my partner in the
conversation. Both of us hear what each says at virtually the same
instant, which makes possible a continuous, synchronized, reciprocal
access to our two subjectivities, an intersubjective closeness in the
face-to-face situation that no other sign system can duplicate. What
is more, I hear *myself* as I speak; my own subjective meanings are
made objectively and continuously available to me and *ipso facto*
become "more real" to me. Another way of putting this is to recall
the previous point about my "better knowledge" of the other as
against my knowledge of myself in the face-to-face situation. This
apparently paradoxical fact has been previously explained by the
massive, continuous and prereflective availability of the other's
being in the face-to-face situation, as against the requirement of
reflection for the availability of my own. Now, however, as I
objectivate my own being by means of language, my own being
becomes massively and continuously available to myself at the same
time that it is so available to him, and I can spontaneously respond
to it without the "interruption" of deliberate reflection. It can,
therefore, be said that language makes "more real" my subjectivity
not only to my conversation partner but also to myself. This capacity
of language to crystallize and stabilize for me my own subjectivity
is retained (albeit with modifications) as language is detached from
the face-to-face situation. This very important characteristic of
language is well caught in the saying that men must talk about
themselves until they know themselves.

Language originates in and has its primary reference to
everyday life; it refers above all to the reality I experience in wide-
awake consciousness, which is dominated by the pragmatic motive

(that is, the cluster of meanings directly pertaining to present or future actions) and which I share with others in a taken-for-granted manner. Although language can also be employed to refer to other realities, which will be discussed further in a moment, it even then retains its rootage in the commonsense reality of everyday life. As a sign system, language has the quality of objectivity. I encounter language as a facticity external to myself and it is coercive in its effect on me. Language forces me into its patterns. I cannot use the rules of German syntax when I speak English; I cannot use words invented by my three-year-old son if I want to communicate outside the family; I must take into account prevailing standards of proper speech for various occasions, even if I would prefer my private "improper" ones. Language provides me with a ready-made possibility for the ongoing objectification of my unfolding experience. Put differently, language is pliantly expansive so as to allow me to objectify a great variety of experiences coming my way in the course of my life. Language also typifies experiences, allowing me to subsume them under broad categories in terms of which they have meaning not only to myself but also to my fellowmen. As it typifies, it also anonymizes experiences, for the typified experience can, in principle, be duplicated by anyone falling into the category in question. For instance, I have a quarrel with my mother-in-law. This concrete and subjectively unique experience is typified linguistically under the category of "mother-in-law trouble." In this typification it makes sense to myself, to others, and, presumably, to my mother-in-law. The same typification, however, entails anonymity. Not only I but *anyone* (more accurately, anyone in the category of son-in-law) can have "mother-in-law trouble." In this way, my biographical experiences are ongoingly subsumed under general orders of meaning that are both objectively and subjectively real.

Because of its capacity to transcend the "here and now," language bridges different zones within the reality of everyday life and integrates them into a meaningful whole. The transcendences have spatial, temporal and social dimensions. Through language I can transcend the gap between my manipulatory zone and that of the other; I can synchronize my biographical time sequence with his; and I can converse with him about individuals and collectivities with whom we are not at present in face-to-face interaction. As a result of these transcendences language is capable of "making present" a variety of objects that are spatially, temporally and socially absent from the "here and now." *Ipso facto* a vast accumulation of experiences and meanings can become objectified in the "here and now." Put simply, through language an entire world can be actualized at any moment. This transcending and integrating power of language is retained when I am not actually conversing with another. Through linguistic objectification, even when "talking to myself" in solitary thought, an entire world can be appresented to me at any moment. As far as social relations are concerned, language "makes present" for me not only fellowmen who are physically absent at the moment, but fellowmen in the remembered or reconstructed past, as well as fellowmen projected as imaginary figures into the future. All these "presences" can be highly meaningful, of course, in the ongoing reality of everyday life.

Moreover, language is capable of transcending the reality of everyday life altogether. It can refer to experiences pertaining to finite provinces of meaning, and it can span discrete spheres of reality. For instance, I can interpret "the meaning" of a dream by integrating it linguistically within the order of everyday life. Such integration transposes the discrete reality of the dream into the reality of everyday life by making it an enclave within the latter. The dream is now meaningful in terms of the reality of everyday life rather than of its own discrete reality. Enclaves produced by such transposition belong, in a sense, to both spheres of reality. They are "located" in one reality, but "refer" to another.

Any significative theme that thus spans spheres of reality may be defined as a symbol, and the linguistic mode by which such transcendence is achieved may be called symbolic language. On the level of symbolism, then, linguistic signification attains the maximum detachment from the "here and now" of everyday life, and language soars into regions that are not only *de facto* but *a priori* unavailable to everyday experience. Language now constructs immense edifices of symbolic representations that appear to tower over the reality of everyday life like gigantic presences from another world. Religion, philosophy, art, and science are the historically most important symbol systems of this kind. To name these is already to say that, despite the maximal detachment from everyday experience that the construction of these systems requires, they can be of very great importance indeed for the reality of everyday life. Language is capable not only of constructing symbols that are highly abstracted from everyday experience, but also of "bringing back" these symbols and appresenting them as objectively real elements in everyday life. In this manner, symbolism and symbolic language become essential constituents of the reality of everyday life and of the commonsense apprehension of this reality. I live in a world of signs *and* symbols every day.

Language builds up semantic fields or zones of meaning that are linguistically circumscribed. Vocabulary, grammar and syntax

are geared to the organization of these semantic fields. Thus
language builds up classification schemes to differentiate objects by
"gender" (a quite different matter from sex, of course) or by
number; forms to make statements of action as against statements
of being; modes of indicating degrees of social intimacy, and so on.
For example, in languages that distinguish intimate and formal
discourse by means of pronouns (such as *tu* and *vous* in French, or
du and *Sie* in German) this distinction marks the co-ordinates of a
semantic field that could be called the zone of intimacy. Here lies
world of *tutoiement* or of *Bruderschaft*, with a rich collection of
meanings that are continually available to me for the ordering of my
social experience. Such a semantic field, of course, also exists for the
English speaker, though it is more circumscribed linguistically. Or,
to take another example, the sum of linguistic objectifications
pertaining to my occupation constitutes another semantic field,
which meaningfully orders all the routine events I encounter in my
daily work. Within the semantic fields thus built up it is possible for
both biographical and historical experience to be objectified,
retained and accumulated. The accumulation, of course, is selective,
with the semantic fields determining what will be retained and what
"forgotten" of the total experience of both the individual and the
society. By virtue of this accumulation a social stock of knowledge
is transmitted from generation to generation and which is available
to the individual in everyday life. I live in the commonsense world
of everyday life equipped with specific bodies of knowledge. What
is more, I know that others share at least part of my knowledge, and
they know that I know this. My interaction with others in everyday
life is, therefore, constantly affected by our common participation
in the available social stock of knowledge.

The social stock of knowledge includes knowledge of my
situation and its limits. For instance, I know that I am poor and
that, therefore, I cannot expect to live in a fashionable suburb. This
knowledge is, of course, shared both by those who are poor
themselves and those who are in a more privileged situation.
Participation in the social stock of knowledge thus permits the
"location" of individuals in society and the "handling" of them in the
appropriate manner. This is not possible for one who does not
participate in this knowledge, such as a foreigner, who may not
recognize me as poor at all, perhaps because the criteria of poverty
are quite different in his society—how can I be poor, when I wear
shoes and do not seem to be hungry?

Since everyday life is dominated by the pragmatic motive, recipe
knowledge, that is, knowledge limited to pragmatic competence in
routine performances, occupies a prominent place in the social stock

of knowledge. For example, I use the telephone every day for specific pragmatic purposes of my own. I know how to do this. I also know what to do if my telephone fails to function—which does not mean that I know how to repair it, but that I know whom to call on for assistance. My knowledge of the telephone also includes broader information on the system of telephonic communication— for instance, I know that some people have unlisted numbers, that under special circumstances I can get a simultaneous hook-up with two long-distance parties, that I must figure on the time difference if I want to call up somebody in Hong Kong, and so forth. All of this telephonic lore is recipe knowledge since it does not concern anything except what I have to know for my present and possible future pragmatic purposes. I am not interested in *why* the telephone works this way, in the enormous body of scientific and engineering knowledge that makes it possible to construct telephones. Nor am I interested in uses of the telephone that lie outside my purposes, say in combination with short-wave radio for the purpose of marine communication. Similarly, I have recipe knowledge of the workings of human relationships. For example, I know what I must do to apply for a passport. All I am interested in is getting the passport at the end of a certain waiting period. I do not care, and do not know, how my application is processed in government offices, by whom and after what steps approval is given, who puts which stamp in the document. I am not making a study of government bureaucracy—I just want to go on a vacation abroad. My interest in the hidden workings of the passport-getting procedure will be aroused only if I fail to get my passport in the end. At that point, very much as I call on a telephone-repair expert after my telephone has broken down, I call on an expert in passport-getting—a lawyer, say, or my Congressman, or the American Civil Liberties Union. *Mutatis mutandis*, a large part of the social stock of knowledge consists of recipes for the mastery of routine problems. Typically, I have little interest in going beyond this pragmatically necessary knowledge as long as the problems can indeed be mastered thereby.

The social stock of knowledge differentiates reality by degrees of familiarity. It provides complex and detailed information concerning those sectors of everyday life with which I must frequently deal. It provides much more general and imprecise information on remoter sectors. Thus my knowledge of my own occupation and its world is very rich and specific, while I have only very sketchy knowledge of the occupational worlds of others. The social stock of knowledge further supplies me with the typificatory schemes required for the major routines of everyday life, not only the typifications of others that have been discussed before, but typifications of all sorts of events

and experiences, both social and natural. Thus I live in a world of
relatives, fellow-workers and recognizable public functionaries. In
this world, consequently, I experience family gatherings, professional
meetings and encounters with the traffic police. The natural
"backdrop" of these events is also typified within the stock of
knowledge. My world is structured in terms of routines applying in
good or bad weather, in the hayfever season and in situations when
a speck of dirt gets caught under my eyelid. "I know what to do"
with regard to all these others and all these events within my
everyday life. By presenting itself to me as an integrated whole the
social stock of knowledge also provides me with the means to
integrate discrete elements of my own knowledge. In other words
"what everybody knows" has its own logic, and the same logic can
be applied to order various things that I know. For example, I know
that my friend Henry is an Englishman, and I know that he is
always very punctual in keeping appointments. Since "everybody
knows" that punctuality is an English trait, I can now integrate
these two elements of my knowledge of Henry into a typification
that is meaningful in terms of the social stock of knowledge.

The validity of my knowledge of everyday life is taken for
granted by myself and by others until further notice, that is, until a
problem arises that cannot be solved in terms of it. As long as my
knowledge works satisfactorily, I am generally ready to suspend
doubts about it. In certain attitudes detached from everyday reality
—telling a joke, at the theater or in church, or engaging in
philosophical speculation—I may perhaps doubt elements of it. But
these doubts are "not to be taken seriously." For instance, as a
businessman I know that it pays to be inconsiderate of others. I may
laugh at a joke in which this maxim leads to failure, I may be moved
by an actor or a preacher extolling the virtues of consideration, and
I may concede in a philosophical mood that all social relations
should be governed by the Golden Rule. Having laughed, having
been moved and having philosophized, I return to the "serious"
world of business, once more recognize the logic of its maxims, and
act accordingly. Only when my maxims fail "to deliver the goods" in
the world to which they are intended to apply are they likely to
become problematic to me "in earnest."

Although the social stock of knowledge appresents the everyday
world in an integrated manner, differentiated according to zones of
familiarity and remoteness, it leaves the totality of that world
opaque. Put differently, the reality of everyday life always appears as
a zone of lucidity behind which there is a background of darkness.
As some zones of reality are illuminated, others are adumbrated. I
cannot know everything there is to know about this reality. Even if,

for instance, I am a seemingly all-powerful despot in my family, and know this, I cannot know all the factors that go into the continuing success of my despotism. I know that my orders are always obeyed, but I cannot be sure of all the steps and all the motives that lie between the issuance and the execution of my orders. There are always things that go on "behind my back." This is true *a fortiori* when social relationships more complex than those of the family are involved—and explains, incidentally, why despots are endemically nervous. My knowledge of everyday life has the quality of an instrument that cuts a path through a forest and, as it does so, projects a narrow cone of light on what lies just ahead and immediately around; on all sides of the path there continues to be darkness. This image pertains even more, of course, to the multiple realities in which everyday life is continually transcended. This latter statement can be paraphrased, poetically if not exhaustively, by saying that the reality of everyday life is overcast by the penumbras of our dreams.

My knowledge of everyday life is structured in terms of relevances. Some of these are determined by immediate pragmatic interests of mine, others by my general situation in society. It is irrelevant to me how my wife goes about cooking my favorite goulash as long as it turns out the way I like it. It is irrelevant to me that the stock of a company is falling, if I do not own such stock; or that Catholics are modernizing their doctrine, if I am an atheist; or that it is now possible to fly non-stop to Africa, if I do not want to go there. However, my relevance structures intersect with the relevance structures of others at many points, as a result of which we have "interesting" things to say to each other. An important element of my knowledge of everyday life is the knowledge of the relevance structures of others. Thus I "know better" than to tell my doctor about my investment problems, my lawyer about my ulcer pains, or my accountant about my quest for religious truth. The basic relevance structures referring to everyday life are presented to me ready-made by the social stock of knowledge itself. I know that "woman talk" is irrelevant to me as a man, that "idle speculation" is irrelevant to me as a man of action, and so forth. Finally, the social stock of knowledge as a whole has its own relevance structure. Thus, in terms of the stock of knowledge objectivated in American society, it is irrelevant to study the movements of the stars to predict the stock market, but it is relevant to study an individual's slips of the tongue to find out about his sex life, and so on. Conversely, in other societies, astrology may be highly relevant for economics, speech analysis quite irrelevant for erotic curiosity, and so on.

One final point should be made here about the social distribution of knowledge. I encounter knowledge in everyday life as socially distributed, that is, as possessed differently by different individuals and types of individuals. I do not share my knowledge equally with all my fellowmen, and there may be some knowledge that I share with no one. I share my professional expertise with colleagues, but not with my family, and I may share with nobody my knowledge of how to cheat at cards. The social distribution of knowledge of certain elements of everyday reality can become highly complex and even confusing to the outsider. I not only do not possess the knowledge supposedly required to cure me of a physical ailment, I may even lack the knowledge of which one of a bewildering variety of medical specialists claims jurisdiction over what ails me. In such cases, I require not only the advice of experts, but the prior advice of experts on experts. The social distribution of knowledge thus begins with the simple fact that I do not know everything known to my fellowmen, and vice versa, and culminates in exceedingly complex and esoteric systems of expertise. Knowledge of *how* the socially available stock of knowledge is distribtued, at least in outline, is an important element of that same stock of knowledge. In everyday life I know, at least roughly, what I can hide from whom, whom I can turn to for information on what I do not know, and generally which types of individuals may be expected to have which types of knowledge.

8

THE NATURE OF SYMBOLIC INTERACTIONISM

Herbert Blumer

Symbolic interactionism[1] rests in the last analysis on three simple premises. The first premise is that human beings act toward things on the basis of the meanings that the things have for them. Such things include everything that the human being may note in his world—physical objects, such as trees or chairs; other human beings, such as a mother or a store clerk; categories of human beings, such as friends or enemies; institutions, as a school or a government; guiding ideals, such as individual independence or honesty; activities of others, such as their commands or requests; and such situations as an individual encounters in his daily life. The second premise is that the meaning of such things is derived from, or arises out of, the social interaction that one has with one's fellows. The

Reproduced by permission from *Symbolic Interactionism: Perspective and Method* by Herbert Blumer (Englewood Cliffs, N.J.: Prentice-Hall, Inc. © 1969), pp. 2–21.

third premise is that these meanings are handled in, and modified through, an interpretative process used by the person in dealing with the things he encounters. I wish to discuss briefly each of these three fundamental premises.

It would seem that few scholars would see anything wrong with the first premise—that human beings act toward things on the basis of the meanings which these things have for them. Yet, oddly enough, this simple view is ignored or played down in practically all of the thought and work in contemporary social science and psychological science. Meaning is either taken for granted and thus pushed aside as unimportant or it is regarded as a mere neutral link between the factors responsible for human behavior and this behavior as the product of such factors. We can see this clearly in the predominant posture of psychological and social science today. Common to both of these fields is the tendency to treat human behavior as the product of various factors that play upon human beings; concern is with the behavior and with the factors regarded as producing them. Thus, psychologists turn to such factors as stimuli, attitudes, conscious or unconscious motives, various kinds of psychological inputs, perception and cognition, and various features of personal organization to account for given forms or instances of human conduct. In a similar fashion sociologists rely on such factors as social position, status demands, social roles, cultural prescriptions, norms and values, social pressures, and group affiliation to provide such explanations. In both such typical psychological and sociological explanations the meanings of things for the human beings who are acting are either bypassed or swallowed up in the factors used to account for their behavior. If one declares that the given kinds of behavior are the result of the particular factors regarded as producing them, there is no need to concern oneself with the meaning of the things toward which human beings act; one merely identifies the initiating factors and the resulting behavior. Or one may, if pressed, seek to accommodate the element of meaning by lodging it in the initiating factors or by regarding it as a neutral link intervening between the initiating factors and the behavior they are alleged to produce. In the first of these latter cases the meaning disappears by being merged into the initiating or causative factors; in the second case meaning becomes a mere transmission link that can be ignored in favor of the initiating factors.

The position of symbolic interactionism, in contrast, is that the meanings that things have for human beings are central in their own right. To ignore the meaning of the things toward which people act is seen as falsifying the behavior under study. To bypass the

meaning in favor of factors alleged to produce the behavior is seen
as a grievous neglect of the role of meaning in the formation of
behavior.

The simple premise that human beings act toward things on
the basis of the meaning of such things is much too simple in itself
to differentiate symbolic interactionism—there are several other
approaches that share this premise. A major line of difference
between them and symbolic interactionism is set by the second
premise, which refers to the source of meaning. There are two well-
known traditional ways of accounting for the origin of meaning.
One of them is to regard meaning as being intrinsic to the thing that
has it, as being a natural part of the objective makeup of the thing.
Thus, a chair is clearly a chair in itself, a cow a cow, a cloud a
cloud, a rebellion a rebellion, and so forth. Being inherent in the
thing that has it, meaning needs merely to be disengaged by
observing the objective thing that has the meaning. The meaning
emantes, so to speak, from the thing and as such there is no process
involved in its formation; all that is necessary is to recognize the
meaning that is there in the thing. It should be immediately
apparent that the view reflects the traditional position of "realism"
in philosophy—a position that is widely held and deeply entrenched
in the social and psychological sciences. The other major traditional
view regards "meaning" as a psychical accretion brought to the
thing by the person for whom the thing has meaning. This psychical
accretion is treated as being an expression of constituent elements
of the person's psyche, mind, or psychological organization. The
constituent elements are such things as sensations, feelings, ideas,
memories, motives, and attitudes. The meaning of a thing is but the
expression of the given psychological elements that are brought into
play in connection with the perception of the thing; thus one seeks
to explain the meaning of a thing by isolating the particular
psychological elements that produce the meaning. One sees this in
the somewhat ancient and classical psychological practice of
analyzing the meaning of an object by identifying the sensations
that enter into perception of that object; or in the contemporary
practice of tracing the meaning of a thing, such as let us say
prostitution, to the attitude of the person who views it. This lodging
of the meaning of things in psychological elements limits the
processes of the formation of meaning to whatever processes are
involved in arousing and bringing together the given psycholoical
elements that produce the meaning. Such processes are psychological
in nature, and include perception, cognition, repression, transfer of
feelings, and association of ideas.

Symbolic interactionism views meaning as having a different source than those held by the two dominant views just considered. It does not regard meaning as emanating from the intrinsic makeup of the thing that has meaning, nor does it see meaning as arising through a coalescence of psychological elements in the person. Instead, it sees meaning as arising in the process of interaction between people. The meaning of a thing for a person grows out of the ways in which other persons act toward the person with regard to the thing. Their actions operate to define the thing for the person. Thus, symbolic interactionism sees meanings as social products, as creations that are formed in and through the defining activities of people as they interact. This point of view gives symbolic interactionism a very distinctive position, with profound implications that will be discussed later.

The third premise mentioned above further differentiates symbolic interactionism. While the meaning of things is formed in the context of social interaction and is derived by the person from that interaction, it is a mistake to think that the use of meaning by a person is but an application of the meaning so derived. This mistake seriously mars the work of many scholars who otherwise follow the symbolic interactionist approach. They fail to see that the use of meanings by a person in his action involves an interpretative process. In this respect they are similar to the adherents of the two dominant views spoken of above—to those who lodge meaning in the objective makeup of the thing that has it and those who regard it as an expression of psychological elements. All three are alike in viewing the use of meaning by the human being in his action as being no more than an arousing and application of already established meanings. As such, all three fail to see that the use of meanings by the actor occurs through *a process of interpretation*. This process has two distinct steps. First, the actor indicates to himself the things toward which he is acting; he has to point out to himself the things that have meaning. The making of such indications is an internalized social process in that the actor is interacting with himself. This interaction with himself is something other than an interplay of psychological elements; it is an instance of the person engaging in a process of communication with himself. Second, by virtue of this process of communicating with himself, interpretation becomes a matter of handling meanings. The actor selects, checks, suspends, regroups, and transforms the meanings in the light of the situation in which he is placed and the direction of his action. Accordingly, interpretation should not be regarded as a mere automatic application of established meanings but as a formative process in which meanings are used and revised as instruments for the guidance and formation of action. It is necessary to see that meanings play their part in action through a process of self-interaction.

It is not my purpose to discuss at this point the merits of the three views that lodge meaning respectively in the thing, in the psyche, and in social action, nor to elaborate on the contention that meanings are handled flexibly by the actor in the course of forming his action. Instead, I wish merely to note that by being based on these three premises, symbolic interaction is necessarily led to develop an analytical scheme of human society and human conduct that is quite distinctive. It is this scheme that I now propose to outline.

Symbolic interactionism is grounded on a number of basic ideas, or "root images," as I prefer to call them. These root images refer to and depict the nature of the following matters: human groups or societies, social interaction, objects, the human being as an actor, human action, and the interconnection of the lines of action. Taken together, these root images represent the way in which symbolic interactionism views human society and conduct. They constitute the framework of study and analysis. Let me describe briefly each of these root images.

NATURE OF HUMAN SOCIETY OR HUMAN GROUP LIFE

Human groups are seen as consisting of human beings who are engaging in action. The action consists of the multitudinous activities that the individuals perform in their life as they encounter one another and as they deal with the succession of situations confronting them. The individuals may act singly, they may act collectively, and they may act on behalf of, or as representatives of, some organization or group of others. The activities belong to the acting individuals and are carried on by them always with regard to the situations in which they have to act. The import of this simple and essentially redundant characterization is that fundamentally human groups or society *exists in action* and must be seen in terms of action. This picture of human society as action must be the starting point (and the point of return) for any scheme that purports to treat and analyze human society empirically. Conceptual schemes that depict society in some other fashion can only be derivations from the complex of ongoing activity that constitutes group life. This is true of the two dominant conceptions of society in contemporary sociology—that of culture and that of social structure. Culture as a conception, whether defined as custom, tradition, norm, value, rules, or such like, is clearly derived from what people do. Similarly, social structure in any of its aspects, as represented by such terms as social position, status, role, authority, and prestige, refers to relationships derived from how people act toward each other. The life of any human society consists necessarily of an ongoing process of fitting together the activities of its members. It is this complex of ongoing activity that establishes and portrays structure or organization. A cardinal principle of symbolic interactionism is that any empirically oriented scheme of human society, however, derived, must respect the fact that in the first and last instances human society consists of people engaging in action. To be empirically valid the scheme must be consistent with the nature of the social action of human beings.

NATURE OF SOCIAL INTERACTION

Group life necessarily presupposes interaction between the group members; or, put otherwise, a society consists of individuals interacting with one another. The activities of the members occur predominantly in response to one another or in relation to one another. Even though this is recognized almost universally in definitions of human society, social interaction is usually taken for granted and treated as having little, if any, significance in its own right. This is evident in typical sociological and psychological schemes—they treat social interaction as merely a medium through which the determinants of behavior pass to produce the behavior. Thus, the typical sociological scheme ascribes behavior to such factors as status position, cultural prescriptions, norms, values, sanctions, role demands, and social system requirements; explanation in terms of such factors suffices without paying attention to the social interaction that their play necessarily presupposes. Similarly, in the typical psychological scheme such factors as motive, attitudes, hidden complexes, elements of psychological organization, and psychological processes are used to account for behavior without any need of considering social interaction. One jumps from such causative factors to the behavior they are supposed to produce. Social interaction becomes a mere forum through which sociological or psychological determinants move to bring about given forms of human behavior. I may add that this ignoring of social interaction is not corrected by speaking of an interaction of societal elements (as when a sociologist speaks of an interaction of social roles or an interaction between the components of a social system) or an interaction of psychological elements (as when a psychologist speaks of an interaction between the attitudes held by different people). Social interaction is an interaction between actors and not between factors imputed to them.

Symbolic interaction does not merely give a ceremonious nod to social interaction. It recognizes social interaction to be of vital importance in its own right. This importance lies in the fact that social interaction is a process that *forms* human conduct instead of being merely a means or a setting for the expression or release of human conduct. Put simply, human beings in interacting with one another have to take account of what each other is doing or is about to do; they are forced to direct their own conduct or handle their situations in terms of what they take into account. Thus, the activities of others enter as positive factors in the formation of their own conduct; in the face of the actions of others one may abandon an intention or purpose, revise it, check or suspend it, intensify it, or replace it. The actions of others enter to set what one plans to do, may oppose or prevent such plans, may require a revison of such plans, and may demand a very different set of such plans. One has to *fit* one's own line of activity in some manner to the actions of others. The actions of others have to be taken into account and cannot be regarded as merely an arena for the expression of what one is disposed to do or sets out to do.

We are indebted to George Herbert Mead for the most penetrating analysis of social interaction—an analysis that squares with the realistic account just given. Mead identifies two forms or levels of social interaction in human society. He refers to them respectively as "the conversation of gestures" and "the use of significant symbols"; I shall term them respectively "non-symbolic interaction" and "symbolic interaction." Non-symbolic interaction takes place when one responds directly to the action of another without interpreting that action; symbolic interaction involves interpretation of the action. Non-symbolic interaction is most readily apparent in reflex responses, as in the case of a boxer who automatically raises his arm to parry a blow. However, if the boxer were reflectively to identify the forthcoming blow from his opponent as a feint designed to trap him, he would be engaging in symbolic interaction. In this case, he would endeavor to ascertain the meaning of the blow—that is, what the blow signifies as to his opponent's plan. In their association human beings engage plentifully in nonsymbolic interaction as they respond immediately and unreflectively to each other's bodily movements, expressions, and tones of voice, but their characteristic mode of interaction is on the symbolic level, as they seek to understand the meaning of each other's action.

Mead's analysis of symbolic interaction is highly important. He sees it as a presentation of gestures and a response to the meaning of those gestures. A gesture is any part or aspect of an ongoing action that signifies the larger act of which it is a part—for example, the shaking of a fist as an indication of a possible attack, or the declaration of war by a nation as an indication of a posture and line of action of that nation. Such things as requests, orders, commands, cues, and declarations are gestures that convey to the person who recognizes them an idea of the intention and plan of forthcoming action of the individual who presents them. The person who responds organizes his response on the basis of what the gestures mean to him; the person who presents the gestures advances them as indications or signs of what he is planning to do as well as of what he wants the respondent to do or understand. Thus, the gesture has meaning for both the person who makes it and for the person to whom it is directed. When the gesture has the same meaning for both, the two parties understand each other. From this brief account it can be seen that the meaning of the gesture flows out along three lines (Mead's triadic nature of meaning): It signifies what the person to whom it is directed is to do; it signifies what the person who is making the gesture plans to do; and it signifies the joint action that is to arise by the articulation of the acts of both. Thus, for illustration, a robber's command to his victim to put up his hands is (a) an indication of what the victim is to do; (b) an indication of what the robber plans to do, that is, relieve the victim of his money; and (c) an indication of the joint act being formed, in this case a holdup. If there is confusion or misunderstanding along any one of these three lines of meaning, communication is ineffective, interaction is impeded, and the formation of joint action is blocked.

One additional feature should be added to round out Mead's analysis of symbolic interaction, namely, that the parties to such interaction must necessarily take each other's roles. To indicate to another what he is to do, one has to make the indication from the standpoint of that other; to order the victim to put up his hands the robber has to see this response in terms of the victim making it. Correspondingly, the victim has to see the command from the stand-point of the robber who gives the command; he has to grasp the intention and forthcoming action of the robber. Such mutual role-taking is the *sine qua non* of communication and effective symbolic interaction.

The central place and importance of symbolic interaction in human group life and conduct should be apparent. A human society or group consists of people in association. Such association exists necessarily in the form of people acting toward one another and thus engaging in social interaction. Such interaction in human society is characteristically and predominantly on the symbolic level; as individuals acting individually, collectively, or as agents of some organization encounter one another they are necessarily required to take account of the actions of one another as they form their own action. They do this by a dual process of indicating to others how to act and of interpreting the indications made by others. Human group life is a vast process of such defining to others what to do and of interpreting their definitions; through this process people come to fit their activities to one another and to form their own individual conduct. Both such joint activity and individual conduct are formed *in* and *through* this ongoing process; they are not mere expressions or products of what people bring to their interaction or of conditions that are antecedent to their interaction. The failure to accommodate to this vital point constitutes the fundamental deficiency of schemes that seek to account for human society in terms of social organization or psychological factors, or of any combination of the two. By virtue of symbolic interaction, human group life is necessarily a formative process and not a mere arena for the expression of pre-existing factors.

NATURE OF OBJECTS

The position of symbolic interactionism is that the "worlds" that exist for human beings and for their groups are composed of "objects" and that these objects are the product of symbolic interaction. An object is anything that can be indicated, anything that is pointed to or referred to—a cloud, a book, a legislature, a banker, a religious doctorine, a ghost, and so forth. For purposes of convenience one can classify objects in three categories: (a) physical objects, such as chairs, trees, or bicycles; (b) social objects, such as students, priests, a president, a mother, or a friend; and (c) abstract objects, such as moral principles, philosophical doctrines, or ideas such as justice, exploitation, or compassion. I repeat that an object is anything that can be indicated or referred to. The nature of an object—of any and every object—consists of the meaning that it has for the person for whom it is an object. This meaning sets the way in which he sees the object, the way in which he is prepared to act toward it, and the way in which he is ready to talk about it. An object may have a different meaning for different individuals: a tree will be a different object to a botanist, a lumberman, a poet, and a home gardener; the President of the United States can be a very different object to a devoted member of his political party than to a member of the opposition; the members of an ethnic group may be seen as a different kind of object by members of other groups. The meaning of objects for a person arises fundamentally out of the way they are defined to him by others with whom he interacts. Thus, we come to learn through the indications of others that a chair is a chair, thus doctors are a certain kind of professional, that the United States Constitution is a given kind of legal document, and so forth. Out of a process of mutual indications common objects emerge—objects that have the same meaning for a given set of people and are seen in the same manner by them.

Several noteworthy consequences follow from the foregoing discussion of objects. First, it gives us a different picture of the environment or milieu of human beings. From their standpoint the environment consists *only* of the objects that the given human beings recognize and know. The nature of this environment is set by the meaning that the objects composing it have for those human beings. Individuals, also groups, occupying or living in the same spatial location may have, accordingly, very different environments; as we say, people may be living side by side yet be living in different worlds. Indeed, the term "world" is more suitable than the word "environment" to designate the setting, the surroundings, and the texture of things that confront them. It is the world of their objects with which people have to deal and toward which they develop their actions. It follows that in order to understand the action of people it is necessary to identify their world of objects— an important point that will be elaborated later.

Second, objects (in the sense of their meaning) must be seen as social creations—as being formed in and arising out of the process of definition and interpretation as this process takes place in the interaction of people. The meaning of anything and everything has to be formed, learned, and transmitted through a process of indication—a process that is necessarily a social process. Human group life on the level of symbolic interaction is a vast process in which people are forming, sustaining, and transforming the objects of their world as they come to give meaning to objects. Objects have no fixed status except as their meaning is sustained through indications and definitions that people make of the objects. Nothing is more apparent than that objects in all categories can undergo change in their meaning. A star in the sky is a very different object to a modern astrophysicist than it was to a sheepherder of biblical times; marriage was a different object to later Romans than to earlier Romans; the president of a nation who fails to act successfully through critical times may become a very different object to the citizens of his land. In short, from the standpoint of symbolic interactionism human group life is a process in which objects are being created, affirmed, transformed, and cast aside. The life and action of people necessarily change in line with the changes taking place in their world of objects.

THE HUMAN BEING AS AN ACTING ORGANISM

Symbolic interactionism recognizes that human beings must have a makeup that fits the nature of social interaction. The human being is seen as an organism that not only responds to others on the non-symbolic level but as one that makes indications to others and interprets their indications. He can do this, as Mead has shown so emphatically, only by virtue of possessing a "self." Nothing esoteric is meant by this expression. It means merely that a human being can be an object of his own action. Thus, he can recognize himself, for instance, as being a man, young in age, a student, in debt, trying to become a doctor, coming from an undistinguished family and so forth. In all such instances he is an object to himself; and he acts toward himself and guides himself in his actions toward others on the basis of the kind of object he is to himself. This notion of oneself as an object fits into the earlier discussion of objects. Like other objects, the self-object emerges from the process of social interaction in which other people are defining a person to himself. Mead has traced the way in which this occurs in his discussion of role-taking. He points out that in order to become an object to himself a person has to see himself from the outside. One can do this only by placing himself in the position of others and viewing himself from that position. The roles the person takes range from that of discrete individuals (the "play stage"), through that of discrete organized groups (the "game stage"), to that of the abstract community (the "generalized other"). In taking such roles the person is in a position to address or approach himself—as in the case of a young girl who in "playing mother" talks to herself as her mother would do, or in the case of a young priest who sees himself through the eyes of the priesthood. We form our objects of ourselves through the way in which others see or define us—or, more precisely, we see ourselves by taking one of the three types of roles of others that have been mentioned. That one forms an object of himself through the ways in which others define one to himself is recognized fairly well in the literature today, so despite its great significance I shall not comment on it further.

There is an even more important matter that stems from the

fact that the human being has a self, namely that this enables him to interact with himself. This interaction is not in the form of interaction between two or more parts of a psychological system, as between needs, or between emotions, or between ideas, or between the id and the ego in the Freudian scheme. Instead, the interaction is social—a form of communication, with the person addressing himself as a person and responding thereto. We can clearly recognize such interaction in ourselves as each of us notes that he is angry with himself, or that he has to spur himself on in his tasks, or that he reminds himself to do this or that, or that he is talking to himself in working out some plan of action. As such instances suggest, self-interaction exists fundamentally as a process of making indications to oneself. This process is in play continuously during one's waking life, as one notes and considers one or another matter, or observes this or that happening. Indeed, for the human being to be conscious or aware of anything is equivalent to his indicating the thing to himself—he is identifying it as a given kind of object and considering its relevance or importance to his line of action. One's waking life consists of a series of such indications that the person is making to himself, indications that he uses to direct his action.

We have, then, a picture of the human being as an organism that interacts with itself through a social process of making indications to itself. This is a radically different view of the human being from that which dominates contemporary social and psychological science. The dominant prevailing view sees the human being as a complex organism whose behavior is a response to factors playing on the organization of the organism. Schools of thought in the social and psychological sciences differ enormously in which of such factors they regard as significant, as is shown in in such a diverse array as stimuli, organic drives, need-dispositions, conscious motives, unconscious motives, emotions, attitudes, ideas, cultural prescriptions, norms, values, status demands, social roles, reference group affiliations, and institutional pressures. Schools of thought differ also in how they view the organization of the human being, whether as a kind of biological organization, a kind of psychological organization or a kind of imported societal organization incorporated from the social structure of one's group. Nevertheless, these schools of thought are alike in seeing the human being as a responding organism, with its behavior being a product of the factors playing on its organization or an expression of the interplay of parts of its organization. Under this widely shared view the human being is "social" only in the sense of either

being a member of social species, or of responding to others
(social stimuli), or of having incorporated within it the organization
of his group.

The view of the human being held in symbolic interactionism
is fundamentally different. The human being is seen as "social" in a
much more profound sense—in the sense of an organism that
engages in social interaction with itself by making indications to
itself and responding to such indications. By virtue of engaging
in self-interaction the human being stands in a markedly different
relation to his environment than is presupposed by the widespread
conventional view described above. Instead of being merely an
organism that responds to the play of factors on or through it, the
human being is seen as an organism that has to deal with what it
notes. It meets what it so notes by engaging in a process of
self-indication in which it makes an object of what it notes, gives
it a meaning, and uses the meaning as the basis for directing its
action. Its behavior with regard to what it notes is not a response
called forth by the presentation of what it notes but instead is an
action that arises out of the interpretation made through the process
of self-indication. In this sense, the human being who is engaging
in self-interaction is not a mere responding organism but an acting
organism—an organism that has to mold a line of action on the
basis of what it takes into account instead of merely releasing a
response to the play of some factor on its organization.

NATURE OF HUMAN ACTION

The capacity of the human being to make indications to himself
gives a distinctive character to human action. It means that the
human individual confronts a world that he must interpret in order
to act instead of an environment to which he responds because of
his organization. He has to cope with the situations in which he is
called to act, ascertaining the meaning of the actions of others
and mapping out his own line of action in the light of such
interpretation. He has to construct and guide his action instead of
merely releasing it in response to factors playing on him or operating
through him. He may do a miserable job in constructing his action,
but he has to construct it.

This view of the human being directing his action by making
indications to himself stands sharply in contrast to the view of
human action that dominates current psychological and social
science. This dominant view, as already implied, ascribes human
action to an initiating factor or a combination of such factors.
Action is traced back to such matters as motives, attitudes,

need-dispositions, unconscious complexes, stimuli configurations, status demands, role requirements, and situational demands. To link the action to one or more of such initiating agents is regarded as fulfilling for the process of self-interaction through which the individual handles his world and constructs his action. The door is closed to the vital process of interpretation in which the individual notes and assesses what is presented to him and through which he maps out lines of overt behavior prior to their execution.

Fundamentally, action on the part of a human being consists of taking account of various things that he notes and forging a line of conduct on the basis of how he interprets them. The things taken into account cover such matters as his wishes and wants, his objectives, the available means for their achievement, the actions and anticipated actions of others, his image of himself, and the likely result of a given line of action. His conduct is formed and guided through such a process of indication and interpretation. In this process, given lines of action may be started or stopped, they may be abandoned or postponed, they may be confined to mere planning or to an inner life of reverie, or if initiated, they may be transformed. My purpose is not to analyze this process but to call attention to its presence and operation in the formation of human action. We must recognize that the activity of human beings consists of meeting a flow of situations in which they have to act and that their action is built on the basis of what they note, how they note, and what kind of projected lines of action they map out. This process is not caught by ascribing action to some kind of factor (for example, motives, need-dispositions, role requirements, social expectations, or social rules) that is thought to initiate the action and propel it to its conclusion; such a factor, or some expression of it, is a matter the human actor takes into account in mapping his line of action. The initiating factor does not embrace or explain how it and other matters are taken into account in the situation that calls for action. One has to get inside of the defining process of the actor in order to understand his action.

This view of human action applies equally well to joint or collective action in which numbers of individuals are implicated. Joint or collective action constitutes the domain of sociological concern, as exemplified in the behavior of groups, institutions, organizations, and social classes. Such instances of societal behavior, whatever they may be, consist of individuals fitting their lines of action to one another. It is both proper and possible to view and study such behavior in its joint or collective character instead of in its individual components. Such joint behavior does not lose its character of being constructed through an interpretative process in meeting the situations in which the collectivity is called on to act. Whether the collectivity be an army engaged in a campaign, a corporation seeking to expand its operations, or a nation trying to correct an unfavorable balance of trade, it needs to construct its action through an interpretation of what is happening in its area of operation. The interpretative process takes place by participants making indications to one another, not merely each to himself. Joint or collective action is an outcome of such a process of interpretive interaction.

INTERLINKAGE OF ACTION

As stated earlier, human group life consists of, and exists in, the fitting of lines of action to each other by the members of the group. Such articulation of lines of action gives rise to and constitutes "joint action"—a societal organization of conduct of different acts of diverse participants. A joint action, while made up of diverse component acts that enter into its formulation, is different from any one of them and from their mere aggregation. The joint action has a distinctive character in its own right, a character that lies in the articulation or linkage as apart from what may be articulated or linked. Thus, the joint action may be identified as such and may be spoken of and handled without having to break it down into the separate acts that comprise it. This is what we do when we speak of such things as marriage, a trading transaction, war, a parliamentary discussion, or a church service. Similarly, we can speak of the collectivity that engages in joint action without having to identify the individual members of that collectivity, as we do in speaking of a family, a business corporation, a church, a university, or a nation. It is evident that the domain of the social scientist is constituted precisely by the study of joint action and of the collectivities that engage in joint action.

In dealing with collectivities and with joint action one can easily be trapped in an erroneous position by failing to recognize that the joint action of the collectivity is an interlinkage of the separate acts of the participants. This failure leads one to overlook the fact that a joint action always has to undergo a process of formation; even though it may be a well-established and repetitive form of social action, each instance of it has to be formed anew. Further, this career of formation through which it comes into being necessarily takes place through the dual process of designation and interpretation that was discussed above. The participants still have to guide their respective acts by forming and using meanings.

With these remarks as a background I wish to make three

observations on the implications of the interlinkage that constitutes
joint action. I wish to consider first those instances of joint action
that are repetitive and stable. The preponderant portion of social
action in a human society, particularly in a settled society, exists
in the form of recurrent patterns of joint action. In most situations
in which people act toward one another they have in advance a
firm understanding of how to act and of how other people will act.
They share common and pre-established meanings of what is
expected in the action of the participants, and accordingly each
participant is able to guide his own behavior by such meanings.
Instances of repetitive and pre-established forms of joint action are
so frequent and common that it is easy to understand why scholars
have viewed them as the essence or natural form of human group
life. Such a view is especially apparent in the concepts of "culture"
and "social order" that are so dominant in social science literature.
Most sociological schemes rest on the belief that a human society
exists in the form of an established order of living, with that order
resolvable into adherence to sets of rules, norms, values, and
sanctions that specify to people how they are to act in their different
situations.

Several comments are in order with regard to this neat
scheme. First, it is just not true that the full expanse of life in a
human society, in any human society, is but an expression of
pre-established forms of joint action. New situations are constantly
arising within the scope of group life that are problematic and for
which existing rules are inadequate. I have never heard of any
society that was free of problems nor any society in which members
did not have to engage in discussion to work out ways of action.
Such areas of unprescribed conduct are just as natural, indigenous,
and recurrent in human group life as are those areas covered by
pre-established and faithfully followed prescriptions of joint
action. Second, we have to recognize that even in the case of
pre-established and repetitive joint action each instance of such
joint action has to be formed anew. The participants still have to
build up their lines of action and fit them to one another through the
dual process of designation and interpretation. They do this in the
case of repetitive joint action, of course, by using the same recurrent
and constant meanings. If we recognize this, we are forced to
realize that the play and fate of meanings are what is important,
not the joint action in its established form. Repetitive and stable
joint action is just as much a result of an interpretative process as
is a new form of joint action that is being developed for the first
time. This is not an idle or pedantic point; the meanings that
underlie established and recurrent joint action are themselves

subject to pressure as well as to reinforcement, to incipient
dissatisfaction as well as to indifference; they may be challenged
as well as affirmed, allowed to slip along without concern as well as
subjected to infusions of new vigor. Behind the facade of the
objectively perceived joint action the set of meanings that sustains
that joint action has a life that the social scientists can ill afford to
ignore. A gratuitous acceptance of the concepts of norms, values,
social rules, and the like should not blind the social scientist to the
fact that any one of them is subtended by a process of social
interaction—a process that is necessary not only for their change
but equally well for their retention in a fixed form. It is the social
process in group life that creates and upholds the rules, not the rules
that create and uphold group life.

The second observation on the interlinkage that constitutes
joint action refers to the extended connection of actions that make
up so much of human group life. We are familiar with these large
complex networks of action involving an interlinkage and
interdependency of diverse actions of diverse people—as in the
division of labor extending from the growing of grain by the farmer
to an eventual sale of bread in a store, or in the elaborate chain
extending from the arrest of a suspect to his eventual release from
a penitentiary. These networks with their regularized participation
of diverse people by diverse action at diverse points yield a picture
of institutions that have been appropriately a major concern of
sociologists. They also give substance to the idea that human group
life has the character of a system. In seeing such a large complex
of diversified activities, all hanging together in a regularized
operation, and in seeing the complementary organization of
participants in well-knit interdependent relationships, it is easy to
understand why so many scholars view such networks or institutions
as self-operating entities, following their own dynamics and not
requiring that attention be given to the participants within the
network. Most of the sociological analyses of institutions and social
organization adhere to this view. Such adherence, in my judgment,
is a serious mistake. One should recognize what is true, namely,
that the diverse array of participants occupying different points
in the network engage in their actions at those points on the basis
of using given sets of meanings. A network or an institution does
not function automatically because of some inner dynamics or
system requirements; it functions because people at different points
do something, and what they do is a result of how they define the
situation in which they are called on to act. A limited appreciation
of this point is reflected today in some of the work on decision-
making, but on the whole the point is grossly ignored. It is necessary

to recognize that the sets of meanings that lead participants to act as they do at their stationed points in the network have their own setting in a localized process of social interaction—and that these meanings are formed, sustained, weakened, strengthened, or transformed, as the case may be, through a socially defining process. Both the functioning and the fate of institutions are set by this process of interpretation as it takes place among the diverse sets of participants.

A third important observation needs to be made, namely, that any instance of joint action, whether newly formed or long established, has necessarily arisen out of a background of previous actions of the participants. A new kind of joint action never comes into existence apart from such a background. The participants involved in the formation of the new joint action always being to that formation the world of objects, the sets of meanings, and the schemes of interpretation that they already possess. Thus, the new form of joint action always emerges out of and is connected with a context of previous joint action. It cannot be understood apart from that context; one has to bring into one's consideration this linkage with preceding forms of joint action. One is on treacherous and empirically invalid grounds if he thinks that any given form of joint action can be sliced off from its historical linkage, as if its makeup and character arose out of the air through spontaneous generation instead of growing out of what went before. In the face of radically different and stressful situations people may be led to develop new forms of joint action that are markedly different from those in which they have previously engaged, yet even in such cases there is always some connection and continuity with what went on before. One cannot understand the new form without incorporating knowledge of this continuity into one's analysis of the new form. Joint action not only represents a horizontal linkage, so to speak, of the activities of the participants, but also a vertical linkage with previous joint action.

SUMMARY REMARKS

The general perspective of symbolic interactionism should be clear from our brief sketch of its root images. This approach sees a human society as people engaged in living. Such living is a process of ongoing activity in which participants are developing lines of action in the multitudinous situations they encounter. They are caught up in a vast process of interaction in which they have to fit their developing actions to one another. This process of interaction consists in making indications to others of what to do and in interpreting the indications as made by others. They live in worlds of objects and are guided in their orientation and action by the meaning of these objects. Their objects, including objects of themselves, are formed, sustained, weakened, and transformed in their interaction with one another. This general process should be seen, of course, in the differentiated character which it necessarily has by virtue of the fact that people cluster in different groups, belong to different associations, and occupy different positions. They accordingly approach each other differently, live in different worlds, and guide themselves by different sets of meanings. Nevertheless, whether one is dealing with a family, a boy's gang, an industrial corporation, or a political party, one must see the activities of the collectivity as being formed through a process of designation and interpretation.

Notes

[1] The term "symbolic interactionism" is a somewhat barbaric neologism that I coined in an offhand way in an article written in Emerson P. Schmidt (ed.), *Man and Society* (Englewood Cliffs, N.J.: Prentice-Hall, 1937). The term somehow caught on and is now in general use.

9

SYMBOLIC STRATEGIES

Sol Worth and Larry Gross

*How do we distinguish "natural" from
"symbolic" events, and how do we assign
meaning to them? A new theory of
communicative performance and
behavior.*

The world does not present itself to us directly. In the process of
becoming human we learn to recognize the existence of the objects,
persons, and events that we encounter, and to determine the
strategies by which we may interpret and assign meaning to them.
   Our encounters with the world can be thought of as being both

Reprinted by permission from "Symbolic Strategies" by Sol Worth and
Larry Gross in the *Journal of Communication*, 24, (1974):27–29. © 1974
by The Annenberg School of Communications.

natural and symbolic since we often make distinctions between
events that we consider natural and events that we will interpret
symbolically. What then are the conditions governing that
assessment? What strategies do we use in order to assign meaning
to natural and symbolic events?

The interpretation of meaning, or the assignment of a natural
event to a place in a scheme of things, is embodied in our
recognition of that event's existence. The interpretation of the
meaning of a symbolic event on the other hand, is embodied in our
recognition of its structure—that is, in our recognition of its possible
communicational significance. In order to recognize the structure
which defines a communication event—as distinguished from a
natural event—we must bring to that act of recognition an
assumption of intention. We must assume that the structure we
recognize is, in a sense, "made," performed, or produced for the
purpose of "symbolizing," or communicating.

The assessment of events as natural or symbolic determines
whether we use an interpretive strategy which we shall call
attribution, or an interpretive strategy which we shall call
communicational inference.

Let us give an example. You are walking along a street, and
from a distance you notice a man lying on the sidewalk. As you
draw closer you notice that he appears to be injured. In assessing
this situation, if you assume it to be a natural event, you will most
likely ask yourself, "What happened?" and "What should I (or can
I) do?" However, if you notice a sign pinned to his shirt which
reads, "sic semper tyrannus," you might make a further and more
complex assessment. Suppose you remember, at that point, either
that a guerrilla theater group has been performing in your
neighborhood or that you read about guerrilla theater in a book.
Your assessment of the situation might now be quite different. As
the possibility of assuming communicative intent enters the
assessment, you might then bring to bear a different set of rules by
which you will interpret the meaning of that event—the conventions
of guerrilla theater. Under these rules, you might ask yourself,
"What does it mean, and how can I tell?"

Now let us take the same situation in a social and formal
context which most clearly labels it as symbolic. You go to the
movies and see a film that you call a "fiction" or "feature" film
which begins with a shot of a street in which the camera moves
towards a man lying on the sidewalk as we have described above.
The film cuts to a closeup of the man's head and then to a shot of
the note pinned to his shirt. There is no question that, in our culture,
a moviegoer, assuming communicative intent, would not ask, "Is it

real?" or "What should I do?" but rather, "What does it mean?" And what's more, in our culture that viewer expects to learn the answer to that and many other questions in the course of the film.

This rather bizarre example can help us differentiate three basic types of situation and the interpretive strategies they evoke.

The first group are what we call *existential meaning* situations. These occur when persons, objects, and events which come to our attention are quickly assessed as having no symbolic meaning beyond the fact of their existence. Problems of communication and the interpretation of meaning will not be particularly relevant in these situations.

The second group are *ambiguous meaning* situations. In these, something in the event or in the context of the event makes us pause and assess it in terms of possible significance and/or signification as a symbolic event. We then seek additional signs on which to base our choice of an appropriate interpretive strategy.

The third group includes situations we clearly "know" to be symbolic and communicative. We call these *"communicational meaning"* situations. We read books, go to the movies, talk to our friends, and interact in ways in which particular strategies for the interpretation of symbolic codes are invoked. These are situations in which there is no ambiguity as to the communicative nature of the event. Being a member of a culture "tells" one that certain events are communicative. Interpretive problems which arise in clearly marked communication situations will concern the assignment of a specific meaning or meanings to be inferred from some specific event.

Persons, objects, and events that we encounter may also be classified as "sign events" or "non-sign events." Non-sign events are those activities of everyday life which do not evoke the use of any strategy to determine their meaning.

Figure 1 describes the larger context in which human beings interact with their environment and with the persons, objects, and events they perceive and recognize. In certain contexts, people learn to treat some of these situations as signs to which they may assign existential or symbolic meaning.

It is important to note that the distinction between sign and non-sign events must not be taken as a categorical classification of persons, objects, and events. Any event, depending upon its context and the context of the observer, may be assigned sign value. By the same token, any event may be disregarded and not treated as a sign.

Sign events may be *natural* or *symbolic* but always have the

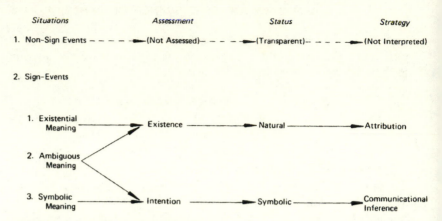

Figure 1   Context of interpretation.

property of being used in the interpretation of meaning. If we
assess them to be natural, we may do no more than tacitly note their
existence and interact with them in a variety of adaptive ways
(requiring little conscious or even tacit interpretation of meaning).
We may further *attribute* to them stable, transient, and/or situational
characteristics. If, on the other hand, we assess them as *symbolic*,
we consciously or tacitly assume *implicative intent* and call into
play those interpretive strategies by which we *infer meaning* from
communicative events.

One further term we will be using in our discussion is
articulation. An articulated event is produced by a person's own
musculature or by his use of tools or both. The articulated event
must be thought of as mediated through the use of a communicative
mode—words, pictures, music, and so on. An articulated event is a
symbolic event. (A natural event may be produced by either human
or non-human agencies, and *may be* treated as symbolic. However,
the signness of a natural event exists only and solely because, within
some context, human beings treat the event as a sign. An example
of a natural event would be a tree bending in the wind, which may
be treated as a sign of a coming storm. An example of the same
event treated as articulated and symbolic would, in a film, be a
close-up of a tree bending in the wind interpreted as an implication
on the part of the director that a storm is coming up.)

An event, then, may be produced by human entities as well as
by natural force, but its "signness" is always *assigned* by an observer
who can tell the difference within his own cultural context between
those events which are articulated, and thus treated as intentional
and communicationally symbolic, and those events which are
existential and natural. Knowing and assessing that difference is
often difficult and problematic. We are concerned with the strategies

people use for solving that problem—are they natural or communicational?

Communication shall therefore be defined as *a social process, within a context, in which signs are produced and transmitted, perceived, and treated as messages from which meaning can be inferred.*

Let us review briefly some of the terms we have introduced earlier and place them within the context of this definition of communication. The concept of articulation and interpretation must be seen as relevant to both the production and transmission of signs, as well as to their perception and subsequent treatment. While the perception and treatment of symbolic events might be thought of as acts of interpretation, and production and transmission seen as acts of articulation, they can most fruitfully be seen as parts of a *process*. We articulate in terms of the subsequent interpretations we expect, just as we imply only in those terms which we expect others to use when they infer.

In such a situation one shifts, mentally, back and forth between articulation and interpretation, asking oneself, "If I say it (or paint it, or sequence it in a film) this way, would I (as well as others) make sense of it—given the conventions, rules, style in which I am working?"

Going back to our definition, it should be clear now that meaning is not inherent within the sign itself, but rather in the social context, whose conventions and rules dictate the articulatory and interpretive strategies to be invoked by producers and interpreters of symbolic forms. It is our view that only when an interpretive strategy assumes that production and transmission are articulatory and intentional can communicational meaning be inferred. In a communicational sense, therefore, articulation is symbolic and implicational, and interpretive strategies are designed within social contexts in order to make inferences from implications.

A critical distinction in terms of social *accountability* must now be made between behavior that is viewed as intentionally communicative and behavior that is not. We are all held accountable for certain aspects of our behavior. In the simplest sense, we are most accountable for our intentionally communicative behavior. A tic of the eye cannot be taken as a social offense; a wink may be so taken in certain circumstances, even though the physical event may be exactly the same in both interpretive contexts. It is our knowledge of the conventions which govern social behavior in general, and communicative behavior in particular, that allows us to determine the intentionality of behavior, and hence the nature and extent of accountability that may be appropriate in a specific situation.

> *Let us now turn to the question of how*
> *people develop the competence to assess*
> *and interpret symbolic intent.*

The distinctions in Figure 2 are meant to explain, not an ideal state
of knowledge or competence, but the actual use of certain abilities
in the articulation and interpretation of meaning in communication
situations.

We learn to articulate in a variety of symbolic modes and
codes, as we similarly learn to interpret in an appropriate set of
ways. As Gross has shown, the competence to perform (either as
creator or interpreter) is dependent upon the acquisition of at least
minimal articulatory ability in that mode (3).

Figure 2 diagrams what we are hypothesizing as a model of
the levels of articulatory and interpretive abilities, and indicates a
series of recognition stages which people apply to sign events. These
stages or levels are seen as both developmental and hierarchical.
They are developmental in that we believe they are acquired
according to a specific order over time, depending on age, cultural
context, and particular communicational or attributional training.
We are not asserting, however, that these articulatory and
interpretive abilities are acquired by all people for all modes, nor
at specific chronological ages. These abilities are hierarchical in that
we see this order as one of increasing articulatory and interpretive
complexity in which each succeeding stage contains within it the
preceding stages. While we are implying, therefore, that the
development of competence to perform on the earlier levels is
necessary for its emergence in the later complex levels, we are not
implying that the earlier levels will disappear or wither away. The
process we envisage is one of elaboration rather than replacement,

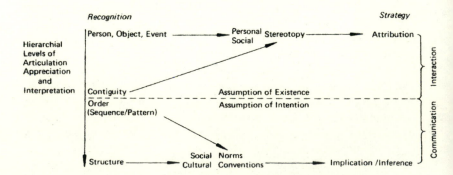

Figure 2   Competence to perform in a communications event.

much like the progression from crawling to walking. Once we learn to walk we do not lose the ability to crawl. Once we have learned to recognize at all levels, we can choose our strategies depending upon our assessment of the sign event situation.

The first stage in the recognition of a sign event shown in Figure 2 occurs at the level of its person-ness, object-ness, or event-ness. This occurs at the simple perceptual level of iconic representation or symbolic reference. The symbolic sign event (word, picture, sound) has as its paired partner a person, object, or event we have learned to juxtapose with it in a simple recognition process. This stage of recognition discrimination is required of a child before the simple sign-reference relationship can develop. The child must learn this recognition technique before he or she actually can articulate or use the concept of sign in any deliberate intentional way. Before any strategy for interpretation is developed, a symbolic consciousness must come into play which allows a child to recognize the relationship between a sign and some referent person, object, or event in the real world.

In Figure 2 note that the arrow moves from person, object, event recognition through personal and psycho-social stereotype to attribution. Thus, if the child sees a picture of a man whom he recognizes as "father," his interpretation of the picture will not be based on the meaning *within* the picture so much as the meaning within the child (viewer) based on what the child knows about "fathers," "his father," and so on.

The next level of development is the recognition of relationships among a number of sign events. The recognition of these relationships is the second major stage in the development of a competence to perform. Relationships, however, can be recognized, and their status assessed (as we show in Figure 2), at two qualitatively distinct levels. We would like to distinguish, therefore, between the recognition of simple existential *contiguity* and the recognition of intentional *order (sequence or pattern)*. It is with the recognition of order that the observer will be able to deal with a sign-event as existential.

Contiguity consists of a juxtaposition of units or events over time, space, or position. The alphabet in this context can be seen as an example of contiguity. Recognizing its contiguity requires that the person grasp that A goes before B which goes before C, and so on. The recognition that shapes repeat themselves in a certain way in a design, or that objects in a room have their places, is a recognition of contiguity. The same shapes in the same design can, in another context discussed below, be seen in different ways. The concept of recognition is one which places emphasis upon the person's cognitive manipulation of signs and their perceptions rather than upon some *intrinsic* quality of events.

Order, on the other hand, is a more complex quality of symbolic arrangement. An order *is a deliberately employed series used for the purpose of implying meaning rather than contiguity to more than one sign event and having the property of conveying meaning through the order itself as well as through elements in that order.*

Order is related to a recognition of an arrangement of elements produced intentionally and purposefully, whereas contiguity is a function of the recognition of existence only. Our use of the term order is meant to include spatial as well as temporal configurations. In painting and the graphic arts, for example, order occurs in space rather than in time and is most closely akin to what is often called "design" or "composition." We shall employ the word "pattern" for such spatial arrangement on the level of order. Temporal orderings, such as occur in aspects of movies, music, or literature, we shall call "sequence."

The recognition of pattern or sequence is the bridge to the level of *structural recognition.* While the earlier levels of recognition deal with single elements or with multiple elements in contiguity, structural recognition calls for an awareness of the *relations between elements* and their implicative-inferential possibilities. Structural recognition enables one to deal with the relations between *noncontiguous* elements: the beginning and end of a story, variations on a theme, differing perspectives on one canvas, and so on. Structure may be thought of as starting with order and being the level of formal organization which links the elements of a communicative event.

We have argued that there is a hierarchy of levels on which the articulation and interpretation of symbolic events can be characterized, and that these represent increasing degrees of complexity as well as different stages of development. They also require, for a person's competence to perform communicatively, the possession of increasingly sophisticated articulatory and performatory skills. The simplest sign events consist of single or unrelated elements; complex sign-events are those wherein the elements are placed in relationships, and in which these relationships are governed according to the organizational principles of a symbolic code. We have also suggested that this hierarchy represents a developmental sequence, in that the competence required to perform on the higher levels of articulation and interpretation will emerge on the basis of prior competence on the lower levels. This analysis parallels that of the development of specific symbolic skills, such as drawing and painting, in which children acquire a repertoire of elements, rational formulae, and, finally, the ability to combine these, intentionally, for the purpose of creating visually meaningful, structurally organized images (5).

We will now deal with the interpretive strategies linked to these levels of recognition as they are applied to mediated representations of behavior.

Sign-events which are recognized as natural events are taken as informative rather than communicative, and interpretations are made of them in terms of what we know, think, or feel about the persons, objects, and events they represent or refer to. That is, we *attribute* characteristics to the recognized sign-elements on the basis of our knowledge of the world in which we "know" they are found. For example, if we view a film of a psychiatric interview taken with a hidden camera we will feel justified in making attributions about the patient, the therapist, and/or the nature of their relationship. We will feel constrained in our interpretations (having assessed the situation as natural because of our knowledge of the hidden camera) because we may not know to what extent the behavior we see is a function of stable characteristics of the patient or therapist (personality, role) or transient characteristics (mood, physical state) or of the situation itself (a psychiatric interview, the *first* interview, and so on).

Most adults in our society are aware of the fact that the appropriateness of such attributional strategies for the interpretation of the film described above derives from the film's status as a record of a natural event that did actually occur in the real world. Were the camera crew to have been in the room during the interview, moving around and filming the event from various positions, or were the film to be clearly edited and rearranged by the filmmaker, most of us would realize that we were seeing a symbolic event which had been intentionally put together for the purpose of implying something the filmmaker wished to communicate. We would recognize that the events we observed had been selected and organized into a "whole," and that the appropriate interpretive strategy was one which analyzed the structure of the film and the relationships of its elements, in addition to incorporating any attributional interpretations which we might make about the people in the film on the basis of our general social knowledge.

If we are correct in our assumption that the levels of recognition and interpretive performance we have described represent a developmental sequence and not merely one of increasing complexity, it would follow that the distinction we have just detailed would not be made by children until they achieve the higher levels of the hierarchy. This assumption has been investigated in a series of studies that we and our students have conducted on the nature and development of interpretive strategies (6, 4, 7, 8, 9).

In much of this research we have been concerned with the development of the child's ability to tell, in words, what he has seen in a series of pictures and what he thinks they "mean." The basic study (7) used pictures which show a sequence beginning with a man (easily recognized as a doctor because of his white coat and stethoscope) doing various tasks in a hospital. He then takes off his white coat, puts on an overcoat, leaves the hospital, and walks down the street. The following picture shows the "doctor" in the background, and in the foreground an obviously damaged automobile from which a man's head and one arm are visible hanging part way out of the door. It is quite clear that the man may be (or is) injured. The next picture shows the "doctor" in the foreground looking at the car and the injured person in the background. The "doctor" crosses the street, continues walking, enters an apartment house, opens a door, and is finally shown relaxed, holding a drink, and smiling at a woman sitting next to him.

Murphy (7) showed these pictures to children in the second, fifth, and eighth grades, who were then interviewed individually in order to elicit their versions of the "story in the pictures." Murphy (7) investigated the evidence the children used in justifying their

A doctor passes by what looks like an accident victim in this picture from a series used by Murphy (7) in a study of children's ability to tell what pictures mean.

interpretations. We have also used the same design and procedure with college students aged 17 to 23.

In the responses of the children and the college students we have distinguished several classes of behavior which appear to parallel our conceptualization of the development of interpretive performance. In the earlier grades, children were able to recognize the persons depicted in terms of conventional attributes (doctor, nurse) and report the events contiguously ("The doctor was talking to the nurse . . . then he left the hospital . . ."). However, when asked about the meaning of the sequence in terms of what is implied about the persons and events depicted, these children gave answers that were completely consistent with and dependent upon the general social knowledge they had about the persons in terms of role attributes, *even when these stereotyped images had been directly contradicted by the information they were given in the pictures*.

For example, all of the second grade children said that they liked the doctor and, when asked why that was so, said they liked him because he was a doctor:

QUESTION: "How do you know that he is a good man?"
ANSWER: "Because doctors are good men."
QUESTION: "How could you tell this one was a good man?"
ANSWER: "Cause he was a doctor."

Similarly, most of the younger children thought that the doctor must have helped the accident victim, not because they saw him do so, but because "that's what doctors do." In fact, most of these children said that the "meaning" of the story was that doctors are good and that they help people:

QUESTION: "What was the most important thing in the story?"
ANSWER: "He was a doctor and he helped people a lot."
QUESTION: "How do you know?"
ANSWER: "Well, I think he helped that person in the car wreck."
QUESTION: "How do you know?"
ANSWER: "Well, I don't know. But I think he helped him, because that's what doctors are for, isn't it, helping people?"

Many of these younger children were aware of the accident, were aware that the doctor didn't help, but still said that the man was a "good doctor" because "doctors are good—because they help people." What they attribtued to the "doctor" on the basis of prior learning about doctors *as a class* was more powerful than any other interpretive strategy which they were able to apply.

We would say that, at this stage, children are using attributional strategies of interpretation. It is not so much the interpretations they give as the reasons they advance for these answers that determines our classification: they are calling into play knowledge they have from outside which is relatively unrelated to the set of pictures they are being shown (1). The children's use of attributional strategies is grounded in their assessment that the events they see in the pictures are real, natural events and must, therefore, have the same meaning that they have learned to assign to such events they have experienced directly:

> QUESTION: "Why do you think (the pictures) are real?"
> ANSWER: "Because doctors walk home."
> QUESTION: "How do you know that?"
> ANSWER: "Cause my uncle's a doctor and he does it himself."

At an older age, the children begin to realize that the pictures do not, in fact, represent a simple record of a natural event. They recognize that it is highly improbable that such a complex sequence could be captured in pictures unless it had been staged: "A guy's going to think something's wrong when every minute a guy pops up in front of him and takes a picture." The younger children took the "realness" of each part of the sequence as evidence for the naturalness of the entire sequence; the older children realized that their assessment must be made in terms of the entire set of elements.

We shall, for illustrative and space-saving purposes, construct a composite interview which will allow us to point out the different kinds of responses that are involved in structural recognition, assumptions of intention, and implicational/inferential interpretations. The following would be such an interview from which we would judge the child to be displaying a knowledge of structure and of implication/inference.

> INTERVIEWER: Could you tell me something about the pictures you saw?
> CHILD: You mean about the story?
> INTERVIEWER: Uh-huh.
> CHILD: Well he didn't help that guy in the accident.
> INTERVIEWER: How do you know?
> CHILD: If they had wanted me to think he helped him they would have had a shot of him with a stethoscope or something bending over the guy in the car. They would have shown him helping somehow.

Notice the concepts involved in this child's interpretation. First, he refers to the set of pictures as "a story"—he recognizes story structure. Then he says, "If they had wanted me to *think* . . ." clearly indicating (a) that the "story" was "given" to him by the experimenter, (b) that the "storyteller" may want him (the viewer) to think along certain lines, and (c) that information comes from "a shot . . ." that is purposefully inserted or omitted.

But most important, his interpretation of the doctor is based on a process that is clearly inferential: he knows that for his interpretation he may use only, or mainly, the information given to him in the communication event. Communicational implication-inference demands just this kind of behavior. The child must subordinate what he already knows about doctors to what he knows about the rules and conventions of communication, and must use the information given in the structure he has recognized (1).

When a child (or an adult for that matter) fails to recognize structure, he will make interpretations through attribution. When he recognizes structure, he knows that implicational/inferential strategies of interpretation are called for. The reasons for this knowledge are imbedded in structural recognition, for basic to that recognition is what we are calling the *assumption of intention*.

Intention is not an empirical datum, nor is it verifiable by the result of an interpretation. The verifying process is the fact that the interpreter gives *reasons* for his inferred meaning, based upon the implications he derives from the messages. It is the *kind of reasons given* for the interpretations that distinguish between attribution of meaning and inferences of meaning. It is important to recognize that an isomorphic relationship between signs and their interpretation does not constitute either sufficient or necessary cause for describing an interpretation either as an act of interaction with the environment or as a communicative event.

Intention is an *assumption* which is made about an event allowing us to treat the elements of that event as sign elements in a structure which *imply*, and from which we may *infer, meaning*. In Figure 2 the assumption of intention is contrasted with the assumption of existence. We are reserving the use of the word communication for those situations where an assumption of intention is made.

It should be clear by now that when we use the term "assumption of intention" we want it understood as an "assumption of intention to mean." Interpretation consists, in a communicational sense, of a process by which X (the interpreter) treats Y (the utterance, sign or message) in such a way that the assumed intention is for X a *reason* (2) rather than a mere cause of his

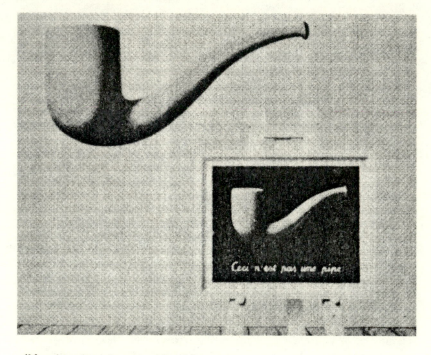

(Magritte: Les deux mystères)

interpretation. It is for this reason that empirical evidence of the asssumption of intention is not the "correctness" of the interpreted intent but rather the *reason* and *reasoning* given by respondents.

The assumption of intention is felt to be within the control of the interpreter as well as within the control of the articulator. The interpreter, further, can distinguish, and finds it important to distinguish between what signs "suggest," what he "attributes" to signs, and what he infers from signs.

This conceptualization of intention and meaning differs from many referential, behavioral, and semiotic theories of meaning which are not concerned with implication, inference, and intention. We are arguing, for example, that a stimulus-response theory or a simple learning (conditioning) theory which defines meaning as the tendency to behave in certain ways upon the presentation of signs or conditioned stimuli is totally inadequate for the interpretation of human symbolic behavior.

We have presented a brief description of a new way to examine the concept of interpretation. First, we are suggesting that interpretation is best seen within a comprehensive framework of communication which distinguishes between "natural" interaction and communication. We have also suggested that the process of interpretation occurs whenever signs are used, and that interpretations can be made in situations that are not communicative. When such interpretations are made we have described them as attributions.

Second, we have presented both a hierarchical and a developmental concept by which the process of interpretation and articulation can be described. We have then described a series of recognition stages culminating in a process of implication and inference within which communication—a social event—takes place.

Third, we have presented, as two basic theoretical constructs, the concept of the assumption of existence leading to attributional strategies of interpretation and the concept of the assumption of intention leading to implicational/inferential strategies of both interpretation and articulation. We have further said that the assumption of intention is very closely allied to the concept of the intention to mean, and that therefore implication and inference as we are using the terms suggest implication to mean and the inference of meaning.

We have argued that intentionality (when used in relation to communication) is always an assumption. The articulator means to imply; the interpreter means to infer. Intention, therefore, is not verified by an isomorphism between implication and inference, nor by an isomorphism between individuals who happen to be articulators or interpreters. Intention is verified by conventions of social accountability, conventions of legitimacy, and rules, genres, and styles of articulation and performance. These are the bases which make our assumptions of intentionality reasonable, justifiable, social, and communicational.

References

1. Donaldson, Margaret. "Preconditions of Inference," in J. K. Cole (ed.). *Nebraska Symposium on Motivation* (Lincoln, Neb.: University of Nebraska Press, 1971), pp. 81–106.
2. Grice, H. P. "Meaning," *The Philosophical Review* **66**, (July 1957):3.
3. Gross, Larry. "Modes of Communication and the Acquisition of Symbolic Competence," in G. Gerbner, L. Cross, and W. Melody (eds.). *Communications Technology and Social Policy* (New York: Wiley, 1973), pp. 189–208.
4. Harlan, Thomas A. "Viewing Behavior and Interpretive Strategies of a Photographic Narrative as a Function of Variation in Story Title and Subject Age." Unpublished

master's thesis, Annenberg School of Communication, University of Pennsylvania, 1972.

5. Lindstrom, Miriam. *Children's Art* (Berkeley, Calif.: University of California Press, 1962).

6. Messatis, S. Paul. "Attribution and Inference in the Interpretation of Filmed Behavior." Unpublished master's thesis, Annenberg School of Communications, University of Pennsylvania, 1972.

7. Murphy, James P. "Attributional and Inferential Strategies in the Interpretation of Visual Communications: A Developmental Study." Unpublished doctoral dissertation, University of of Pennsylvania, 1973.

8. Pallenik, Michael J. "The Use of Attributional and Inferential Strategies in the Interpretation of 'Staged' and 'Candid' Events." Unpublished master's thesis, Annenberg School of Communications, University of Pennsylvania, 1973.

9. Wick, Thomas M. "Attributional and Inferential Interpretive Strategies and Variation in Their Application to Written Communications as a Function of Training and Format." Unpublished master's thesis, Annenberg School of Communications, University of Pennsylvania, 1973.

10
FACIAL ENGAGEMENTS

Erving Goffman

1. CIVIL INATTENTION

When persons are mutually present and not involved together in
conversation or other focused interaction, it is possible for one
person to stare openly and fixedly at others, gleaning what he can
about them while frankly expressing on his face his response to what
he sees—for example, the "hate stare" that a Southern white
sometimes gratuitously gives to Negroes walking past him.[1] It is
also possible for one person to treat others as if they were not there
at all, as objects not worthy of a glance, let alone close scrutiny.
Moreover, it is possible for the individual, by his staring or his "not
seeing," to alter his own appearance hardly at all in consequence of
the presence of the others. Here we have "nonperson" treatment; it

may be seen in our society in the way we sometimes treat children, servants, Negroes, and mental patients.[2]

Currently, in our society, this kind of treatment is to be contrasted with the kind generally felt to be more proper in most situations, which will here be called "civil inattention." What seems to be involved is that one gives to another enough visual notice to demonstrate that one appreciates that the other is present (and that one admits openly to having seen him), while at the next moment withdrawing one's attention from him so as to express that he does not constitute a target of special curiosity or design.

In performing this courtesy the eyes of the looker may pass over the eyes of the other, but no "recognition" is typically allowed. Where the courtesy is performed between two persons passing on the street, civil inattention may take the special form of eyeing the other up to approximately eight feet, during which time sides of the street are apportioned by gesture, and then casting the eyes down as the other passes—a kind of dimming of lights. In any case, we have here what is perhaps the slightest of interpersonal rituals, yet one that constantly regulates the social intercourse of persons in our society.

By according civil inattention, the individual implies that he has no reason to suspect the intentions of the others present and no reason to fear the others, be hostile to them, or wish to avoid them. (At the same time, in extending this courtesy he automatically opens himself up to a like treatment from others present.) This demonstrates that he has nothing to fear or avoid in being seen and being seen seeing, and that he is not ashamed of himself or of the place and company in which he finds himself. It will therefore be necessary for him to have a certain "directness" of eye expression. As one student suggests, the individual's gaze ought not to be guarded or averted or absent or defensively dramatic, as if "something were going on." Indeed, the exhibition of such deflected eye expressions may be taken as a symptom of some kind of mental disturbance.[3]

Civil inattention is so delicate an adjustment that we may expect constant evasion of the rules regarding it. Dark glasses, for example, allow the wearer to stare at another person without that other being sure that he is being stared at.[4] One person can look at another out of the corner of his eyes. The fan and parasol once served as similar aids in stealing glances, and in polite Western society the decline in use of these instruments in the last fifty years has lessened the elasticity of communication arrangements.[5] It should be added, too, that the closer the onlookers are to the individual who interests them, the more exposed his position (and theirs), and the more obligation they will feel to ensure him civil inattention. The further they are from him, the more license they will feel to stare at him a little.

In addition to these evasions of rules we also may expect frequent infractions of them. Here, of course, social class subculture and ethnic subculture introduce differences in patterns, and differences, too, in the age at which patterns are first employed.

The morale of a group in regard to this minimal courtesy of civil inattention—a courtesy that tends to treat those present merely as particiapnts in the gathering and not in terms of other social characteristics—is tested whenever someone of very divergent social status or very divergent physical appearance is present. English middle-class society, for example, prides itself in giving famous and infamous persons the privilege of being civilly disattended in public, as when the Royal children manage to walk through a park with few persons turning around to stare. And in our own American society, currently, we know that one of the great trials of the physically handicapped is that in public places they will be openly stared at, thereby having their privacy invaded, while, at the same time, the invasion exposes their undesirable attributes.[6]

> The act of staring is a thing which one does not ordinarily do to another human being; it seems to put the object stared at in a class apart. One does not talk to a monkey in a zoo, or to a freak in a sideshow—one only stares.[7]
>
> An injury, as a characteristic and inseparable part of the body, may be felt to be a personal matter which the man would like to keep private. However, the fact of its visibility makes it known to anyone whom the injured man meets, including the stranger. A visible injury differs from most other personal matters in that anyone can deal with it regardless of the wish of the injured person; anyone can stare at the injury or ask questions about it, and in both cases communicate to and impose upon the injured person his feelings and evaluations. His action is then felt as an intrusion into privacy. It is the visibility of the injury which makes intrusion into privacy so easy. The men are likely to feel that they have to meet again and again people who will question and stare, and to feel powerless because they cannot change the general state of affairs. . . .[8]

Perhaps the clearest illustration both of civil inattention and of the infraction of this ruling occurs when a person takes advantage of another's not looking to look at him and then finds that the object of his gaze has suddenly turned and caught the illicit looker looking. The individual caught out may then shift his gaze, often with embarrassment and a little shame, or he may carefully act as if

he had merely been seen in the moment of observation that is
permissible; in either case we see evidence of the propriety that
should have been maintained.

To behave properly and to have the *right* to civil inattention
are related: Propriety on the individual's part tends to ensure his
being accorded civil inattention; extreme impropriety on his part is
likely to result in his being stared at or studiously not seen.
Improper conduct, however, does not automatically release others
from the obligation of extending civil inattention to the offender,
although it often weakens it. In any case, civil inattention may be
extended in the face of offensiveness simply as an act of tactfulness,
to keep an orderly appearance in the situation in spite of what is
happening.

Ordinarily, in middle-class society, failure to extend civil
inattention to others is not negatively sanctioned in a direct and
open fashion, except in the social training of servants and children,
the latter especially in connection with according civil inattention
to the physically handicapped and deformed. For examples of such
direct sanctions among adults one must turn to despotic societies
where glancing at the emperor or his agents may be a punishable
offense,[9] or to the rather refined rules prevailing in some of our
Southern states concerning how much of a look a colored male can
give to a white female, over how much distance, before it is
interpreted as a punishable sexual advance.[10]

Given the pain of being stared at, it is understandable that
staring itself is widely used as a means of negative sanction, socially
controlling all kinds of improper public conduct. Indeed it often
constitutes the first warning an individual receives that he is "out of
line" and the last warning that it is necessary to give him. In fact,
in the case of those whose appearance tests to the limit the capacity
of a gathering to proffer civil inattention, staring itself may become
a sanction against staring. The autobiography of an ex-dwarf
provides an illustration:

> There were the thick-skinned ones, who stared like hill people come
> down to see a traveling show. There were the paper-peekers, the
> furtive kind who would withdraw blushing if you caught them at it.
> There were the pitying ones, whose tongue clickings could almost
> be heard after they had passed you. But even worse, there were the
> chatterers, whose every remark might as well have been "How do
> you do, poor boy?" They said it with their eyes and their manners
> and their tone of voice.
>
> I had a standard defense—a cold stare. Thus anesthetized against
> my fellow man, I could contend with the basic problem—getting in
> and out of the subway alive.[11]

2. THE STRUCTURE OF FACE ENGAGEMENTS

When two persons are mutually present and hence engaged together in some degree of unfocused interaction, the mutual proffering of civil inattention—a significant form of unfocused interaction—is not the only way they can relate to one another. They can proceed from there to engage one another in focused interaction, the unit of which I shall refer to as a *face engagement* or an *encounter*.[12] Face engagements comprise all those instances of two or more participants in a situation joining each other openly in maintaining a single focus of cognitive and visual attention—what is sensed as a single *mutual activity*, entailing preferential communication rights. As a simple example—and one of the most common—when persons are present together in the same situation they may engage each other in a talk. This accreditation for mutual activity is one of the broadest of all statuses. Even persons of extremely disparate social positions can find themselves in circumstances where it is fitting to impute it to one another. Ordinarily the status does not have a "latent phase" but obliges the incumbents to be engaged at that very moment in exercising their status.

Mutual activities and the face engagements in which they are embedded comprise instances of small talk, commensalism, love-making, gaming, formal discussion, and personal servicing (treating, selling, waitressing, and so forth). In some cases, as with sociable chats, the coming together does not seem to have a ready instrumental rationale. In other cases, as when a teacher pauses at a pupil's desk to help him for a moment with a problem he is involved in, and will be involved in after she moves on, the encounter is clearly a setting for a mutual instrumental activity, and this joint work is merely a phase of what is primarily an individual task.[13] It should be noted that while many face engagements seem to be made up largely of the exchange of verbal statements, so that conversational encounters can in fact be used as the model, there are still other kinds of encounters where no word is spoken. This becomes very apparent, of course, in the study of engagements among children who have not yet mastered talk, and where, incidentally, it is possible to see the gradual transformation of a mere physical contacting of another into an act that establishes the social relationship of jointly accrediting a face-to-face encounter.[14] Among adults, too, however, nonverbal encounters can be observed: The significant acts exchanged can be gestures[15] or even, as in board and card games, moves. Also, there are certain close comings-together over work tasks which give rise to a single focus of visual and cognitive attention and to intimately coordinated contributions, the order and kind of contribution being determined by shared appreciation of what the task-at-the-moment requires as the next act. Here, while no word of direction or socialibity may be spoken, it will be understood that lack of attention or coordinated response constitutes a breach in the mutual commitment of the particiapnts.[16]

Where there are only two participants in a situation, an encounter, if there is to be one, will *exhaust* the situation, giving us a *fully-focused gathering*. With more than two participants, there may be persons officially present in the situation who are officially excluded from the encounter and not themselves so engaged. These unengaged[17] participants change the gathering into a *partly-focused* one. If more than three persons are present, there may be more than one encounter carried on in the same situation—a *multifocused* gathering. I will use the term *participation unit* to refer both to encounters and to unengaged participants; the term *bystander* will be used to refer to any individual present who is not a ratified member of the particular encounter in question, whether or not he is currently a member of some other encounter.

In our society, face engagements seem to share a complex of properties, so that this class of social unit can be defined analytically, as well as by example.

An encounter is initiated by someone making an opening move, typically by means of a special expression of the eyes but sometimes by a statement or a special tone of voice at the beginning of a statement.[18] The engagement proper begins when this overture is acknowledged by the other, who signals back with his eyes, voice, or stance that he has placed himself at the disposal of the other for purposes of a mutual eye-to-eye activity—even if only to ask the initiator to postpone his request for an audience.

There is a tendency for the initial move and the responding "clearance" sign to be exchanged almost simultaneously, with all participants employing both signs, perhaps in order to prevent an initiator from placing himself in a position of being denied by others. Glances, in particular, make possible this effective simultaneity. In fact, when eyes are joined, the initiator's first glance can be sufficiently tentative and ambiguous to allow him to act as if no initiation has been intended, if it appears that his overture is not desired.

Eye-to-eye looks, then, play a special role in the communication life of the community, ritually establishing an avowed openness to verbal statements and a rightfully heightened mutual relevance of acts.[19] In Simmel's words:

Of the special sense-organs, the eye has a uniquely sociological function. The union and interaction of individuals is based upon mutual glances. This is perhaps the most direct and purest reciprocity which exists anywhere. This highest psychic reaction, however, in which the glances of eye to eye unite men, crystallizes into no objective structure; the unity which momentarily arises between two persons is present in the occasion and is dissolved in the function. So tenacious and subtle is this union that it can only be maintained by the shortest and straightest line between the eyes, and the smallest deviation from it, the slightest glance aside, completely destroys the unique character of this union. No objective trace of this relationship is left behind, as is universally found, directly or indirectly, in all other types of associations between men, as, for example, in interchange of words. The interaction of eye and eye dies in the moment in which directness of the function is lost. But the totality of social relations of human beings, their self-assertion and self-abnegation, their intimacies and estrangements, would be changed in unpredictable ways if there occurred no glance of eye to eye. This mutual glance between persons, in distinction from the simple sight or observation of the other, signifies a wholly new and unique union between them.[20]

It is understandable, then, that an individual who feels he has cause to be alienated from those around him will express this through some "abnormality of the gaze," especially averting of the eyes.[21] And it is understandable, too, that an individual who wants to control others' access to him and the information he receives may avoid looking toward the person who is seeking him out. A waitress, for example, may prevent a waiting customer from "catching her eye" to prevent his initiating an order. Similarly, if a pedestrian wants to ensure a particular allocation of the street relative to a fellow pedestrian, or if a motorist wants to ensure priority of his line of proposed action over that of a fellow motorist or a pedestrian, one strategy is to avoid meeting the other's eyes and thus avoid cooperative claims.[22] And where the initiator is in a social position requiring him to give the other the formal right to initiate all encounters, hostile and teasing possibilities may occur, of which Melville's *White Jacket* gives us an example:

But sometimes the captain feels out of sorts, or in ill-humour, or is pleased to be somewhat capricious, or has a fancy to show a touch of his omnipotent supremacy; or, peradventure, it has so happened that the first lieutenant has, in some way, piqued or offended him, and he is not unwilling to show a slight specimen of his dominion over him, even before the eyes of all hands; at all events, only by some one of these suppositions can the singular circumstance be accounted for, that frequently Captain Claret would pertinaciously promenade up and down the poop, purposely averting his eye from the first lieutenant, who would stand below in the most awkward suspense, waiting the first wink from his superior's eye.

"Now I have him!" he must have said to himself, as the captain would turn toward him in his walk; "now's my time!" and up would go his hand to his cap; but, alas! the captain was off again; and the men at the guns would cast sly winks at each other as the embarrassed lieutenant would bite his lips with suppressed vexation.

Upon some occasions this scene would be repeated several times, till at last Captain Claret, thinking that in the eyes of all hands his dignity must by this time be pretty well bolstered, would stalk toward his subordinate, looking him full in the eyes; whereupon up goes his hand to the cap front, and the captain, nodding his acceptance of the report, descends from his perch to the quarter-deck.[23]

As these various examples suggest, mutual glances ordinarily must be withheld if an encounter is to be avoided, for eye contact opens one up for face engagement. I would like to add, finally, that there is a relationship between the use of eye-to-eye glances as a means of communicating a request for initiation of an encounter, and other communication practices. The more clearly individuals are obliged to refrain from staring directly at others, the more effectively will they be able to attach special significance to a stare, in this case, a request for an encounter. The rule of civil inattention thus makes possible, and "fits" with, the clearance function given to looks into others' eyes. The rule similarly makes possible the giving of a special function to "prolonged" holding of a stranger's glance, as when unacquainted persons who had arranged to meet each other manage to discover one another in this way.[24]

Once a set of participants have avowedly opened themselves up to one another for an engagement, an eye-to-eye ecological huddle tends to be carefully maintained, maximizing the opportunity for participants to monitor one another's mutual perceivings.[25] The participants turn their minds to the same subject matter and (in the case of talk) their eyes to the same speaker, although of course this single focus of attention can shift within limits from one topic to another and from one speaker or target to another.[26] A shared definition of the situation comes to prevail. This includes agreement concerning perceptual relevancies and irrelevancies, and a "working consensus," involving a degree of mutual considerateness, sympathy, and a muting of opinion differences.[27] Often a group atmosphere develops—what Bateson has called—ethos.[28] At the same time, a heightened sense of moral responsibility for one's acts also seems to develop.[29] A "we-rationale" develops, being a sense of the single thing that we the participants are avowedly doing together at the time. Further, minor ceremonies are likely to be employed to mark the termination of the engagement and the entrance and departure of particular participants (should the encounter have more than two members). These ceremonies, along with the social control exerted during the encounter to keep participants "in line," give a kind of ritual closure to the mutual activity sustained in the encounter. An individual will therefore tend to be brought all the way into an ongoing encounter or kept altogether out of it.[30]

Engagements of the conversational kind appear to have, at least in our society, some spatial conventions. A set of individuals caused to sit more than a few feet apart because of furniture arrangements will find difficulty in maintaining informal talk;[31] those brought within less than a foot and a half of each other will find difficulty in speaking directly to each other, and may talk at an off angle to compensate for the closeness.[32]

In brief, then, encounters are organized by means of a special set of acts and gestures comprising communication about communicating. As a linguist suggests:

> There are messages primarily serving to establish, to prolong, or to discontinue communication, to check whether the channel works ("Hello, do you hear me?"), to attract the attention of the interlocutor or to confirm his continued attention ("Are you listening?" or in Shakespearean diction, "Lend me your ears!"— and on the other end of the wire "Um-hum!").[33]

Everyday terms refer to different aspects of encounters. "Cluster," "knot," "conversational circle"—all highlight the physical aspects, namely, a set of persons physically close together and facially oriented to one another, their backs toward those who are not participants. "Personal encounter" refers to the unit in terms of the opportunity it provides or enforces for some kind of social intimacy. In the literature, the term "the interaction" is sometimes used to designate either the activity occurring within the cluster at any one moment or the total activity occurring from the moment the cluster forms to the moment at which it officially disbands. And, of course, where spoken messages are exchanged, especially under informal circumstances, the terms "chat," "a conversation," or "a talk" are employed.

It may be noted that while all participants share equally in the rights and obligations described, there are some rights that may be differentially distributed within an encounter. Thus, in spoken encounters, the right to listen is one shared by all, but the right to be a speaker may be narrowly restricted, as, for example, in stage performances and large public meetings. Similarly, children at the dinner table are sometimes allowed to listen but forbidden to talk;[34] if not forbidden to talk, they may be "helped out" and in this way denied the communication courtesy of being allowed to finish a message for themselves.[35] And in other engagements, one category of participant may be allowed to say only "Yes, sir," or "No, sir," or restricted to the limited signalling that a modulation of applause allows. The differential rights of players vis-à-vis kibitzers in games provide another example.

When the communion of a face engagement has been established between two or more individuals, the resulting state of ratified mutual participation can last for varying periods. When a clearly defined task is involved, the engagement may last for hours. When no apparent work or recreational task is involved, and what is perceived as sociability alone holds the participants, certain durations seem to be favored. The contact may be very brief, as brief, in fact, as the opening meeting of eyes itself. In our own middle-class society there are "chats," where two individuals pause in their separate lines of action for what both recognize to be a necessarily brief period of time; there are greetings, whereby communion is established and maintained long enough for the participants to exchange brief interpersonal rituals; and, briefest of all, there are recognitional or "friendly" glances. (Of course, a recognitional glance may be merely the first interchange in an extended greeting, and a greeting merely the opening phase of a chat, but these extensions of coparticipation are not always found.) Except for the ritual of civil inattention, the mere exchange of friendly glances is perhaps the most frequent of our interpersonal rituals.

Encounters of an obligatory kind are linked to the world of domestic convivial occasions. In some social circles, a guest entering a party has a right to be greeted by the host or hostess and convoyed into the proceedings in visible contact with the authorizing person, this encounter thereby legitimating and celebrating the newcomer's participation in the occasion. His departure may be marked with the same kind of ceremony, officially bringing his participation to an end.[36] The occasion then closes in and over the place he has left, and if he should have to return for something he has forgotten, embarrassment is likely to be felt, especially if the ethos of the occasion has changed, and especially if marked ceremonial attention had been given his leave-taking.[37]

Encounters, of course, tend to be taken as an expression of the state of a social relationship. And, as will be considered later, to the degree that contact is practical, it may have to be made so as not to deny the relationship.[38] Further, each engagement tends to be initiated with an amount of fuss appropriate to the period of lapsed contact, and terminated with the amount appropriate to the assumed period of separation. There results a kind of tiding over, and a compensation for the diminishing effects of separation.[39] At a party, then, a version of Mrs. Post's ruling is likely to prevail:

> In meeting the same person many times within an hour or so, one does not continue to bow after the second, or at most third meeting. After that one either looks away or merely smiles.[40]

The same mere smile between the same two persons newly coming within range of each other in a foreign country may constitute a grievous affront to their relationship.

I have suggested that a face engagement is a sufficiently clear-cut unit that an individual typically must either be entirely within it or entirely outside it. This is nicely borne out by the trouble caused when a person attempts to be half-in and half-out. Nonetheless, there are communication arrangements that seem to lie halfway between mere copresence and full scale coparticipation, one of which should be mentioned here. When two persons walk silently together down the street or doze next to each other at the beach, they may be treated by others as "being together," and are likely to have the right to break rather abruptly into spoken or gestured communication, although they can hardly be said to sustain continuously a mutual activity. This sense of being together constitutes a kind of lapsed verbal encounter, functioning more as a means of excluding nonmembers than as a support for sustained focused interaction among the participants.[41]

Persons who can sustain lapsed encounters with one another are in a position to avoid the problem of "safe supplies" during spoken encounters—the need to find a sufficient supply of inoffensive things to talk about during the period when an official state of talk prevails. Thus, in Shetland Isle, when three or four women were knitting together, one knitter would say a word, it would be allowed to rest for a minute or two, and then another knitter would provide an additional comment. In the same manner a family sitting around its kitchen fire would look into the flames and intersperse replies to statements with periods of observation of the fire. Shetland men used for the same purpose the lengthy pauses required for the proper management of their pipes.

To these comments on the structure of engagements I would like to add a brief remark on the information that encounters convey to the situation as a whole. In an earlier section, it was suggested that an individual divulges things about himself by his mere presence in a situation. In the same way, he gives off information about himself by virtue of the encounters in which others do or do not see him. Involvement in focused interaction therefore inevitably contributes to unfocused interaction conveying something to all who are present in the situation at large.

In public places in our society, what is conveyed by being in or out of encounters differs appreciably according to sex and the periods of the week. Morning and lunchtime are times when anyone can appear alone almost anywhere without this giving evidence of how the person is faring in the social world; dinner and other evening activities, however, provide unfavorable information about unaccompanied participants, especially damaging in the case of female participants. Weekend nights, and ceremonial occasions such as Thanksgiving, Christmas, and, especially, New Year's Eve, are given special weight in this connection, being times when an unearned individual in a semipublic place may feel very much out of place.

It should be added, finally, that in so far as others judge the individual socially by the company he is seen in, for him to be brought into an engagement with another is to be placed in the position of being socially identified as the other is identified.

3. ACCESSIBILITY

In every situation, those present will be obliged to retain some readiness for potential face engagements. (This readiness has already been suggested as one way in which situational presence is expressed.) There are many important reasons why the individual is usually obliged to respond to requests for face engagements. In the first place, he owes this to himself because often it will be through such communication that his own interests can be served, as when a stranger accosts him to tell him he has dropped something, or that the bridge is out. For similar reasons he owes this accessibility to others present, and to persons not present for whom those present may serve as a relay. (The need for this collective solidarity is heightened in urban living, which brings individuals of great social distance within range of one another.) Further, as previously suggested, participation in a face engagement can be a sign of social closeness and relatedness; when this opportunity to participate is proffered by another, it ought not to be refused, for to decline such a request is to reject someone who has committed himself to a sign of desiring contact. More than this, refusal of an offer implies that the refuser rejects the other's claim to membership in the gathering and the social occasion in which the gathering occurs. It is therefore uncommon for persons to deny these obligations to respond.

Although there are good reasons why an individual should keep himself available for face engagements, there are also good reasons for him to be cautious of this.

In allowing another to approach him for talk, the individual may find that he has been inveigled into a position to be attacked and assaulted physically. In societies where public safety is not firmly established, especially in places such as the desert, where the traveler is for long periods of time remote from any source of help, the danger that a face engagement may be a prelude to assault becomes appreciable, and extensive avoidance practices or greetings at a distance tend to be employed.[42] Here, of course, the "physical safety" component of civic order and the communication component overlap. But apart from this extreme, we should see that when an individual opens himself up to talk with another, he opens himself up to pleadings, commands, threats, insult, and false information. The mutual considerateness characteristic of face engagements reinforces these dangers, subjecting the individual to the possibility of having his sympathy and tactfulness exploited, and causing him to act against his own interests.

Further, words can act as a "relationship wedge"; that is, once an individual has extended to another enough consideration to hear him out for a moment, some kind of bond of mutual obligation is established, which the initiator can use in turn as a basis for still further claims; once this new extended bond is granted, grudgingly or willingly, still further claims for social or material indulgence can be made. Hence, in one important example, a man and a woman can start out as strangers and, if conditions are right, progress from an incidental encounter to matrimony. We need only trace back the history of many close relationships between adults to find that something was made of face engagements when it need not have been. Of course, persons usually form "suitable" relationships, not allowing casual encounters to be a wedge to something else. But there is sufficient slippage in systems of conviviality segregation to give mothers concern about their daughters and to provide one of the basic romantic themes of light fiction.

I have suggested some reasons why individuals, at least in our own society, are obliged to keep themselves available for face engagement, and I have also suggested some of the dangers persons open themselves up to in so doing. These two opposing tendencies are reconciled in society, apparently, by a kind of implicit contract or gentleman's agreement that persons sustain: Given the fact that the other will be under some obligation, often unpleasant, to respond to overtures, potential initiators are under obligation to stay their own desires. A person can thus make himself available to others in the expectation that they will restrain their calls on his availability and not make him pay too great a price for his being accessible. Their right to initiate contact is checked by their duty to take his point of view and initiate contact with him only under circumstances that he will easily see to be justified; in short, they must not "abuse" their privileges.

This implicit communication contract (and the consequence of breaking it) receive wide mythological representation, as in our own "cry wolf" tale. Understandably, infractions of the rule against undesired overture do cause some anxiety, for the recipient must either accede to the request or demonstrate to himself and the others present that his availability for face engagements was not part of his character but a false pose, to be maintained only when no price was involved in maintaining it.

In noting the implicit contract that makes persons present delicately accessible and inaccessible to each other, we can go on to note a basic margin of appetite and distaste to be found in social situations. The reasons why individuals are obliged to restrain themselves from making encounter overtures provide many of the reasons why they might want to do so. And the obligation to be properly accessible often covers a desire to be selectively quite unavailable. Hence, many public and semipublic places, such as cocktail lounges and club cars, acquire a special tone and temper, a special piquancy, that blurs the communication lines, giving each participant some desire to encroach where perhaps he does not have a right to go, and to keep from being engaged with others who perhaps have a right to engage him. Each individual, then, is not only involved in maintaining the basic communication contract, but is also likely to be involved in hopes, fears, and actions that bend the rules if they do not actually break them.

It has been suggested, then, that as a general rule the individual is obliged to make himself available for encounters even though he may have something to lose by entering them, and that he may well be ambivalent about this arrangement. Here mental patients provide a lesson in reverse, for they can show us the price that is paid for declining to make oneself available and force us to see that there are reasons why someone able to be accessible should be willing to pay the price of remaining inaccessible.

In brief, a patient who declines to respond to overtures is said to be "out of contact," and this state is often felt to be full evidence that he is very sick indeed, that he is, in fact, cut off from all contact with the world around him. In the case of some "organic" patients, this generalization from inaccessibility appears quite valid, as it does with certain "functionals." There are patients, for example, who, before admission, had progressively withdrawn from responding to such things as the telephone and doorbell, and, once in the hospital, decline all staff overtures for engagement, this being but one instance of a general withdrawal of concern for the life about them.

In the case of other patients, however, refusal to enter proffered engagements cannot be taken as a sign of unconcern for the gatherings, but rather as a sign of alienation based on active feelings such as fear, hate, and contempt, each of which can be understandable in the circumstances, and each of which can allow the patient to show a nice regard for other situational proprieties.

Thus, there are patients who coldly stare through direct efforts to bring them into a state of talk, declining all staff overtures, however, seductive, teasing, or intensive, who will nonetheless allow themselves face engagements carefully initiated and terminated by themselves without the usual courtesies. Still other patients who are out of contact to most persons on the ward will engage in self-initiated encounters with a small select number of others, by means of coded messages, foreign language, whispering, or the exchange of written statements. Some patients, unwilling to engage in spoken encounters with anyone, will be ready to engage in other types of encounters, such as dancing or card playing. Similarly, I knew a patient who often blankly declined greetings extended him by fellow-patients on the grounds, but who could be completely relied upon not to miss a cue when performing the lead in a patient dramatic production.

As might then be expected, a patient declining to conduct himself properly in regard to face engagements might be well conducted in regard to unfocused interaction.[43] One illustration was provided by a patient I observed, a young woman of thirty-two, who at one point in her "illness" was ready to handle her dress and deportment with all the structured modesty that is required of her sex, while at the same time her language was foul. During another phase of her illness, this patient, in the company of a friendly nurse, enjoyed shopping trips to the neighboring town, during which she and her keeper got wry pleasure from the fact that the patient was "passing" as a "normal" person. Had anyone made an opening statement to the patient, however, the masquerade would have been destroyed, for this was a time when the patient was mute in all verbal interaction or, at best, spoke with very great pressure.

A touching illustration of the same difference in capacity for focused and unfocused interaction was provided at Central Hospital by patients who were fearful and anxious of their whole setting, but who nonetheless made elaborate efforts to show that they were still what they had been before coming to the hospital and that they were in poised, businesslike control of the situation. One middle-aged man walked busily on the grounds with the morning newspaper folded under one arm and a rolled umbrella hooked over the other, wearing an expression of being late for an appointment. A young man, having carefully preserved his worn grey flannel suit, bustled similarly from one place he was not going to another. Yet both men stepped out of the path of any approaching staff person, and painfully turned their heads away whenever someone proffered an exchange or greeting of some kind, for both employed the tack of being mute with many of the persons whom they met. The management of a front of middle-class orientation in the situation, in these circumstances, was so precarious and difficult that (for these men) it apparently represented the day's major undertaking.[44] In other cases, of course, it is not fear that seems to account for inaccessibility of otherwise properly mannered persons, but rather hostility: To acknowledge a staff overture is partly to acknowledge the legitimacy of the staff person making the overture, and if he is a serious worthy person then so must be his implied contention that the individual with whom he is initiating contact, namely, oneself, is a mental patient properly confined to a mental ward. To strengthen one's feeling that one is really sane, it may thus seem reasonable to disdain encounters in which the opposite will be assumed—even though this results in exactly the kind of conduct, namely, inaccessibility, that confirms the hospital's view that one is mentally ill.

A final point about accessibility should be mentioned. As previously suggested, conversational engagements are often carried out as involvements subordinated to some other business at hand, just as side involvements, such as smoking, are often carried out as activities subordinated to a conversational main involvement. The question arises as to the limits placed upon this coexistence in middle-class society. There are, for example, records of middle-class Navy personnel postponing a visit to the "head" until others have left so as not to have to defecate while being accessible to others for talk. I have also been told by a middle-class informant that she was always uneasy about painting her toenails while in the presence of her husband, since the painting involved too much attention to leave her sufficiently respectful of the talk.

4. LEAVE-TAKING RIGHTS

Just as the individual is obliged not to exploit the accessibility of
others (else they have to pay too large a price for their obligation to
be accessible), so he is obliged to release those with whom he is
engaged, should it appear, through conventional cues, that they
desire to be released (else they have to pay too great a price for
their tact in not openly taking leave of him). A reminder of these
rules of leave-taking can be found in elementary school classrooms
where leave-taking practices are still being learned, as, for example,
when a teacher, having called a student to her desk in order to
correct his exercise book, may have to turn him around and gently
propel him back to his seat in order to terminate the interview.

   The rights of departure owed the individual, and the rule of
tactful leave-taking owed the remaining participants, can be in
conflict with each other. This conflict is often resolved, in a way
very characteristic of communication life, by persons active in
different roles tacitly cooperating to ease leave-taking. Thus,
business etiquette provides the following lesson:

> *On when to go*—your exit cues are many. The range from clear-cut
> closing remarks, usually in the form of a "thank you for coming in,"
> to a vacant and preoccupied stare. But in any case they should come
> from the interviewer. It should not be necessary for him to stand,
> abruptly; you should have been able to feel the goodbye in the air
> far enough in advance to gather up your gear, slide forward to the
> edge of your chair and launch into a thank-you speech of your own.
> Nor should it be necessary to ask that embarrassing question, "Am I
> taking too much of your time?"; if that thought crosses your mind,
> it's time to go.[45]

In fact, persons can become so accustomed to being helped out by
the very person who creates the need for help, that when cooperation
is not forthcoming they may find they have no way of handling the
incident. Thus, some mental patients may characteristically hold a
staff person in an encounter regardless of how many hints the
latter provides that termination ought now to occur. As the staff
person begins to walk away, the patient may follow along until the
locked door is reached, and even then the patient may try to
accompany him. At such times the staff person may have to hold
back the patient forcibly, or precipitously tear himself away,
demonstrating not merely that the patient is being left in the lurch,
but also that the staff show of concern for the patient is, in some
sense, only a show. Pitchmen and street stemmers initiate a similar
process; they rely on the fact that the accosted person will be
willing to agree to a purchase in order not to have to face being the

sort of person who walks away from an encounter without being officially released.

Notes

1. Griffin, J. H., *Black Like Me* (Boston: Houghton Mifflin, 1961), pp. 54, 128.
2. Goffman, Erving, *The Presentation of Self in Everyday Life* (Garden City, N.Y.: Doubleday Anchor, 1959) 151–153.
3. Riemer, M. D., "Abnormalities of the Gaze—A Classification," *Psychiatric Quarterly* 29, (1955):659–672.
4. A notable observer of face-to-face conduct, the novelist William Sansom, disputes this point in "Happy Holiday Abroad," in *A Contest of Ladies* (London: Hogarth Press, 1956), p. 228:

   Slowly he walked the length of the beach, pretending to saunter, studying each bather sideways from behind his black spectacles. One would think such dark glasses might conceal the inquisitive eye: but Preedy knew better, he knew they do the opposite, as soon as they are swivelled anywhere near the object it looks like a direct hit. You cannot appear to glance just beyond with your dark guns on.

5. See P. Binder, *Muffs and Morals* (New York: Morrow, n.d.), chap. 9, "Umbrellas, Walking Sticks, and Fans," pp. 178–196. The author suggests, p. 193:

   Another quizzing fan [in eighteenth-century England] had an inset of mica or gauze, so that a lady might cunningly use her fan as a lorgnette while her face appeared to be screened from view. This type of fan was intended for use at a risqué play, where modesty required some equivalent to the earlier face-mask.

   Successive devices of this kind must incorporate three features: The user must be able to look at the other, be able to give the appearance of not being ashamed of being seen by the other, and be able to conceal that he is in fact spying. Children in Shetland Isle primary schools handle visiting strangers with something like a fan—but one that fails in the last two counts —by shyly hiding their faces behind their two hands while peeking out at the visitor from a crack between two fingers.

6. See the very useful paper by R. K. White, B. A. Wright, and T. Dembo, "Studies in Adjustment to Visible Injuries: Evaluation of Curiosity by the Injured," *Journal of Abnormal and Social Psychology* 43, (1948):13–28.
7. Ibid., 22.

8. Ibid., 16–17.

9. Douglas, R. K., *Society in China* (London: Innes, 1894), p. 11.

10. See, for example, the notable Webster-Ingram case reported November 12–13, 1952 (AP). In many societies in Africa and Asia, a similar taboo exists regarding glances that males cast on females.

11. Viscardi, H., Jr., *A Man's Stature* (New York: Day, 1952), p. 70, as cited in B. A. Wright, *Physical Disability—A Psychological Approach* (New York: Harper & Row, 1960), p. 214.

12. The term "encounter," which is much the easier of the two to use, has some common-sense connotations that ought here to be ruled out. First, the term is sometimes used to refer to mediated, as well as to direct, contact between two persons, as when persons have correspondence with each other. Secondly, the term is sometimes used with an implication of there having been difficulty or trouble during the interaction, as in the phrase "a run-in." Finally, the term is sometimes used to cover occasions which bring two persons into easy access to each other, regardless of how many times they may come together in a joint conversation during this time, as in the phrase, "I next encountered him at the Jones's party." I have attempted to consider the internal dynamics of encounters in "Fun in Games" in *Encounters*, 17–81.

13. Suggested by Arthur Stinchcombe.

14. See, for example, the early study by A. Beaver, *The Initiation of Social Contacts by Preschool Children* (New York: Bureau of Publications, Teachers College, Columbia University, Child Development Monographs, No. 7, 1932), pp. 1–14.

15. Efron, D., *Gesture and Environment* (New York: King's Crown, 1941), p. 38.

16. The kind of intimate coordination consequent on involvement in the same task is nicely described in F. B. Miller, " 'Situational' Interactions—A Worthwhile Concept?" *Human Organization* **17**, (Winter 1958–1959):37–47. After pointing out the differences between this kind of focused interaction and the kind necessarily involving speech or gestures, the writer does not, however, go on to consider the similarities, such as the fact that withdrawal of attention, or ineptness, can give rise to the same kind of corrective social control in both cases. A well-described illustration of a task activity as an engagement may be found in T. Burling, *Essays on Human Aspects of Administration* (New York State School of Industrial and

Labor Relations, Cornell University, Bulletin 25, August, 1953), pp. 10–11:

> What is actually happening is that the changing needs of the patient, as they develop in the course of the operation, determine what everybody does. When a surgical team has worked long enough to have developed true teamwork, each member has such a grasp of the total situation and of his role in it that the needs of the patient give unequivocal orders. A small artery is cut and begins to spurt. In a chain-of-command organization the surgeon would note this and say to the assistant, "Stop that bleeder." The assistant, in turn would say to the surgical nurse, "Give me a hemostat," and thus, coordinated effort would be achieved. What actually happens is that the bleeder gives a simultaneous command to all three members of the team, all of whom have been watching the progress of the operation with equal attention. It says to the surgeon, "Get your hand out of the way until this is controlled." It says to the instrument nurse, "Get a hemostat ready," and it says to the assistant, "Clamp that off." This is the highest and most efficient type of cooperation known. It is so efficient that it looks simple and even primitive. It is possible only where every member of the team knows not only his own job thoroughly, but enough about the total job and that of each of the other members to see the relationship of what he does to everything else that goes on.

17. An "unengaged" participant may of course be involved in a task or other main focus of attention and hence not be "disengaged" in the situation.

18. When the individual is socially subordinated to the one to whom he is about to initiate an encounter overture, he may be required to use a minimal sign so that the superior can easily continue to overlook it, or can respond to it at his own convenience. For example, *Esquire Etiquette* (New York: Lippincott, 1953), p. 24, in listing the habits of a good secretary, includes "waiting to be recognized, when she has stepped in to speak to you, before interrupting whatever you are doing." In such cases the fiction is maintained that the superordinate alone can initiate an engagement. The classic case here is the mythical butler who coughs discreetly so that his master will take note of his presence and allow him to deliver a message.

19. In face engagements embodying a formal sports activity, opening moves may take other forms, as when boxers touch gloves, or swordsmen touch foils, in order to establish a sporting bracket or frame, as it were, around the oncoming encounter. Where participants know each other well, clearance

signs may be taken for granted, and the initiator may pause slightly or in other ways modify his opening action, as a courtesy, and then proceed as if clearance had been granted.

Interestingly enough, some face engagements are of the kind in which coordination of activity is typically embodied in the usual ritual brackets of eye-recognition and exchange of words, but which, under special circumstances, are carefully initiated, maintained, and terminated *without* usual verbal or gestural overlay. Thus, in many mental hospitals, patients expect to be able to call on *any* patient who is smoking for a light, regardless of how withdrawn or regressed the smoker may appear to be. The gestured request for a light seems to be invariably complied with, but very often the complier addresses himself to the technical task alone, declining any other kind of negotiation or business. A similar kind of deritualized encounter is found where a man holds a door open for a woman he does not know, under circumstances that could imply an overture or could bring home undesirable facts about the woman for being in the region; under such circumstances the male may be careful to proffer civil inattention even while nicely adjusting his physical behavior to the movements of the woman. Emily Post, *Etiquette* (New York: Funk & Wagnalls, 1937) p. 26, suggests a similar courtesy:

Lifting the hat is a conventional gesture of politeness shown to strangers only, not to be confused with bowing, which is a gesture used to acquaintances and friends. In lifting his hat, a gentleman merely lifts it slightly off his forehead—by the brim of a stiff hat or by the crown of a soft one—and replaces it; he does not smile or bow, nor does he even look at the object of his courtesy. No gentleman ever subjects a lady to his scrutiny or his apparent observation if she is a stranger.

20. From his *Soziologie*, cited in R. E. Park and E. W. Burgess, *Introduction to the Science of Sociology*, 2nd ed. (Chicago: University of Chicago Press, 1924), p. 358. An interesting statement of some of the things that can be conveyed through eye-to-eye contact alone is given by Ortega y Gasset in his *Man and People* (New York: Norton, 1957), pp. 115–117. He implies that there is a whole vocabulary of glances, describing several of them.
21. Riemer, M. D., "The Averted Gaze," *Psychiatric Quarterly* **23**, (1949):108–115. It would be very interesting to examine techniques employed by the blind and the dumb to provide

functional substitutes for clearance cues and other eye
contributions to the structure of face-to-face communication.

22. The general point behind this example has been made by
T. C. Schelling in his analysis of the bargaining power of the
individual who can convincingly commit himself to a line of
action, in this case by communicating his inability to receve
demands and threats through messages. See Schelling's "An
Essay on Bargaining," *The American Economic Review* **46**,
(1956):281–306, esp. 294–295.

23. Melville, Herman, *White Jacket* (New York: Grove Press,
n.d.), p. 276.

24. Evelyn Hooker, in an unpublished Cophenhagen address,
August 14, 1961, titled "The Homosexual Community,"
suggests: "It is said by homosexuals that if another catches
and holds the glance, one need know nothing more about him
to know that he is one of them."

25. This may not be a universal practice. According to an early
report on the Northwest Coast Amazons:

> When an Indian talks he sits down, no conversation is ever carried
> on when the speakers are standing unless it be a serious difference
> of opinion under discussion; nor, when he speaks, does the Indian
> look at the person addressed, any more than the latter watches the
> speaker. Both look at some outside objects. This is the attitude also
> of the Indian when addressing more than one listener, so that he
> appears to be talking to some one not visibly present.

Whiffen, T., *The North-West Amazons* (London: Constable,
1915), p. 254. In our own society, however, we can readily
understand that when convicts are forbidden to talk to one
another but desire to do so, they can effectively shield their
joint involvement by talking without moving their lips and
without looking at each other. See, for example, J. Phelan, *The
Underworld* (London: Harrap, 1953), pp. 7–8 and 13. We
can also understand that when technical considerations prevent
eye-to-eye accessibility (as in the case of a surgical nurse
receiving orders from a surgeon who must not take his eyes
from the surgical field), considerable discipline will be
required of the recipient if communication is to be maintained.
Finally, we can appreciate that the blind will have to learn to
act as if the speaker is being watched, even though in fact the
blind recipient could as well direct his sightless gaze
anywhere. In the latter connection see H. Chevigny, *My Eyes
Have a Cold Nose* (New Haven, Conn.: Yale University Press,
1962), p. 51.

26. Cf. R. F. Bales et al., "Channels of Communication in Small

Groups," *American Sociological Review* 16, (1951):461–468, p. 461:

> The conversation generally proceeded so that one person talked at a time, and all members in the particular group were attending the same conversation. In this sense, these groups might be said to have a "single focus," that is, they did not involve a number of conversations proceeding at the same time, as one finds at a cocktail party or in a hotel lobby. The single focus is probably a limiting condition of fundamental importance in the generalizations reported here.

To this the caution should be added that the multiple focuses found in places like hotel lobbies would occur simultaneously with unfocused interaction.

27. Hence, as Oswald Hall has suggested to me, when closeness and symapthy are to be held to a minimum, as when a butler talks to a house guest, or an enlisted man is disciplined by an officer, eye-to-eye communion may be avoided by the subordinate holding his eyes stiffly to the front. An echo of the same factor is to be found even in mediated conversation, where servants are obliged to answer the telephone by saying "Mrs. So-and-So's residence" instead of "Hello."

   This tendency for eye-to-eye looks to involve sympathetic accommodation is nicely suggested in Trotsky's description of street disturbances during the "five days" in *The History of the Russian Revolution*, trans. Max Eastman (New York: Simon and Schuster, 1936), pp. 1, 109:

> In spite of the auspicious rumors about the Cossacks, perhaps slightly exaggerated, the crowd's attitude toward the mounted men remains cautious. A horseman sits high above the crowd; his soul is separated from the soul of the demonstrator by the four legs of his beast. A figure at which one must gaze from below always seems more significant, more threatening. The infantry are beside one on the pavement—closer, more accessible. The masses try to get near them, look into their eyes, surround them with their hot breath. A great role is played by women workers in the relation between workers and soldiers. They go up to the cordons more boldly than men, take hold of the rifles, beseech, almost command: "Put down your bayonets—join us." The soldiers are excited, ashamed, exchange anxious glances, waver; someone makes up his mind first, and the bayonets rise guiltily above the shoulders of the advancing crowd. The barrier is opened, a joyous and grateful "Hurah!" shakes the air.

A more formalized version of the same tendency is described as obtaining among the Bedouins. See A. Musil, *The Manners and Customs of the Rwala Bedouins* (New York: American

Geographical Society, Oriental Explorations and Studies No. 6, 1928), p. 455:

A salutation, if returned, is a guarantee of safety in the desert, *as-salâm salâme*. If a stranger travels unaccompanied by a *hawi* through the territory of a tribe unknown to him and salutes someone —be it only a little girl—and is saluted in return, he may be reasonably certain that he will be neither attacked nor robbed, for even a little girl with all her kin will protect him. Should the fellow tribesmen of the girl attack and rob him, *mâhûd* he has only to ask the help of her kinsfolk, who must take his part. The girl is the best witness: "A traveler saluted me at such and such a place of about such and such an age, dressed thus and so, riding on a she-camel," of which she also gives a description. Frequently even an enemy saves himself in this manner when hotly pursued. Realizing that he cannot escape, he suddenly changes his course, returns by a roundabout way to the camp of his pursuers, salutes a child, and, taking its hand, allows himself to be led to the tent of the parents. The adult Bedouins, being more cautious, do not answer at once when saluted by a man they do not know. Especially if two or three are riding together and approach a camp at night, the guard replies to their salute thus:
 "Ye are outlawed; I shall not return your salutation; *tarâkom mwassedin w-lâ 'alejkom radd as-salâm*." For an outlawed one, *mwassed*, is treated like an enemy to whom a salutation is of no use whatever.

Because of the obligation of considerateness among members of an engagement, and especially between a speaker and the particular member to whom he addresses his remarks, individuals sometimes "talk into the air" or mutter, pointedly addressing their remarks to no one, or to a child or pet. The person for whose benefit the remarks are intended may thus be half forced into the role of overhearer, allowing greater liberties to be taken with him than could be comfortably managed in direct address.

28. Bateson, G., *Naven* (Cambridge: Cambridge University Press, 1936), pp. 119–120:

When a group of young English men or women are talking and joking together wittily and with a touch of light cynicism, there is established among them for the time being a definite tone of appropriate behavior. Such specific tones of behavior are in all cases indicative of an ethos. They are expressions of a standardized system of emotional attitudes. In this case the men have temporarily adopted a definite set of sentiments towards the rest of the world, a definite attitude towards reality, and they will joke about subjects which at another time they would treat with seriousness. If one of the men suddenly intrudes a sincere or realist remark it will be received with no enthusiasm—perhaps with a moment's silence and a slight feeling that the sincere person has committed a solecism. On another occasion the same group of persons may adopt a different ethos; they may talk realistically and sincerely. Then if the blunderer makes a flippant joke it will fall flat and feel like a solecism.

29. And so we find that bringing someone into a face engagement can be used by the initiator as a form of social control, as when a teacher stops a student's *sotto voce* comments by looking him in the eye and saying, "What did you say?" or when failure to accord civil inattention is handled as Norman Mailer describes in his novel *The Deer Park* (New York: Signet Books, 1957), p. 212:

> Beda [a celebrity] looked at a woman who had been staring at him curiously and when he winked, she turned away in embarrassment, "Oh God, the tourists," he said.

Interestingly enough, since joint participation in an encounter allows participants to look fully at each other—in fact, enjoins this to a degree—we find that one strategy employed by an individual when he is caught out by the person he is staring at is to act as if this staring were the first move in an overture to engagement, thereby ratifying and legitimating the failure to accord civil inattention.

30. One well-established way of confirming and consolidating a leave-taking is for the leave-taker to move away physically from the other or others. In places like Shetland Isle this can cause a problem when two persons pause for a moment's sociability and then find that their directions of movement do not diverge sharply. If the two persons walk at a normal pace, they find themselves attempting to close out the encounter while still having easy physical access to each other. Sometimes one individual offers an excuse to break into a run; sometimes, even if it takes him out of his way, he may take a path diverging sharply from that taken by his erstwhile coparticipant.

31. Sommer, R., "The Distance for Comfortable Conversation: A Further Study," *Sociometry* 25, (1962):111–116. See also his "Studies in Personal Space," *Sociometry* 22, (1959):247–260.

32. See E. T. Hall, *The Silent Language* (New York: Doubleday, 1959), pp. 204–206. In B. Schaffner (ed.), *Group Processes*, Transactions of the Fourth (1957) Conference (New York: Josiah Macy, Jr. Foundation, 1959), p. 184, R. Birdwhistell comments as follows in a symposium discussion:

It appears that Americans, when standing face to face, stand about arm's length from each other. When they stand side by side, the distance demanded is much less. When "middle majority Americans" stand closer than this in a face-to-face position they will either gradually separate or come toward each other and begin to emit signs of irritation. However, if they are put in a situation in which they are not required to interact—say on a streetcar—they can stand quite closer, even to the point of making complete contact.

The amount of this territory seems to vary culturally. So, there can be a situation where two or three ethnic groups occupy different territories, that is, varying amounts of personal space. For example, put together a Southeastern European Jew (who occupies about half the area of personal space) and a middle-class American and a high degree of irritation results, particularly if the middle-class American keeps drifting around to the side, in order not to be insulting, and the Southeastern European Jewish man tries to move around to get face-to-face relationship. You get an actual dance, which very often turns into what is practically a fight.

From all of this it follows that among persons arranged in a discussion circle, persons adjacent to each other may tend not to address remarks to each other, except to pass side comments, since a voice full enough to embrace the circle would be too full for the distance between them. For experimental evidence, see B. Steinzor, "The Spatial Factor in Face to Face Discussion Groups," *Journal of Abnormal and Social Psychology* **45**, (1950):552–555.

33. Jakobson, R., "Closing Statement: Linguistics and Poetics," in T. A. Sebeok (ed.), *Style in Language* (New York: Wiley, 1960), p. 355. Cf. the concept of metacommunication in J. Ruesch and G. Bateson, *Communication* (New York: Norton, 1951).

34. Bossard, J. H. S., "Family Modes of Expression," *American Sociological Review* **10**, (1945):226–237, p. 229.

35. Ibid.

36. Here there is an interesting difference between Anglo-American and French custom; in France, the entering or departing person ratifies his entrance or departure not only through contact with the person managing the occasion but often also by a hand-shaking engagement with some or all of the other guests present.

37. The same sort of embarrassment occurs when a member of an organization, who has been given a farewell party and gift to mark a termination of his membership and to set the stage for the group's developing a new relation to a substitute, then finds that he must remain with or return to the organization.

He finds that the group has "worked through" his membership, leaving him present but socially not there.

38. Face engagements, of course, are not the only kinds of contact carrying ceremonial functions. Gifts, greeting cards, and salutatory telegrams and telephone calls also serve in this way. Each social circle seems to develop norms as to how frequently and extensively these ought to be employed to affirm relationships among geographically separated people, depending on the costs faced by each group in using these several devices. Just as friends at the same social party are obliged to spend at least a few moments chatting together, so a husband out of town on business may be considered "in range" and be obliged to telephone home in the evening.

39. Goffman, E., "On Face-Work," *Psychiatry* **18**, (1955):229.

40. Post, *Etiquette*, p. 29.

41. Being "with" someone at a given moment is to be distinguished from the party relationship of having "come with" someone to the occasion, the latter representing a preferential claim as to whom one will leave with, be loyal to, and the like.

42. The case of desert contacts is vividly described in a short story by Paul Bowles, "The Delicate Prey," in *The Delicate Prey and Other Stories* (New York: Random House, 1950), pp. 277–289, esp. 279–280.

43. Manner books contain the same suggestion. See, for example, *Good Manners* (New York: Garrity, 1929), p. 31:

   Many people whose "acting" manners are good have poor "talking" manners. They may be gossipy or they may tell off-color stories; or say things that hurt people's feelings, or they may chatter on so continuously that no one else can get a word in "edgewise."

44. Just as it is evident that the individual may comply with rules regarding unfocused interaction while failing to comply with regulations regarding focused interaction, so cases can be found of mental patients who dress in a spectacularly improper manner but who are none the less ready to be socially tractable as conversationalists. Here are two pieces of evidence in favor of distinguishing conceptually between focused and unfocused interaction.

45. *Esquire Etiquette*, p. 59.

11

WHEN PEOPLE TALK WITH PEOPLE

John C. Condon, Jr.

Years ago, a popular phonograph record produced by Stan Freberg
presented a short conversation between two persons, Marsha and
John. The conversation began like this:

"John . . ."

"Marsha . . ."

"John . . ."

"Marsha . . ."

"John . . ."

"Marsha . . ."

(Using the above dialogue as a basis, the clever reader can
extrapolate the entire three-minute conversation.)

Reprinted with permission of Macmillan Publishing Co., Inc. from
Semantics and Communication by John C. Condon, Jr., pp. 87–107.
Copyright by John C. Condon, Jr., 1965.

The printed form does not convey what the recording artists did with only two words. They were able to indicate differences in meaning by speaking the words with varied inflections and in different tones of voice. In fact, so skillful was the performance that several radio stations banned the harmless record from the air as "too suggestive."

The vocal variations on a theme of two words illustrate a simple but important point about communication: That one word or sentence may serve many purposes and have many meanings, depending on its context and on how it is said. The sensitive conversant, the diplomat, the therapist are well aware of the many purposes of communication that any word or phrase may serve, functions our language serves for us each day. In this chapter we will very briefly look at eight of these functions of communication.

PHATIC COMMUNION

Small talk, uninspired greetings, and idle chatter are among the descriptions of a fundamental type of communication that Bronislaw Malinowski called *phatic communion*. To show that we welcome communication, that we are friendly, or that we at least acknowledge the presence of another person, we exchange words. In English we do not have special words for this function of communication, though phatic communion tends to be rather unimaginative. We say, "How are you?" or "Hello," or "Nice day." There may be variations based on geography ("Howdy!") or familiarity ("Hi ya, Baby!") or specific conditions ("Cold enough for ya?"). Whatever the words, the speaker is saying, in effect, "I see you and I am friendly." The channels of communication are opened.

In phatic communion, the specific words exchanged are not important. This is illustrated in the story of a U.S. businessman who, while traveling to Europe for the first time, finds himsef seated across from a Frenchman at lunch. Neither speaks the other's language, but each smiles a greeting. As the wine is served, the Frenchman raises his glass and gesturing to the American says, "*Bon appétit!*" The American does not understand and replies, "Ginzberg." No other words are exchanged at lunch, That evening at dinner, the two again sit at the same table and again the Frenchman greets the American with the wine, saying, "*Bon appétit!*" to which the American replies, "Ginzberg." The waiter notices this peculiar exchange and, after dinner, calls the American aside to explain that "the Frenchman is not giving his name—he is wishing you a good appetite; he is saying that he hopes you enjoy your meal." The following day the American seeks out the Frenchman at lunch, wishing to correct his error. At the first opportunity the American raises his glass and says, *"Bon appétit!"* To which the Frenchman proudly replies, "Ginzberg."

Although in this story the ignorance of a common language made more significant communication impossible, it was the exchange of simple words like *bon appétit* (and Ginzberg) that broke the tension of silence and expressed friendship. Without the small talk first there can be no "big talk" later.

The only rule that seems to apply to phatic communion is that the "subject" of the communication be such that each party can say something about it. That is why everybody talks about the weather. The important thing is to talk—and this is why so much of phatic communion begins with a question, for a question requires a reply.

We do not request specific information in phatic communion and we are not expected to reply with precision or accuracy. If we are greeted with a "How are you?" we do not reply as we might if our doctor asked the question. When we are precise the result is likely to be humorous, as when James Thurber was once asked, "How's your wife?" and replied, "Compared to *what?*"

Specific information is sought in one kind of greeting, however. Members of secret organizations sometimes speak in code when they meet to determine whether each knows the password, special handshake, or other symbol. If the answer to the secret question is not precise, then the other is not regarded as a brother Mason or sister Theta or whatever, and subsequent communication will be prevented. Such coded phatic communion dates from times when members of such organizations might be persecuted if discovered. Among some "secret organizations" today, the reverse seems to be true. The coded greeting is often expressed loudly, more for the benefit of the outsiders than for the "secret" members. Phatic communion is usually the most casual, even careless, form of communication. The stories of persons passing through receiving lines and saying something like "I just killed my mother-in-law," which is met with a smile and a "Fine, I hope you're enjoying yourself" are well known. They illustrate what little significance is attached to phatic communion, so little that the speaker is not even listened to. In such extreme cases, however, we may wonder to what extent the channels of communication have been opened after that exchange of noises. In any case, it seems that we prefer some noise to no noise.

PREVENTION OF COMMUNICATION

A second function of communication is the opposite of the first.
Just as we rarely open a conversation with "I see you and I am
friendly," when this may be the real "message" of our greeting,
we rarely prevent further communication by saying directly, "I
don't want to talk to you anymore." This is said sometimes, to
be sure. But there are more sophisticated ways that we have
mastered.

There are the dismissal reactions "Ha!" "That's crazy!"
"Yeah, I'll bet!" and so forth. Whether the speaker intends these
to stop communication or whether they merely function in this
way is often difficult to determine. In either case it takes but a
few chosen reactions to end a conversation—and a few more to
end a friendship.

Then there are the guarded utterances or verbal grunts that
seem to show a lack of interest in speaker or subject: "Oh,
really?" "I see—," "Indeed," or "Hmm."

These brief snips of uninterested responses will end a
conversation, and often large hunks of verbiage will achieve the
same end. Either the language seems to say nothing or it is so
difficult to decipher that it does not seem worth the effort. A
favorite technique of naughty children, students taking
examinations, and some U.S. Senators is to talk on and on about
anything irrelevant to the subject at hand.

RECORD-TRANSMITTING FUNCTIONS

One definition of teaching goes something like this: "Teaching
is the transmission of the professor's notes into the students'
notebooks without their having passed through the minds of either."
A few years ago it was reported that a professor at a large mid-
western college put his lectures on tape and had the tape recorder
sent into his classroom and played every day. Weeks later, when
he stopped into the room to see if all was going well, he found,
on each student's desk, another machine recording the lectures.
Allowing for the hyperboles here, these stories illustrate a basic
function of communication, where the individual performs like a
precise and self-contained transmitting and recording machine.

In one sense, all communication is a process of transmitting
some information that is received by another. This is one
definition of communication. But as we note the variety of ways
in which we can describe the kind and purpose of a message sent,
the category of transmitting-recording seems insufficient. The

category is useful only for the most neutral exchanges of
information, messages without intent to be instrumental, compliment
the listener, let off steam, and so on. Thus, asking when the next
bus leaves and being told; asking what time it is, and being told;
reporting or hearing the news, weather, classroom lectures, and
so on, all might be examples of this function of communication.

INSTRUMENTAL COMMUNICATION

When we say something and something happens as the result of
our speaking, then our comments have been instrumental in
causing that event to happen. The instrumental function of
communication is one of its most common purposes. We request
a secretary to type three copies of a letter. We ask a friend at
dinner to pass the butter. We order a salesman out of the house.

The category of instrumental communication is loose enough to
allow for several kinds of statements. There are statements that are
clearly instrumental in their wording, for which the result correlates
with the language. If we say "Shut the door" and the door is
then shut, we may assume that the noise we made was influential
in the shutting of the door. There are also statements for which
the results cannot be so easily attributed to our utterances. If on
a day planned for a picnic it is raining and so we sing, "Rain,
rain go away"—and the rain does stop—it would be immodest
to assume that our words caused that action. Much of prayer
has been traditionally instrumental, and if the faithful believe
that some prayers "have been answered," we could say that for
these people the prayer was an instrumental communication. We
will touch on this subject again when we discuss ritual and the
magic function of communication.

Some statements are instrumental in intent or effect, but are
not phrased as such. For example, if you want the salt passed to
you, you may request it directly (instrumental) or you might
comment that the food needs salt (transmitting information). If
a wife wants a new fur coat, she may request it directly or she
may comment on how well dressed her husband seems, especially
when compared to her (apparently an effective technique). One
instrumental request may result in a different instrumental action,
as when commercial airlines do not ask passengers to stop
smoking but to "observe the no smoking sign."

One characteristic of some instrumental statements is a faint
resemblance between manner of speaking and the requested
action itself. One sometimes speaks as if his words *were*
instruments, as a belaying pin or rawhide whip are instruments.

The voice (see metacommunication) does its best to imitate the desired action, as do voices instrumentally cheering at a football game, "Push 'em back, push 'em back, w-a-a-a-a-y back!"

AFFECTIVE COMMUNICATION

Communication in which the message is the emotional feelings of the speaker toward a listener is known as *affective communication*. Compliments, praise and flattery, and also snide and cutting remarks may be so classified.

There are affective elements in many of the functions of communication. Phatic communion may contain praise, as when old friends greet by saying, "You're looking great!" As noted in the previous section, instrumental purposes are often best served through affective communication, too.

It seems to be part of the woman's role in our society to use more affective communication than does the opposite sex. Where tradition has not given women authority in all situations, women have had to achieve their goals indirectly. And this indirection may be reflected in instrumental desires disguised in affective language. The wife who says to her husband, "You look so handsome all dressed up," might be requesting a new wardrobe for herself or be asking to go out to dinner, rather than just complimenting her husband.

The nonaffective language of fact and description or the language of clear and explicit requests need not be any more desirable than it is common in interpersonal communications. We admire and respect the clarity of the scientist in writing his report, but we may find him less explicit during his courtship. Perhaps the reason is that whereas the scientist communicates to himself and to others pursuing one goal, the diplomats or the lovers may not be sure they are pursuing the same goal.

A study of the social gestures of dating, which I once made in an attempt to discover what was "meant" when a man held the door for his date or failed to open the door, and so on, certainly indicated this. Each sex had its own mythology for the purpose of the gesture. To the woman, the man performed the task out of respect for Woman. To the man, he performed the task because he "had to" if he was going to get anywhere. Again, the man's purpose even in the nonverbal language was far more instrumental than the woman's. If the words and actions were more specific, it would not be possible for the sexes to maintain their mutual self-delusion.

Affective language is also *convincing* language. In many cases a person would not do something if asked to do it directly; he would be too aware of reasons that he might not be able to accept. We seem to prefer to do things we think we want to do, not things we are told to do. There is a story of an experiment performed by a university class on its professor. The class set out as a group to apply simple learning theory (reward-punishment) on the professor in order to force him to do something he would not ordinarily do and certainly not do if requested. The emotional rewards and "punishments," though nonverbal in this case, are comparable to the use of affective language for instrumental purposes. The class decided it would try to move the professor into a corner from which he would deliver his lectures. The reinforcement was of the kind professors like best, interested expressions on student faces, passionate note taking at his every word, smiles at his whimsy and laughter at his wit. These responses, when appropriate, were made whenever the professor moved in the direction of the desired corner. When he moved in the other direction the class responded with looks of boredom, gazing out the windows, shuffling of feet, and the other academic behaviors one has rehearsed since childhood. As the story goes, by the end of the semester the professor was, indeed, giving his lectures from the corner of the room.

Although this story may be apocryphal, affective communication in a variety of situations does "move" the listener in a way that direct requests would not. The salesman knows it ("I'll make a special deal just for you"), the professor knows it ("I'm sure that your studies of Artaud and Beckett have led you to ask . . ."), the lover knows it. Most persons recognize the influence of words on the ego. (I'm sure that *you*, dear reader, are very sensitive to the communication process. . . .) To make another person feel good (or bad) through language is a rather common and vital function of communication.

It is possible to characterize attitudes of speakers toward their listeners on the basis of instrumental-affective content. One unpublished study[1] of Mexican attitudes toward male and female members of the Holy Family discovered that the language used toward male statues in a church was almost entirely instrumental in content, whereas the language used before the statue of the Virgin was highly affective. This distinction mirrored the differences in language used by children toward their parents in the average Mexican home. It is possible that degrees of anger, hostility, authority, and so on, can be measured by the comparative content of instrumental and affective language in our everyday expressions.

Many criticisms of the U.S. visitors or resident abroad have their basis in a lack of affective communication and a preponderance of instrumental commnunication. As a pragmatic people, we may have a cultural tendency to "get down to business," to be impersonal. Former Secretary of State John Foster Dulles is often quoted in Latin America as having said with some pride that "the U.S. does not have friends; it has interests." If others are treated as "interests" when they are more accustomed to being treated as "brothers" or at least "cousins," surely they will resent the change. The nonaffective communication may be honest, fair, sincere. But to one who does not expect it, the communication is cold, unfeeling, mechanical.

"Better understanding through communication" is a popular slogan. Too often what is meant is an improvement in semantics, an increase in the clarity of what we *mean*. We must not forget the affective aspects of communication, and must strive for an increase in the interpersonal attraction that we *feel*.

CATHARSIS

When you are angry or disturbed or hurt, physically or mentally, probably you give expression to your feelings. It is curious that expressions, which could be as personal as the feelings that evoke them, are rather stylized and predictable within a language. Words like *ouch!* or *oh!* are spoken by a people who speak English, whereas our neighbors who speak Spanish will say *ay!* when they express a comparable feeling. Grunts may be the only universal expression of catharsis.

When pain or frustration is sufficient, our cathartic expression becomes more obviously symbolic. We move from the "ouch!" to words that might be used in other ways, most often words that are socially disapproved of. We swear or curse or substitute words that sound something like the popular curses we long ago learned were "adult" and special. We find that different kinds of expressions for releasing tension are appropriate among different ages and occupations. A sailor who is angry is not expected to say "Oh, goodness me!" and an angry nun is not expected to sound like a sailor.

The physical stimulus finds expression in a symbol. This symbol eventually ceases to stand for, directly, anything in the outside world except an attitude toward whatever produced it. We move from physical sensation to verbal assault on that sensation ("Damn it!") to mere release of tension.

The idea of cursing a situation dates to times when the belief

in magic language was more common. There was a time when
"God damn you" was meant as a magic curse to bring about
suffering. The transference into such symbols was a step above the
infantile reaction of actually attacking the offending person or
object. Children may be observed to run into a wall and then
physically retaliate against the wall, kicking it and saying "you
mean old wall." But when the child's father runs into the wall and
says "damn it!" (or, if the child is there, "darn it!") he probably is
not talking to the wall. He is simply relieving his tension in symbols
that have long evolved from their literal meaning.

Because expressions of catharsis have no referential meaning,
any word may serve the cathartic function. Probably each person
has some favorite expressions for releasing anger. If you were to
prepare a list of cathartic expressions, ranking them according to
the degree of tension to be released, you might find it an easy task,
too, which indicates that there are personal favorites for a hierarchy
of catharsis. The meaning of any of these expressions is to be found
in what they do for us, not in a dictionary or in what they do for
anybody else. Through repetition we give our select swear words
added significance, so that with each new experience and repeated
expression we may recall the release of tension from past
experiences.

If you have studied another language, you may have learned
the kinds of swear words that are most common in that language. In
the literal translation they may not seem to "do much for you."
Obviously, they cannot, for they have not yet come to be associated
with the experiences that give them meaning. This same observation
might be made for all words, but the language of catharsis,
associated with the strongest of emotions, is the most extreme
example of the general principle.

MAGIC[2]

The belief in the magic power of words exists in all cultures and
takes the form of superstitions, instrumental curses, aspects of most
religions, and minor forms of wishful thinking. At the root of the
attitude of magic is the assumption that words are part of the thing
to which they refer and, often, that words precede the "thing"
(such as expressed in the Bible, "In the beginning was the Word").
Another quality of the magic attitude of words is that words "stand
for things" in the sense that a friend "stands for" a bride or groom
in a marriage by proxy. With this belief it follows that one can alter
a thing by altering its word. If I write your name on a piece of

paper and burn it, you, too, will burn, or at least suffer. Words, in the magical interpretation, must be treated with the same care as one would treat what the words stand for.

A common example of the belief in word-magic is the hesitancy to speak of possible dangers. If, on an airplane, you remark about the possibility of crashing, fellow passengers may turn on you as if your utterance of the possibility might just cause that to happen. In some cases, of course, it may be simply that others do not wish to think of unpleasant things; but the manner and intensity of the reply often indicates a very real fear of the words. If the belief in a magic function of communication seems immature (that is, not at all what *you* would think or do), ask yourself whether in a plane you ever avoided such "thoughts" or whether you ever thought "we will not crash, we will not crash." For better or for worse, the belief that thinking or saying words will have some effect on what the words stand for is an example of the magic function of communication.

In many religions the magic function of language is still present. One would expect this of any institution that is centuries old and seeks to conserve the language and ritual of the past. The distinction between transubstantiation and consubstantiation of the Roman Catholic and Protestant sects is, in part, the difference in attitude toward the magic function of language. Do the bread and wine become the body and blood of Christ, or do they merely symbolize the body and blood? There are other examples in religions. The Anglican and Roman Catholic Faiths retain rituals for the exorcising of spirits from a haunted house. One may wish to make a distinction between these examples and examples of words that call for the intercession of a divine spirit (such as prayers of petition) where the effect is produced not by the utterance of the words but by the action upon the words by another being. The difference is the difference between Ali Baba saying "Open Sesame!" (and having the cave door open because of the magic in the words) and having the words heard by a god who then opens the door. In the latter case we have an example of instrumental communication.[3]

Symbols associated with persons have long been recognized for their magical associations. Personal names have been regarded as "part of the person," so that what is done to the name results in affecting the person. (Elements of this attitude are still very common today, as when parents give their child the name of somebody important to them so that the child will be like his namesake.) The magical attitude toward personal names requires that these names not be taken in vain or, in some cases, not even uttered.

> Here the name is never a mere symbol, but is part of the personal property of its bearer; property which is exclusively and jealously reserved to him. . . . Georg von der Gabelentz, in his book on the science of language, mentions the edict of a Chinese emperor of the third century B.C. whereby a pronoun in the first person, that had been legitimately in popular use, was henceforth reserved to him alone. . . . It is said of the Eskimos that for them man consists of three elements—body, soul, and name. And in Egypt, too, we find a similar conception, for there the physical body of man was thought to be accompanied, on the one hand by his Ka, or double, and on the other, by his name, as a sort of spiritual double. . . . Under Roman law a slave had no legal name, because he could not function as a legal person.[4]

Cassirer points out, too, that this attitude toward personal names was held by the early Christians, and hence today Christians still say "In Jesus' name" instead of "In Christ."

The belief in the magic function of language is based on assumptions that are quite opposed to the discipline of semantics, which regards words as conventional and convenient and without necessary associations with persons or objects in themselves. There is a sense, however, in which words do have "power." Words have the "power" to limit our thought, for example, though this is a different sense of the word "power." With rumor, with labels that evoke signal reactions, and with labels we try to live up to, we see some effects of the "power" of words. Such powers, however, are not magical, for they are not to be found *in* the words. Rather, the powers are social, and thus they are effective only to the degree that we accept our language without evaluation and respond to words without evaluation. When we understand and evaluate our language habits this social magic spell of words is broken.

RITUAL

The scene is a Senate Subcommittee hearing room on October 1, 1963. A 60-year-old convicted murderer, Joseph M. Valachi, calmly reports to the investigators some of the history and methods of the crime organization known as Cosa Nostra. According to the press reports, the witness appeared comfortable throughout his testimony until he described his induction into the organization. Emanuel Perlmutter[5] of the *New York Times* reports:

Valachi said he had been taken into a large room, where 30 or 35 men were sitting at a long table.

"There was a gun and a knife on the table," Valachi testified. "I sat at the edge. They sat me down next to Maranzaro. I repeated some words in Sicilian after him." . . .

"You live by the gun and knife, and die by the gun and knife." . . .

The witness said Maranzaro had then given him a piece of paper that was set afire in his hand.

"I repeated in Sicilian, 'This is the way I burn if I betray the organization.' " . . .

Valachi said the men at the table then "threw out a number," with each man holding up any number of fingers from one to five. The total was taken. Starting with Maranzaro, the sum was then counted off around the table. The man on whom the final number fell was designated as Valachi's "godfather" in the family. Valachi said the lot had fallen to Bonanno.

The witness said that he had then had his finger pricked by a needle held by Bonanno to show he was united to Bonanno by blood. Afterward, Valachi continued, all those present joined hands in a bond to the organization.

Valachi said he was given two rules in Cosa Nostra that night— one concerning allegiance to it and another a promise not to possess another member's wife, sister or daughter.

For the first time, the witness grew grim. "This is the worst thing I can do, to tell about the ceremony," he said. "This is my doom, telling it to you and press."

If the ceremony Valachi described seems strange to us, stranger still is the fear of his "doom" caused by revealing that secret. For a tough-minded criminal who reported that for him "killing was like breathing," who gave evidence about the methods and men of the Cosa Nostra, why should the most fearful disclosure be his report of some remote and grisly rite performed years ago? The answer to that question is part of the answer to why some rituals affect almost all of us.

Few organizations or institutions have rituals quite like the Cosa Nostra. The language of the rituals of secret organizations, social fraternities, lodges, and some religious or political organizations is kept secret, known only to their members. But the language of other rituals—patriotic, religious, academic, and so on—is not kept private. Nevertheless, an oath of allegiance or a communal prayer can affect the nervous system as no statement of fact or judgment can.

Ritual is sometimes described as the behavioral part of a mythology. The mythology may be for almost any purpose, but consistently it emphasizes a sense of community among its members and a sense of permanence. To participate in a ritual is to participate in a community, often one that claims a tradition of centuries. The sense of timelessness is quite important. When the anthropologist asks the primitive why he performs a certain ritual, the answer might be, "because our ancestors have always done this." If in the modern-day United States our sense of tradition is a short one, we may find the same comfort in rituals realizing that we as individuals have always said the pledge or sung the hymn.

There appears to be little that is instrumental in the performance of a ritual, with some notable exceptions. Sociologist Robert Merton has noted that activities originally conceived as instrumental often become transmuted into ends in themselves. What was originally obtained through certain words or acts is no longer needed or desired. If at one time meat had to be prepared in a certain way to avoid contamination, meat may still be prepared in such a way because "that's the way our ancestors have always done it." If certain prayers were recited with the hope of rewards, the same prayers may be repeated even though a congregation no longer expects those rewards. In many, perhaps most, cases, a new mythology will develop to explain certain words and actions of a ritual. It is not clear whether rituals continue to exist by virtue of constant repetition or whether the participants in a ritual feel that some ends are being served.

Three characteristics of most rituals are most important: The rituals must be performed with others (immediately or symbolically present); they must be performed on some occasion; and they must be performed with special care to details.

This last characteristic makes ritual somewhat different from other forms of communication. Many children have difficulty with the high-level abstractions and archaic language often present in ritual. The usual vocabulary of children contains few high-level abstractions. But a child will learn to imitate or approximate the sounds of the rituals in which he finds himself participating. Frequently these words become translated in his own vocabuluary without conflict. My niece and nephew, when very young, sang their favorite Christmas carol in church. The boy concluded "Silent Night" with the words "Sleep in heavenly beans." "No," his sister corrected, "not beans, peas."

Most of us have association with aspects of some rituals from our earliest memories. Perhaps you have had the sudden awareness of what some words you have been saying all your life were really supposed to be. It can be both a startling and amusing realization. But it is one that characterizes a form of communication in which repetition of certain words over an expanse of time is most important.

For some persons, part of the appeal of ritual may be the pleasure of solemnly repeating words that seem to have no referent; this may evoke a mood of mystery for such persons. Other persons may find a deep satisfaction in discovering the meaning of what they have been saying for years. Such attitudes, if they exist, would seem to be unhealthy, not only as regards an understanding of the purpose of language but also for the significance of the ritual itself.

There are other characteristics of ritual that make it distinct from other functions of language in communication. One of these is the sublimation function of ritual. Through ritual, a person may symbolically take part in an event that would exclude his actual participation. During wartime, rituals tend to become more common and more significant. The displaying of the flag, the reciting of the pledge of allegiance, even the rationing of food and gasoline are ways of symbolically participating in the war effort. Or, to take a happier example, during a football game the fans who wish to help their team may better do so by cheering than by assisting on the field. It is common, for example, that at the kick-off the fans will go "sssssssspoooom!" as if their noise will help to carry the ball farther down field.

Some rituals last longer than their mythologies. At a time when some persons begin to question religious beliefs, they may find it relatively easier to "lose the faith" than to lose the habit of prayer or church attendance on certain holy days. A sense of compulsiveness frequently attends ritual, and a sense of guilt may enter when ritual has gone. As a nation becomes what is called a "nontraditional society" the rituals that are a part of the tradition die. This finds expression as "alienation," the subject of many books, dramas, and films of recent years. It may also explain, in part, the current attraction for many philosophies of the "absurd." If a society's stability has been largely dependent on ritual and the rituals fall, it is an easy out to label the world as "absurd."

A final point should be made and emphasized. That is that what was intended for some purpose other than ritual can take on a ritual function. This may be a healthy addition to some other instrumental purpose, or it may be unhealthy if it substitutes for that other purpose. An example of the former might be the lasting effect of the Negro Civil Rights March on Washingtgon of 1963. No legislation was passed as a direct result of the march, but there was produced an important sense of community among white and black that had not been exhibited so dramatically before.

Conventions of many kinds, political, social, and academic, many times serve more of a ritual function than the function of exchanging information or achieving some instrumental goal. To see the participants cheer or clap as the speaker speaks the holy jargon and drops the right names at the right time is amusing and a little sad at the same time. What is called a report may better serve as an incantation. No group can maintain itself without strong cohesiveness, it is true. But if the main result of the group's effort is only cohesiveness then surely we have the origins of a new ritual.

METACOMMUNICATION

In communication there are always more than words that pass between persons. There are also cues that indicate to the persons how the spoken words are to be interpreted. These communications about communications are called *metacommunication cues.* These may be vocal inflections (as in the spoken John-Marsha dialogue) or nonverbal indicators, such as gestures and expressions (pounding the table or frowning). Even clothing and the distance between speakers may provide clues for interpreting the message correctly and thus may also be classified as metacommunication.

These cues may reinforce the meaning of the words, may sometimes distract from the words spoken, or may even contradict what the words seem to mean. When the cues are different from the words, a listener has difficulty in accepting the spoken message. Sometimes, for example, the words sound like phatic communion, but the way in which they are spoken sounds more like the straight transmission of information with, perhaps, a vague hint of some ulterior instrumental purpose. If you have ever answered the telephone and found yourself in what sounded like a friendly conversation until you began to realize you were being solicited for magazine subscriptions, you know the feeling. A friend once found himself in such a conversation. The words were familiar but the metacommunication was mechanical. When he asked the anonymous voice, "Are you *reading* that?" the woman became so startled, she hung up.

Not only may a message be interpreted differently because of metacommunication cues, some messages may be greatly altered or even not spoken because the speaker has received such cues from the listener. A friend who is a priest in Brazil says that one definition of the priest there might be "the person you lie to." When the Roman collar and clerical garb is seen the communication changes completely. For some persons in the United States, unfortunately, a person's skin color serves as a cue to others. John Howard Griffin's *Black Like Me* is an excellent account of the change in communication that was forced on the white author when he traveled in the South disguised as a Negro.

One other function served by metacommunication is that of feedback. Feedback, a term borrowed from the field of cybernetics, refers to signals sent from the listener to the speaker in order to tell the speaker how he is being understood. Upon receiving such signals, which are usually nonverbal, the speaker alters his message accordingly. If a listener wrinkles his brow, the speaker explains more carefully; if a listener nods knowingly, the speaker may speed up or skip over parts of his message, assuming that the listener understands clearly. As with all metacommunication cues, those associated with feedback may conflict or be confusing. One smiles as if he is friendly to the message, while at the same time he taps his foot impatiently.

ON SAYING WHAT YOU MEAN, AND MEANING WHAT YOU SAY

Semanticists are sometimes thought to desire complete honesty of expression, directness, and "no beating around the bush." An understanding of the many purposes of communication should dispel that view. We use language for too many purposes and find ourselves forced to make some comment in too many difficult situations to hold to such a goal. Simple friendship, not to mention diplomacy and tact, prohibits us from always saying what we are thinking.

Suppose, for example, some friends are in a drama. You attend the opening-night performance, which is, as accurately as you can judge it, a real turkey. Then, as you leave the theater you encounter your friends and the director. Do you say what you are thinking and maybe hurt a friendship? Do you betray your critical integrity? No. Assuming that you cannot avoid comment, you equivocate, you speak in ambiguities. The popular expressions for this moment of untruth are many: (to the director): "Well, you've done it again!"; (to the actors): "You should have been in the audience!"; (to the elderly bystander who may be the dean, the director's father, or the playwright): "It was an unforgettable evening!"

If you feel that the potential ridicule of these expressions is too strong, you may equivocate further with the always safe "Congratulations!"

One may protest that these comments, however deft, are still lies¬and should not be excused. I think, however, that to so regard them is to confuse standards of different functions of communication. Affective communication directed to the emotional responses of the listener does not require the accuracy, even of judgments, that the transmission of specific information does. The purpose is often friendship, not a critical evaluation. Often it is much more important to tell a person that you like his tie, coat, smile, voice, and so on, than to be bound by some standards of judgment which would severely limit your affective communications. A kind or friendly remark often does more for human understanding than a diplomatic silence or a hundred "honest" judgments.

To be aware of the many functions of communication is to be alive and sensitive to the most basic of human needs. As our needs for bodily health and comfort are met, we become more aware of (and create new) needs for symbolic health and comfort. To be loved or respected, to help others, to feel trust—the list could be elaborated greatly—becomes extremely important. Each communication situation both reveals our frailty and offers some promise for support.

Notes

1. Nelson, Cynthia, "Saints and Sinners: Parallels in the Sex-Role Differentiation in the Family of Saints and in the Family of Man in a Mexican Peasant Village," mimeographed, n.d.
2. Susanne Langer includes the magic function of language as part of "ritual." She writes, "Magic . . . is not a method, but a language; it is part and parcel of that greater phenomenon, ritual, which is the language of religion." (*Philosophy in a New Key* [Cambridge, Mass.: Harvard University Press, 1942], p. 39.) Although this may have a historical basis, and although magic and ritual are also clearly related today, I find it useful to make a distinction between the two.
3. Some students are unimpressed by the distinction.
4. Cassirer, Ernst, *Language and Myth* (New York: Dover, n.d.), pp. 50–51.
5. Perlmutter, Emanuel, "Valachi Names 5 as Crime Chiefs in New York Area," *New York Times*, 2 October, 1963, p. 28.

RECOMMENDED READING

Barnlund, Dean C., and Haiman, Franklyn S., *The Dynamics of Discussion* (Boston: Houghton Mifflin, 1960).

Berlo, David K., *The Process of Communication: An Introduction to the Theory and Practice* (New York: Holt, Rinehart and Winston, 1960).

Cassirer, Ernst, "Word Magic," in *Language and Myth* (New York: Dover, n.d.), pp. 44–62.

Goffman, Erving, *The Presentation of Self in Everyday Life* (Garden City, N.Y.: Doubleday Anchor, 1959).

Hayakawa, S. I., *Language in Thought and Action*, 2nd ed. (New York: Harcourt Brace Jovanovich, 1964) chapters six through nine, especially.

Hayakawa, S. I. (ed.), *The Use and Misuse of Language* (Greenwich, Conn.: Fawcett Premier Books, 1962).

Johnson, Wendell, *Your Most Enchanted Listener* (New York: Harper & Row, 1956).

Malinowski, Bronislaw, "The Problem of Meaning in Primitive Languages," supplement I in C. K. Ogden and I. A. Richards, *The Meaning of Meaning* (New York: Harcourt Brace Jovanovich, Harvest Books, 1923), pp. 296–336.

Ruesch, Jurgen, and Bateson, Gregory, *Communication: The Social Matrix of Psychiatry* (New York: Norton, 1951).

12

LANGUAGE WITHIN LANGUAGE

Albert Mehrabian

VERBAL IMMEDIACY

Beyond its use for categorizing posture and position cues, the
concept of immediacy broadly describes the extent to which any
communication behavior reflects or involves a closer interaction. For
the posture and position cues, greater immediacy is the result of
increasing physical proximity and/or perceptual availability of the
communicator to the addressee. Thus, a face-to-face conversation
is more immediate than one via video tape, which in turn is more
immediate than a conversation over the telephone. Less immediate
still is a communication, such as a letter, involving the written
medium only. The basic hypothesis relating immediacy to attitudes
predicts that less immediacy is selected by a communicator when he

Reprinted by permission of Aldine Publishing Company from *Nonverbal
Communication* by Albert Mehrabian, pp. 31–39, 1972.

has negative feelings toward his addressee, toward the contents of his communication, or toward the act of communicating those contents (Wiener and Mehrabian, 1968). An employer is using less immediate communication when he expresses discontent to an employee via an intermediary rather than in a face-to-face confrontation. In line with the hypothesis, the employer's choice illustrates his difficulty or discomfort in expressing what he has to say. The 'Dear John" letter also exemplifies the preference for a less immediate medium to convey contents that are distressing to express in person.

In this chapter we will deal primarily with verbal immediacy, or those variations which occur within speech itself. The variations to be discussed include linguistic components, such as pronouns, tense, or kinds of symbols (words) used to refer to an object. The linguistic components considered in these analyses include words that designate (1) the object(s) of the communication, (2) a relationship among these objects, (3) an implied or explicit relationship of the speaker to the objects or to their relationships, or (4) a relationship of the speaker to the entire message. The word *object* is used here to refer to persons, inanimate entities, or events, and specific characteristics or attributes of any of these instances.

The following example illustrates some of the components within a statement that are possible sources of immediacy variation. If a speaker is describing a party that he attended, several constructions of the event are possible. For instance, he could say, "I think they enjoyed themselves." By varying one pronoun, it can be specified as to who is enjoying the party: "I think I enjoyed myself," "I think we enjoyed ourselves," "I think you enjoyed yourself (yourselves)." In these variations the speaker either includes or excludes himself from the referent group. Another set of variations results from specifying the different objects of enjoyment: "I think they enjoyed themselves," "I think they enjoyed each other," or "I think they enjoyed the party." There are also variations which specify differences in the speaker's relationship to the objects in the statement, such as "I think I enjoyed their company," "I think they enjoyed my company," "I think we enjoyed each other's company," or "I think I enjoyed the party."

Another verbal component which is amenable to this form of analysis is verb tense. The temporal organization of a statement may vary, as in "I think they enjoy themselves," "I think they were enjoying themselves," "I think they have enjoyed themselves," or "I think they enjoyed themselves."

Variations denoting the speaker's relationship to his message can be seen in the different modifiers he uses. For example, he may ascribe ambiguity to the event ("They acted as if they enjoyed themselves"), or to himself and his particular interpretation of the event ("I think they enjoyed themselves"). On the other hand, he may indicate certainty about the event ("It is obvious that they enjoyed themselves") or within himself ("I am sure they enjoyed themselves"). Each of these examples is a contrast to the simple declarative statement, "They enjoyed themselves."

Instead of attributing all such verbal variations to style or chance, one can consider them a basis for analyzing a communicator's (1) particular experience of an event, (2) relationship to his addressee, or (3) relationship to his message. Wiener and Mehrabian (1968) related immediacy variations to communicator affect on the basis of several complementary considerations. Verbal communications seem to have evolved to denote an "objective" world. Consequently, experiences of affect, evaluation, or preference, which are concomitant with the experience of a complex stimulus, cannot be readily and verbally expressed. That is, in most cultures there are restraints imposed on the communication of affect, evaluation, or preference, particularly when these are negative. If a person experiences affect about an event and does not describe it, then there is an additional component accruing to his experience— the relative uncommunicability of that affect. The unverbalized affect can interfere with the communication process, resulting in ambiguous or idiosyncratic references to internal states. It can also lead to speech disruptions such as the slips, errors, or false starts analyzed by Mahl (1959), or to blocking and hesitation. For example, if someone cannot use the direct form, "Jack makes me anxious," sequencing may be evident in his statements as follows: "I see Jack. . . . I don't feel so good." In this instance both components are present in the communication, but they are not related.

When reflected in speech, the separation of internal-affect and external-object can have instrumental value for a speaker. If, like other behaviors, speech patterns are learned, then it follows that the forms learned for conveying relatively inexpressible affects are more acceptable, likely to be positively received, or less likely to evoke negative response or punishment from others. The separation of affect from the object with which it is associated can thus have value in communications about negative experiences. Separation of events (that is, discrimination of affect from objects, or objects from each other) in speech can take many forms, such as spatial or temporal separation, or separation through exclusion.

In sum, the various forms of separation, nonidentity, or nonimmediacy that occur in speech are expected to be most frequently associated with negative affect. The degree of nonimmediacy in statements about neutral, in contrast to positive, experiences will depend on the possibility for direct expression of positive affect. Such possibility is determined by the kind of addressee (peer of authority) or communication situation (formal or informal setting).

Some of the nonimmediacy forms indicate a nonidentity with, or dissimilarity from, the addressee. There is a considerable amount of evidence showing that more dissimilar persons like each other less, because they are less likely to positively reinforce one another (Byrne, 1969; Mehrabian and Ksionzky, 1971a). The inference of negative affect from verbal statements that show dissimilarity is therefore consistent with well-established findings.

There are still other conceptual bases for relating nonimmediacy in speech to positive, neutral, and negative feelings: the approach-avoidance framework is one example (Dollard and Miller, 1950; Lewin, 1935; Miller, 1964). Briefly, approach-avoidance behaviors are associated with positive-negative affect, evaluation, and preference. A speaker's separation of himself from the object of his message, from his addressee, or from the message itself is an instance of avoidance behavior which is motivated by negative affect toward the object, the addressee, or the message respectively. Several categories of speech nonimmediacy are informally described in the following sections.

Spatio-Temporal Indicators

One set of variations in speech literally describes the relationship between a speaker and the object of his communication in spatial or temporal terms. The use of the demonstratives *this, that, these, those, here,* and *there* denotes specific spatial relations. If the actual spatio-temporal situation (near and/or now, far away and/or long ago) is inconsistent with the demonstrative used to describe it, then the statement is readily interpreted. The use of a demonstrative that is incongruous for the actual event of "long ago and far away" is seen in a statement about the Renaissance which starts "This period of history. . . ." A demonstrative that is incongruous for the event "here and now" is noted in the comment, "I don't understand those people . . ." when the people are in the same room as the speaker. In instances where either set of demonstrative pronouns or adjectives can be used for a given condition, the particular selection is considered significant and interpretable. The following statements exemplify this point:
(1) Two people are waiting for a third person to arrive. When

they see her, one says, "Here's (there's) Jean"; (2) a person responding to another says, "I know this (the, that) person you are talking about"; (3) "These (those) people need help."

Another set of spatio-temporal variations is evident in certain forms of introductory phrases or terms that are not required by the events described (for example, over and above, on the other hand, elsewhere, in the beginning, before, at that time, such time). Specific examples are: "In the beginning, I was writing" in contrast to "I was writing"; or "I know of several problems over and above yours" in contrast to "I know of several problems also." The first instance in each example is considered less immediate because it includes a temporal or spatial separation.

Temporal referents in speech are another source of nonimmediacy. Temporal relationships are most often expressed through verb tense. If the context allows some variation in tense usage, the specific tense used is interpretable. For example, consider a person who is no longer a member of a particular political party. Asked about his membership, he may say "I have been a member," "I was a member," or "I had been a member." In this example, the successive instances exhibit increasing temporal nonimmediacy between the speaker and the event that is described. As with spatial variations, increasing temporal nonimmediacy is also interpreted as signifying lack of preference, or negative affect and evaluation. The inclusion of spatio-temporal variations in the analysis of nonimmediacy seems to require little further justification or rationale. These variations in our language are often used explicitly to designate the degree of separation of a person from the object of his communication.

Denotative Specificity

Another set of variations, denotative specificity, is a function of the amount of ambiguity in the symbol used to denote a specific referent—the communicated object. A symbol (word) may in the literal sense denote a single object (John Smith) or a class of objects (a person). As the number of possible additional referents (other than the specific object that is being referred to) increases, ambiguity increases and denotative specificity decreases. For instance, parents referring to their son's fiancée might say, "our daughter-to-be," "our son's fiancée," "his fiancée," "his lady friend," "his friend," "she," "the person," or "that thing." These examples show decreasing degrees of denotative specificity and are interpreted as expressing decreasing degrees of liking.

Variations in the personal pronouns used to denote a referent are also included under denotative specificity. For example, a person may say, "I smoke because I enjoy it." "We smoke because we enjoy it," "People smoke because they enjoy it," "One smokes because one enjoys it," or "You (meaning *I*) smoke because you enjoy it." In these examples, there is a progressive decrease in denotative specificity for the specific subject who smokes and who enjoys it (that is, *I*). Thus, denotative specificity varies with the different symbols that show the communicator's inclusion or exclusion from the group of people referred to in his statement.

Some additional examples may be helpful. A speaker describing an event in which he participated can say: "I danced," "We danced," "The gang danced," or "There was dancing," with decreasing degrees of inclusion and, therefore, decreasing denotative specificity in denoting *I*. Similarly, in a psychotherapeutic setting, a client who recalls an earlier interchange between himself and the therapist may say, "Remember we said," "Remember you said," or "Remember it was said." In these examples, the decreasing denotative specificity is interpreted as showing decreasing positive or more negative attitudes toward the communication, toward the therapy, or toward the therapist.

Apart from varying the degree of ambiguity of the symbol that is used to designate the referent, the use of an overspecific or overexclusive symbol which refers to only a part of the referent is also significant. Overexclusive references to the object are seen in the following instances: "I like the print of this book," where *book* is the object; or "John's manners irritate me," where *John* is the object.

Denotative specificity may also be lacking because of the use of negation. We frequently hear, "It wasn't bad" instead of "It was good." Other examples are: "I am not sad about going" in contrast to "I am happy about going"; "The chair is not red" versus "The chair is maroon." Such negation lacks specificity because negating and occurrence, object, or quality fails to unambiguously identify what is in fact present.

Selective Emphasis

Variations of selective emphasis are manifested in the order in which objects are introduced into a communication; the frequency, intensity, or extensity attributed to an event; and over- and underresponsiveness to specific contents within a complex stimulus. "My mother and father" versus "my father and mother" is an example of sequencing. The numerous ways of referring to a married couple exemplify both sequence and emphasis: "Let's go see the Smiths," "Let's go see Mary and John," "Let's go see John and Mary," "Let's go see John," or "Let's go see Mary." In these cases, the interpretation of sequencing is evident, but the selective emphasis requires some explanation. If a couple is referred to as "the Smiths," the unity or nonseparateness of the pair is emphasized. The latter form of reference results from a lack of differential experience with the members of the pair. If the same couple is identified as "John and Mary" or "Mary and John," then the separateness of the members of the pair is made more focal, and different attitudes toward the two are implied.

Sequencing and selective emphasis are also evident in the following description of a complex event with multiple attributes and components: "We had a busy day; we went shopping, to the movies, met people, and had lunch." If a speaker identifies the people who were present at a gathering, the order in which he gives the names can vary. Incidentally, such variations in speech are paralleled in other forms of behavior, as in the order in which people are served at a gathering.

A speaker's affect toward objects can be inferred from the sequential order in which he narrates them when alternative sequences are possible for a given condition. As in the other immediacy interpretations, it is hypothesized that objects experienced more positively, or less negatively, occur earlier in the sequence.

Selective emphasis is also evident in the particular attribute constellation implied by the term used to denote the referent. In referring to a specific psychotherapist, the speaker can say "the psychotherapist," "the therapist," "the doctor," "the ward physician," "the man," or "the headshrinker." In referring to a party he can say "I enjoyed the party," "I enjoyed the dancing," "I enjoyed the food," "I enjoyed the people," "I enjoyed the conversation," or "I enjoyed the place." A colleague can be referred to as "my collaborator," "my colleague," "my associate," "my coworker," "my assistant," "my helper," or "my student." In all of these instances the particular attribute that is emphasized signifies its differential significance for the speaker. When there is a shift from a consensual referent (*party*) to a component of it (*conversation*) the interpretation is as follows: the attributes that are de-emphasized through exclusion are less preferred or are disliked. Alternatively, the denoted attribute constellation is disliked least, or is liked and preferred most (Mehrabian, 1967). In general, though, inferences of negative affect for the excluded aspects of the referent are more likely to be valid.

Agent-Action-Object Relationships

In our discussion of agent-action-object relationships, the person who initiates the activity will be referred to as the agent and the receiver of the action as the object. For example, in the statement "John is looking at Mary," *John* is the agent and *Mary* is the object. There are at least three loci of possible variation in the agent-action-object reationships within a statement.

One set of variations in this relationship is indicated by the specific words used by the communicator for designating the agent(s) and object(s) for an "objective" event. A quarrel between two people can be reported as follows: "They were fighting," "She was fighting with him," or "He was fighting with her."

A second set of variations occurs when responsibility for an activity is attributed to sources other than the ostensible agent(s), when it is possible to attribute responsibility to the latter. "I should go," "I have to go," "I must go," "I am compelled (or driven) to go" in contrast to "I want to go," "I would like to go," or "I will go" illustrate these variations. The attribution of the action to some part or characteristic of the agent in the "objective" situation is also considered part of this set of variations. "It is my desire to go," "Something in me makes me want to go," "My legs automatically carry me there" in contrast to "I want to go" or "I will go."

A third set of variations arises from the use of the passive rather than the active voice. Note, for example, the difference between "I drove the car" and "The car was driven by me," or between "I went to school with my mother" and "I was taken to school by my mother."

All variations in agent-action-object relationships are interpreted as showing different degrees of positive-negative affect toward the activity involved, the persons in the act, or the addressee. For example, if the speaker says, "I had to go" instead of "I went," affect is inferred about "'going," or about having to report "the going" to the specific addressee. When an external agent is introduced, it indicates a greater separation of the communicator from the agent, object, or activity in his statement because the source of involvement is other than the consensual agent (*I*). Consider another example. The speaker describes someone dancing with his girl friend as follows: "He was dancing with her" or "She was dancing with him" instead of "They were dancing." The less interactive agent-object relationships in the first two statements, as compared to "They were dancing," indicate the speaker's negative experience of the activity, of the agent and object in the activity, or of his reporting the event. The emphasis on separation, when separateness is not a quality of the event, is what allows the inference of negative communicator affect.

There is less immediacy when the number of responsible agents indicated in a statement is less than what the context implies. For example, a communication describing a mutual activity can be organized to convey only a unilateral relationship. Such variations are possible whether or not the speaker is one of the agents in the event. Thus, "They (we) are dancing" can be expressed as "She dances with him (me)." With such a unilateral relationship, different degrees of participation of the agents are implied. The following sentences are listed in the order of the implied decreasing mutual interaction: "We (they) danced," "She and I (he) danced," "I (he) danced with her," or "The dancing I (he) did was with her." Whereas in the *we* or *they* example the mutuality is explicit, in the *she and I* or *she and he* example the implied mutuality is somewhat decreased through the separation of the two agents. In "I danced with her," the mutuality is only implicit and the communicator (*I*) is the ostensible agent. Finally, in "The dancing I (he) did was with her," the mutuality is not only implicit, but there is also a further separation of the activity "dancing" from the agent—the major focus is on the dancing, and the other person's participation is almost incidental. This decrease in reported mutuality can be a function of the speaker's negative affect about dancing, a quality of his dancing, or her dancing. If the speaker is not one of the agents, the corresponding change may be a function of the the speaker's negative affect about *his dancing, their dancing together,* or *them.*

Modifiers

Qualifications of a communication include expressions of the speaker's doubt about his opinion, as in "I think (believe, feel) that you are correct," or of his uncertainty about the event, as in "It could be (it seems to be, it might be) that you are correct." With the use of such qualifications, a speaker implies that others, especially the listener, experience the same event differently.

Objectifications of a communication take the form of introductory phrases such as "It is obvious," "It is evident," or "It is simply true," all of which imply certainty on the part of the speaker. He emphasizes a consensus for his experience by asserting the reality of the event, thereby separating himself from the object of the communication.

In sum, qualification introduces a separation of the speaker from others, including the addressee. In objectification, there is a separation of the speaker from the objects in his message. Both forms decrease immediacy and indicate the speaker's less positive attitude toward the event described, or his reluctance to relay this information to that particular addressee. Either may be a function of the specific communicator-addressee relationship; that is, it may occur with one addressee but not with another. Furthermore, uncertainty as expressed in qualification and certainty as expressed in objectification may also signify different personality characteristics of speakers.

Incidentally, the specific localization of uncertainty within a speaker as to feeling (*I feel*), belief (*It is my opinion*), or thought (*I think*) offers intriguing speculative possibiliites for trying to change the commitment of a speaker to his message. Thus, if the content of a message is qualified with "I feel," the most successful approach to a change of attitude may require emotionally oriented arguments and emphases, in contrast to a statement qualified with "I think," where a rational or logical approach might be most effective.

Automatic Phrasing

Automatic phrasing occurs with the use of words such as *just* or *simply*, phrases such as *you know*, nonsemantic sounds as *uh*, and pauses that are linguistically unnecessary.

The occurrence of words like *just* or *simply* signifies an attempt by the speaker to minimize his association with, or his responsibility for, the communication or the actions described. Some examples are, "I just borrowed it for a moment or two," "It's only a minor damage," "It's really unimportant," or "It's simply unnecessary." These forms are interpreted as showing negative attitudes toward the objects in the message or the reporting of the events to the addressee.

When a speaker uses phrases and words such as *you know, you understand, right?* or *all right?* he implicitly requests verification from the listener that the latter understands what is said. We assume that, in an immediate communication, the speaker takes for granted the listener's understanding. Thus, phrases like *you know* or *I mean* show that the speaker regards himself as separate or different (nonimmediate) from the listener, and therefore imply negative affect.

Other automatic phrases, sounds, pauses such as *well, uh, that is,* and slips or false starts (Freud, 1938) can reflect inconsistent experiences, ambivalence toward the event being described, or ambivalence toward the description of the event to the particular addressee. For example, in "How did you like the party?" "Well (ah, or uh) (pause) it was fine," uncertainty or ambivalence is conveyed by the use of automatic phrases (*well*) and by the pause. Temporal delay in these instances is considered a prime index of separation or nonimmediacy between a speaker and his message. Whereas Mahl (1959) interpreted speech disruptions as anxiety indicators, aborted starts in speech in our context are yet another case of nonimmediacy and are interpreted wihin a more general framework.

References

Byrne, D., "Attitudes and Attraction, in L. Berkowitz (ed.), *Advances in Experimental Social Psychology*, vol. 4 (New York: Academic Press, 1969), pp. 35–89.

Dollard, J., and Miller, N. E., *Personality and Psychotherapy* (New York: McGraw-Hill, 1950).

Freud, Sigmund, "The Psychopathology of Everyday Life" (1904) in *The Basic Writings of Sigmund Freud* (New York: Random House, 1938).

Lewin, K., *A Dynamic Theory of Personality: Selected Papers.* (New York: McGraw-Hill, 1935).

Mahl, G. F., "Measuring the Patient's Anxiety during Interviews from 'expressive' Aspects of His Speech," *Transactions of the New York Academy of Sciences* 21, (1959):249–257.

Mehrabian, A., "Substitute for Apology: Manipulation of Cognitions to Reduce Negative Attitude toward Self," *Psychological Reports* 20, (1967):687–92.

Mehrabian, A., and Ksionzky, S., "Models for Affiliative and Conformity Behavior," *Psychological Bulletin* 74, (1970): 110–26.

Miller, N. E., "Some Implications of Modern Behavior Therapy for Personality Change and Psychotherapy," in P. Worchel and D. Byrne (eds.), *Personality Change* (New York: Wiley, 1964), pp. 149–175.

Wiener, M., and Mehrabian, A., *Language within Language: Immediacy, a Channel in Verbal Communication* (New York: Appleton, 1968).

13

COMMUNICATION WITHOUT WORDS

Albert Mehrabian

Suppose you are sitting in my office listening to me describe some
research I have done on communication. I tell you that feelings
are communicated less by the words a person uses than by certain
nonverbal—means that, for example, the verbal part of a spoken
message has considerably less effect on whether a listener feels
liked or disliked than a speaker's facial expression or tone of voice.

So far so good. But suppose I add, "In fact, we've worked out
a formula that shows exactly how much each of these components
contributes to the effect of the message as a whole. It goes like
this: Total Impact = .07 verbal + .38 vocal + .55 facial."

What would you say to *that*? Perhaps you would smile
good-naturedly and say, with some feeling, "Baloney!" or perhaps
you would frown and remark acidly, "Isn't science grand." My

own response to the first answer would probably be to smile back: The facial part of your message, at least, was positive (55 percent of the total). The second answer might make me uncomfortable: Only the verbal part was positive (eleven percent).

The point here is not only that my reactions would lend credence to the formula but that most listeners would have mixed feelings about my statement. People like to see science march on, but they tend to resent its intrusion into an "art" like the communication of feelings, just as they find analytical and quantitative approaches to the study of personality cold, mechanistic, and unacceptable.

The psychologist himself is sometimes plagued by the feeling that he is trying to put a rainbow into a bottle. Fascinated by a complicated and emotionally rich human situation, he begins to study it only to find in the course of his research that he has destroyed part of the mystique that originally intrigued and involved him. But despite a certain nostalgia for earlier, more intuitive approaches, one must acknowledge that concrete experimental data have added a great deal to our understanding of how feelings are communicated. In fact, as I hope to show, analytical and intuitive findings do not so much conflict as complement each other.

It is indeed difficult to know what another person really feels. He says one thing and does another; he seems to mean something but we have an uneasy feeling it isn't true. The early psychoanalysts, facing this problem of inconsistencies and ambiguities in a person's communications, attempted to resolve it through the concepts of the conscious and the unconscious. They assumed that contradictory messages meant a conflict between superficial, deceitful, or erroneous feelings on the one hand and true attitudes and feelings on the other. Their role, then, was to help the client separate the wheat from the chaff.

The question was, how could this be done? Some analysts insisted that inferring the client's unconscious wishes was a completely intuitive process. Others thought that some nonverbal behavior, such as posture, position, and movement, could be used in a more objective way to discover the client's feelings. A favorite technique of Frieda Fromm-Reichmann, for example, was to imitate a client's posture herself in order to obtain some feeling for what he was experiencing.

Thus began the gradual shift away from the idea that communication is primarily verbal, and that the verbal message includes distortions or ambiguities due to unobservable motives that only experts can discover.

Language, though, can be used to communicate almost anything. By comparison, nonverbal behavior is very limited in range. Usually, it is used to communicate feelings, likings, and preferences, and it customarily reinforces or contradicts the feelings that are communicated verbally. Less often, it adds a new dimension of sorts to a verbal message, as when a salesman describes his product to a client and simultaneously conveys, nonverbally, the impression that he likes the client.

A great many forms of nonverbal behavior can communicate feelings: Touching, facial expression, tone of voice, spatial distance from the addressee, relaxation of posture, rate of speech, number of errors in speech. Some of these are generally recognized as informative. Untrained adults and children easily infer that they are liked or disliked from certain facial expressions, from whether (and how) someone touches them, and from a speaker's tone of voice. Other behavior, such as posture, has a more subtle effect. A listener may sense how someone feels about him from the way the person sits while talking to him, but he may have trouble identifying precisely what his impression comes from.

Correct intuitive judgments of the feelings or attitudes of others are especially difficult when different degrees of feeling, or contradictory kinds of feeling, are expressed simultaneously through different forms of behavior. As I have pointed out, there is a distinction between verbal and vocal information (vocal information being what is lost when speech is written down— intonation, tone, stress, length and frequency of pauses, and so on), and the two kinds of information do not always communicate the same feeling. This distinction, which has been recognized for some time, has shed new light on certain types of communications. Sarcasm, for example, can be defined as a message in which the information transmitted vocally contradicts the information transmitted verbally. Usually the verbal information is positive and the vocal is negative, as in "Isn't science grand."

Through the use of an electronic filter, it is possible to measure the degree of liking communicated vocally. What the filter does is eliminate the higher frequencies of recorded speech, so that words are unintelligible but most vocal qualities remain. (For women's speech, we eliminate frequencies higher than about 200 cycles per second; for men, frequencies over about 100 cycles per second.) When people are asked to judge the degree of liking conveyed by the filtered speech, they perform the task rather easily and with a significant amount of agreement.

This method allows us to find out, in a given message, just how inconsistent the information communicated in words and the information communicated vocally really are. We ask one group to judge the amount of liking conveyed by a transcription of what was said, the verbal part of the message. A second group judges the impact of the complete recorded message. In one study of this sort we found that, when the verbal and vocal components of a message agree (both positive or both negative), the message as a whole is judged a little more positive or a little more negative than either component by itself. But when vocal information contradicts verbal, vocal wins out. If someone calls you "honey" in a nasty tone of voice, you are likely to feel disliked; it is also possible to say "I hate you" in a way that conveys exactly the opposite feeling.

Besides the verbal and vocal characteristics of speech, there are other, more subtle, signals of meaning in a spoken message. For example, everyone makes mistakes when he talks— unnecessary repetitions, stutterings, the omission of parts of words, incomplete sentences, "ums" and "ahs." In a number of studies of speech errors, George Mahl of Yale University has found that errors become more frequent as the speaker's discomfort or anxiety increases. It might be interesting to apply this index in an attempt to detect deceit (though on some occasions it might be risky: Confidence men are notoriously smooth talkers).

Timing is also highly informative. How long does a speaker allow silent periods to last, and how long does he wait before he answers his partner? How long do his utterances tend to be? How often does he interrupt his partner, or wait an inappropriately long time before speaking? Joseph Matarazzo and his colleagues at the University of Oregon have found that each of these speech habits is stable from person to person, and each tells something about the speaker's personality and about his feelings toward and status in relation to his partner.

Utterance duration, for example, is a very stable quality in a person's speech; about 30 seconds long on the average. But when someone talks to a partner whose status is higher than his own, the more the high-status person nods his head the longer the speaker's utterances become. If the high-status person changes his own customary speech pattern toward longer or shorter utterances, the lower-status person will change his own speech in the same direction. If the high-status person often interrupts the speaker, or creates long silences, the speaker is likely to become quite uncomfortable. These are things that can be observed outside the laboratory as well as under experimental conditions. If you have an employee who makes you uneasy and seems not to respect you, watch him the next time you talk to him—perhaps he is failing to follow the customary low-status pattern.

Immediacy or directness is another good source of information about feelings. We use more distant forms of communication when the act of communicating is undesirable or uncomfortable. For example, some people would rather transmit discontent with an employee's work through a third party than do it themselves, and some find it easier to communicate negative feelings in writing than by telephone or face to face.

Distance can show a negative attitude toward the message itself, as well as toward the act of delivering it. Certain forms of speech are more distant than others, and they show fewer positive feelings for the subject referred to. A speaker might say "Those people need help," which is more distant than "These people need help," which is in turn even more distant than "These people need our help." Or he might say "Sam and I have been having dinner," which has less immediacy than "Sam and I are having dinner."

Facial expression, touching, gestures, self-manipulation (such as scratching), changes in body position, and head movements—all these express a person's positive and negative attitudes, both at the moment and in general, and many reflect status relationships as well. Movements of the limbs and head, for example, not only indicate one's attitude toward a specific set of circumstances but relate to how dominant, and how anxious, one generally tends to be in social situations. Gross changes in body position, such as shifting in the chair, may show negative feelings toward the person one is talking to. They may also be cues: "It's your turn to talk," or "I'm about to get out of here, so finish what you're saying."

Posture is used to indicate both liking and status. The more a person leans toward his addressee, the more positively he feels about him. Relaxation of posture is a good indicator of both attitude and status, and one that we have been able to measure quite precisely. Three categories have been established for relaxation in a seated position: Least relaxation is indicated by muscular tension in the hands and rigidity of posture; moderate relaxation is indicated by a forward lean of about 20 degrees and a sideways lean of less than 10 degrees, a curved back, and, for women, an open arm position; and extreme relaxation is indicated by a reclining angle greater than 20 degrees and a sideways lean greater than 10 degrees.

Our findings suggest that a speaker relaxes either very little or a great deal when he dislikes the person he is talking to, and to a moderate degree when he likes his companion. It seems that extreme tension occurs with threatening addresses, and extreme relaxation with nonthreatening, disliked addresses. In particular, men tend to become tense when talking to other men whom they dislike; on the other hand, women talking to men *or* women and men talking to women show dislike through extreme relaxation. As for status, people relax most with a low-status addressee, second-most with a peer, and least with someone of higher status than their own. Body orientation also shows status: In both sexes, it is least direct toward women with low status and most direct toward disliked men of high status. In part, body orientation seems to be determined by whether one regards one's partner as threatening.

The more you like a person, the more time you are likely to spend looking into his eyes as you talk to him. Standing close to your partner and facing him directly (which makes eye contact easier) also indicate positive feelings. And you are likely to stand or sit closer to your peers than you do to addressees whose status is either lower or higher than yours.

What I have said so far has been based on research studies performed, for the most part, with college students from the middle and upper-middle classes. One interesting question about communication, however, concerns young children from lower socioeconomic levels. Are these children, as some have suggested, more responsive to implicit channels of communication than middle- and upper-class children are?

Morton Wiener and his colleagues at Clark University had a group of middle- and lower-class children play learning games in which the reward for learning was praise. The child's responsiveness to the verbal and vocal parts of the praise-reward was measured by how much he learned. Praise came in two forms: The objective words "right" and "correct"; and the more affective or evaluative words "good" and "fine." All four words were spoken sometimes in a positive tone of voice and sometimes neutrally.

Positive intonation proved to have a dramatic effect on the learning rate of the lower-class group. They learned much faster when the vocal part of the message was positive than when it was neutral. Positive intonation affected the middle-class group as well, but not nearly as much.

If children of lower socioeconomic groups are more responsive to facial expression, posture and touch as well as to vocal communication, that fact could have interesting applications to elementary education. For example, teachers could be explicitly trained to be aware of, and to use, the forms of praise (nonverbal or verbal) that would be likely to have the greatest effect on their particular students.

Another application of experimental data on communication is to the interpretation and treatment of schizophrenia. The literature on schizophrenia has for some time emphasized that parents of schizophrenic children give off contradictory signals simultaneously. Perhaps the parent tells the child in words that he loves him, but his posture conveys a negative attitude. According to the "double-bind' theory of schizophrenia, the child who perceives simultaneous contradictory feelings in his parent does not know how to react: Should he respond to the positive part of the message, or to the negative? If he is frequently placed in this paralyzing situation, he may learn to respond with contradictory communications of his own. The boy who sends a birthday card to his mother and signs it "Napoleon" says that he likes his mother and yet denies that he is the one who likes her.

In an attempt to determine whether parents of disturbed children really do emit more inconsistent messages about their feelings than other parents do, my colleagues and I have compared what these parents communicate verbally and vocally with what they show through posture. We interviewed parents of moderately and quite severely disturbed children, in the presence of the child, about the child's problem. The interview was video-recorded without the parents' knowledge, so that we could analyze their behavior later on. Our measurements supplied both the amount of inconsistency between the parents' verbal-vocal and postural communications, and the total amount of liking that the parents communicated.

According to the double-bind theory, the parents of the more disturbed children should have behaved more inconsistently than the parents of the less disturbed children. This was not confirmed: There was no significant difference between the two groups. However, the *total amount* of positive feeling communicated by parents of the more disturbed children was less than that communicated by the other group.

This suggests that (1) negative communications toward disturbed children occur because the child is a problem and therefore elicits them, or (2) the negative attitude precedes the child's disturbance. It may also be that both factors operate together, in a vicious circle.

If so, one way to break the cycle is for the therapist to create situations in which the parent can have better feelings toward the child. A more positive attitude from the parent may make the child more responsive to his directives, and the spiral may begin to move up instead of down. In our own work with disturbed children, this kind of procedure has been used to good effect.

If one puts one's mind to it, one can think of a great many other applications for the findings I have described, though not all of them concern serious problems. Politicians, for example, are careful to maintain eye contact with the television camera when they speak, but they are not always careful about how they sit when they debate another candidate of, presumably, equal status.

Public relations men might find a use for some of the subtler signals of feeling. So might Don Juans. And so might ordinary people, who could try watching other people's signals and changing their own, for fun at a party or in a spirit of experimentation at home. I trust that does not strike you as a cold, manipulative suggestion, indicating dislike for the human race. I assure you that, if you had more than a transcription of words to judge from (seven percent of total message), it would not.

14

DEFENSIVE COMMUNICATION

Jack R. Gibb

One way to understand communication is to view it as a people
process rather than as a language process. If one is to make
fundamental improvement in communication, he must make
changes in interpersonal relationships. One possible type of
alteration—and the one with which this paper is concerned—
is that of reducing the degree of defensiveness.

DEFINITION AND SIGNIFICANCE

Defensive behavior is defined as that behavior which occurs when
an individual perceives threat or anticipates threat in the group.

Reprinted by permission of Jack R. Gibb and International Communication
Association from "Defensive Communication" by Jack R. Gibb in the
Journal of Communication 2 (1961):141–148.

The person who behaves defensively, even though he also gives some attention to the common task, devotes an appreciable portion of his energy to defending himself. Besides talking about the topic, he thinks about how he appears to others, how he may be seen more favorably, how he may win, dominate, impress, or escape punishment, and/or how he may avoid or mitigate a perceived or an anticipated attack.

Such inner feelings and outward acts tend to create similarly defensive postures in others; and, if unchecked, the ensuing circular response becomes increasingly destructive. Defensive behavior, in short, engenders defensive listening, and this in turn produces postural, facial, and verbal cues which raise the defense level of the original communicator.

Defense arousal prevents the listener from concentrating upon the message. Not only do defensive communicators send off multiple value, motive, and affect cues, but also defensive recipients distort what they receive. As a person becomes more and more defensive, he becomes less and less able to perceive accurately the motives, the values, and the emotions of the sender. The writer's analyses of tape recorded discussions revealed that increases in defensive behavior were correlated positively with losses in efficiency in communication.[1] Specifically, distortions become greater when defensive states existed in the groups.

The converse, moreover, also is true. The more "supportive" or defense reductive the climate, the less the receiver reads into the communication distorted loadings which arise from projections of his own anxieties, motives, and concerns. As defenses are reduced, the receivers become better able to concentrate upon the structure, the content, and the cognitive meanings of the message.

CATEGORIES OF DEFENSIVE AND SUPPORTIVE COMMUNICATION

In working over an eight-year period with recordings of discussions occurring in varied settings, the writer developed the six pairs of defensive and supportive categories presented in Table 1. Behavior which a listener perceives as possessing any of the characteristics listed in the left-hand column arouses defensiveness, whereas that which he interprets as having any of the qualities designated as supportive reduces defensive feelings. The degree to which these reactions occur depends upon the personal level of defensiveness and upon the general climate in the group at the time.[2]

Table 1   CATEGORIES OF BEHAVIOR CHARACTERISTIC OF
SUPPORTIVE AND DEFENSIVE CLIMATES IN SMALL GROUPS

DEFENSIVE CLIMATES	SUPPORTIVE CLIMATES
1. Evaluation	1. Description
2. Control	2. Problem orientation
3. Strategy	3. Spontaneity
4. Neutrality	4. Empathy
5. Superiority	5. Equality
6. Certainty	6. Provisionalism

Evaluation and Description

Speech or other behavior which appears evaluative increases
defensiveness. If by expression, manner of speech, tone of voice,
or verbal content the sender seems to be evaluating or judging the
listener, then the receiver goes on guard. Of course, other factors
may inhibit the reaction. If the listener thought that the speaker
regarded him as an equal and was being open and spontaneous, for
example, the evaluativeness in a message would be neutralized
and perhaps not even perceived. This same principle applies
equally to the other five categories of potentially defense-producing
climates. The six sets are interactive.

Because our attitudes toward other persons are frequently,
and often necessarily, evaluative, expressions which the defensive
person will regard as nonjudgmental are hard to frame. Even the
simplest question usually conveys the answer that the sender
wishes or implies the response that would fit into his value system.
A mother, for example, immediately following an earth tremor
that shook the house, sought for her small son with the question:
"Bobby, where are you?" The timid and plaintive "Mommy, I
didn't do it" indicated how Bobby's chronic mild defensiveness
predisposed him to react with a projection of his own guilt and in
the context of his chronic assumption that questions are full of
accusation.

Anyone who has attempted to train professionals to use
information-seeking speech with neutral affect appreciates how
difficult it is to teach a person to say even the simple "who did
that?" without being seen as accusing. Speech is so frequently
judgmental that there is a reality base for the defensive
interpretations which are so common.

When insecure, group members are particularly likely to
place blame, to see others as fitting into categories of good or bad,
to make moral judgments of their colleagues, and to question the

value, motive, and affect loadings of the speech which they hear. Since value loadings imply a judgment of others, a belief that the standards of the speaker differ from his own causes the listener to become defensive.

Descriptive speech, in contrast to that which is evaluative, tends to arouse a minimum of uneasiness. Speech acts which the listener perceives as genuine requests for information or as material with neutral loadings is descriptive. Specifically, presentations of feelings, events, perceptions, or processes which do not ask or imply that the receiver change behavior or attitude are minimally defense producing. The difficulty in avoiding overtone is illustrated by the problems of news reporters in writing stories about unions, communists, Negroes, and religious activities without tipping off the "party" line of the newspaper. One can often tell from the opening words in a news article which side the newspaper's editorial favors.

Control and Problem Orientation

Speech which is used to control the listener evokes resistance. In most of our social intercourse someone is trying to do something to someone else—to change an attitude, to influence behavior, or to restrict the field of activity. The degree to which attempts to control produce defensiveness depends upon the openness of the effort, for a suspicion that hidden motives exist heightens resistance. For this reason attempts of nondirective therapists and progressive educators to refrain from imposing a set of values, a point of view, or a problem solution upon the receivers meet with many barriers. Since the norm is control, noncontrollers must earn the perceptions that their efforts have no hidden motives. A bombardment of persuasive "messages" in the fields of politics, education, special causes, advertising, religion, medicine, industrial relations, and guidance has bred cynical and paranoidal responses in listeners.

Implicit in all attempts to alter another person is the assumption by the change agent that the person to be altered is inadequate. That the speaker secretly views the listener as ignorant, unable to make his own decisions, uninformed, immature, unwise, or possessed of wrong or inadequate attitudes is a subconscious perception which gives the latter a valid base for defensive reactions.

Methods of control are many and varied. Legalistic insistence on detail, restrictive regulations and policies, conformity norms, and all laws are among the methods. Gestures, facial expressions, other forms of nonverbal communication, and even such simple acts as holding a door open in a particular manner are means of imposing one's will upon another and hence are potential sources of resistance.

Problem orientation, on the other hand, is the antithesis of persuasion. When the sender communicates a desire to collaborate in defining a mutual problem and in seeking its solution, he tends to create the same problem orientation in the listener; and, of greater importance, he implies that he has no predetermined solution, attitude, or method to impose. Such behavior is permissive in that it allows the receiver to set his own goals, make his own decisions, and evaluate his own progress—or to share with the sender in doing so. The exact methods of attaining permissiveness are not known, but they must involve a constellation of cues and they certainly go beyond mere verbal assurances that the communicator has no hidden desires to exercise control.

Strategy and Spontaneity

When the sender is perceived as engaged in a stratagem involving ambiguous and multiple motivations, the receiver becomes defensive. No one wishes to be a guinea pig, a role player, or an impressed actor, and no one likes to be the victim of some hidden motivation. That which is concealed, also, may appear larger than it really is with the degree of defensiveness of the listener determining the perceived size of the supressed element. The intense reaction of the reading audience to the material in the *Hidden Persuaders* indicates the prevalence of defensive reactions to multiple motivations behind strategy. Group members who are seen as "taking a role," as feigning emotion, as toying with their colleagues, as withholding information, or as having special sources of data are especially resented. One participant once complained that another was "using a listening technique" on him!

A large part of the adverse reaction to much of the so-called human relations training is a feeling against what are perceived as gimmicks and tricks to fool or to "involve" people, to make a person think he is making his own decision, or to make the listener feel that the sender is genuinely interested in him as a person. Particularly violent reactions occur when it appears that someone is trying to make a stratagem appear spontaneous. One person has reported a boss who incurred resentment by habitually using the gimmick of "spontaneously" looking at his watch and saying, "My gosh, look at the time—I must run to an appointment." The belief was that the boss would create less irritation by honestly asking to be excused.

Similarly, the deliberate assumption of guilelessness and natural simplicity is especially resented. Monitoring the tapes of feedback and evaluation sessions in training groups indicates the surprising extent to which members perceive the strategies of their colleagues. This perceptual clarity may be quite shocking to the strategist who usually feels that he has cleverly hidden the motivational aura around the "gimmick."

This aversion to deceit may account for one's resistance to politicians who are suspected of behind-the-scenes planning to get his vote, to psychologists whose listening apparently is motivated by more than the manifest or content-level interest in his behavior, or to the sophisticated, smooth, or clever person whose "one-upmanship" is marked with guile. In training groups the role-flexible person frequently is resented because his changes in behavior are perceived as strategic maneuvers.

In contrast, behavior which appears to be spontaneous and free of deception is defense reductive. If the communicator is seen as having a clean id, as having uncomplicated motivations, as being straightforward and honest, and as behaving spontaneously in response to the situation, he is likely to arouse minimal defense.

Neutrality and Empathy

When neutrality in speech appears to the listener to indicate a lack of concern for his welfare, he becomes defensive. Group members usually desire to be perceived as valued persons, as individuals of special worth, and as objects of concern and affection. The clinical, detached, person-is-an-object-of-study attitude on the part of many psychologist-trainers is resented by group members. Speech with low affect that communicates little warmth or caring is in such contrast with the affect-laden speech in social situations that it sometimes communicates rejection.

Communication that conveys empathy for the feelings and respect for the worth of the listener, however, is particularly supportive and defense reductive. Reassurance results when a message indicates that the speaker identifies himself with the listener's problems, shares his feelings, and accepts his emotional reactions at face value. Abortive efforts to deny the legitimacy of the receiver's emotions by assuring the receiver that he need not feel bad, that he should not feel rejected, or that he is overly anxious, though often intended as support giving, may impress the listener as lack of acceptance. The combination of understanding and empathizing with the other person's emotions with no accompanying effort to change him apparently is supportive at a high level.

The importance of gestural behavioral cues in communicating empathy should be mentioned. Apparently spontaneous facial and bodily evidences of concern are often interpreted as especially valid evidence of deep-level acceptance.

Superiority and Equality

When a person communicates to another that he feels superior in position, power, wealth, intellectual ability, physical characteristics, or other ways, he arouses defensiveness. Here, as with the other sources of disturbance, whatever arouses feelings of inadequacy causes the listener to center upon the affect loading of the statement rather than upon the cognitive elements. The receiver then reacts by not hearing the message, by forgetting it, by competing with the sender, or by becoming jealous of him.

The person who is perceived as feeling superior communicates that he is not willing to enter into a shared problem-solving relationship, that he probably does not desire feedback, that he does not require help, and/or that he will be likely to try to reduce the power, the status, or the worth of the receiver.

Many ways exist for creating the atmosphere that the sender feels himself equal to the listener. Defenses are reduced when one perceives the sender as being willing to enter into participative planning with mutual trust and respect. Differences in talent, ability, worth, appearance, status, and power often exist, but the low defense communicator seems to attach little importance to these distinctions.

Certainty and Provisionalism

The effects of dogmatism in producing defensiveness are well known. Those who seem to know the answers, to require no additional data, and to regard themselves as teachers rather than as co-workers tend to put others on guard. Moreover, in the writers' experiment, listeners often perceived manifest expressions of certainty as connoting inward feelings of inferiority. They saw the dogmatic individual as needing to be right, as wanting to win an argument rather than solve a problem, and as seeing his ideas as truths to be defended. This kind of behavior often was associated with acts which others regarded as attempts to exercise control. People who were right seemed to have low tolerance for members who were "wrong"—i.e., who did not agree with the sender.

One reduces the defensiveness of the listener when he communicates that he is willing to experiment with his own behavior, attitudes, and ideas. The person who appears to be taking provisional attitudes, to be investigating issues rather than taking sides on them, to be problem solving rather than debating, and to be willing to experiment and explore tends to communicate that the listener may have some control over the shared quest or the investigation of the ideas. If a person is genuinely searching for information and data, he does not resent help or company along the way.

CONCLUSION

The implications of the above material for the parent, the teacher, the manager, the administrator, or the therapist are fairly obvious. (Arousing defensiveness interferes with communication and thus makes it difficult—and sometimes impossible—for anyone to convey ideas clearly and to move effectively toward the solution of therapeutic, educational, or managerial probems.)

Notes

1. Gibb, J. R., "Defense Level and Influence Potential in Small Groups," in L. Petrullo and B. M. Bass (eds.), *Leadership and Intereprsonal Behavior* (New York: Holt, Rinehart and Winston, 1961), pp. 66–81.
2. Gibb, J. R., "Sociopsychological Processes of Group Instruction," in N. B. Henry (ed.), *The Dynamics of Instructional Groups,* Fifty-ninth Yearbook of the National Society for the Study of Education, Part II, 1960, pp. 115–135.

Part III
THE STRUCTURE OF COMMUNICATIVE ACTS

Neither the translation of human events nor the symbolic significance of behavior can be determined in a chaotic, unpredictable environment. Whenever information unfolds in a random fashion, with no apparent pattern or underlying order, the importance of the content cannot be readily interpreted. The human organism strives to impose order on experience and to disregard as insignificant those features in the physical surroundings that reveal no apparent connection with other changes that are taking place. The central nervous system functions as an intricate classificational system, searching for pattern and orderly configuration, then assimilating and assigning significance to the *pattern* of change in the visual, auditory, and kinetic stream. The same principle of pattern recognition applies to sensory activity we create for others. There is order not only in the flow of words, but also in the continuity of movement and gesture. To be in a state of dissynchrony with another is a serious liability, for such a lack of interpersonal integration indicates that one is separated from the ordering principles the other uses to make sense of their experience.

All of us have our own style, our own organizing logic or slant, and our own unique way of representing and enacting our personalized constructions of reality. Hence, face-to-face interaction always entails some accommodation to the inevitable differences that arise in the way each person seeks to provide structure to his or her behavior. The essays in this section discuss the organization of communication from several vantage points. The progression of ideas moves from the structure of the human environment to the successively more specific levels of order that are maintained in a conversation, looking patterns, posture, movement, and silence.

"Communication Boundaries" by Erving Goffman shows how the immediate physical surroundings shape the unfolding organization of what people say and do. The arrangement of rooms, walls, doors, windows, stairways, lighting fixtures, and even furniture may have a decisive influence on the pattern of interaction, on the restrictions imposed, and on the physical orientations and attitudes conveyed by various participants. Each situation imposes its own assumptions on the location, accessibility, and perspectives of those present. Situation also shapes behavior through subtle obligations that accompany states of personal inattention, noninvolvement, and recognition. Individuals tends to maintain a network of space that assures "cooperative distribution" and open "talk lines."

Another source of structure in communication develops out of the sheer willingness of interactants to engage in what John Wiemann and Mark Knapp discuss—"Turn-taking in Conversations." Turn-taking refers to the *way* the participants switch from talk to silence and back again from silence to talk. The process varies in degree of synchrony and the sequencing devices used. Natural word endings, verbal requests, "stutter starts," simultaneous talking, pauses, silence, interruptions, hand gestures, looking patterns, shifts in posture, and head nodding all help shape the rhythm of exchange and thereby serve a symbolic function in defining relationships.

Intuitively, it is easier to sense the structure of verbal activity than the order of visual experience. Words, after all, are categories; they occur in a sequence, one after another, in clusters and classifications determined by rules that specify "what follows what." Visual images, on the other hand, do not fall into any conventional categories. The visual world has no natural order or syntax. Nonetheless, visual information and verbal information do have important structural features in common. Both create order through the very nature of the boundaries that are maintained in each mode of experience. Words, phrases, sentences, and utterances are bounded off in varying frequencies and durations, and visual images are bounded in much the same way. We decide whether to talk or not to talk, and we also decide whether to look or not to look; in each case our decisions create a sense of order and pattern. The sequence of looking behavior regulates the flow of interaction in ways no less powerful than the intervals of talk. In "Visual Behavior in Social Interaction," Phoebe Ellsworth and Linda Ludwig show how visual behavior helps regulate the flow of conversation and the sequence and pace of speech. The eyes send information and, in so doing, reveal how a person is collecting it as well. The authors also document wide variation and individual differences that exist in looking style, the accuracy levels in visual discrimination, regulative and information-seeking functions, together with the intricate role of eye contact in the assumptions, inferences, attitudes, and personal involvements of interactants.

The structure of behavior extends from the boundaries of the physical environment to the ritual of conversation, looking patterns, right down to the particular movements and postures of the body. In "Hand Movements" by Paul Ekman and Wallace Friesen, and "The Significance of Posture in Communication Systems" by Albert Scheflin, the spontaneity of bodily activitiy is shown to be an expression of one's own style of organization. What the patterned features of the human body reflect is nothing less significant than the complex, ongoing transaction between internal translation and external situation. Postures, Scheflin claims, tend to cluster into repetitive "points" and "positions," and constitute the basis of one's "presentational" style. Basic bodily orientations are sometimes congruent and at other times incongruent with those conveyed by other interactants. Hence, even the way people move their bodies may express something of their attitude and orientation to other participants in a face-to-face situation. Hand movements, for example, convey personal attitudes in three basic ways. Some movements are *emblematic*—their meanings can be translated in conventional verbal terms; others are *illustrators*— they accompany, underscore, or qualify the meanings associated with the flow of conversation; still other movements function as *adaptors*—their meanings closely identified with physical and emotional needs. In short, the body performs a multiple set of functions that acquire communicative significance only within the larger content of verbal interaction and interpersonal relations.

The importance of what people say and do cannot be

separated from what is left unsaid. In "Communicative Silences: Forms and Functions," Thomas Bruneau discusses three different types of silence. Psycholinguistic silence consists of hesitations and pauses in the flow of speech. Interactive silences are pausal interruptions in the dialogue between interactants. Sociolinguistic silence refers to all of the characteristic ways that a given culture or subculture'refrains from speech and thereby regulates the pattern of psycholinguistic and interactive silence. Patterns of silence have immense communicative significance. In subtle ways we use the absence of bodily sound to convey and to attribute emotion, attitude, status and authority cues, and intentions to regulate and control relationships. The total configuration of silence, sound, and sight, creates a unique set of interactive boundaries and limits imposed on the process of symbolic interaction.

15

COMMUNICATION BOUNDARIES

Erving Goffman

1. CONVENTIONAL SITUATIONAL CLOSURE

Whether an individual is allowed to enter a region, such as a room,
or is excluded from it, he will often be required to show some kind
of regard for the physical boundary around it, when there is one.
Of course, theoretically it is possible for boundaries like thick walls
to close the region off physically from outside communication;
almost always, however, some communication across the boundary
is physically possible. Social arrangements are therefore recognized
that restrict such communication to a special part of the boundary,
such as doors, and that lead persons inside and outside the region
to act *as if* the barrier had cut off more communication than it
does. The work walls do, they do in part because they are honored

Reprinted by permission of The Free Press from *Behavior in Public
Places* by Erving Goffman, pp. 151–165, 1963.

or socially recognized as communication barriers, giving rise, among properly conducted members of the community, to the possibility of "conventional situational closure" in the absence of actual physical closure.

A glimpse of these conventions can be obtained by noting a fact about socialization: children in our middle-class society are firmly taught that, while it is possible to address a friend by shouting through the walls, or to get his attention by tapping on the window, it is none the less not permissible, and that a desire to engage anyone in the region must be ratified by first knocking at the door as the formal means of making entry.

Windows themselves may provide an opportunity for partial participation in a situation and are typically associated with an understanding that such a possibility will not be exploited. Deviations from this rule can, of course, be found. In Shetland Isle, visiting Norwegian seamen, described by some islanders as "of the lowest type," would sometimes walk around cottages and peer directly into the windows. Dickens provides a similar illustration from the America of a century ago:

> After dinner we went down to the railroad again, and took our seats in the cars for Washington. Being rather early, those men and boys who happened to have nothing particular to do, and were curious in foreigners, came (according to custom) round the carriage in which I sat; let down all the windows; thrust in their heads and shoulders; hooked themselves on conveniently by their elbows; and fell to comparing notes on the subject of my personal appearance, with as much indifference as if I were a stuffed figure. I never gained so much uncompromising information with reference to my own nose and eyes, the various impressions wrought by my mouth and chin on different minds, and how my head looks when it is viewed from behind, as on these occasions.[1]

In the many mental hospitals where the nurses' station is a glass-enclosed observation post, patients must be trained to keep from lingering around the windows and looking in on the life inside. (Interestingly enough, no hospital rule prohibits staff from looking out at a patient through these windows, thus maintaining an official form of eavesdropping.) The fashion of using "picture windows" for walls has, of course, introduced its own social strains, requiring great morale on both sides of the window to ensure conventional closure; there are many cartoon illustrations of consequent problems. It may be added (as the citation from Dickens suggests) that failure to recognize a region boundary is often associated with, according to those who are improperly observed, the status of nonpersons.

Where walls between two regions are known to be very thin, problems of reticence become pronounced.[3] Sometimes open recognition will be given to the communication possibilities, with persons talking through the wall almost as though they were all in the same social situation, as an analysis of a British semidetached housing development suggests:

> Developing our picture of neighbour linkage by car from the comments of residents, we find that it is possible in these houses to entertain a neighbour's wife by playing her favorite records with the gramophone tuned to loud, or to mind her child or invite her to tea, all through the party wall.[3]

Here, of course, we see some of the special functions of sight: those on the other side of the party wall may not be present, or, if present, may not be attending, but it will be impossible to *see* that this is the case.

2. ACCESSIBLE ENGAGEMENTS

When a face engagement exhausts the situation—all persons present being accredited participants in the encounter—the problem of maintaining orderly activity will be largely internal to the encounter: the allocation of talking time (if the engagement is a spoken one); the maintenance of something innocuous to talk or act upon (this being describable as the problem of "safe supplies"); the inhibition of hostility; and so forth.

When there are persons present who are not participants in the engagement, we know that inevitably they will be in a position to learn something about the encounter's participants and to be affected by how the encounter as a whole is conducted. When a face engagement must be carried on in a situation containing bystanders, I will refer to it as *accessible*.

Whenever a face engagement is accessible to nonparticipants there is a fully shared and an unshared participation. All persons in the gathering at large will be immersed in a common pool of unfocused interaction, each person, by his mere presence, manner, and appearance, transmitting some information about himself to everyone in the situation, and each person present receiving like information from all the others present, at least in so far as he is willing to make use of his receiving opportunities. It is this possibility of widely available communication, and the regulations arising to control this communication, that transform a mere physical region into the locus of a sociologically relevant entity, the situation. But above and beyond this fully common participation, the ratified members of a particular engagement will *in addition* be participating in interaction of the focused kind, where a message conveyed by one person is meant to make a specific contribution to a matter at hand, and is usually addressed to a particular recipient, while the other members of the encounter, and only these others, are meant to receive it too. Thus, there will be a fully shared basis of unfocused interaction underlying one or more partially shared bases of focused interaction.

The difference between participation in the unfocused interaction in the situation at large and participation in the focused interaction in a face engagement is easy to sense but difficult to follow out in detail. Questions such as choice of participants for the encounter or sound level of voices have relevance for the situation as a whole, because anyone in the situation will be (and will be considered to be) in a position to witness these aspects of the face engagement, which are the unfocused part of the communication flowing from it. But the specific meanings of *particular* statements appropriately conveyed within a face engagement will not be available to the situation at large, although, if a special effort at secrecy be made, this furtiveness, as a *general* aspect of what is going on, may in fact become quite widely perceivable and an important time in the unfocused interaction that is occurring. That part of the communication occurring in a face engagement that could not be conveyed through mediating channels is situational; but this situational aspect of the encounter becomes part of the unfocused communication in the situation at large only when some of the grosser improprieties, such as shouting, whispering, and broad physical gestures, occur.

In considering accessible engagements, it is convenient to take a vantage point within such an encounter, and to describe the issues from this point of view. The persons present in the gathering at large can then be divided up into participants and bystanders, depending on whether or not they are official members of the engagement in question; and the issues to be considered can be divided up into obligations owed the encounter and obligations owed the gathering at large (and behind the gathering, the social occasion of which it is an expression).

In order for the engagement to maintain its boundaries and integrity, and to avoid being engulfed by the gathering, both participant and bystander will have to regulate their conduct appropriately. And yet even while cooperating to maintain the privacy of the given encounter, both participant and bystander will be obligated to protect the gathering at large, demonstrating that in certain ways all those within the situation stand together, undivided by their differentiating participation.

3. CONVENTIONAL ENGAGEMENT CLOSURE

By definition, an accessible engagement does not exhaust the situation; there is no situational closure, physical or conventional, to cut it off from nonparticipants. What we find instead is some obligation and some effort on the part of both participants and bystanders to act as if the engagement were physically cut off from the rest of the situation. In short, a "conventional engagement closure" is found. I want now to consider some of the elements of social organization this closure entails.

a. Bystanders extend a type of civil inattention, but one that is designed for encounters, not for individuals. Bystanders are obliged to refrain from exploiting the communication position in which they find themselves, and to give visible expression to the participants of the gathering that they are focusing their attention elsewhere—a courtesy of some complexity, since a too studied inattention to what one is in a position to overhear can easily spoil a show of inattention.[4]

Since there are many reasons why an individual might want to overhear the content of an engagement of which he is not a member, he may often simulate inattention, giving the impression that conventional closure has been obtained, while in fact he is furtively attending to the talk. How much of this eavesdropping actually does go on, and in what situations, is difficult to assess.

The expression of inattention and noninvolvement exhibited by those who are physically close to an encounter in which they are not participants can be observed in an extreme form at times when an individual could join the encounter (as far as its participants are concerned), but finds himself "psychologically" incapable of doing so. What can then result is a kind of conversational parasitism, often observable on mental hospital wards. For example, one psychotic young woman I observed would sit alongside her mother and look straight ahead while the latter was engaged in conversation with a nurse, maintaining what appeared to be civil inattention in regard to the neighboring engagement. But while attempting to keep her face composed like that of an uninvolved, uninterested bystander, she would keep up a running line of derisive comment on what was being said, uttering these loud stake whispers under great verbal pressure, from the side of her mouth. The psychological issue here, presumably, was that of "dissociation." But the direction of flow taken by the two dissociated lines of conduct—conversational participation and civil inattention—seemed entirely determined by the social organization of communication that is standard for social situations in our society. In a social situation, then, an individual may find himself torn apart, but torn apart on a standard rack that is articulated in a standard way.

There are circumstances in which it is difficult for participants to show tactful trust of bystanders and for bystanders to extend civil inattention in brief, there are times when conventional closure is difficult to manage.

For one example of this we can turn to small enclosed places like elevators, where individuals may be so closely brought together that no pretense of not hearing can possibly be maintained. At such times, in middle-class America at least, there seems to be a tendency for participants of an encounter to hold their communication in abeyance, with only an occasional word to stabilize their half-lapsed encounter. A similar kind of issue seems to arise in near-empty bars, as novelists have pointed out:

> We were alone in that bar, it was still the middle of the morning and the presence of the barman there was embarrassing. He could not help overhearing. In his white impassive coat he was a figure of reticent authority. But he probably realised this too, he was nice enough to keep bobbing down behind the bar and shovelling about his glasses and his little trays of ice. So Harry ordered two more as it were from no-one, and soon these bobbed up.[5]

The cabdriver has something of the same kind of problem here as the bar man.[6] So too has the individual who is momentarily left to his own resources while a person to whom he has been talking answers a telephone call; physically close to the engaged other and patently unoccupied, he must yet somehow show civil inattention.[7]

Where civil inattention is physically difficult to manage, the scene is set for a special kind of dominance. In an elevator, for example, those in one of the engagements may continue fully engaged, forcing the others present to accept the role of nonpersons. Similarly, when two unacquainted couples are required to share the same booth in a restaurant, and they elect to forego trying to maintain an inclusive face engagement, one couple may tactily give way to the louder interaction of the other. In these situations, the submissive couple may attempt to show independence and civil inattention by beginning a talk of their own. But while it may appear convincing to the other couple, this weaker talk is not likely to convince its own participants, who, in carrying it on, will

be admitting to each other not only that they have been upstaged
but that they are willing to try to pretend that they have not.[8] It
may be added that strength in these cases derives not from muscle,
but, typically, from social class.

    b. Given the fact that participants and bystanders are required
to help maintain the integrity of the encounter, and given the
complicating fact that bystanders of this encounter may well be
participants of another, we may expect some tacit cooperation in
maintaining conventional closure. First, if bystanders are to desist
in some way from exploiting their communication opportunities,
then it will fall upon the participants to limit their actions and
words to ones that will not be too hard to disattend. And this
keeping down of the excitement level is, in fact, what is generally
found. Interestingly enough, this tendency is matched by another
that moves in the opposite direction, namely, acting in such a way
as to show confidence in the willingness of bystanders not to exploit
their situation. Thus, as already suggested, whispering or obvious
use of code terms will often be thought impolite, in part because
it casts a doubt on bystanders' willingness to be inattentive.

    One consequence of the combination of these rules of
conventional closure may be mentioned. It is a rule of conversation
that participants show consideration for one another, by, for
example, avoiding facts about which the other might be touchy, or
by showing constraint in raising criticism, and so forth.
Disparagement of persons not present, on the other hand, is
usually quite acceptable, offering a basis of preferential solidarity
for those in the encounter. In addition, the conversation may well
involve business matters that an absent other cannot safely be
made privy to. It follows, therefore, that the run of comments in a
conversational encounter may have to be altered strategically when
a relevantly excluded person approaches, lest the content of the
talk put too much strain upon his willingness to offer civil
inattention; when he approaches with the intention of entering the
encounter, even more delicacy is required. The well-known
example is that of the individual who comes into a room to find that
conversation has suddenly stopped and that others present are
seeking in a flustered way to find a new and tenable topic.
Sometimes, as a relevantly excluded other approaches, a particular
physical point is reached where the conversation can be altered
without either letting the oncomer hear what would be embarrassing
to him (or what would embarrass the speakers for him to hear)
or giving him an impression that something embarrassing regarding
him has been suppressed. This distance will, of course, vary with
the social skill of the participants. Sometimes, too, a given room

will have a special "safe region," from which vantage point any newcomer can be spied in time to safely alter the content of talk without showing that an alteration was necessary. In these circumstances we sometimes find skill-showing, where the talkers daringly and coolly continue their talk up to the very last moment for altering it safely.

   c. The care that a bystander is obliged to exert for an accessible encounter extends past civil inattention to the question of how and when he can present himself for official participation. Even at social parties, where every encounter is supposed to be conducted in a fashion that makes it joinable by any guest, the entrant is expected to exert tact and, when cues suggest, not exercise his rights. When he does enter he is expected to accept the current topic and tone, thus minimizing the disruption he causes. Thus, early American etiquette suggests:

> If a lady and gentleman are conversing together at an evening party, it would be a rudeness in another person to go up and interrupt them by introducing a new topic of observation. If you are sure that there is nothing of a particular and private interest passing between them, you may *join* their conversation and strike into the current of their remarks; yet if you then find that they are so much engaged and entertained by the discussion that they were holding together, as to render the termination or change of its character unwelcome, you should withdraw. If, however, two persons are occupied with one another upon what you guess to be terms peculiarly delicate and particular, you should withhold yourself from their company.[9]

Welcome or not, the entrant today is usually expected to knock at the door of the encounter before he enters, thus giving the encounter advance warning of his intention and the participants a moment to straighten their house for the newcomer.

   d. One of the most interesting forms of cooperation in the maintenance of conventional closure is what might be called *spacing*:[10] the tendency for units of participation in the situation—either face engagements or unengaged individuals—to distribute themselves cooperatively in the available space so as physically to facilitate conventional closure. (Often this seems to involve a maximization of the sum of the squares of the physical distance among the various units.[11]) Of course, where the units of participation owe one another some expression of mutual trust and comradeship, full spacing may be specifically avoided.[12]

   Spacing will of course ensure that "talk lines" are open, that is, that persons addressing one another in an encounter will have no physical obstruction to block the free exchange of glances. A bystander finding himself interposed in such a line (in American society, at least) is likely to offer an apology and quickly shift his position.

While the phenomenon of spacing may be difficult to see because one takes it for granted, a tracing of it in reverse can be obtained by observing children and mental patients—those communication deliquents who sometimes play the game of "attack the encounter." On many wards, for example, a patient will follow a pair of talkers around the room until they have stopped moving, and then slide right up to the edge of the encounter and lean into it. One adolescent patient I studied would intercept talk lines between two persons by waving her knitting needles in the way, or by swinging her upraised arms, or by thrusting her face into the face of one of the participants, or by sitting in his lap.

Along with physical spacing, we also find control of sound so that the various units in the situation can proceed with their business at hand without being jammed out of operation. In many cases this will mean restriction on the volume of sound, although, at occasions like social parties, where persons may be crowded close to others not in the same encounter, a general raising of voices may be found; this allows coparticipants to hear each other, but jams the opportunities of eavesdroppers. Here, too, accurately designed delicts can be observed, as when an adolescent mental patient, in a spirit of fun, places her face up against the face of someone engaged in talk with another at a distance, and then shouts so that he can neither hear nor be heard.

The requirement that visually open talk lines be maintained and that sound level not interfere with neighboring encounters, sets a limit to the distance over which spoken encounters can ordinarily be sustained. For example, should two persons carry on a conversation from one end of a crowded streetcar to the other, all the intervening passengers would have to remain out of the line of talk and modulate their own conversation so as not to jam the one being maintained over a distance. Such a conversation would necessarily also be fully available to everyone between the two speakers, and would therefore be likely to constitute an embarrassment, even were one of the speakers the conductor. Thus, engagements that must be carried on over such a populated distance are likely to be limited to the exchange of silent gestures, for these neither interfere with other encounters nor expose what is being conveyed. As might be expected, therefore, deaf and dumb persons who board a streetcar together and find themselves seated apart need not discontinue their exchange of messages, but are able to carry on conversation as long as sight lines are clear, their "talk" neither jamming the other talkers nor being accessible to them.

While physical spacing and sound control certainly have relevance to occasions such as social parties that are carried on within a relatively small physical region, they are perhaps even more important in public streets and roads and in semipublic regions. In Western society, the development of middle-class dominance is expressed in the rise of a relatively equalitarian use of public places. Even today, however, funerals, weddings, parades, and some other ceremonies are allowed to press their spirit momentarily upon the public at large. Technical units, such as ambulances, police cars, and fire engines cut through public traffic with an amount of sound not permitted to other units of traffic; and guests of a city may be given a motor escort. Some of these prerogatives, however, are but small remnants of practices that were once more general, such as the entourage and train associated with "clientage,"[13] which led a worthy to demonstrate his status by the cluster of dependent supporters that accompanied him through a town or a house of parliament, shouldering his way for him wherever he went. Nor are these rules uniform within Western society, as is suggested by the response of King Edward (of Britain) and his party during a 1906 visit to the Emperor of Germany:

> The Emperor had a standard attached to his motor and a trumpeter on the box who blew long bugle-calls at every corner. The inhabitants thus had no difficulty in making out where the Emperor was, and all the traffic cleared out of the way when they heard the trumpets blow. The King, however, detested what he called "theatrical methods" and drove about like anybody else.[14]

e. In terminating this discussion of conventional closure, I want to mention the kind of restructuring that can occur when a situation is transformed from one containing many encounters—a multifocused situation—to one that is exhausted by a single all-encompassing engagement. For example, at noontime on a ward of Central Hospital, when the attendant shouts, "Chow time!" he is addressing the whole place, and wherever the sound level of his voice reaches, the meanings of his words are meant to carry too. Similarly, at a small social party, the arrival of a couple may cause the hostess to interrupt the separateness of all the separate encounters in order to introduce the newcomers to the assembly. So also, at formal dinners, the moment the hostess indicates that the conversation will be "general," she opens up whatever is being said to all the guests. And, of course, whenever public speeches are given, the speaker's words, as well as the heat with which he speaks them, are meant to impinge on the situation at large. In all such cases, there is the understanding that the situation at large is properly open to the content of the words of an appropriate single speaker; he has, as we say, the floor.

The transformation of a multifocused situation into one that is exhausted by one face engagement is an interesting process to consider. At social parties we can observe a singer or guitar player make an effort to incorporate more and more of the room's population into his audience, until a point is reached where his singing officially exhausts the chamber, and the party is momentarily transformed into a performance.[15] At the same time, as a particular encounter comes to include a larger and larger number of persons, side involvements increasingly occur in which a subordinate byplay is sustained, sometimes furtively, its volume and character modulated to allow the main show to prevail unchallenged as the dominating one.

In mental hospitals there is a special kind of "symptomatic" behavior that takes recognition of how the situation as a whole can be "talked to." Many patients talk to someone, present or not, in a voice loud enough for everyone in the situation to hear and be somewhat distracted. But those on the ward implicitly distinguish this kind of impropriety from that which occurs when a patient "addresses the situation," haranguing everyone present in a tone and direction of voice that suggests he is purposedly breaching the barriers designed to render clusters of talkers and game players safe in their own focused interactions. (Interestingly, although the actual volume of sound may be greater in the case of a patient insufficiently modulating his contribution to a private conversation than in the case of a patient "addressing the situation," it is the latter that is likely to cause the greater disturbance.)[16]

Notes

1. Dickens, Charles, *American Notes* (Greenwich, Conn.: Premier Americana, Fawcett Publications, 1961), pp. 136–137.
2. *The Presentation of Self* (Garden City, New York: Anchor Books, 1957), pp. 119–120.
3. Kuper, L., "Blueprint for Living Together," in L. Kuper (ed.), *Living in Towns* (London: The Cresset Press, 1953), p. 14.
4. Here I do not want to overstress rational intent in situational behavior. An individual is supposed to be entirely in or entirely

out of an encounter. But even the individual who wants to follow this rule cannot completely control the expressed direction of his attention. If his attention is attracted to an accessible encounter, then his attempt to conceal the fact is likely to be visible both to those with whom he ought to be participating and to those whom he ought to be disattending.

5. Sansom, William, *The Face of Innocence* (New York: Harcourt Brace Jovanovitch, 1951), p. 12.

6. Davis, F., "The Cabdriver and His Fare: Facets of a Fleeting Relationship," *American Journal of Sociology* 65, (1959):160.

7. Similarly, in a three-person engagement, when a talker interrupts his talk to answer the phone, the two remaining persons may attempt a quiet, and often very limp, conversation.

8. In Britain, it is my impression that where one of the units present is of "good" speech, that is, received pronunciation, then it is this group that is likely to talk openly, as if the others could easily offer civil inattention and could easily stop their own conversation. This is one of the ways in which a visitor to Britain is struck by the startling vulgarity (according to American standards) of the British upper middle class.

9. Anon., *The Canons of Good Breeding* (Philadelphia: Lee and Blanchard, 1839), p. 68.

10. The term "individual distance" was apparently introduced by the ethologist Hediger to describe the tendency of birds on a fence or railing to stay a particular distance from each other, the distance apparently varying with the species. He also employs the term "flight distance" to refer to the closeness with which an animal of a given species can be approached before taking flight. See H. Hediger, *Studies of the Psychology and Behavior of Captive Animals in Zoos and Circuses* (London: Buttersworth Scientific Publications, 1955), pp. 40 ff. and 66. An interesting application of these and other ethological concepts may be found in R. Sommer, "Studies in Personal Space," *Sociometry* 22, (1959):247–260.

11. In a useful paper, "The Anthropology of Manners," *Scientific American* (April 1955):84–90, E. T. Hall cautions against cross-cultural generalizations on the matter of spacing:

In the U.S. we distribute ourselves more evenly than many other people. We have strong feelings about touching and being crowded; in a streetcar, bus or elevator we draw ourselves in. Toward a person who relaxes and lets himself come into full contact with others in a crowded place we usually feel reactions that could not be printed on this page. It takes years for us to train our children not to crowd and lean on us. . . .

In Latin America, where touching is more common and the basic units of space seem to be smaller, the wide automobiles made in the U.S. pose problems. People don't know where to sit.

12. A useful ethological analysis of types of mutual physical distance is provided by J. H. Crook, "The Basis of Flock Organisation in Birds," in W. H. Thorpe and O. L. Zangwill (eds.), *Current Problems in Animal Behaviour* (Cambridge: Cambridge University Press, 1961), pp. 138 ff.
13. For example, J. E. Neale, *The Elizabethan House of Commons* (New Haven, Conn.: Yale University Press, 1950), pp. 24–26.
14. Ponsonby, Sir Frederick, *Recollections of Three Reigns* (New York: Dutton, 1952), p. 261.
15. I am here indebted to an unpublished paper by Robert Martinson on the transformation of informal engagements into performances.
16. Attacks on the situation should be compared with the attacks on encounters, previously mentioned, which children, mental patients, and other communication delinquents perform. Many middle-class parents in our society have experineced times when their child, forbidden to interrupt or even to enter a room where adults are talking, stealthily stalks the situation in self-conscious mimicry of stealthiness and stalking, resulting in much more disturbance to the gathering than his mere presence might entail.

16

TURN-TAKING IN CONVERSATIONS

John M. Wiemann and Mark L. Knapp

The mechanisms by which people take turns speaking in a conversation are both spoken and nonverbal, open and subconscious.

A child of five enters a room where his mother and another woman are talking. The child tugs on his mother's skirt for attention and, without waiting for her to respond, he begins talking to her. The mother becomes irritated and scolds the child for interrupting while she is talking.

Five college students are sitting in a dorm room talking. One of the five students has been talking for about ten minutes when another member of the group says, "Jim, why don't you shut up! I can't get a word in edgewise."

In each of the preceding stories, the central figure is guilty of

Reprinted with permission from "Turn-Taking in Conversations" by John M. Wiemann and Mark L. Knapp in the *Journal of Communication*, 25 (1975):75–92. © 1975 by The Annenberg School of Communications.

violating a communicative norm in our culture. And, in each case, the response was in the form of a reprimand. At least two explanations account for the reprimands given to the central figures in the stories: (a) they did not provide for a smooth transition of the speaking turn from one person to the next, and (b) they forced a definition of the situation that the other interactants present were not willing to accept. The nature of this conversational "turn-taking" or "floor apportionment" will be the focus of this essay.

The phenomenon by which one interactant stops talking and another starts in a smooth, synchronized manner is considered the most salient feature of face-to-face conversation by some researchers (12, 19, 20). The fact that we usually make judgments about people based on the *way* they interact argues that the structure of a conversation—the way it "comes off"—is at least as important as the content.

Goffman (10) recognized that when two or more people come together to interact, they are making a symbolic commitment to one another to respect the role that each chooses to play. One role that is basic to almost all other roles that an interactant can present is the role of human being, one worthy and deserving of consideration and respect.

In order to help insure that one receives the respect that each person considers his due, most cultures have developed rather elaborate (in unelaborated) rules[1] to govern what should and should not be said and done in interactions. From this perspective, Goffman defines a rule as a "guide for action, recommended not because it is pleasant, cheap, or effective, but because it is suitable or just" (11, p. 48).

Unlike other societal rules (e.g., criminal laws), interaction rules are seldom specified, and consequently the actions they govern are usually carried out unthinkingly. For the most part, it is only when a rule is broken that the interactants become aware that something is amiss with the interaction, and attention is then usually directed away from the content of the conversation and toward putting the interaction back on the right track (11). Thus, in the earlier examples, the interactants interrupted their partners to remind the offenders of two existing rules: (a) one person speaks at a time, and (b) speaker-changes should reoccur (20). One result of the sanctioning action might have been embarrassment for *all* present—a culturally undesirable state of affairs and a rule violation in its own right.

This leads to an important aspect of rule-governed interaction behavior: *the manner in which specific rules are employed provides us with information about the nature of the relationship between the interactants*. This seems to underline the importance of interaction rules: they directly impinge on each interactant's presented self. For example, interruptions or inattention may convey disrespect and "must be avoided unless the implied disrespect is an accepted part of the relationship" (11, p. 36).

Interaction rules can be considered from the perspective of communication theory. Communication consists of manipulating symbols; if these symbols are to be understood as intended, rules must exist for their encoding and decoding. Cushman and Whiting differentiate between two types of rules that are necessary if an interaction is to come off successfully: "(1) those which specify the action's content (its meaning, what it is to count as) and (2) those which specify the procedures appropriate to carrying out the action" (14, p. 217).

Included in Cushman and Whiting's procedural rules category are the interaction rules that have been discussed above. When a rule (or symbol by which a rule is implemented) has gained wide acceptance by a particular culture, it can be said that that rule (symbol) has achieved "standardized usage." In other words, certain situations or symbols have particular meanings and require particular responses. If an individual fails to respond correctly to a situation or symbol (because the individual either does not know the appropriate rules to govern his response or does not wish to respond in the appropriate fashion), that person is alienating him or herself from those present.[2]

The way interaction is regulated in an elementary school classroom is an example of what we have been discussing. When children enter first grade, they are often told they must raise their hands before speaking. The rule is: "You may not speak unless the teacher gives you permission." The symbol by which the rule is implemented—by which permission is requested and gained—is the upraised hand. New students may be given some amount of time in which to learn the rule. Note that learning the rule and learning the symbol to implement the rule are, for all practical purposes, one and the same thing. During the learning period, violations of the rule are corrected, but tolerated. The assumption is that the children are not yet part of the school-culture. After a certain period, the teacher decides that all of the first graders have had enough time to become acculturated—that is, they have had enough time to learn the rules. Now when the hand-raising is violated, the children are likely to be punished; disrespect and disregard for the school-culture is assumed.

This rather ordinary example illustrates that people often rely on conformity to interaction rules—particularly turn-taking rules—

for information about an individual's relationship with or orientation —towards a group or individual. Speier states this same point more strongly:

> *Cultural competence in using conversational procedures in social interaction not only displays adequate social membership among participants in the culture, but more deeply*, it provides a procedural basis for the ongoing organization of that culture *when members confront and deal with one another daily* (19, p. 398, emphasis in original).

The conversational procedures Speier is concerned with are the turn-taking phenomena.

In order to communicate successfully, an interactant must understand and subscribe to the interaction rules of his culture. The violation of interaction rules provides us with information about an individual's orientation toward his or her fellow interactants.

> *Our specific topic is the process of deciding who will speak and who will listen in an interaction.*

With the exception of people in classrooms or those attending formal meetings, individuals usually devote little conscious time to deciding who will speak. In our culture we have no formal system for determining who will speak at "informal" gatherings. In other words, there is no cultural norm that states, for example, that when adults are sitting around the dinner table, the person sitting on the north side of the table will speak first and thereafter the speaking turn will rotate in a clockwise direction.

Yet we often evaluate our interactions in terms of the allocation of speaking roles. A person who dominates a conversation is often judged a "boor" (particularly if the "judge"—the other interactant —had something to say and did not get the opportunity). The person who constantly interrupts is judged "rude." Thus, it may be embarrassing and rude to tell the boor to give someone else a chance to speak.

In spite of this seeming paradox, there are numerous encounters in which the need to interrupt someone else to get the floor does not confront us. If interactants need not resort to violence—either verbal or physical—to get the floor, how do they decide who will speak and who will listen? In other words, how are the numerous interaction rules governing the respect of the speaker implemented?

The behavior by which an exchange of speaking turns is accomplished will be referred to here as the turn-taking mechanism.

While a number of studies have dealt with various behaviors which may be part of the turn-taking mechanism, only Duncan (6, 7, 8) has dealt directly with it in its entirety. Taking an inductive approach, Duncan observed interactions, and then described the behavior that accompanied speaking-role changes.[4]

Duncan (7, 8) posits three rules operating during successful exchanges of the speaking turn: (1) turn-yieding cues, which are used by speakers to signal that they are concluding their remarks and that the auditors can take the floor; (2) suppression of speaking-turn claims, which are exhibited by speakers in conjunction with turn-yielding cues, when they intend to maintain their speaking turn; and (3) back channel cues, which are displayed by the auditors to indicate that they do not wish the floor, even though the speaker is displaying yielding cues.

• *Turn-yielding.* The rule for turn-yielding states that the auditor may take his speaking turn when the speaker emits any one of a number of verbal or nonverbal turn-yielding cues. The display of a turn-yielding cue does not require the auditor to take the floor; he may remain silent or reinforce the speaker with a back channel cue. The absence of simultaneous turns (i.e., both participants in the conversation claiming the speaking turn at the same time) during the exchange of speaking roles is considered a successful exchange. If the turn-taking mechanism is operating properly, the auditor will take his turn in response to a turn-yielding cue emitted by the speaker, and the speaker will immediately yield his turn.

Duncan (8) defines a turn-yielding signal as the display of at least one of a set of cues (see Table 1) either singly or in clusters. He notes that, while some of the cues may be displayed at any time during the conversation, they are only considered part of the turn-taking mechanism if they occur at the end of a phonemic clause. Others have found, however, that the change in frequency of cues over a speaking turn or the intensity of cue display may be the determining factor in how a behavior is interpreted by the other interactant (cf. 21).

• *Suppression of speaking-turn claims.* This cue serves to maintain the turn for the speaker by counteracting any turn-yielding cues emitted simultaneously. It consists of "one or both of the speaker's hands being engaged in gesticulation" (8, p. 38). Self- and object-adaptors[5] do not function as claim suppressors.

• *Back channel cues.* These cues, exhibited by the auditor, are related to various speaker signals, either within-turn signals (8) or turn-yielding cues. In relation to turn-yielding cues, they serve to signal the speaker that the auditor does not wish to take the speaking role (cf. 22).

• *Turn-requesting.* Personal experience tells us that participants in a conversation are not at the mercy of the speaker, in spite of the interaction rules. To account for this, Wiemann (21) proposed that a turn-requesting rule exists, and that auditors employ such a rule to let the speaker know that they want the floor without violating the respect due the speaker because he or she is the speaker.

Turn-requesting consists of the display of one or more of a number of verbal or nonverbal cues (cf. Table 1) by the author. If the turn-taking mechanism is functioning correctly, the speaker should relinquish the speaking role upon completion of the thought unit he or she is communicating at the time the request is made.

Wiemann (21) took a more deductive approach than Duncan in studying the floor yielding and requesting aspects of the turn-taking mechanism. In light of the concept of "standardized usage" mentioned earlier, he asked if (in a given homogeneous group of subjects) certain verbal and nonverbal behaviors would manifest themselves in such a way that they might be interpreted to be operating as turn-taking cues.

Subjects were 18 Purdue University students, each paired with an acquaintance such that there were three all-male dyads, three all-female dyads, and three dyads composed of one male and one female.

Dyads were videototaped while they discussed a topic suggested by them and approved by the researcher. A random sample of 72 interaction sequences or exchanges was drawn from the tapes and analyzed twice, once for each subject as a speaker and once for each subject as the auditor.

A review of literature, observation in a number of different settings, and introspection led to the construction of two analysis systems, one for verbal behavior and one for nonverbal behavior (cf. Table 2).

The verbal behaviors that played a role in turn-yielding were (in order of incidence): completions, interrogative requests, and buffers.

The only nonverbal behavior that seemed to play a role in turn-yielding was other-directed gaze. An analysis of the time spent in other-directed gazes indicated that speakers steadily increased the amount of time spent looking at the auditor as their speaking turn approached completion. This phenomenon was also

Table 1 TURN-TAKING CUES AND INVESTIGATORS

	INVESTIGATORS			
CUES	DUNCAN (6, 7, 8)	WIEMANN (21)	KENDON (13, 14, 15)	SPEIER (19, 20)
TURN-YIELDING				
Intonation[a]	yes			
Drawl	yes			
Buffers[b]	called "socio-centric sequences"	yes		
Pitch/loudness	yes			
Sentence completions	yes	yes		yes
Interrogatives[b]	yes	yes		
Gesticulations[b]	yes	yes	yes	
Auditor-directed gaze[b]	yes	yes	yes	
Silence	yes	yes	yes	
TURN-REQUESTING				
Speaker-directed gaze[b]		yes	yes	
Reinforcers[b]		yes		
Head nods[b]		yes		
Forward lean[b]		yes		
Buffers		yes		
Interruption[b]		yes		yes
Simultaneous talking[b]	yes, but not as a requesting cue			yes, but not as a requesting cue
Stutter starts[b]		yes		
BACK CHANNEL				
Reinforcers	yes	yes		
Sentence completion by auditor	yes	yes		Called "tying procedures"
Request for clarification	yes	considered a reinforcer		
Head nods and Shakes	yes			

ADDITIONAL POSSIBLE TURN-TAKING BEHAVIORS (either not studied or studied inconclusively)

Up-raised index finger; deep inspiration of breath accompanied by straightening posture; backward lean and other relaxation cues; smiles; contain self-adaptors, particularly those which might be considered "preening"

a. The use of any pitch level-terminal juncture combination other than 2 2 21 at the end of a phonemic clause.
b. Operationalized in Table 2.

	INVESTIGATORS			JAFFE &	
SCHEGLOFF (18)	SCHEFLEN (17)	KNAPP ET AL. (15)	DITMANN (5)	FELDSTEIN (12)	YNGVE (22)

under "summons sequences"

"summons sequences"

				yes	yes, but says it plays role
		yes			
yes		yes, but in terms of ending interaction	yes		
					yes
					yes

Table 2 BEHAVIORAL ANALYSIS CATEGORIES FOR THE TURN-TAKING MECHANISM

NONVERBAL	VERBAL
1. Other-directed gazes. The amount of time spent looking at the facial area around the eyes of the other person.	1. Interrogative request. A question specifically directed to the other dyad member.
2. Smiles. A positive facial expression marked by upturned corners of the mouth (as opposed to a straight or downturned mouth)	2. Completion. The completion of a declarative "statement" with no attempt being made by the speaker to continue.
3. Reclining angle. When that plane defined by a line from the communicator's shoulders to his hips is away from the vertical plane, such that the communicator is leaning backward to some degree.	3. Buffers. Short words or phrases which are "content-free," more or less stereo-typical, and which either precede or follow substantive statements (e.g., "but uh," "you know," "or something," "um," "well," and "uh-well").
4. Forward-leaning angle. When that plane defined by a line from the communicator's shoulders to his hips is away from the vertical plane, such that the communicator is bending forward at the waist.	4. Interruption. The attempt to assume the speaking role before it has been relinquished by the current speaker.
5. Gesticulations. Hand and arm movements (excluding self-manipulations), including side-to-side, forward-back, and up-and-down movements (e.g., an up-raised and pointed index finger).	5. Simultaneous talking. Speaking by both interactants at the same time. (This includes simultaneous turns, where both speakers attempt to hold the floor at the same time.)
6. Head nods. Cyclical up-and-down movements of the head.	6. Stutter starts. Short words (including nonfluencies) or phrases repeated with increasing frequency by one interactant while the other interactant holds the speaking role (e.g., "I . . . I . . . I . . . I think we should vote now.")
	7. Reinforcers. Words that provide feedback to the speaker, but do not necessarily attempt to gain the speaking role for the interactant emitting them. Short questions asking for clarification are coded in this category. (Examples include: "Yeah," "yes," and "um-hm.")

noted by Kendon (13). Other nonverbal behaviors observed, including the termination gestures specified by Duncan (8), seemed to play little or no role in the turn-yielding of these subjects.

Verbal turn-requesting behavior included (again, in order of occurrence): simultaneous talking, buffers, reinforcers, interrogative requests, and stutter starts.

Nonverbal turn-requesting behavior included other-directed gazes and head nods. While the other nonverbal behaviors included in the study were emitted by the auditors, they seemed to play little or no role in turn-requesting for these subjects.

In the Weimann study, the two verbal behaviors that seemed to play a significant role in the turn-yielding mechanism were completions and interrogative requests. Both of these behaviors can be considered "natural" endings to utterances; the speaker is allowed to complete the utterance he or she is engaged in before the other interactant assumes the floor. In fact, the speaker was allowed to come to a "natural" conclusion in 67 of the 72 interaction episodes studied—93 percent of the time.

There is little need to discuss the effectiveness of the interrogative "statement" in causing a change in the speaking role. One of our cultural norms seems to be that we answer questions that are asked of us (18).

The tendency to effect a change in the speaking turn by ending an utterance with a declarative "statement" is not as easily explained. The declarative statement does not have the same "demand" characteristics as either an interrogative or an imperative statement. Schegloff (18), however, contends that certain declaratives—which he calls summonses—do possess the same demand characteristics as questions.

One possible explanation for the high incidence of "completion" endings is that the silence of the speaker at the end of an utterance (failure to continue speaking) operates as a yielding strategy. Jaffe and Feldstein (12) have systematically investigated silence or length of pauses as part of the turn-taking mechanism. They report that the longer the silence during a conversation, the more likely it is that a change in speaker will take place. Further, they found that pacing depends on silences and that "the pacing of conversational interaction is (a) characteristic of the speakers involved, (b) stable within any conversation, and (c) consistent from one conversation to the next for the same two speakers" (p. 116).

Thus, it seems probable that two acquaintances would develop a rhythm of exchange of turns; because of their experiences interacting with each other, they would learn each other's style and could "predict" when each would stop talking. Jaffe and Feldstein's findings are not supported by Yngve (22), who in a preliminary report of his research on turn-taking states that silence alone does not play a major role in speaker switches.

Buffers apparently had little to do with turn-yielding for Wiemann's informed dyads. Speakers seemed to emit buffers in attempts either to hold the floor while planning their next statements or to elicit feedback from the auditor without yielding the floor (i.e., eliciting head nods or reinforcers for continuing to talk). "She's gonna wear, *you know*, that low-cut dress . . ." is an example of this use of buffers. The interactant uttering this statement was responding to a question and continued the description of the wardrobe for several more seconds. The purpose of the "you know" was clearly *not* to yield the floor.

The fact that, in our culture, auditors pay respect to the speaker simply because he is the speaker has been discussed at length. The high frequency of "natural" completions and the use of occasional buffers by the speakers seems to indicate that speakers feel a certain responsibility to their auditors—almost as if they had a "the show must go on" attitude toward the speaking turn. This is not to deny that speakers talk for a variety of other reasons as well. They do, however, seem to feel a need to fill the silence. If this tentative proposal has some validity, it helps to explain the general lack of verbal yielding behavior. Speakers feel it is their "duty" to keep the interaction alive; if auditors want to talk, then they must let the speakers know that they are ready to assume responsibility for the interaction.

A competing explanation for the reluctance to yield the floor is the demand characteristic of the experimental situation. The students who served as subjects might have felt they had to keep the conversation going or the "experiment" would fail.

Since the nonverbal channel is often more subtle than the verbal, speakers can be expected to make more use of it. Probably the most frequently occurring nonverbal yielding behavior is auditor-directed gazes. The percentage of time spent by the speaker looking at the face of the auditor increases steadily as the speaking turn approaches finality from 61 percent in the first third of the interaction episode to 83 percent in the final third.[6] Conversely, the percentage of time the auditor spends looking at the speaker increases from the first third to the second third of the interaction episode, and then drops off in the final third (see Figure 1).

As the speaker comes to the end of an utterance, he or she looks at the auditor in search of feedback. If this feedback is in the

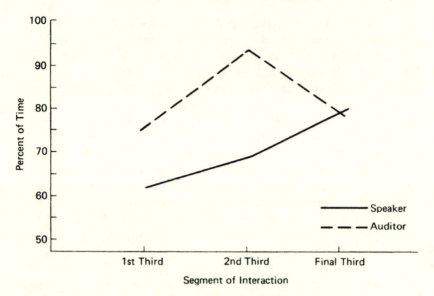

Figure 1   Percentage of time spent in other-directed gazes.

form of a verbal response, then the speaking role is likely to be exchanged. The looking away by the auditor seems to be a response to the speaker—acknowledging the turn-yielding cue and the acceptance of the speaking turn.

It seems that other-directed gazes function more as a turn-yielding device than as a turn-requesting device, but they can function as both. It is possible that there must be mutual gaze at, or very near, the point where the speaking roles are exchanged. That is, for other-directed gaze to be successful as a turn-taking strategy, the two interactants must have eye contact at or near the exchange point. The increasing percentage of time the speaker spends in auditor-directed gazes as the episode draws to an end seems to indicate that the speaker is making himself more available for the bit of eye-contact that will aid in the exchange of the speaking turn.

The role that gesticulations play in the turn-taking mechanism is not entirely clear. Duncan (6, 7, 8) reports that his subjects used gesticulations as turn-yielding signals. On the other hand, Wiemann (21) found a very low incidence of gesticulations—too low to draw any meaningful conclusions. A number of factors may account for low incidence of gesticulations in some situations. The setting may encourage interactants to tone down their behaviors—not just gesticulations, but all overt behaviors. Also, the topic may or may not encourage excited or animated behavior. For example, conversations concerned with describing an unknown event to an auditor or one that is particularly salient to either party may encourage more animated behavior.

The role that shifts of posture play in the turn-taking mechanism is unclear. The available data—which are unconvincing—suggest that it plays no role at all. However, Kendon (14, 15) and our own natural-state observations argue this interpretation. People do not really sit still in their seats for an appreciable length of time. Auditors may be reclining for a time and then, as they prepare to take the speaking role, move to an upright position or even to a forward-leaning position. Likewise, speakers at times, "punctuate" their yielding of the floor by leaning back in their chairs as they finish their utterances.

Situational variables may influence the way postural shifts are used as turn-taking cues. Gross postural shifts may be unnecessarily harsh or obvious forms of conversation regulation in some situations. Interactants who know each other may find the more subtle turn-taking cues (head nods, other-directed gazes, buffers) sufficient to effect changes in the speaking turn.

Auditors seem to make more use of the verbal channel in turn-taking than do speakers. This is probably true, in part, because the speakers are using the verbal channel to convey the substance of their message. Some form of verbal behavior accompanied 49 percent of the exchanges of the speaking turn in the Wiemann study. That is, auditors engaged in some form of talking immediately prior to assuming the speaking turn.[7]

The generalized requesting cue which appeared most frequently was simultaneous talking. Because simultaneous talking can take a variety of forms (buffing, reinforcing, etc.), it can serve a variety of purposes in the conversation, not all of which have to do with the turn-taking mechanism. However, the high percentage of simultaneous talking immediately before exchanges of speaking roles indicates that people use it as a requesting strategy.

Buffers and reinforcers are frequently-used turn-requesting strategies. Buffers generally constitute a clear attempt by the auditor to get the floor. Occasionally, the buffers are uttered while the speaker is talking; but more often they are uttered while the speaker is silent, either during a pause or after the speaker has clearly ended his utterance. In the latter case, they seem to be a signal by the auditor that he is ready to talk; the buffers allow the other interactant time to attend to the new speaker before he begins his "message." The use of buffers by the auditor at this point may also constitute a signal to the speaker that he has accepted the speaker's offer of the floor.

The role of reinforcers in turn-requesting differs from that of buffers. While these two phenomena are similar, reinforcers have usually been considered a form of encouragement for the speaker to continue talking (cf. 6, 7, 8). However, the subjects in this study seemed to use reinforcers in order to effect a "request" for the floor as often as they used them to encourage the speaker to continue talking. Knapp et al (16) speculate that reinforcers are used in this way when one interactant wants to get the floor or when "we interact with verbose persons, where conversational 'openings' are difficult to find." In instances such as these, the reinforcers may be used to encourage the speaker to "hurry up and get finished" so the auditor can assume the speaking role.

The behavior of the auditor that accompanies the utterance of the reinforcer, or the behavior of the speaker to which the reinforcer is a response, probably determines how the speaker interprets the reinforcer. If the utterance of the reinforcer is accompanied by a postural shift (e.g., a move from a reclining to an upright position), prolonged eye contact, or rapidly repeated and demonstrative head nods, the reinforcer is more likely interpreted as a request for the floor. Reinforcers aso seem to have the force of a request when they are uttered while the speaker is talking (rather than during a pause) or if they are uttered while the speaker is not looking at the auditor. On the other hand, if the speaker has somehow requested feedback from the auditor (e.g., by the use of a buffer like "you know"); if the reinforcer comes during a pause by the speaker; or if it is delivered in a slow, thoughtful manner, the speaker seems to interpret it as encouragement to continue talking. It may be that a dramatic increase on an "activity dimension" differentiates between turn request and back channel cues.

At times, an utterance seems to function both as a reinforcer and as a buffer.

For example, after a speaker makes a "statement" (or during the speaker's utterance), the other interactant might use a "hybrid" reinforcer-buffer to effect a change in the speaking role. An example of this type of expression is "yeah, well." The auditor is giving the speaker a strong indication that he (the auditor) wants the floor. The use of the buffer seems to be an attempt to soften the impact of the request (particularly if it is an interruption) and to maintain the integrity of the interaction. The use of "well" "but" might not soften the request for the floor at all. Such a a requesting strategy often causes speakers to try harder not to let the requester "in" because they know disagreement is coming. It is a clear signal, but not necessarily subtle, soft, or effective.

More than any of the other verbal behaviors mentioned here, buffers and reinforcers seem to bind the interactants together. Not only do they serve as attention signals and turn-taking signals, but reinforcers and buffers also provide the auditor a means of participating in the conversation in an overt, verbal manner even when he or she doesn't have the floor. Using these two behaviors as a means of participation, the auditor does not violate the "don't interrupt the speaker" norm; and, therefore, this form of participation is acceptable in our culture.

Interrogative requests, when used by the auditor, seem to serve a function similar to those served by reinforcers. That is, interrogative requests are in the back channel and encourage the speaker to continue by asking for explanation or clarification. They are included here as part of turn-requesting behavior because, in some instances, the auditors append *their* answer to the question asked; thus, they allow the auditor to briefly hold the floor without actually taking the speaking turn. For example, one interactant described to his partner a Purdue basketball game he had seen the night before. He said, in part, ". . . the guards played well last night." Before he finished the utterance, the auditor said, "You mean Parkinson? He's great." The speaker continued speaking "over" the auditor's comment (he recognized the comment with a head nod); he did not slow down but he did go on to elaborate on Parkinson's play. While this may have been the direction the conversation would have taken anyway, it seems that the auditor's comment about Parkinson encouraged the speaker to talk about Parkinson. This interaction episode ended with an exchange of the speaking turn a few "statements" later when the speaker asked the auditor what he thought about Parkinson.

Stutter-starts appear to be similar to buffers as far as the role they play in turn-requesting. Stuttering-starts may constitute more of a demand for the floor than do buffers, however. They are usually emitted by the auditor only after the speaker has had the floor for some time (15 to 20 seconds) or when the speaker pauses longer than usual. This could be because the speaker is not attending to the more subtle requesting cues of the auditor or because he inadvertently gives a turn-yielding cue and then continues to talk—"faking out" the auditor, so to speak.

The role speaker-directed gazes play in turn-taking has already been discussed. It seems worth repeating that mutual gaze is necessary if this is to serve as a turn-taking strategy.

Head nodding appears to play a major role in turn-requesting, while having little or no significance in turn-yielding. Speakers do not systematically increase the amount of nodding as the episode progresses. On the other hand, there is a dramatic increase in nodding by the auditor.

The rapidity of the head nods and whether or not they are accompanied by any verbal behavior seems to determine how speakers interpret them. Closely placed, successive nods, and nods that accompany short, rapid-fire reinforcers (e.g., "yeah, yeah") or buffers (e.g., "uh, uh"), constitute requests for the floor by the auditor. On the other hand, nods that serve as responses to a request for feedback from the speaker seem to be interpreted by the speaker as support for his maintaining the floor.

Both nodding and other-directed gazes appear to be important to the turn-taking mechanism because of the dual role they play. These behaviors indicate support for and interest in the other interactant when they are displayed by one member of the dyad. They also provide both the speaker and the auditor with a means of either yielding or requesting the floor. Their supportive nature "softens" the terms of the exchange. The nodding auditor is signaling the speaker his agreement and reinforcement at the same time the request is being made; the respect of the speaking role is maintained because, in effect, the auditor is letting the speaker know that there is no threat or disrespect intended by the takeover of the floor. In like manner, the speaker can use nodding and auditor-directed gazes to inform the auditor that he is looking for feedback and that he is receiving the auditor's messages. All this can be accomplished without interrupting the flow of the "conversation."

While primarily yielding cues, gesticulations may also be used by auditors to signal in a rather dramatic way their desire to get the floor. An example of this use of gesticulation is the pointed and raised index finger—usually accompanied by an open mouth, poised to speak, or other such behavior that is similar to school-trained hand-raising.

Other nonverbal cues not yet specifically studied, but whose co-occurrence with reinforcers might influence the interpretation of reinforcers, include a deep inspiration of breath immediately before the reinforcer is uttered and the holding open of the mouth for a brief period before the reinforcer is uttered (21).

As is the case with most exploratory work, the results of these investigations are more suggestive than conclusive. Some of the behaviors studied were used in the same ways consistently enough to warrant the tentative conclusion that they play a role in the turn-taking mechanism.

Many of the behaviors mentioned above are emitted simultaneously. In some instances, it appears that emission of two or more cues at the same time may determine the other interactant's interpretation of the cues. For example, a head nod by the auditor is interpreted as a back channel cue or reinforcer if displayed alone, but when the nod is accompanied by "yeah, but," it becomes a request for the floor. The appearance of multiple cues may also be related to the perceived urgency or strength of turn-yielding or turn-requesting. For example, when the auditor leans forward in his chair, raises and points his finger and says "yeah . . . yeah . . . yeah, yeah" while nodding his head, he is giving the speaker a very strong indication that he would like the floor.

Auditors displayed a wider variety of verbal and nonverbal behavior and display those behaviors more frequently than do speakers. A possible expanation for this was touched on earlier. Speakers may feel an obligation to keep the conversation going; it is their way of reciprocating the respect auditors show them (by not interrupting). This, in turn, might be one reason why auditors' respect is due the speaker. Any behavior by the speaker that might be interpreted as a unilateral move to end the encounter might be offensive (cf. 16). Turn-yielding, therefore, must be executed carefully. In normal conversation the bulk of the burden for initiating exchanges of the speaking turn—at least in terms of frequency and variety of cues displayed—falls to the auditors.

The line of thinking developed here suggests that a "grammar" of dyadic interaction exists. This is not to imply that there is any relationship between this grammar and that proposed for spoken languages. Rather, the term "grammar," as used here, implies the existence of a structure of interaction. By correctly applying the rules of this structure, interactants can accurately express their relationship to the other interactants without interrupting the flow of the content of the conversation.

Argyle (2, 3) has suggested that social competence can be studied much as motor skills are, with similar implications. If the components of "successful" interaction can be isolated, they can be analyzed and taught. Argyle lists four components of social competence: (1) perceptual sensitivity, (2) basic interaction skills, (3) rewardingness, and (4) poise. While all of these come into play even in something so elementary as negotiating the speaking turn, basic interaction skills seem to be at the heart of the matter: "To be socially competent it is necessary to be able to establish a smoothly meshing pattern of interaction with other people" (3, p. 68).

A competence paradigm may provide communication scholars with a theoretical framework for the study of interpersonal communication.

Turn-taking in conversations not only helps us apportion the floor, but also serves a symbolic function of helping the interactants to define their relationship. The way in which this ritual is managed by one interactant will affect the judgments made about him or her by the other interactant. Thus, research may show that it is the management of the small, unnoticed, ritualistic behaviors that has the greatest effect upon our attributions about others; it may be these behaviors that determine whether or not we are successful interactants.

Notes

[1] The term "rules" is used here in the descriptive, rather than prescriptive sense.

[2] Goffman (11, pp. 113–136) treats this type of alienation in great detail.

[3] This is not the case in all cultures, however. Albert (1), for example, reports that the Barundi of Africa do have such a formal system. When in a conversational gathering, the person from the highest caste (or status) will speak first, followed by the person from the second highest caste, etc., until everyone present has had a speaking turn. Then the interactants repeat this sequence of speakers until the interaction is terminated.

[4] The data consist of the first 19 minutes of two dyadic conversations one between a therapist and his patient and the other between the same therapist and one of his colleagues.

[5] Ekman and Friesen (9) discuss self- and object-adaptors in detail. Generally adaptors consist of manipulation of either the self (i.e., scratching) or personal objects (e.g., rearranging one's clothes or handling a pipe).

[6] A review of the video tapes of subjects conversing indicated that changes in the duration of some nonverbal behaviors might present a more accurate picture of the role these behaviors play in the turn-taking mechanism than did the frequency counts originally computed. Therefore, the duration of other-directed gazes, smiles, reclining angle, and forward-leaning angle was calculated for each interaction segment (i.e., for each person during any one speaking turn). In order to make interaction segments of different lengths comparable, they were divided

into thirds. Thus, what happened in the beginning of one interaction segment in the first third, could be compared with all other segments.

[7] A person is considered to "have the floor" when, through tacit, but mutual agreement of those participating in the interaction, he has the "right" to speak uninterrupted. This agreement is inferred from some signal by one of the other participants or by their attentive silence. An interactant's turn begins when his speech becomes audible and ends when another interactant takes over the floor.

References

1. Albert, E. M. "Cultural Patterning in Speech Behavior." In J. J. Gumperz and D. Hymes (eds.), *Directions in Sociolinguistics* (New York: Holt, Rinehart and Winston, 1972).

2. Argyle, M. *Social Interaction* (Chicago: Aldine Atherton, 1969).

3. Argyle, M. *The Psychology of Interpersonal Behaviour*, 2d ed. (Baltimore: Penguin, 1972).

4. Cushman, D., and Whiting, G. "An Approach to Communication Theory: Toward Consensus on Rules." *Journal of Communication* 22, (1972):217–238.

5. Dittman, A. T. "Developmental Factors in Conversational Behavior." *Journal of Communication* 22, (1972):404–423.

6. Duncan, S. "Towards a Grammar for Floor Apportionment: A System Approach to Face-to-Face Interaction." In *Proceedings of the Second Annual Environmental Design Research Association Conference*. Philadelphia: Environmental Design Research Association, 1970.

7. Duncan, S. "Some Signals and Rules for Taking Speaking Turns in Conversations." *Journal of Personality and Social Psychology* 23, (1972):283–292.

8. Duncan, S. "Toward a Grammar for Dyadic Conversation." *Semiotica* 9, (1973):29–64.

9. Ekman, P., and Friesen, W. V. "The Repertoire of Nonverbal Behavior: Categories, Origins, Usage, and Coding." *Semiotica* 1, (1969):49–98.

10. Goffman, E. *The Presentation of Self in Everyday Life* (Garden City, N.Y.: Doubleday Anchor, 1959).

11. Goffman, E. *Interaction Ritual* (Garden City, N.Y.: Doubleday Anchor, 1967).

12. Jaffe, J., and Feldstein, S. *Rhythms of Dialogue* (New York: Academic Press, 1970).

13. Kendon, A. "Some Functions of Gaze-Direction in Social Interaction." *Acta Psychologica* 26, (1967):22–63.

14. Kendon, A. "Movement Coordination in Social Interaction: Some Examples Described." *Acta Psychologica* **32**, (1970): 101–125.
15. Kendon, A. "Some Relationships between Body Motion and Speech: An Analysis of an Example." In A. W. Siegman and B. Pope (eds.), *Studies in Dyadic Communication* (Elmsford, N.Y.: Pergamon Press, 1972).
16. Knapp, M. L., Hart, R. P., Friedrich, G. W., and Shulman, G. M. "The Rhetoric of Goodbye: Verbal and Nonverbal Correlates of Human Leave-Taking." *Speech Monographs* **40**, (1973):182–198.
17. Scheflen, A. E. "The Significance of Posture in Communication Systems." *Psychiatry* **17**, (1964):316–331.
18. Schegloff, E. A. "Sequencing in Conversational Openings." In J. J. Gumperz and D. Hymes (eds.), *Directions in Sociolinguistics* (New York: Holt, Rinehart and Winston, 1972).
19. Speier, M. *How to Observe Face-to-Face Communication: A Sociological Introduction* (Pacific Palisades, Calif.: Goodyear, 1973).
20. Speier, M. "Some Conversational Problems for Interactional Analysis." In D. Sudnow (ed.), *Studies in Social Interaction* (New York: Free Press, 1972).
21. Wiemann, J. M. "An Exploratory Study of Turn-Taking in Conversations: Verbal and Nonverbal Behavior." Unpublished M.S. thesis, Purdue University, 1973.
22. Yngve, V. H. "On Getting a Word in Edgewise." In M. A. Campbell, et al. (eds.), *Papers from the Sixth Regional Meeting, Chicago Linguistics Society* (Chicago: Department of Linguistics, University of Chicago, 1970).

17

VISUAL BEHAVIOR IN SOCIAL INTERACTION

Phoebe C. Ellsworth and Linda M. Ludwig

Abstract

Visual behavior appears to provide information at several different communicational levels in social interaction. As a dependent variable, it has been used to measure stable individual and group differences, the regulation of the flow of conversation, and the search for feedback in an interaction. As an independent variable, it has been shown to influence emotional responses and cognitive attributions. Research efforts to specify and understand the functioning of visual behavior at each level are reviewed. An example of a multi-level approach to an area is provided by a survey of the research on visual behavior in relation to interpersonal attraction and involvement. Finally, some speculations about future questions and concerns are presented.

Reprinted by permission of the International Communication Association from "Visual Behavior in Social Interaction" by Phoebe C. Ellsworth and Linda M. Ludwig in *Journal of Communication* 22:4 (1972):375–403.

The study of visual behavior in social interaction (or "eye contact," or "gaze direction," or "visual interaction") has become increasingly popular during the last decade; interest is high, articles are numerous, and the topic is clearly eligible for review. The difficulty in writing such a review is that visual behavior is not properly a "topic" at all. Different investigators have been concerned with different kinds of psychological events and processes, and their methods have varied accordingly. Nor is the diversity simply a function of different points or view; by this time it is apparent that visual behavior can convey several different kinds of information, and can serve several different functions in social interaction.

Most of the research on visual behavior in humans has been studied as a consistent, and sometimes potentially informative attribute of individuals, gender, and personality. Insofar as this research has been concerned with the implications of the visual behavior, it has focused on information potentially available to an outside observer (e.g., a therapist), and has so far set aside the question of whether the same (or different) information is available to other naive interactants. Second, visual behavior like vocal intonation, has been studied as one of the major *regulators* of the flow of conversation, of the sequencing and pacing of speech. Unless an interactant deviates markedly from the normal regulatory patterns, this type of visual behavior probably does not convey much higher-level psychological information about the individuals involved or their relationship, either to outside observers or to the participants themselves. Third, looking for information and shutting out information have been taken to be important determinants of gaze direction—reminding us that one of the basic complications of research on visual behavior is that the eyes not only send information, but are one of the primary systems for collecting it.

These three areas of research have been approached by similar methods: eye contact is typically a variable which is *measured*, either as a response to a manipulated independent variable, or as one of a set of measured variables which are then correlated. Other research has been concerned with higher-level interactive functions of visual behavior within the relationship, and thus has typically varied the visual behavior of one interactant and observed its effect on the other. Most broadly conceived, these studies involve the *influence* of one member's visual behavior on the behavior of another member. The behavior influenced can be verbal or nonverbal, and the manipulated visual behavior can be conceived as a stimulus or as a reinforcer. When dealing with questions of influence, it is also possible to ask how the visual behavior of one member affects the *cognitions* of the other member: what does he think about the person looking; what sorts of attributions does he make? Finally, it is possible to study the communicative aspects of visual behavior, where "communication" implies that the sender's visual signal is intentional, and the receiver's interpretation assumes that intentionality. This is an area which has not yet been researched successfully, probably largely due to the difficulty of dealing with intentionality as a variable in psychological research.

Thus research on visual behavior involves a series of questions at different levels of communication: 1) What does the behavior tell a trained (or untrained) outside observer about the subject? 2) How is the flow of conversation regulated? 3) What is the looker looking for? 4) How does gaze direction influence the receiver? 5) What attributions does a receiver make on the basis of the other person's visual behavior? 6) To what extent is visual behavior "communicative" in the narrow sense set forth above?

The first thing to recognize about these questions is that they are different questions. Not all of the research on visual behavior is relevant to any given question, and the researcher must have a clear idea of his question and its communicational level in order to determine which of the research on visual behavior is directly related. The second thing to recognize is that questions at different levels may be mutually relevant. Information gained at one level may be applicable to research at another level. However, an element isolated as meaningful at one level—say, the regulatory level, may be meaningless at another level, or, as Argyle and Kendon put it, "what we refer to as an element will depend on the level in the hierarchy we are discussing" (3:59). It is also possible that an element may reappear as relevant again at a more global level. For example, a significant scrap of regulatory visual behavior may tell us nothing about the psychological attributions made by the interactants or about the affective tone of the interaction, but it may be extremely informative in inferring the subculture of the interactants.

Finally, a single set of questions may be studied at many levels, thereby enriching our understanding. For example, cutting across these levels of analysis is the variable of interpersonal attraction, which many researchers have taken to be the main affective domain covered by visual behavior in social interaction. While the various research strategies used in research on visual behavior are appropriate to questions at different levels of communication, their combined application to the particular area of visual behavior in interpersonal attraction and involvement has contributed considerably to our understanding of that area, and has served as a demonstration of how the levels may be coordinated in relation to a specific issue.

In this review, we will discuss research done at each of these communicational levels—individual differences, regulation of conversation, information-seeking, influence, and attribution—in turn. Then we will examine applications of techniques to the area of interpersonal attraction at several levels. Finally, we will raise some unanswered questions and speculate about some directions which the study of visual behavior might take in the future. Regrettably, space limitations dictate that a good deal will be left out. Most notably, this review is primarily restricted to experimental research involving at least two adult human beings (although that traditional semi-human, the experimental confederate, will be admitted). In other words, we are omitting most studies of non-human primates and lower species, nonexperimental studies, developmental studies, and experiments involving human beings "interacting" with photographs or with thin air.

CONSISTENT PATTERNS OF VISUAL BEHAVIOR WITHIN INDIVIDUALS OR CATEGORIES OF PEOPLE

Studies falling into this category are not concerned with the transmission of information among the members of an interaction; instead, the researcher looks for stable patterns of visual behavior which may inform him about other aspects of the user. In general, these studies are descriptive, with little interpretation of why a person or type of person consistently adopts a particular visual style.

Individual Differences

Large individual differences in looking behavior during dyadic conversations have been found. Kendon (31) found that gaze directed at the other varied from 28% of the time to over 70% of the time, depending on the individual. Nielson (45), studying gaze direction in stressful interactions, found individual variation in amount of time spent looking at the other from 8% to 73%. Because of the close relationship between length of gaze and rate of change in gaze direction for the two members of a conversing dyad, Kendon (31) questioned how much this wide variation really reflected stable individual differences. Kendon and Cook (32), however, studying subjects in dyadic conversation with a number of different partners, found that most gaze patterns were consistent for subjects across the different interactions. Gaze patterns varied as a function of the identity of the partner on only a few measures: length and frequency of gazes while listening, and, to a lesser degree, while speaking.

Libby (37) also investigated individual differences in maintaining eye contact and direction of looking. Subjects were given a structured interview of 54 questions, and instructed to look at the interviewer until she finished asking each question. Four ocular responses were recorded: 1) maintaining eye contact with the interviewer while answering the question; 2) breaking eye contact before the interviewer finished asking the question; 3) vertical direction of gaze aversion after the question; and 4) horizontal direction of gaze aversion after the question. All four looking variables proved to have high inter-observer reliability, intra-individual consistency, and temporal stability over the course of the interview.

Sex Differences

In research on visual behavior, sex differences are the rule, rather than the exception. In the most common experimental arrangement, where the subject interacts with a steadily-gazing partner, women have been found to engage in more overall eye contact (17, 19, 20), more eye contact while speaking (17, 19, 37), more eye contact while listening (20), and more eye contact during silences (17). Argyle and Dean (2) found trends in the same direction, and Exline (15) found similar results in three-person groups. Kendon and Cook (32) found a slight tendency for females to look more and to be looked at more, but there was a great deal of variability, and on several variables an interaction between subject identity and partner sex we found, such that some subjects looked more at females and others looked more at males, the former tendency being observed more frequently.

Argyle, Lalljee, and Cook (4) found that females were more uncomfortable than males when talking to an unseen partner. Unlike males, females preferred to see their partners even when they could not be seen themselves. Exline (15) suggested that (1) visual information plays a greater role in the social field of women than of men, and (2) the visual activity of women is more sensitive to social field conditions than that of men. Argyle and Williams (5) found that females feel more observed than males, and suggested that with regard to visual appearance females are the performers and males the audience. People who feel observed are expected to have the perceptual goal of watching for visual feedback in order to adjust their social performances (5). If females feel more observed than males, they may rely more on visual feedback; without such feedback they may feel unable to adjust their social performances in response to their audiences. In general, these studies indicate that in a neutral or positive interaction at a given level of intimacy, females engage in more eye contact and possibly depend more on visual feedback than do males.

Personality Differences

The data on personality correlates of visual behavior are weaker and less consistent than the data on sex differences, often showing as interactions with other variables rather than as main effects. Exline (15) obtained a sex by need for Affiliation interaction such that females high in need for Affiliation look more while speaking and share more mutual glances than low *n Aff* women, while males show the opposite tendency. Internal analysis further suggested that mutual glances were greater in high affiliative dyads in a non-competitive situation, while among low affiliative dyads eye contact was greater in the competitive situation. This effect was considerably stronger for female groups than for male groups. Somewhat similar dimensions were tapped by Exline, Gray and Schuette (17), who found that subjects high on the inclusion and affection scales of Schutz's FIRO test engaged in more eye contact with an interviewer than subjects low on both dimensions. Kendon and Cook (32) also used the FIRO scales, and found that of 90 correlations, no more reached significance than would be expected by chance. No significant relationship was found between affiliation, wanted or given, and gaze patterns. Inclusion, wanted and given correlated positively with mean length of eye contact. Gray (26) also failed to find a relationship between affiliative orientation, measured by the FIRO scale, and amount of gaze at the interviewer during a low stress interview. Efran and Broughton (9) found that need for approval measured by the Marlowe-Crown scale, was positively correlated with amount of eye contact with two listening confederates, but Efran (8) was unable to replicate this finding. Thus the relationship between affiliation/inclusion/approval needs and eye contact continues dubious, and probably depends largely on some third variable, such as the subject's *expectations* of approval.

In a correlational study of freely interacting dyads, Kendon and Cook (32) found that, contrary to prediction, field dependence (Embedded Figures Test) correlated negatively with the amount of gaze while speaking. Scores on the Rod and Frame test did not correlate significantly with gaze or action patterns. Neuroticism as measured by MPI correlated negatively with frequency of gaze while speaking and frequency of eye contact correlated positively with length of action. Extraversion (on the MPI) correlated positively with frequency of gaze while speaking. Mobbs (43) also found that extraverts engaged in significantly more eye contact than introverts, looking more often while speaking and more (in overall duration) while listening. Exline et al. (19) found that high Mach subjects decreased eye contact less than low Mach subjects after being implicated in cheating.

Perhaps as a consequence of the importance of visual behavior in maintaining dominance hierarchies in primates, several studies have examined correlations between interpersonal dominance and visual behavior in humans. Strongman and Champness (51) paired ten subjects with each other in all combinations of two. The pair interacted briefly with each other and the frequency of breaking eye contact was taken as a measure of submission. On each trial, the subject having fewer visual submissions was defined as the dominant member of the pair. The investigators found a highly consistent dominance hierarchy. Although a wide range of within-subject variation was found, it seemed to be operating within limits imposed by the dominance hierarchy. Argyle (1) suggested that dominant and/or socially poised persons look more at others than submissive and/or socially anxious persons. In a questionnaire study, Argyle and Williams (5) found that dominant males reported feeling less observed than females or dependent males when meeting younger people of the same sex. Dependent males felt more observed with females than with males, and most of all if the female was their own age. Insecure males reported feeling more observed in the same-age, opposite-sex condition, while insecure females felt less observed in the younger, same-sex condition. None of these correlations was particularly strong. In a study by Exline and Messick (18), dependent subjects in the low social-reinforcement condition engaged in significantly more eye contact than did either dependent subjects given high reinforcement or dominant subjects given low reinforcement. Dominant subjects tended to engage in more eye contact in the high, compared to the low, reinforcement condition, though the difference was not statistically significant.

On the whole, these results suggest that features of the situation and the relationship probably have a greater effect on visual behavior than personality-test variables, not a unique finding in Social Psychology by any means (see 42). The high degree of individual consistency found by Kendon and Cook (32) does not seem to be strongly related to any test variable. In cases of severe psychopathology, deviations from normal gaze patterns may be more striking (35, 43), often taking the form of refusal to establish or maintain eye contact. Hutt and Ounsted (27) found that autistic children are charcterized by extreme gaze aversion, which they interpreted as reflecting fear of rejection and/or an attempt to reduce their chronically high emotional arousal. Rutter and Stephenson (49) studied the visual interaction patterns of 20 schizophrenics, 20 depressives, and normal control subjects in a standardized interview situation. The patterning of looking in relation to periods of speech, listening, and silence did not differ between groups. As predicted, the overall amount of looking at the interviewer was significantly less for both schizophrenic and depressive subjects than for their normal controls. No differences were found between the groups for frequency of looks. Depressives and controls did not differ in mean length of looks, but schizophrenics looked in significantly shorter glances. The investigators suggest that the decrement in looking for schizophrenic and depressive patients may be an aspect of social withdrawal serving to communicate a lack of desire for social intercourse, although an arousal-reducing function may be equally plausible in the case of the schizophrenics.

VISUAL BEHAVIOR RELEVANT WITHIN THE CONTEXT OF AN INTERACTION

In studying visual behavior as a diagnostic cue or a consistent attribute of persons or groups, the researcher need not concern himself with its functions within a social interaction. For this type of study it does not matter whether the other participants in the interaction make the same attributions as the researcher, or even whether they notice the visual behavior at all. When we come to ask questions about the consequent behavior or cognitions of the other interactant(s), however, evidence that these interactants can accurately discriminate the other's gaze direction becomes a fundamental prerequisite.

Observer Awareness of Visual Behavior

Many studies of interactive visual behavior have cited the results of Gibson and Pick (23) and of Cline (6) in assuming that their subjects could discriminate changes in gaze direction with high accuracy. Gibson and Pick (23) found a high degree of accuracy in the ability to discriminate whether or not one is being looked at. They required subjects to attend directly to the other's gaze direction: there was no ongoing social interaction between the two persons. Cline (6) also found accurate discrimination of eye contact from other gaze directions. Both studies indicated that discrimination was poorer when the looker's head was not oriented directly toward the subject. In a careful review of the literature on discrimination of gaze direction, Vine (53) found that accurate discrimination by interactants and outside observers may be considerably less than the high values obtained by Gibson and Pick and by Cline. He concludes, however, that "in real-life interactions we tend either to give a direct eye gaze or to look well away from the face of the other person. If this is the case, then observer judgment can be expected to be fairly adequate in studies where eye gaze vs. non-eye gaze is monitored . . ." (53:16).

It is also quite possible that subjects in a social interaction may not be able to *describe* the other's visual behavior accurately, even when it can be demonstrated that this behavior has had an effect on their behavior (as in studies where a confederate's visual behavior is a manipulated independent variable). Ellsworth and Ross (14), for example, found that subjects could tell whether their partners looked at them a lot or hardly at all, but they could not tell whether or not the eye contact was contingent upon their own behavior. Argyle and Williams (5) found that subjects, when questioned, could not even discriminate between high- and low-looking confederates. Thus subjective report may not be a very good measure in social interaction, since it can be demonstrated that "unnoticed" visual behavior can have important psychological effects (e.g., 11).

THE REGULATORY FUNCTION OF VISUAL BEHAVIOR

The regulatory function (31) of visual interaction, variously termed "visual rhetoric" (45), "channel control" (1, 2), and "synchronizing of speech" (4), is suggested by the consistent relation between visual and verbal interaction. Wiener et al, suggest that the functions of regulators emitted by the speaker are "a) to serve as cues for the addressee that encoding is occurring and continuing, b) to check on whether listening and decoding are occurring, and c) to indicate when the addressee is to speak" (55:207), while the listener's regulators serve to inform the speaker that "decoding, understanding, agreement, or disagreement are occurring" (55:208). The regulators indicate that communication is taking place, though they themselves are not part of the content of communication. People may make attributions about another, however, if his regulatory pattern deviates substantially from the norm for the group.

Looking at or away from the listener at the beginning and end of utterances signals the speaker's intentions and expectations, and thus serves to regulate who holds the floor (31, 45). The speaker tends to look away at the beginning and slightly before the beginning of his utterances, thus inhibiting a response or interruption from his auditor. The speaker often looks up after completed thoughts, to check on the listener's response. At the end of his utterance the speaker looks up at his auditor to signal that he is about to stop speaking (31). In a seven-member discussion group, the member at whom a speaker last looked is more likely than other group members to speak next.

Argyle, Lalljee, and Cook (4) studied synchronization of verbal interaction under conditions of reduced visibility. One member of a pair interviewed the other under one of four visibility conditions: only eyes visible (both wore masks); only face visible· (both work dark glasses); only body visible (screen for head); no vision. More speech pauses occurred in the face-only condition than in the no-vision condition; fewest pauses occurred in the body-only and eyes-only conditions. Slightly more interruptions occurred in the no-vision condition, and the fewest interruptions in the eyes-only condition. For synchronization of speech, then, it seems to be most useful to see the eyes. However, subjects were still able to synchronize speech under conditions of reduced vision. The investigators suggested that factors such as familiarity with the telephone may have enabled people to develop alternative methods of speech regulation when vision is absent.

In addition to providing information about the communicative flow, studies of regulatory patterns (as well as studies of discrimination of gaze direction) are methodologically useful to the investigator planning to program the visual behavior of one interactant. Many studies of visual interaction which measure looking as a dependent variable standardize the visual behavior of the subject's interactant by having him maintain a steady gaze directed at the subject's eyes. When the subject returns the other's gaze, mutual eye contact is recorded as present. A number of investigators have commented on the artificiality of the continuously-staring confederate or interviwer (7, 11, 32, 37). Exline and Winters (20) noted that large differences in visual interaction appear to depend on whether or not the subjects are interacting with a steadily-gazing confederate. When subjects interact with a steadily-gazing confederate, mutual glances occurred between 35% and 55% of the time (17, 20), whereas when subjects interact with other subjects whose looking behavior is uncontrolled (e.g., 15), mutual gazing is much less frequent, usually under 10% of the time. By taking into account the results of studies of regulatory patterns in visual behavior, it is possible to eliminate the steadily-gazing confederate while still retaining a high degree of control over the occurrence of eye contact. For example, Ellsworth and Carlsmith (11) used Kendon's (31) research to schedule the gazes of the experimenter so that they occurred at times when the subject would be most likely to be looking at her. The sequence was arranged so that the subject was looking at the experimenter slightly over 95% of the total time that the experimenter was looking at the subject, and thus the independent variable could legitimately be called "eye contact," and not simply "being looked at."

THE INFORMATION-SEEKING FUNCTION OF VISUAL BEHAVIOR

The "information-seeking" function (2) of visual interaction is variously labelled "monitoring" (31), or "feedback" (1, 4). The questions subsumed under these rubrics are somewhat similar to those asked by researchers who study individual differences: the focus of attention is the person doing the looking—what he is looking for, why he is looking, what he sees, and how he uses it. Argyle and Kendon (3) have put forth a model of social interaction as a serial motor skill. The social skill performer uses the verbal and nonverbal cues of others in the interaction to change and correct his performance, in much the same way as the motor skill performer uses perceptual feedback from the environment to correct his performance (1). In social interaction each person is continually looking for feedback from the others in order to modify his behavior (1, 3).

While a person is speaking, most of the feedback he receives typically comes through nonverbal channels. Kleck (33) writes that "a person's behavior while listening to us is used by us as feedback regarding his evaluation of our own behavior." As we mentioned earlier in our discussion of sex differences, several authors have suggested that the information-seeking or monitoring function of visual interaction plays a greater role in the visual activity of women than in that of men (4, 15). Many of the regulatory behaviors discussed in the last section probably also serve the function of looking for feedback on the *content* of the message, a good example being the tendency of the speaker to look at his auditor more frequently at the ends of utterances. It may be that cues emitted by the auditor at this point are more likely to be noticed and given meaning by the speaker than identical behavior occurring elsewhere during the verbal flow.

In the research on various levels of reduced visibility by Argyle et al. (4), scales were administered designed to measure a) how well the subject could discriminate the experimenter's reactions to him, b) how much the subject desired more information about the experimenter's reaction, and c) how comfortable the subject felt in the situation. Ratings on all scales were significantly affected by the visibility conditions: comfort and ease of communication decline as visibility of either self or other declines, and the effect is greater when it is the other who is invisible. Argyle et al. concluded on the basis of these and other results that the face is the most useful area to see in gathering feedback on the other's reactions to the self (see also 12, 52). However, when visual feedback is reduced for both interactants, rather than just for one, there is in general little difficulty or discomfort in interacting. Argyle et al (4) suggest an alternative theory regarding the effects of reduced visibility, namely that *asymmetry* of visual feedback is the cause of communication difficulty and discomfort.

In order to get a clearer idea of the information-seeking function of visual behavior it would seem important to vary the subject's *motivation* for information and/or the availability of the type of information he is seeking. For example, if a person is getting plenty of verbal feedback relevant to his concerns, he may not need to look as much. It would also be interesting to find out whether the subject who looks frequently does in fact pick up more information, and whether this information is accurate. The motivational question was touched upon by Exline and Messick (18). They found that dependent, but not dominant, subjects engaged in more eye contact while speaking with an experimenter who gave little social reinforcement than with one who gave substantial amounts of reinforcement. The investigators proposed that dependent subjects in the low reinforcement condition, not satisfied in their need for approval, spend more time in visual search of the experimenter's facial expressions and gaze in the hope of finding other cues of approval.

Approaching the same question from a different angle, looking away from the other person may be expected to occur when the information communicated by the other person's face would be distracting or undesirable. Exline and Winters (21) found that subjects discussing cognitively difficult topics looked at their partners less than subjects discussing easy topics, possibly to avoid distracting visual feedback. In general, during long utterances, the speaker looks at his auditor during fluent, more rapid speech and at the ends of phrases, while he looks away during slow or hesitant speech (31). Similarly, Nielsen (45) noted that looking away during speaking expressed uncertaintly about what was being said and helped to avoid distractions, while looking at the other during speaking expressed certainty or served a feedback-seeking function. Gaze aversion may also be motivated by a desire to avoid seeing another's facial affect in reaction to one's own emotional arousal or other aspects of the self. Simmel (50) proposed that when feeling ashamed one looks away both to hide his own affect and to spare himself the sight of the other's responsive affect.

THE INTERACTIVE INFLUENCE OF VISUAL BEHAVIOR

If the investigator is interested exclusively in the information-seeking properties of visual behavior, he views the visual behavior as a window on the interaction, but not as a force within the interaction. The information-seeking behavior may be responsive to other aspects of the situation, but it is not usually viewed as influential. Other researchers have been interested in visual behavior as a variable which itself influences the other person or the course of the interaction. We use the term "influence" advisedly, in order to avoid the difficulties surrounding the term "communication." It is a global term used to describe an effective input into the sequence of the interaction. In much of the research on visual behavior, the receiver's response is an *evaluative* one; responses such as liking for the sender, comfort in the situation, and feelings of satisfaction are measured. Often this influence will be a more cognitive one; the person receiving the visual behavior will make some *attributon* about the other person, or about some aspect of the relationship. This attribution may be the dependent variable of the research, or it may be an intervening variable inferred from a study which demonstrates an influence on action. Finally, one can envision research in which the influence is clearly communicational in the narrowest sense of the word: the sender intentionally sends a message, and the receiver, in interpreting the message, assumes intentionality on the part of the sender (55). Studies of evaluative responses to visual behavior have been around for some time; studies of attributional responses are a new focus of interest; to our knowledge, studies of

communicational influences in this strict sense have so far not
been successfully conducted.

A good example of a finding which demonstrates an influence
of visual behavior is the research indicating the effects of eye
contact on physiological arousal. Kleinke and Pohlen (34) found
that subjects paired with a steadily-gazing confederate had
significantly higher heart rates than subjects paired with a
confederate who averted his gaze. Similarly, Nichols and
Champness (44) reported GSR increases for direct eye contact.
In this case, the emotional arousal may be taken as a basic
element which may produce or interact with more cognitive
elements. In some of our own current research, we have found
these to be key studies in linking research on visual behavior
with theories of emotional attribution in order to explore the
attribution process in social interaction.

Another example of a direct influence of visual behavior on
other behavior is a study by Ellsworth et al. (13) in which
staring elicited an avoidance response. In each of five experiments,
experimenters stared or did not stare at people who were stopped
at a traffic light. Experimenters were standing on a street corner
or riding a motor scooter; subjects were pedestrians or automobile
drivers. Subjects' speed across the intersection when the light
changed was measured. As predicted, crossing time was significantly
shorter in the stare conditions. Here the authors postulated
involvement and appropriateness as intervening variables: "if it
is assumed that staring is a salient stimulus which forcibly involves
the subject in an interpersonal encounter and demands a response,
the fact that there is no appropriate response becomes very
important to the subject, arousing tension and eliciting avoidance
at the earliest possible moment" (13:311).

Finally, Ellsworth and Carlsmith (12) found that consistent
eye contact from the victim inhibited aggressive responses
(shocks) from angered subjects. However, when the victim's
behavior was variable (inconsistent) subjects gave *more* shocks
to the victim when he established eye contact than when he
looked away. The results were interpreted on the basis of the
subjects' efforts to avoid or eliminate the aversive eye contact.

Taken together, these studies indicate that a direct gaze has
an arousing effect on the target. Presumably such a gaze must
deviate from the normal background of regulatory visual behavior,
or must occur outside of the context of a verbal interaction in order
to be arousing. How the subject copes with the arousal, and
what implications he draws probably depend on other aspects of

the situation: affective tone, appropriate level of involvement, and so on.

VISUAL BEHAVIOR AS A SOURCE OF ATTRIBUTION

In studying visual behavior as a source of attribution, we are asking what the visual behavior tells the receiver (as opposed to the more general influence question: "how does the visual behavior affect the receiver?"). A person may attribute stable characteristics, or more transient moods, reactions, or attitudes to the other person on the basis of his visual behavior. He will rarely hold the other person accountable for information received in this manner, however, and he will usually assume that the other person did not deliberately intend to convey this type of information. Research on the attribution question is fairly recent and scattered. Much of it involves fairly simple evaluative responses, so that it is difficult to separate the attributional "She is a nice person" or "She likes me" from the more immediate emotional response, "I like her." These studies will be discussed below in the section on interpersonal attraction and involvement.

LeCompte and Rosenfeld (36) exposed groups of subjects to one of two conditions of visual attention. Male experimenters, presented on videotape, read eight minutes of task instructions to the subjects. In one condition, the experimenter read without glancing up; in the other condition, the experimenter glanced up twice, looking toward the subject for two seconds. Experimenters who glanced up were rated as slightly less formal and less nervous than experimenters who did not look up.

Receiving a look and withholding a look have each been related to perceived power. Weisbrod (54) investigated visual interaction in a seven-member group discussion. A speaker rated individuals who looked at him as valuing him more, and the more an individual was looked at, the greater he himself and others in the group rated his power. Exline and Kendon (reported in 3) found that a listener who does not look at a speaking subject is perceived as more "potent" (i.e., having more authority and control) than one who does look. This may be related to control of reinforcement contingencies; Kendon (reported in 3) found that when an interviewer did not look at the subject for part of the time, the subject thought that the interviewer had lost interest in what the subject was saying.

Exline and Eldridge (16) hypothesized that a verbal message accompanied by eye contact with the addressee would be interpreted as more authentic than a message accompanied by an averted gaze. Subjects interacted with a confederate who subsequently gave them his impressions of them. The impressions were favorable, and dealt with social poise and individuality; as the confederate finished one impression and began another, he changed from direct gaze at the subject to gaze aversion, or vice versa. Subjects judged the verbal message to be more favorable when it was accompanied by direct gaze. They also rated their perceptions a) of the confederate's *confidence* in the correctness of his impressions, and b) of the *believability* of his manner. When eye contact accompanied the second message rather than the first, the confederate was judged as more confident of *both* messages. A similar trend, though not statistically significant, was found for ratings of the confederate's believability. This may reflect a recency effect or the perception of the meaning of the transition, but it is difficult to say in the absence of conditions where the confederate's behavior remains the same for both messages.

A recent extension of attribution theory (29) developed by Jones and Nisbett (28) proposes that an actor's perceptions of the causes of his behavior are different from the perceptions of an observer of the behavior, such that "there is a pervasive tendency for actors to attribute their actions to situational requirements, whereas observers tend to attribute the same actions to stable personal dispositions" (28:2). The extension of this hypothesis to dyadic interaction in which there are two actors observing each other opens up intriguing possibilities for research, and ties in with research on visual behavior in social interaction. We have already discussed the effects of reduced visibility and asymmetry of visual feedback in the section on information seeking; when A sees B better than B sees A, A feels himself to be the "perceiver" or "observer" and B feels himself the "perceived" or "observed" (4).

While physical conditions of visibility between two interactants may affect the extent to which they feel observer or observed, so may the role relationships between persons. In a study by Argyle and Williams (5), subject dyads interacted in brief face-to-face interviews, one member designated the interviewer and the other the interviewee. Subjects reported being more the observer when they were the interviewer, and more the observed when they were the interviewee. Females felt more observed than males. The more one subject felt observed, the more the other felt he was the observer. Argyle and Williams also found that subjects who felt observed looked less at the confederate in the experimental situation. The authors suggested that feeling observed is a cognitive set affected by role relationships, and that observer and observed have different perceptual goals in the interaction. The observer is trying to perceive the other's performance in order to evaluate it; the observed is watching for feedback on the reactions of the other to his own performance. Linking these findings with the propositions of Jones and Nisbett, we may hypothesize that a person who feels himself an observer will interpret the other's visual behavior and other nonverbal cues as indicators of the other's stable dispositions or internally-motivated moods, while a person who feels himself observed will interpret the same cues as reactions to himself and as influences on his own behavior. We are currently conducting research on this hypothesis.

Another hypothesis which follows from Jones and Nisbett's formulation is that an actor may not only attribute his actions to situational requirements,; but may define and describe his behavior on the basis of situational cues. In a study by Ellsworth and Ross (14), there were three people involved: a *talker* (actor) whose task was to talk about himself in intimate terms to a *listener* (observer #1), who gave him high or low amounts of eye contact, in a situation where an experimenter (observer #2), unaware of the eye contact manipulation, monitored the interaction from behind a one-way mirror. For females, all three participants agreed: the talker was more intimate under conditions of high eye contact. For males, however, the two observers agreed that the male talker was *less* intimate under conditions of high eye contact. But the male talker thought that he was *more* intimate. Given Jones and Nisbett's hypothesis about the perceptions of actors, we would expect the subject's perception of his own intimacy to reflect situational factors, and since the only feature of the situation which changes systematically is the listener's visual behavior, we may tentatively infer that the subject thinks he is being very intimate because the listener is looking at him during an unusually large proportion of the time. In other words, he assesses his own level of intimacy on the basis of the listener's perceived response to him.

Attribution theory has also led to the hypothesis that an important factor mediating interpersonal perception and behavior may be the perceiver's assumptions about whether the other person's behavior is homogeneous or variable (30). If the other person's behavior is perceived as relatively invariant, a person should be more likely to make dispositional attributions than situational attributions, and should feel relatively powerless to change the course of the interaction. Once the perceiver sees the other person's behavior as variable, he can look for its causes in the situation and in himself. The results of a study of Ellsworth and Carlsmith (12) indicate that the assumption of variability may lead the perceiver to see himself as an influential agent in the interaction, even when the other's variable responses are not in fact contingent upon the perceiver's behavior. Angered subjects in an aggressive situation who were faced with invariant eye contact from their victims responded by delivering fewer shocks than subjects whose victims consistently averted their gaze. The eye contact was aversive to the subjects, and they felt powerless to eliminate it, so they tended to withdraw from the interaction, figuratively speaking. When the victim's visual behavior was variable, however, subjects repsonded to the aversive eye contact with punishing shocks, delivering more shock on the occasions when the victim looked than when he averted his gaze, presumably acting on the assumption that the behavior was responsive to situational factors and thus could be eliminated by negative reinforcement.

As should be evident from the amount of space allotted to relatively few studies, these and other questions raised by studying attribution in an interactive context seem particularly fruitful and interesting to us, and reflect one of our primary current research interests. One reason is that our major concern is with meaningful social psychological variables, such as influence and attribution and communication, and not with visual behavior *per se*. Relating the study of nonverbal behavior to more traditional areas of social psychological research has the advantages of 1) suggesting fruitful research questions which may speed progress in both areas, 2) suggesting methodological innovations in both areas (e.g., the use of visual behavior as an unobtrusive dependent variable measure or manipulation check), and 3) possibly reducing or redefining the "areas" themselves.

The other major area in which visual behavior has become involved with traditional social psychological variables is that of interpersonal attraction. This research reflects the application of methods from several of the communicational levels laid out in this paper, and shows a faint but gratifying tendency to progress and develop through time.

VISUAL BEHAVIOR IN RELATION TO INTERPERSONAL ATTRACTION AND INVOLVEMENT

The intuition that friendly relationships with attractive people should be characterized by high eye contact provided the initial hypotheses in research on visual behavior and interpersonal attraction. In the early studies the approach was similar to that used in the study of individual differences, except that situational differences were used as the main independent variable. Eye contact was expected to vary as a function of the affective tone of the interaction, and thus to serve as a signal of that tone to an outside observer. Exline and Winters (20) found that subjects receiving negative evaluations from an interviewer significantly decreased eye contact with him; subjects evaluated positively showed a tendency (not statistically significant) to increase eye contact. A manipulation check indicated that the favorability of the subjects' rating of the interviewer varied with the positiveness of the interviewer's treatment. In a second study, after some interaction with a pair of confederates, all subjects were taken to another room, and experimental group subjects were asked to state a preference for one of the two confederates. Post-experimental preference ratings showed that subjects in the experimental group increased their liking more for the evaluator chosen at the mid-point in the experiment than for the non-chosen evaluator. As predicted, positive affect influenced women only for looking while speaking, and men only for looking while listening. During speaking, experimental group women greatly increased eye contact with the preferred evaluator and decreased eye contact with the non-preferred evaluator. During listening, males decreased eye contact with the non-preferred evaluator more than they did with the preferred evaluator. Similarly, Goldberg, Kiesler, and Collins (25) found that subjects with higher scores on questionnaire items judged to measure socioemotional evaluations of the interviewer spent more time gazing into the interviewer's eyes. Kendon and Cook (32), studying subject dyads engaged in friendly conversations, found that partners were evaluated more positively the longer their gazes and the less frequent their gazes; short, frequent gazes were disliked. No correlation was found between sheer amount of looking and evaluation. Exline and Eldridge (16) found that a favorable verbal message was interpreted as more favorable when accompanied by eye contact than when accompanied by gaze aversion. Finally, Rubin (48) found a tendency—not particularly surprising—for couples in love to spend more time looking into each other's eyes than couples not so smitten.

Studies in which subjects role-play like or dislike for an interactant show significant effects for eye contact. Gatton (22) found that subjects engaged in more eye contact with the confederate when instructed to behave as if they liked him than when instructed to behave as if they disliked him. In studies where subjects were instructed to role-play responses to imaginary

partners Mehrabian has found rather more complicated results
(38, 39, 40, 41)). Pellegrini, Hicks, and Gordon (46) hypothesized
that approval seeking is characterized by increased eye contact,
and approval avoiding by decreased eye contact. Subjects
instructed to seek approval were told to act as if they thought
the confederate was a nice person whose liking they wanted;
subjects in the approval-avoiding condition were given opposite
instructions, and control subjects were given no instructions
regarding approval. More frequent and longer glances were
obtained in the approval-seeking condition, compared to both the
approval-avoiding and the control conditions.

Other research, however, indicates that a direct relation
between eye contact and liking or affiliation may be restricted to
certain types of persons and certain types of situations. Exline (15)
found that persons oriented towards affiliation engaged in more
eye contact in affiliative, than in competitive, situations; for persons
oriented towards achievement and control, the reverse findings
were obtained. Kendon (31) proposed that mutual gaze functions
as an intensifier of the specific affect aroused in a particular social
interaction. In line with this proposal, Ellsworth and Carlsmith
(11) hypothesized that eye contact interacts with the favorability
of the verbal message, making a positive encounter more positive
and a negative encounter more negative. Two levels of favorability
of interview were varied with two levels of eye contact. Subjects
receiving the favorable interview evaluated the interviewer and
interview more highly when she looked into their eyes; subjects in
the unfavorable condition evaluated both interview and interviewer
more highly in the "no look" condition. The hypothesis that eye
contact intensified the negative tone of the unfavorable condition
proved insufficient, however, since the unfavorable-no-look
condition was rated as positively as the favorable-look condition.

Argyle and Dean (2) proposed an "affiliative conflict theory"
to account for eye contact in situations which are primarily
cooperative and therefore potentially affiliative. According to this
hypothesis, both approach and avoidance motivations are involved
in engaging in eye contact and other components of interpersonal
intimacy. An equilibrium level develops in any dyad, as a function
of various elements of intimacy: eye contact, physical proximity,
smiling, intimacy of topic. If the equilibrium level for intimacy is
exceeded, anxiety results; if intimacy is below equilibrium, the
dyad feels affiliation-deprived. It is proposed that if any element of
intimacy is above or below equilibrium level, efforts are made to
attain equilibrium by adjusting other elements (1, 2).

Thus it appears that the relationship between eye contact and interpersonal attraction is but one aspect of a more general relationship between eye contact and affect. Emotional arousal is produced by eye contact (34, 44), perhaps even by the perception that one is being looked at (13). This arousal may take the form of liking, as frequently happens in the neutral to slightly positive interactions characteristic of laboratory dyads, but liking is by no means an inevitable consequence. The arousal produced by eye contact is not specifically positive; on the other hand, it is probably not so general as to be easily attributed to *any* stimulus that happens to be present. We believe that an interpersonal cause will be sought. While interpersonal attraction is not implied, interpersonal *involvement* is (11, 14, 24), and the subject's interpretation of the arousal will almost always be focused on his relationship with the other person. He may find the arousal rewarding, as in many of the liking studies, or adversive, in situations which are aggressive (12) or overly intimate (2, 14), but he will always find it interpersonally involving. As an aside, it might be pointed out that many of the sex differences found in previous research might be a function of different "acceptable" levels of involvement for dyads of different sex compositions (14).

SOME FURTHER CONCERNS AND SPECULATIONS

Communication

Like most research on nonverbal "communication," the research on visual behavior has not been "communicational" in the strict sense of the word (55). There has been little discussion of shared codes, intentionally used, and understood as intentional. Instead, the studies deal with influence, and with attributions made by observers or, more recently, participants. In part, this bias probably reflects the clinical origins of the psychological study of nonverbal cues; the cues were regarded as symptoms, no more "intentional" than a tie or a rash. In part, it reflects the difficulty of studying intentionality without sacrificing either acceptable methodology or the essence of the concept. In the early studies the subject emitted behaviors and the experimenter, or the therapist, interpreted them. More recently, nonprofessional interactants who see the cues have been allowed the status of interpreters, and their cognitions have become appropriate matters for research. So far, except in role-playing studies, the sender has not been granted intentionality or awareness. It seems that one of the important future directions for studies of visual behavior, and for nonverbal communication research in general, is toward the study of the communicative properties of nonverbal "communication." An easy step is the study of the receiver's attributions of intentionality on the part of the sender. A more difficult step is the study of the sender's own intentional use of cues. Our own belief is that the level of intentionality involved is somewhere between the unconscious leakage of revealing cues and the deliberate planning of messages, and that the ambiguity of intention is of positive value to the sender, allowing him to send tentative messages for which he will rarely be held accountable.

Visual Behavior and Social Psychology

Our own interest is primarily in person perception and social interaction. Thus we are especially interested in how the receiver interprets the cues he receives and what he does with them. Thus we hope to see more studies in which visual behavior, and nonverbal behavior in general, are related to other areas of research in social interaction. Visual behavior in relation to interpersonal attraction is one area which has been fruitfully explored, and the concept of involvement has emerged as an important basic characteristic of eye contact, one which has helped us to understand its effects in mediating attraction, and one which may prove to be useful even in studies of interpersonal attraction which do not involve the study of visual behavior. The current research linking visual behavior to observer-observed distinctions and other areas of attribution theory also promises to be exciting and fruitful— in relating the information-seeking function of eye contact to the attributional function, in bringing attribution theory into an interactive context, and perhaps even in revitalizing the fascinating and frustrating area of person perception.

Cultural Factors

Always repeated, rarely heeded, the old reminder that cultural factors exist is extremely important in relation to visual behavior. Deviations from cultural norms in overlearned areas like spacing, timing, and looking create unanticipated, unrecognized, inescapable, and thus excruciatingly annoying sources of cross-cultural communication difficulties and ill-feelings. It is not simply a matter of a member of one culture looking "too much" or "too little" for someone of another culture, but more likely a matter of a conflict between two highly complex, totally overlearned *patterns* of behavior. Nor is it a matter of the suburban American and the Bushman; quite often cultural communication difficulties can arise between the surburban American and the suburban American next door.

Nonverbal Behavior and Nonverbal Cues

Research on visual behavior, like almost all research on nonverbal "communication," has so far avoided a question which to us seems central: what cues influence the perceiver and to what cues does he attribute meaning? Research which simply records the nonverbal behavior in an interaction, whether the interaction is naturally occurring or manipulated, does not provide direct information about reactions to the behavior. It tells us that a vast number of discriminable behaviors are constantly occurring, but it does not tell us which of these actually are discriminated by the interacting perceiver. In studies where a single cue is varied, on the other hand, the variation typically affects the perceiver, but we have no way of knowing whether the same cue would be influential or meaningful or salient in any way if it were embedded in the noise of an uncontrolled interaction. The fact that a cue can be made salient does not give us much information about when it is salient.

The perceiver cannot possibly attend to everything that happens in the nonverbal channels and still follow the conversation. One possibility, which we are currently exploring, is that aside from certain extreme nonverbal behaviors (e.g., facial expressions of strong emotion [10]), a cue is not salient or meaningful solely by virtue of its configuration, but by virtue of its temporal placement in a sequence of events in an interaction. In other words, there are moments within the sequence of events, probably largely defined in relation to events in the vocal-verbal channel, when the receiver *looks for* cues, *responds* to them, and *interprets* them, and other times when the same movement or configuration will be unnoticed or disregarded. The study of this temporal patterning is currently one of our primary research concerns.

References

1. Argyle, M. *Social Interaction* (London: Methuen & Co., 1969).
2. Argyle, M., and Dean, J. "Eye Contact, Distance, and Affiliation." *Sociometry* 28, (1965):289–304.
3. Argyle, M., and Kendon, A. "The Experimental Analysis of Social Performance." In L. Berkowitz (ed.), *Advances in*

Experimental Social Psychology, vol. 3 (New York Academic Press, 1967), pp. 55–99.

4. Argyle, M., Lalljee, M., and Cook, M. "The Effects of Visibility on Interaction in a Dyad." *Human Relations* 21, (1968):3–17.
5. Argyle, M., and Williams, M. "Observer or Observed? A Reversible Perspective in Person Perception." *Sociometry* 32, (1969):396–412.
6. Cline, M. G. "The Perception of Where a Person is Looking." *American Journal of Psychiatry* 80, (1967): 41–50.
7. Duncan, S. "Nonverbal Communication." *Psychological Bulletin* 72, (1969):118–137.
8. Efran, J. S. "Looking for Approval: Effects on Visual Behavior of Approbation from Persons Differing in Importance." *Journal of Personality and Social Psychology* 10, (1968):21–25.
9. Efran, J. S., and Broughton, A. "Effect of Expectancies for Social Approval on Visual Behavior." *Journal on Personality and Social Psychology* 4, (1966): 103–107.
10. Ekman, P., Friesen, W. V., and Ellsworth, P. *Emotion in the Human Face* (New York: Pergamon Press, 1972).
11. Ellsworth, P. C., and Carlsmith, J. M. "Effects of Eye Contact and Verbal Content on Affective Response to a Dyadic Interaction." *Journal of Personality and Social Psychology* 10, (1968):15–20.
12. Ellsworth, P. C., and Carlsmith, J. M. "Eye Contact and Gaze Aversion in an Aggressive Encounter." *Journal of Personality and Social Psychology*, in press.
13. Ellsworth, P. C., Carlsmith, J. M., and Henson, A. "The Stare as a Stimulus to Flight in Human Subjects: A Series of Field Experiments." *Journal of Personality and Social Psychology* 21, (1972):302–311.
14. Ellsworth, P. C., and Ross, L. D. "Eye Contact and Intimacy." Unpublished manuscript, 1972.
15. Exline, R. V. "Explorations in the Process of Person Perception: Visual Interaction in Relation to Competition, Sex, and the Need for Affiliation." *Journal of Personality* 31, (1963):1–20.
16. Exline, R. V., and Eldridge, C. "Effects of Two Patterns of a Speaker's Visual Behavior upon the Perception of the Authenticity of His Message." Paper presented at the meeting of the Eastern Psychological Association, Boston, April, 1967.
17. Exline, R. V., Gray, D., and Schuette, D. "Visual Behavior in a Dyad as Affected by Interview Content and Sex of Respondent." *Journal of Personality and Social Psychology* 1, (1965):201–209.

18. Exline, R. V., and Messick, D. "The Effects of Dependency and Social Reinforcement upon Visual Behavior during an Interview." *British Journal of Social and Clinical Psychology* **6**, (1967):256–266.
19. Exline, R. V., Thibaut, J., Brannon, C., and Gumpert, P. "Visual Interaction in Relation to Machiavellianism and an Unethical Act." *American Psychologist* **16**, (1961):396.
20. Exline, R. V., and Winters, L. "Affective Relations and Mutual Glances in Dyads." In S. S. Tomkins and C. E. Izard (eds.), *Affect, Cognition, and Personality* (New York: Springer, 1965), pp. 319–350.
21. Exline, R. V., and Winters, L. (eds.), "The Effects of Cognitive Difficulty and Cognitive Style upon Eye-to-eye Contact in Interviews." Paper presented at the meeting of the Eastern Psychological Association, Atlantic City, April, 1965.
22. Gatton, M. J. "Behavior Aspects of Interpersonal Attraction." Unpublished doctoral dissertation, Purdue University, 1970.
23. Gibson, J. J., and Pick, A. D. "Perception of Another Person's Looking Behavior." *American Journal of Psychology* **76**, (1963):686–694.
24. Goffman, E. *Behavior in Public Places* (New York: Macmillan, 1963).
25. Goldberg, G. N., Kiesler, C. A., and Collins, B. E. "Visual Behavior and Face-to-face Distance During Interaction." *Sociometry* **32**, (1969):43–53.
26. Gray, S. L. "Eye Contact as a Function of Sex, Race, and Interpersonal Needs." *Dissertation Abstracts* Sep. Vol. 32 (3-B):1842, 1971.
27. Hutt, C., and Ounsted, C. "The Biological Significance of Gaze Aversion with Particular Reference to the Syndrome of Infantile Autism." *Behavioral Science* **11**, (1966):346–356.
28. Jones, E. E., and Nisbett, R. E. "The Actor and the Observer: Divergent Perceptions of the Causes of Behavior." General Learning Press, 1971.
29. Kelley, H. H. "Attribution Theory in Social Psychology." *Nebraska Symposium on Motivation* **14**, (1967):192–241.
30. Kelley, H. H., and Stahelski, A. J., "Social Interaction Basis of Cooperators' and Competitors' Beliefs about Others." *Journal of Personality and Social Psychology* **16**, (1970):66–91.
31. Kendon, A. "Some Functions of Gaze-direction in Social Interaction." *Acta Psychologica* **26**, (1967):22–63.
32. Kendon, A., and Cook, M. "The Consistency of Gaze Patterns in Social Interaction." *British Journal of Psychology* **60**, (1969):481–494.

33. Kleck, R. "Physical Stigma and Nonverbal Cues Emitted in Face-to-face Interaction." *Human Relations* **21**, (1968):19–28.
34. Kleinke, C. L., and Pohlen, P. D. "Affective and Emotional Responses as a Function of Other Person's Gaze and Cooperativeness in a Two-person Game." *Journal of Personality and Social Psychology* **17**, (1971):308–313.
35. Laing, R. D. *The Divided Self* (London: Tavistock Publications, 1960).
36. LeCompte, W. F., and Rosenfeld, H. M. "Effects of Minimal Eye Contact in the Instruction Period on Impressions of the Expermenter." *Journal of Experimental Social Psychology* **7**, (1971):211–220.
37. Libby, W. L. "Eye Contact and Direction of Looking as Stable Individual Differences." *Journal of Experimental Research in Personality* **4**, (1970):303–312.
38. Mehrabian, A. "Inference of Attitude from the Posture, Orientation, and Distance of a Communicator." *Journal of Consulting and Clinical Psychology* **32**, (1968):296–308.
39. Mehrabian, A. "Relationship of Attitude to Seated Posture, Orientation, and Distance." *Journal of Personality and Social Psychology* **10**, (1968):26–30.
40. Mehrabian, A. "Significance of Posture and Position in the Communication of Attitude and Status Relationships." *Psychological Bulletin* **71**, (1969):359–372.
41. Mehrabian, A., and Friar, J. T. "Enconding of Attitude by a Seated Communicator via Posture and Position Cues." *Journal of Consulting and Clinical Psychology* **33**, (1969):350–336.
42. Mischel, W. *Personality and Assessment* (New York: Wiley, 1968).
43. Mobbs, N. A. "Eye Contact and Introversion-Extraversion." Reading B. A. thesis, 1967. Cited by A. Kendon and M. Cook, "The Consistency of Gaze Patterns in Social Interaction." *British Journal of Psychology* **60**, (1969): 481–494.
44. Nichols, K. A., and Champness, B. G. "Eye Gaze and the GSR." *Journal of Experimental Social Psychology* **7**, (1971): 623–626.
45. Nielsen, G. *Studies in Self-Confrontation* (Copenhagen: Munksgaard, 1962).
46. Pellegrini, R. J., Hicks, R. A., and Gordon, L. "The Effects of an Approval-Seeking Induction on Eye-Contact in Dyads." *British Journal of Social and Clinical Psychology* **9**, (1970): 373–374.
47. Reimer, M. D. "Abnormalities of the Gaze—A Classification." *Psychiatric Quarterly* **29**, (1955):659–672.

48. Rubin, Z. "Measurement of Romantic Love." *Journal of Personality and Social Psychology* 16, (1970):265–273.
49. Rutter, D. R., and Stephenson, G. M. "Visual Interaction in a Group of Schizophrenic and Depressive Patients." *British Journal of Social and Clinical Psychology* 11, (1972):57–65.
50. Simmel, G. "Sociology of the Senses: Visual Interaction." In R. E. Park and E. W. Burgess (eds.), *Introduction to the Science of Sociology* (University of Chicago Press, 1921).
51. Strongman, K. T., and Champness, B. G. "Dominance Hierarchies and Conflict in Eye Contact." *Acta Psychologia* 28, (1968):376–386.
52. Tomkins, S. S. *Affect, Imagery, Consciousness*, vol. II: *The Negative Affects* (New York: Springer, 1963).
53. Vine, I. "Judgment of Direction of Gaze: An Interpretation of Discrepant Results." *British Journal of Social and Clinical Psychology* 10, (1971):320–331.
54. Weisbrod, R. M. "Looking Behavior in a Discussion Group." Unpublished paper, Cornell University, Ithaca, N.Y. Cited by M. Argyle and A. Kendon, "The Experimental Aanlysis of Social Performance." In L. Berkowitz (ed.), *Advances in Experimental Social Psychology* (New York: Academic Press, 1967), pp. 55–98.
55. Wiener, M., Devoe, S., Rubinow, S., and Geller, J. "Nonverbal Communication." *Psychological Review* 79, (1972):185–214.

18

HAND MOVEMENTS

Paul Ekman and Wallace V. Friesen

Abstract

A revision of our theoretically based classification of nonverbal
behavior is presented, as it relates to the interpretation and
measurement of hand movements. On the basis of the origins, usage
and coding of the behavior distinctions are drawn and hypotheses
offered about three classes of behavior: emblems, illustrators and
adaptors. Findings from our own cross-cultural studies, our studies
of psychiatric patients, and our studies of deceptive interactions,
together with research by Kumin and Lazar, and a study by Harrison
and Cohen are summarized to demonstrate the utility of this
classification of hand movements. The differences between our
formulation and those proposed by Freedman and Hoffman, Mahl,
and Rosenfeld are discussed.

Reprinted by permission of the International Communication Association
from "Hand Movements" by Paul Ekman and Wallace V. Friesen in
Journal of Communication 22:4 (1972):353–374.

INTRODUCTION

Our effort over the past fifteen years has been to develop methods and a theoretical framework for studying nonverbal behavior. Our aim has been both to increase understanding of the individual, his feelings, mood, personality, and attitudes, and to increase understanding of any given interpersonal interaction, the nature of the relationship, the status or quality of communication, what impressions are formed, and what is revealed about interpersonal style or skill. While the study of interpersonal interactions can reveal information about each of the individual interactants, as when, for example, their interactive behavior is seen as a prime manifestation or index of their personality, we draw a distinction between individual and interpersonal concerns, and study people both when they are alone and when they are "with" (Goffman: 16) another person. People have experiences as individuals when alone, changes in feelings and mood. Nonverbal behavior may then be the only source of information about their experience, since people rarely speak when alone; and nonverbal behavior may be an especially rich source in such circumstances, because when the individual is alone his nonverbal behavior is less subject to inhibition or control for social reasons. If we are to understand the influence of social rules about nonverbal behavior in interpersonal interactions, particularly about the management of what we have defined as affect displays and self-adaptors, we must also examine the individual when he is alone.

Our interest in what nonverbal behavior can tell us about individual experience as well as social interaction led to certain decisions about the size of the units we study. If we had been concerned only with the role of nonverbal behavior in social interaction, we might have focused only on what can be easily perceived by persons engaged in such an interaction. Micro-events not easily seen without slowed or repeated viewing would have been omitted. Our interest in the experience of the individual when alone has led to including such micro-events, while our interest in how nonverbal behavior functions in social interaction has required our examining molar units of behavior.

Throughout our studies we have emphasized a comprehensive approach, considering not just one aspect of motor behavior, such as facial expression, or eye contact, or hand movements, or posture, or leg movements, but all of these, if possible, on the same subject in the same settings. This comprehensive approach is based on our assumption that because activities in different areas of the body can serve equivalent or substitutive functions, studies of just one type of activity may provide an incomplete picture of what is occurring. Further, we believe that studies of the sequence of nonverbal behavior requires study of activities across the face and body. And, to the extent that we are interested in one person's impression of another, we must consider the entire range of nonverbal behavior (and voice and words as well), since that is what is available to each participant in most interactions. Finally, some of our theoretical work has proposed major differences between the face and body, particularly when there is conflict about communication (6, 8).

This may seem to be a strange way to introduce a paper which discusses just one area of the body, hand movements, but we want to emphasize that we are reporting here just part of our work. We are conducting studies with the same materials on facial expression, posture, eye contact, and leg movement. The comprehensive approach, we believe, will provide the most important findings and a theoretical breakthrough in the study of nonverbal communication. In the last three years, most of our publications have reported our studies of facial expression (2, 7, 11, 12, 13). During that time we have continued to analyze body movement as well. Here we will report an up-date of our theoretically based classification of hand movements, and some of our first results on the measurement of hand movements.

A THEORETICALLY BASED CLASSIFICATION OF HAND MOVEMENTS

We were anti-theoretical when we began our measuring body movements, blaming the sorry state of this field of research on an over-abundance of theory with too few facts. Rather than considering anything about the origins of the behavior, its coding, or its usage, we were determined simply to measure the behavior itself, free of any theoretical guidance. The unit of behavior we proposed (3) was the nonverbal *act*, which was defined as a movement within any body area(s) which has visual integrity and is visually distinctive from another act. Acts which looked similar to our coders were given the same designation and their frequency and duration were measured. In studies of psychiatric in-patients, we found that some acts so defined were systemmatically related to concomitant verbal behavior and some acts conveyed specific information to observers when judged out of context. While we found that the frequency of particular acts differed between time of admission and time of discharge to a mental hospital for individual patients, we failed to find similarity across these patients in the particular acts which occurred with the greatest frequency at either admission or discharge from the hospital (4). Thus, analyzing behavior as separate acts provided information on an idiosyncratic but not a shared basis; the acts shown varied with ego states for each individual, but the same acts were not shown by individuals who were presumably similar in ego state. At about this time we re-read David Efron's (1) pioneering work on nonverbal behavior, in which he studied the conversational behaviors of Jewish and Italian immigrants in New York.[1] Greatly influenced by the fact that Efron's classification of body movements yielded findings which held across persons, we developed a theoretical scheme to classify body movement and facial expression, not solely on the basis of visual appearance as we did with the act, but on the basis of the *origin, coding* and *usage* of the act.

Origin refers to how the nonverbal behavior initially became part of the person's repertoire. We distinguished three origins: innate or built-in to the nervous system; species-constant experiences, that is, experiences always entailed when the human equipment interacts with any environment and survival results; and experiences which vary with culture, class, family, or individual.

Coding refers to the principle of correspondence between the act and its meaning, the rule which characterizes the relationship between the act and its significant. We distinguished three types of coding. An abitrarily coded act has no visual resemblance to its significant; the movement in no way looks like or contains a clue to what it means. An iconically coded act carries the clue to its decoding in its appearance; the sign looks in some way like what it means.[2] An intrinsically coded act is like an iconic one, visually related to what it signifies, but here the act does not resemble its significant; it *is* its significant. For example, if one person hits another during conversation, the hitting act is not iconic but intrinsic; the act is the significant.

Usage refers to the regular and consistent circumstances surrounding the occurrence of a nonverbal act. Usage includes the external conditions found whenever the act occurs, the relationship of the act to the associated verbal behavior, whether the person is aware of performing the act, whether the person consciously intended the performance of the act to communicate to another person, feedback from the other interactant, and the type of information conveyed by the act, whether it be shared or idiosyncratic, and whether it also is communicative or interactive. Idiosyncratic acts are meaningful, not random, activity, but the meaning is specific to one person. Among acts which have shared meaning there are those which were consciously intended to send a message to another person, communicative acts, and those which typically lead to a consistent change in the behavior of the other interactant, interactive acts. A given movement can be both communicative and interactive, or either—or neither. If an act has shared meaning but is neither communicative nor interactive, we call it informative.

On the basis of their origin, coding and usage, we then described five classes of nonverbal behavior. We will describe here just the three classes which are relevant to distinguishing among most hand movements: emblems; illustrators; and adaptors.

Emblems are those nonverbal acts (a) which have a direct verbal translation usually consisting of a word or two, or a phrase, (b) for which this precise meaning is known by most or all members of a group, class, subculture, or culture, (c) which are most often deliberately used with the conscious intent to send a particular message to the other person(s), (d) for which the person(s) who sees the emblem usually not only knows the emblem's message but also knows that is was deliberately sent to him, and (e) for which the sender usually takes responsibility for having made that communication. A further touchstone of an emblem is whether it can be replaced by a word or two, its message verbalized, without substantially modifying the conversation.

People are usually aware of their use of an emblem, just as aware as they are of the words they emit. However, there can be emblematic slips, like slips of the tongue, when the sender apparently does not deliberately choose to make the emblem and may be unaware that he has done so. Emblems most often occur when verbal discourse is prevented by external circumstance (e.g., between pilot and landing crew), by distance (e.g., between hunters spaced apart from each other in the field), by agreement (e.g., while playing charades), or by organic impairment. Emblems of course also occur during conversation, repeating a verbalized message, replacing a word or two, adding a separate message not necessarily part of the verbal discourse, or contradicting the verbalization. Emblems, as we have defined them, are communicative and interactive acts.

The origin of emblems is culture specific learning. Efron (1) found major differences in the emblems used by Italian and Jewish immigrants to the United States. Saitz and Cervenka (25) have catalogued differences in emblematic behaviors between Colombia and the U.S. We have found major differences in the emblems used in urban Japan, urban Argentina, and a preliterate culture in

New Guinea (10). As we expected, there are a few emblems which are the same across these groups; these are ones which are similar because of our anatomy—referring to a body part, or to a bodily action which, because of anatomical constraints, can only be performed in one way. We have found the number of emblems in each group to vary, but in each group we discovered more than 50 different emblems, and in some more than 100.

Emblems can be either arbitrarily or iconically coded. In our studies of emblems we have uncovered both types. Emblems can involve actions in any part of the body, although typically they involve the hands, head orientation, facial muscular movement, or posture.

Illustrators are those acts which are intimately related on a moment-to-moment basis with speech, with phrasing, content, voice contour, loudness, etc. Illustrators usually augment what is being said verbally, but they may contradict the verbalization or be used as a subscitute for a word. Illustrators are similar to emblems in that they are used with awareness and intentionality, although the use of illustrators is usually in peripheral, not focal, awareness. Illustrators differ from emblems in a number of ways. Many of the illustrators do not have as precise a verbal definition as the emblems, and for some illustrators there is actually no obvious or agreed upon verbal translation of the act. Also, illustrators do not occur without conversation, or the rehearsal of conversation. And, illustrators are only shown by the speaker in a conversation, not by the listener, while emblems may be shown by either speaker or listener.

Changes in the frequency of illustrator activity for any given individual depends upon mood and problems in verbal communication. When a person is demoralized, discouraged, tired, unenthusiastic, concerned about the other person's impression, or in a nondominant position in a formal interaction and setting, the rate of illustrators is less than is usual for that person. With excitement, enthusiasm about the topic or process of communication, when in the dominant role in a formal interaction, or in a more informal interaction where there is little concern about the impression being conveyed, a person uses more illustrators. When difficulty is experienced in finding the right words, or when feedback from the listener suggests he is not comprehending what is being said, illustrators increase. Illustrators can fill pauses, and maintain the role of speakers for the speaker if that is in doubt, and they can serve to command renewed attention from the listener if that is flagging.[3] While illustrators aid in managing the behavior of the other conversant, and help the speaker explain and the listener understand what is said, illustrators also serve a self-priming function, helping the speaker past an awkwardness in his speech or thought, accelerating the flow of his ideas. We should note the qualification that these ideas about changes in the rate of illustrator activity are based on and meant to apply to middle class white Americans, and we do not know how much of this is general to other groups. Certainly we do know that the type of illustrator varies with ethnic background, and it may also vary with social class and age. We distinguish the following eight types of illustrators.

> *batons:* movements which accent or emphasize a particular word or phrase
> *ideographs:* movements which sketch the path or direction of thought
> *deictic-movements:* pointing to an object, place, or event
> *spatial movements:* movements which depict a spatial relationship
> *rhythmic movements:* movements which depict the rhythm or pacing of an event
> *kinetographs:* movements which depict a bodily action, or some non-human physical action
> *pictographs:* movements which draw a picture in the air of the shape of the referrent
> *emblematic movements:* emblems used to illustrate a verbal statement, either repeating or substituting for a word or phrase

Some of the terminology and some of the sub-types were first described by Efron (1), who found that the type of illustrator employed differed for Italian and Jewish immigrants to the U.S. We know of no further study of illustrator sub-types in the last thirty years.

By including emblematic illustrators as one sub-type, we wish to make clear that illustrators are not an exclusive category; the classification of a behavior as an illustrator depends upon its usage in a given context. An act can be both an emblem and because of its particular usage at a particular time also an illustrator. Our classification of illustrator sub-types should emphasize that there are many illustrators which do not involve emblematic acts. Further, illustrators may in a particular instance be also designated as regulators, if they manage the conversational flow (cf. footnote 3).

The eight illustrator sub-types are also not mutually exclusive. Although many illustrators fall neatly into one or another category, others are combinations of sub-types. The need to distinguish the sub-types rather than simply measure the presence of any type of illustrators will depend upon the purposes of the experiment. If, for example, the investigator is interested in just how body movement is interrelated on a moment-to-moment basis with verbal behavior, or if he is interested in ethnic or social class differences in nonverbal behavior, distinguishing the illustrator sub-types should be profitable.

Illustrators are informative acts, and some could be considered communicative as well, although their explicit intentionality is not always certain. Illustrators can be interactive depending upon whether there is a response by the other interactant in a given context.

Illustrators are socially learned, presumably many of them early in life during language acquisition. Their chief function early in life is probably to command the adults' attention, and to aid in explaining matters for which the child has no words. The self-priming function could also occur early, but probably becomes more important after the child has a moderate vocabulary, when there is verbal material to prime. Most illustrators are iconically coded, the type of iconic coding varying with the sub-type. Some of the emblematic illustrators may be arbitrarily coded. Like emblems, illustrators may involve any part of the body, although typically they involve the hands, head, facial muscular movement, or postural shift.

Adaptors are movements first learned as part of an effort to satisfy self needs or body needs, or to perform certain bodily actions, or to manage and cope with emotions, or to develop or maintain prototypic interpersonal contacts, or to learn instrumental activities. Emitted in private, or even in public if the individual is alone, not with another person, and not the conspicuous objects of anyone's attention, the adaptive act (i.e., nose-picking, head-scratching) will be manifest in its entirety, carried through to completion, so that it is obvious what need is being satisfied, what the person is about. When the person is aware that he is being watched, or is with another person, and particularly when he is speaking in a conversation, adaptor acts will be reduced or fragmented, so that they are not nearly as conspicuous, nor is it always obvious what need is being met. These fragmented adaptors do not serve completely to accomplish their goal (the hand may go to the nose but the nostril may not be entered or cleansed, the scalp may be touched but the itch not thoroughly scratched).

The management of adaptors when the person is conversing, the process of reducing them in time, scope and completeness, seems to occur with little awareness, and the reduced adaptor is emitted with little cognizance by the performer. Adaptors are either iconically or intrinsically coded. If the movement is reduced or fragmented it approaches the iconic, but it could be considered intrinsically coded if the movement is not altered.

We distingiush *self-adaptors*, *object-adaptors*, and *alter-adaptors*. The last is discussed elsewhere (5).

Self-adaptors are learned and utilized in condition with a variety of problems or needs. Some are relevant to facilitating or blocking sensory input; some are relevant to ingestive, excretive, or autoerotic activity; some are relevant to grooming, cleansing, or modifying the attractiveness of the face and body; some are relevant to facilitating or blocking sound making and speech; and some appear to be aggression directed against the self.

All other things being equal, self-adaptors occur more frequently when the person is in a private rather than a public place, when alone rather than in the presence of others, when not in any way involved with others rather than "with" others, when listening rather than speaking in conversation. No matter when it occurs, the adaptor is never deliberately employed to communicate information to another person. Self-adaptors have no intrinsic relationship to concomitant speech, but they may be triggered by the motives or affects which are being verbalized, or by discomfort or anxiety about conversation.

When the individual is alone in a private place, he may or may not be aware of his adaptor activity. When he is in conversation, although he will reduce or fragment his adaptor acts, the individual is rarely aware of either managing or performing the adaptor acts. The performance of self-adaptors during conversation rarely receives direct attention or comment from others, except for the parents' comments to the child. The person showing a self-adaptor will break visual contact with the other interactants, and they will not look at him in any sustained fashion until he finishes the adaptor activity.

Adaptors are unlike both emblems and illustrators in intentionality and awareness, having little of either. While emblems and illustrators will almost never be shown when the individual is totally alone, or disengaged from some form of communication with another person, self-adaptors will occur, often with high frequency and in their most complete form, when the person is alone.

In any given conversational setting people differ markedly in their rate of self-adaptor activity. Self-adaptors will increase with psychological discomfort or anxiety, although some people will show a decrease in self-adaptors when discomforted or anxious, instead freezing movement in muscularly tense immobility. We believe that specific types of self-adaptors are associated with specific feelings and attitudes. Two examples can illustrate our thinking. Picking or squeezing part of the body is aggression against the self or aggression towards others temporarily displaced onto the self; covering the eye with a hand is relevant to preventing input, avoiding being seen, and shame. Both the action and location of the self-adaptor must be considered to decode the specific meaning of the act, although certain actions, such as the picking or squeezing, may have meaning in themselves regardless of location. When many parts of the body can perform an adaptor action (lips, teeth, legs, feet) we will discuss here only self-adaptors in which the hand is performing the action in contact with some part of the body. We classify the actions of the hand as rub, squeeze, pick-scratch, holds, supports, covers, grooms, massages and plays (plays are small movements where it is difficult to say just what the action is). Our list of locations which the hand may contact is based on both biological and psychological functions associated with different parts of the body. For example, we distinguish the eyes, ears, nose and mouth, but do not make locational distinctions within the cheek. While we make no distinctions within the forehead, we do distinguish the temple because it can symbolize thought. Additional locations are lips, chin, hair, neck, general torso, breasts, crotch, rump, arms, hands, fingers, legs, feet.

Object-adaptors involve the use of some object or prop, e.g., a pencil, part of the clothing, matchbook, etc. If the object is used to accomplish an instrumental task, we do not consider the act an object-adaptor. If the object is held or moved without serving an instrumental goal, the act is classified as an object-adaptor. For example, taking notes during a conversation is not an object-adaptor, but holding or playing with the pencil is. Doodling is intermediate, and we classify it as an object-adaptor. Similarly, smoking is not an object-adaptor, but playing with the cigarette, when lit or unlit, or playing with matches or lighter are object-adaptors. Object-adaptors are usually more within awareness than self-adaptors, and their meaning is more general—restlessness. Some object-adaptors can have more specific meaning, depending on the action involved (21). For example, the prop can be used in an attack on the body, or to soothe or stroke part of the body.

Let us turn now to consider some of the research in which we and others have utilized this scheme for distinguishing different classes of hand movements.

RESEARCH ON EMBLEMS

Our initial work on emblems was a survey of emblems in different cultures. Our procedure was fairly simple. We started with an *a priori* list of messages which might be emblematic. The concept of emblems was explained to a subject, who was asked if he had a way of saying each message with his body. Subjects were asked to volunteer emblems not on the original list and these were added to the list for the next subject. The emblematic performances were filmed or videotaped. An emblem was established for a cultural group if (a) the majority of subjects made the same movement for the same message, (b) a new group of subjects when shown the emblem correctly decoded the message, and (c) they agreed it was an intentional act used within their culture to communicate the message. As mentioned earlier, some emblems have appeared across the cultures we have studied. These are the ones which involve a message describing a bodily activity which, for anatomical reasons, must be performed in similar ways. For example, if a culture has an emblem for sleeping, we have found it will involve moving the head into a lateral position, perpendicular to the body, with or without bringing one or both hands below the head as a kind of pillow.

Many messages are emblematic in more than one culture, but a different movement is used in each culture. With many of these the message involves the use of tools. For example, in the U.S. the emblem for suicide is placing the hand to the temple, with the hand in the "gun-shooting" emblem position (index finger extended, thumb raised and moved towards and away from the index finger, and the other fingers curled into the palm). In the Fore of New Guinea the emblem for suicide is grabbing the throat with an open hand and pushing up, a representation of hanging, which is how these people commit suicide. In Japan the suicide emblem is either to plunge one fist into the stomach, a representation of hari-kari, or to draw the index finger across the neck, a representation of slitting the throat.

Many messages are emblematic in one culture, and not in another. Efron, in the republication of his book (1), has included a list of Sicilian emblems. We are comparing these with our surveys in the U.S., Japan and the Fore of New Guinea.

Kumin and Lazar (20) have conducted a developmental study of emblems. Comparing 3 to 3½-year-old with 4 to 4½-year-old children, they found that the number of emblems performed and recognized increased with age. No work has yet appeared to our knowledge on the earliest appearance of emblems before and during language acquisition, although one of our students has written a theoretical paper on this topic (18).

We have studied a particular emblem as a clue to the occurrence of deception. Twenty-one student nurses were subjects in this experiment. They honestly described their reactions to a pleasant film in one interview and dishonestly attempted to deceive the interviewer in another session, pretending pleasant feelings when they had seen a stressful film[4] Pilot studies had suggested that a particular emblem, the hand shrug which has the meaning of helplessness or inability (see Figure 1), would appear as a clue to the occurrence of deception.[5] Our theory of nonverbal leakage and clues to deception (6) had specified that hand and leg movements would not be as closely monitoried or disguised as the face during deception. Hand movements could provide either leakage of the concealed information, or a clue that deception was in progress without revealing what was concealed. In this instance, we expected that the hand-shrug emblem was occurring as a nonverbal slip of

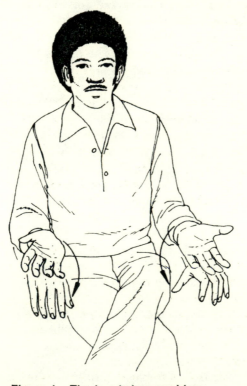

Figure 1   The hand shrug emblem.

the tongue, with little awareness on the part of the subject, and that it was a deception clue.

All of the hand movements shown by the subjects in the honest and deceptive interviews were located, each was classified as an emblem, illustrator or adaptor, and the frequency of each was determined. As predicted, the hand shrug emblem increased in the deceptive session from a mean of 13.1 (expressed as a percent of total hand activity) in the honest interview to a mean of 23.5 in the deceptive interview, and this difference was significant at the .05 level.

RESEARCH ON ILLUSTRATORS

Harrison and Cohen (17) compared the frequency of illustrators used when subjects were given directions to a person visibly present and, over an intercom, to a person in another room. Illustrators occurred more often when the recipient was visibly present. They interpreted their findings as consistent with our explanation of the function of illustrators—they are intended to communicate information to another person and, at least in part, are used to help explain the verbalized message.

We know of no work pursuing Efron's discovery that the type of illustrator activity shown varies with ethnic origin. We have found some relationships between the frequency of illustrators disregarding the type employed, and personality. Among the student nurses who participated in our deception experiment frequency of illustrating in the honest session was positively not related with the femininity scale of the California Personality Inventory (.61) and with cooperativeness on the Interpersonal Check List (.53), but negatively with dominance (−.54 on the CPI, −.48 on the ICL). These findings must be viewed with great caution; although they are consistent, the sample was small and the relationships had not been predicted.

We did predict on the basis of our leakage theory that illustrators would decrease in the deceptive session. We expected fewer illustrators then because there would be less enthusiasm when witnessing the stress film. Although a perfect deceiver would still maintain illustrator activity when pretending a pleasant film was being viewed, our theory stated that hand activity is not used to simulate. The mean frequency for illustrators was 23.9 (expressed as a percent of total activity) in the honest session and 14.7 in the deceptive session, a difference significant at the .05 level.

Our studies of interviews conducted at the beginning and end of psychiatric hospitalization have also provided information about illustrators (19).[6] The hand movements in the admission and discharge interviews with 31 female patients were classified. Nine of the patients had been diagnosed as psychotic depressive, seven as neurotic depressive and 15 as schizophrenic. We predicted an increase in illustrators from admission to discharge for the psychotic depressives because of the shift away from a dysphoric mood, but no difference in the schizophrenics. This prediction was confirmed, and there was a trend for illustrators to increase at discharge for the neurotic depressives; the psychotic depressives showed a mean of 2.7 illustrators at admission and 12.3 at discharge, a difference significant at less than the .05 level, and there was no change in illustrator activity for the schizophrenics. The patients were also rated on Overall and Gorham's (22) Brief Psychiatric Rating Scale, and these ratings were factor analyzed. We called the first factor "out of it," since the Overall and Gorham scales of withdrawal and motor retardation had the highest factor loadings. Scores on this factor were negatively correlated with illustrator activity (−.67). These findings were not affected when a control was introduced for number of words emitted in each interview.

RESEARCH ON ADAPTORS

Our deception experiment also provided data relevant to adaptors. We expected an increase in self-adaptors and object-adaptors in the deceptive interview, because subjects should be more uncomfortable and anxious than in the honest session. This prediction was not confirmed. When all self- and object-adaptors were considered, regardless of the type of action and the location of the action, there was no difference between the honest and deceptive sessions. Our sample was too small to compare many of the self-adaptor sub-types. One of the few sub-types which did occur with some frequency across subjects showed the predicted increase in activity. Face-play increased from the honest session (.33 mean percent of total hand activity) to the deceptive session (2.6); this difference was significant beyond the .01 level.

We also explored whether self-adaptor activity is related to how observers evaluate nonverbal behavior. A group of observers were told the nature of the situation, saw a sample of the subject's behavior during the honest session, which was identified as being honest behavior, and then saw an additional sample of behavior, which was from either the honest or deceptive session. They had to judge whether this unidentified sample came from the honest or deceptive session. The observers saw only the body; the face was blocked off from their view. From our interpretation of self-adaptors we expected that observers who viewed the body would tend to call people deceptive if they showed many self-adaptors (thus appearing anxious, fidgety, nervous) and honest if they did not. That is what did occur. The rate of self-adaptors was positively correlated (.75) with the observers' judgments of deception.

In another part of our analysis of the deception experiment we found that the subject's facial behavior during the honest and deceptive session was related to their work in the School of Nursing over the following year, both to their clinical grades (that is, ratings of how well they worked with patients), and to their academic grades. Untrained observers were shown just the facial behavior of each subject and asked to judge whether the subject was being honest or deceptive. Subjects whose honest facial behavior was judged as honest did well in the School of Nursing over the next year, earning good academic and clinical grades. We may infer that those who were judged honest were those who appeared relaxed and that persons who can relax, or appear relaxed, in this situation are likely to be best able to do well in the nursing situation.

More important for our interests we found that skill in facial deceiving (that is, the observers were misled when they judged the subject's face during the deception session) was significantly correlated (.63) with clinical grades one year later when a partial correlation technique was employed to remove the influence of the relationship between grades and how the face during the honest session was judged. (The correlations between facial deceiving and academic grades were not significant when the partial correlation technique was applied.) We had expected to find such a relationship and had designed our deception situation in part to tap clinically relevant interpersonal skills and had explained the experiment and recruited subjects in those terms. These findings provided the basis for testing a hypothesis about self-adaptors.

Our interpretation of self-adaptors during deceptive interaction led to the prediction that the frequency of their occurrence would be negatively correlated with nursing grades in the following year. Our reasoning was that showing self-adaptors when deceiving was to be a poor deceiver. If deceptive skill is correlated with success in nursing, then those who show many self-adaptors when deceiving would not do well in the School of Nursing. An alternative prediction could be made, based on our interpretation that self-adaptors generally are a sign of discomfort or anxiety. This hypothesis would argue that subjects who were uncomfortable or nervous in the experiment would be those who would not do well in the School of Nursing quite independently of deceptive skill. The significance of self-adaptors in this context would be in their revelation of discomfort not of a lack of deceptive skill. From this viewpoint the correlation between self-adaptors and subsequent school performance should be found regardless of whether the self-adaptor occurred in the honest or deceptive part of the experiment. The data support the first hypothesis, not the second. Self-adaptors in the deceptive session were negatively correlated with the combined clinical and academic grade (− .54) one year later, but self-adaptors in the honest session were unrelated to subsequent achievement in nursing school.

Our last source of evidence on self-adaptors came from the analysis of hand movements during the interviews with psychiatric patients. It will be remembered that the patients had been rated on the Overall and Gorham scales, and these ratings were then factor analyzed. The scales with the highest loading on the second factor were *anxiety* and *guilt feelings,* and scores on this factor were positively correlated (.38) with self-adaptor activity when the type of self-adaptor activity was disregarded. The scales with the highest loading on the fourth factor were *hostility* and *suspiciousness*; scores on this factor were positively correlated (.33) with self-adaptors in which the action was picking or scratching.[7]

CONCLUSION

We have presented our classification of hand movements, explaining the theoretical basis for the distinctions we make, and offering a number of hypotheses about the origins, usage and coding of three different classes of nonverbal behavior. The research reported does not test all of our hypotheses, but the evidence to date is consistent with our theory and most of the hypotheses tested have been supported. Most important, the studies briefly summarized here should serve to demonstrate the utility of our classifatory scheme in converting a seemingly vague area of behavior, hand movements, into data which can be examined quantitatively, yielding findings relevant to culture, personality and the nature of the interaction.

Our framework is posited on the notion that nonverbal behavior is not all of one kind. Even when dealing only with one area of the body, hands, it is crucial to make distinctions among some of the very different kinds of things people do. There is now some consensus among those studying hand behavior about the need to make some distinctions. All have a category similar to our self-adaptors; Rosenfeld (24) called this category *self-manipulations*, Mahl (21) called it *autistic*, and Freedman and Hoffman (15) called it *body-focused*. All agree that this behavior related to negative feelings. There is disagreement about the specific negative feelings involved, their functions and meanings, and the usefulness of drawing further distinctions within this sphere of activity. All have a category similar to what we have called illustrators; Rosenfeld called this category *gesticulation*. Mahl called it *communicative*, and Freedman and Hoffman called it *object-focused*. All agree that this behavior is related to speech, and serves to explain what is being said verbally. There is considerable disagreement about what the sub-classes of this type of activity are, and how they function in conversation. Efron, ourselves, and Kumin and Lazar have worked with emblems, although the other investigators of hand movements describe behavior which we would categorize as emblems. As yet there is no data base for determining the relative utility of these different approaches, for deciding whether they are alternatives and which is more useful, or whether they are approaching different levels or aspects of the phenomena.[8]

In closing we reiterate that our distinction between illustrators, emblems and adaptors applies not only to the hands, but also to facial behavior and leg movements. In addition, we have proposed two other classes of behavior not described here, *affect* displays and *regulators* (5). We believe that progress in the study of nonverbal behavior requires consideration of all five classes of behavior, all parts of the organism's motor activity—in the face, hands, legs, posture—and the interrelationship of these nonverbal behaviors with measures of voice and language.

Notes

[1] Efron's book, long out of print, has just been republished with additional materials not available in the original publication.

[2] We further distinguished five types of iconic coding. For a complete explanation of what we mean by origin, coding and usage, and a complete description of our classification scheme, we refer the reader to Ekman and Friesen (5). While we have updated some of our thinking in this article, we have also by necessity had to simplify or omit many aspects of our theory which are crucial to fully understanding it, or applying it in research.

[3] This function of illustrators would fit our definition of another class of movement, "regulators," acts which manage the flow of conversation (5). We have purposefully allowed for overlap among our classes of behavior, when a particular instance is considered—some illustrators, but

not all, and some emblems, but not all, in particular instances also should be designated as regulators because they are functioning primarily to regulate the conversational flow; but some acts which are not either emblems or illustrators, such as the affect displays, will also on occasion be employed as regulators; and, as will be explained shortly, an emblem can in particular instances be used as an illustrator.

[4] For a complete description of the experimental situation see (9); for a report of a study which showed that observers can more accurately judge the occurrence of deception from the body than from the face, see (8).

[5] Mahl (21) has described this emblem and attributed the same meaning to it, although his theoretical scheme does not distinguish emblems as a separate class of nonverbal behavior.

[7] The third factor was one where the highest loadings were on the scales *unusual thought* and *concept disorganization*. Scores on this factor were not related to either self-adaptors or illustrators.

[8] For recent work on hand movements, see Freedman et al. (14) and Rosenfeld (23).

References

1. Efron, D. *Gesture and Environment* (New York: King's Crown, 1941); (current ed.) *Gesture, Race and Culture* (The Hague: Mouton, 1972).
2. Ekman, P. "Universals and Cultural Differences in Facial Expressions of Emotion." In *Nebraska Symposium on Motivation, 1971* (edited by J. Cole). University of Nebraska Press, 1972.
3. Ekman, P., and Friesen, W. V. "The Nonverbal Act: A Visual Unit of Nonverbal Behavior." Paper presented at the American Psychological Association Symposium, New York, September, 1966.
4. Ekman, P., and Friesen, W. V. "Nonverbal Behavior in Psychotherapy Research." In J. Shlien (ed.), *Research in Psychotherapy*, vol. III (Washington, D.C.: American Psychological Association, 1968).
5. Ekman, P., and Friesen, W. V. "The Repertoire of Nonverbal Behavior: Categories, Origins, Usage, and Coding." *Semiotica* 1, (1969): 49–98.
6. Ekman, P., and Friesen, W. V. "Nonverbal Leakage and Clues to Deception." *Psychiatry* 32, (1969):88–105.
7. Ekman, P., and Friesen, W. V. "Constants Across Cultures in the Face and Emotion." *Journal of Personality and Social Psychology* 17, (1971):124–129.
8. Ekman, P., and Friesen, W. V. "Detecting Deception from the

Body or Face." *Journal of Personality and Social Psychology,* in press.

9. Ekman, P., and Friesen, W. V. "Nonverbal Behavior and Psychopathology." In R. J. Friedman and M. M. Katz (eds.), *The Psychology of Depression: Contemporary Theory and Research,* 1973, in press.
10. Ekman, P., and Friesen, W. V. "Cross-Cultural Survey of Emblems." Manuscript in preparation.
11. Ekman, P., Friesen, W. V., and Ellsworth, P. *Emotion in the Human Face: Guidelines for Research and an Integration of Findings* (New York: Pergamon, 1972).
12. Ekman, P., Friesen, W. V., and Tomkins, S. S. "Facial Affect Scoring Technique: A First Validity Study," *Semiotica 3,* (1971):37–58.
13. Ekman, P., Sorenson, E. R., and Friesen, W. V. "Pan-Cultural Elements in Facial Displays of Emotions." *Science* **164,** (1969):86–88.
14. Freedman, N., Blass, T., Rifkin, A., and Quitkin, F. "Body Movements and Verbal Encoding of Aggressive Affect." *Journal of Personality and Social Psychology,* 1973, in press.
15. Freedman, N., and Hoffman, S. P. "Kinetic Behavior in Altered Clinical States: Approach to Objective Analysis of Motor Behavior During Clinical Interviews." *Perceptual and Motor Skills* **24,** (1967):527–539.
16. Goffman, E. *Relations in Public* (New York: Basic Books, 1971).
17. Harrison, R., and Cohen, A. A. "Intentionality in the Use of Hand Illustrators in Face-to-Face Communication Situations." *Journal of Personality and Social Psychology,* 1972, in press.
18. Johnson, H. G. "Infant Communication." Qualifying examination paper, University of California, San Francisco, 1972.
19. Kiritz, S. A., Ekman, P., and Friesen, W. V. "Hand Movements and Psychopathology." In preparation.
20. Kumin, L., and Lazar, M., "Acquisition of Nonverbal Behavior: The Encoding and Decoding of Emblems in Young Children." Presented at the Speech Communication Association, December, 1971.
21. Mahl, G. F. "Gestures and Body Movements in Interviews." In J. Shlien (ed.), *Research in Psychotherapy,* vol. III (Washington, D.C.: American Psychological Association, 1968).
22. Overall, J. E., and Gorham, E. R. "The Brief Psychiatric Rating Scale." *Psychological Reports* **10,** (1962):799–812.

23. Rosenfeld, H. M. "The Experimental Analysis of Interpersonal Influence Processes." *Journal of Communication* **22**, (1972): 353–374.
24. Rosenfeld, H. M. "Instrumental Affiliative Functions of Facial and Gestural Expressions." *Journal of Personality and Social Psychology* **4**, (1966):65–72.
25. Saitz, R. L., and Cervenka, E. J. *Colombian and North American Gestures: An Experimental Study* (Bogota, Colombia: Centro Colombo-Americano, 1962); (current ed.) *Handbook of Gesture: Colombia and the United States*. In *Approaches to Semiotics* (The Hague: Mouton Publishers, 1972, [1973]), vol. 31.

19

THE SIGNIFICANCE OF POSTURE IN COMMUNICATION SYSTEMS

Albert Scheflin

INTENTION AND FUNCTION IN COMMUNICATION

In psychiatry, human group behavior has traditionally been examined in terms of the personal, unique life experiences and behavioral expressions of each subject. This is a psychological view. More recently, the interaction *between* individuals has become of interest to psychiatrists. The social psychological approach to such interaction examines how one person's behavior affects another. The sociological viewpoint considers the organization of individuals as a group. All of these approaches focus upon the individual or group, in contrast with the cultural approach, which emphasizes the discovery of the traditional formats or templates, learned and used by each member of a culture, that determine behavior. These varying views in no way

Reprinted by special permission of The William Alanson White Psychiatric Foundation, Inc. from *Psychiatry* 27 (1964), 317–331.
© 1964 by The William Alanson White Psychiatric Foundation, Inc.

represent in themselves competitive or alternative truths; but whichever one is used determines how researchers approach the quest for the function or meaning of an element of human behavior.

The psychological approach traditionally answers any question about meaning with a statement about the motivations or intention of the individual who performs the actions. But this type of explanation is too narrow in itself to account for the meaning or *function* of behavior in a group. In the first place, human behavior can be communicative whether or not it is *intended* to communicate. To one who recognizes it, the rash of measles is informative, but does not, of necessity, signify that the patient means to convey that he is ill. . . . *The intent of an interactant and the function that a behavior actually has in a group process must be conceptually distinguished.*

The behaviors in a group combine to serve social purposes beyond the instinctual aims of any member. The fact that the activities of a group ultimately satisfy the needs of an individual member is not construed to mean that this is the purpose of the group. Group activity is concerned primarily with minute-by-minute control, negotiation of aims and relationships, adherence to form, and so on—the equilibrium of the group itself.

As specific groups have evolved, each has developed traditional forms of interaction which the individual must learn to use and recognize if he is to meet his personal needs. He must negotiate his position within the given forms of a given society.

Thus, every American speaker generally raises his head slightly at the end of statements to which he expects an answer. He does so because all other Americans recognize this postural form for eliciting an answer. It may be that raising the head has other, strictly personal or fanciful meanings for a particular person; but this is beside the point in terms of what is commonly understood by the communicative signal of head-raising. To elicit an answer to his questions, the speaker must perform the head movement in the customary and recognized manner. If he wishes the personal meaning of the movement to be understood, he will have to learn another way of communicating it.

Communication, then, includes *all behaviors by which a group forms, sustains, mediates, corrects, and integrates its relationships.* In the flow of an interaction, communicative behaviors serve to give continuous notification of the states of each participant and of the relationships that obtain between them. Individuals growing up in a culture must learn these communicative behaviors and perform them correctly if they are to be comfortable, perhaps even if they are to survive, in their world.

POSTURAL INDICATORS OF UNITS

Observed through time, the behaviors that make up communicative programs appear to be a continuous stream of events, but actually they are grouped into standard units of structure. These units are not arbitrary divisions made up spontaneously by an interactant or imposed presumptively by an investigator; *they are specific constellations of behavior built into a culture, learned and perceived in communication as Gestalten.*

The structure of language provides a familiar example of this kind of arrangement. Every school child learns about units of language. Syllables are formed into words, and the words are arranged in a given context from which meaning can be derived. These characteristics—components, organization, and context—allow identification of the structural units of language, and their hierarchical arrangement.

This type of hierarchical arrangement is characteristic for any phenomenon of nature. Planets are part of solar systems, which, in turn, are parts of galaxies. Organizations of molecules make up cells, which, in turn, are parts of larger structural units called organs, which make up organisms and so on. In music, certain combinations of rests and notes constitute a measure, so many measures a passage, so many passages a movement, and so on.

Just as language consists of a hierarchy of increasingly more inclusive units, so a communications system as a whole is an integrated arrangement of structural units deriving from kinesic, tactile, lexical, and other elements. This extended view of communication beyond language is new and only slightly bolstered by research, but investigators already note that the system is organized hierarchically into larger and larger structural units. I have designated the units that we have identified beyond the syntactic sentence as the point, the position, and the presentation.

These complex units seem to occur generally in American communication. I am going to describe each of them briefly here, and show how posture and postural shifts mark their duration and termination. Even a sketchy knowledge of them enables one to make practical use of postural observations in understanding interactions such as psychotherapy. Such knowledge brings into awareness what American interactants know unconsciously—when the steps of a communicative stream begin and end and how long each unit is in effect.

It is well known in structural linguistics that the unit known as the syntactic sentence is marked by a terminal change in pitch. These "markers" are called junctures. There are three types in

English: A rise in pitch, indicating a question; a fall in pitch, indicating completion; and a holding of pitch, indicating that the speaker will continue.

In 1962 Birdwhistell demonstrated that these junctures were also accompanied by a movement of the head, eyes, or hands. While the attitudes of head, eyes, and hands are not in traditional usage considered "posture," such actions are analogous to the use of posture in the larger units to be described. The occurrence of this pitch and kinesic activity at the termination of each syntactic sentence is illustrated in Fig. 1.

The Point

When an American speaker uses a series of syntactic sentences in a conversation, he changes the position of his head and eyes every

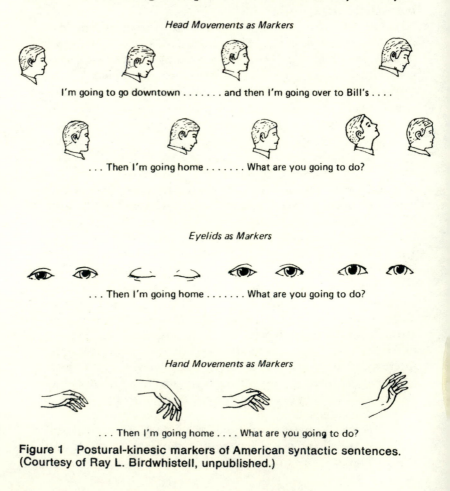

Head Movements as Markers

I'm going to go downtown . . . . and then I'm going over to Bill's . . . .

. . . Then I'm going home . . . . What are you going to do?

Eyelids as Markers

. . . Then I'm going home . . . . What are you going to do?

Hand Movements as Markers

. . . Then I'm going home . . . . What are you going to do?

Figure 1   Postural-kinesic markers of American syntactic sentences. (Courtesy of Ray L. Birdwhistell, unpublished.)

few sentences. He may turn his head right or left, tilt it, cock it to one side or the other, or flex or extend his neck so as to look toward the floor or ceiling. Regardless of the kind of shift in head posture, the attitude is held for a few sentences, then shifted to another position. Each of these shifts I believe marks the end of a structural unit at the next level higher than the syntactic sentence. This unit I have tentatively named a "point" because it corresponds crudely to making a point in a discussion. The maintenance of head position indicates the duration of the point. The use of head-eye postural markers in points is illustrated in Fig. 2.

Most interactants in a given psychotherapy session show a repertoire of three to five points, which they use over and over. For example, the therapist in Fig. 2 used two points repeatedly.

While there may be great variety in the manifest content of the speech accompanying each type of point, it is usually possible to abstract some theme that belongs with each category. For instance, explanations may occur with one type of head position, interruption with another, interpretations with yet another, and listening with a fourth. Or there may be different modes of relating corresponding to each type of point. The patient in Fig. 2 accompanied head cocking to the right with baby talk and other regressive behavior, while in head-erect postures he spoke aggressively and in stilted formal language.

It is difficult to believe that the head-eye points for a person during a thirty-minute interview are thus stereotyped and repetitive. Yet, the participants in this and other interactions that I have studied rarely show greater range or variability. They use the same cluster of postures again and again.

The Position

A sequence of several points constitutes a larger unit of communication that I call the "position." This unit corresponds roughly to a point of view that an interactant may take in an interaction. The position is marked by a gross postural shift involving at least half the body. Positions generally last from about half a minute to five or six minutes, although psychoanalytic therapists may hold the position in which they listen without speaking or moving grossly twenty minutes or more. Most interactants in the social situations that we have observed show about two to four positions.

Everyone is familiar in a general way with the markers of positions. Imagine a participant in a conference leaning back in his chair, smoking, remaining silent as another person expresses a point

The Psychotherapist

Point 1. Head slightly downward, cocked to the right, averting eyes from patient. Used while listening to patient.

Marker. Head lifted up. Marks termination of Point 1 and transition to Point 2. Signals preparation to interpret.

Point 2. Head erect, looking directly at patient. Used while making an interpretation.

Marker. Head turned far to the right, away from patient. Marks termination of Point 2.

The Patient

Point 1. Head erect, turned to his right. Used while therapist is interpreting, and avoids her gaze.

Point 2. Head facing directly toward therapist. Used during response to interpretation. Stares at therapist as he minimizes interpretation's importance.

Point 3. Head cocked, gaze to therapist's left. Patient takes up narrative of another incident not manifestly related to therapist's interpretation, accompanied by childlike manner of speech.

Figure 2   Head placements and markers of points in a psychotherapist and patient.

of view. The listener experiences growing disagreement and decides finally that he must state his viewpoint. His shift begins. He tamps out his cigarette, uncrosses his legs, leans forward, and, perhaps with some gesture, begins his exposition. Two markers of positions for a psychotherapy session are illustrated in Fig. 3.

In Fig. 3 the therapist shifted from an initial position in which he listened to free associations, to a position in which he interpreted and reassured the patient actively. Later he shifted back to his original position and resumed clinical "inactivity." This is a characteristic sequence in psychotherapy.

The largest unit we have studied, the presentation, consists of the totality of one person's positions in a given interaction. Presentations have a duration of from several minutes to several hours, and the terminals are a complete change in location. For example, the participant may leave the meeting altogether or change his place in the room. Such familiar acts as going to the bathroom, going to get cigarettes, or going to make a telephone call, are, in fact, often markers of presentations. After such an interruption, the re-entrant usually assumes a different role or engages in a new type of interaction.

There appear, then, to be at least three levels of structural units above the syntactic sentence that are marked by postural activities. Whether or not there are other actions that can substitute for postural markers we do not yet know, nor do we know for certain whether or not there are other levels or larger units that have not yet been visualized. And we do not yet have clear-cut knowledge about differences incident to ethnic backgrounds or class.

| The therapist begins the session seated, with legs and arms crossed, and leaning backward, away from the patient. In this posture, he uses the clinical tactic of not answering and "eliciting free associations." | After about five minutes, he leans toward the patient, uncrossing his legs. After this postural shift, he is more active—reassuring, interpreting, conversing. He is likely to think of his tactic as "establishing rapport." |

Figure 3 Body postures of a psychotherapist, indicating positions.

Our research shows that the function of an individual's posture in communication is to mark or punctuate the units at multiple levels. The unconscious observation of postures and shifts seems to help American communicants orient themselves in interaction. . . .

POSTURAL INDICATORS OF RELATIONSHIPS

If one directs attention away from individuals in a group and toward the relations between and among members, one feels that posture has another order of communicative significance. At this level, the research question is not how the posture of Mr. X relates to his other activities, but how the posture of Mr. X relates to that of Mr. Y. At this level of relationship one again finds that postural configurations are orderly and standard for a culture.

Although at first glance there seems to be an infinite variety of postural relationships, these can be abstracted to a few basic types, which are regularly associated with given social activities. In fact, even when no words are being spoken (or the sound track of a movie is turned off) it is possible to identify the kinds of human relationship that are in progress by means of the postural configurations and other kinesic movements.

The markers of relationships are mechanically the same postures and shifts that are used by individuals to mark units. But here postural shifts mark the beginning and end of units and some aspects of the relationship as well. It is not unusual for multiple units or activities to be continuous, so that one and the same marker signals the completion of one or more structural divisions and a change in the relationship. For instance, the gun at the end of a football game may mark the end of a play, a quarter, a game, and a season, and at the same time mark the end of a particular relationship between two quarterbacks and another between two teams.

There are three basic dimensions of postural relations in interaction, easily observable, that grossly indicate aspects of the relationships. The three dimensions, which occur simultaneously, are not different types of postural relation but are abstractable from any configuration of posture. They are:

1. Inclusiveness or noninclusiveness of posture—defines the space for the activities and delimits access to and within the group.
2. Vis-à-vis or parallel body orientation—gives evidence about the types of social activities.
3. Congruence or noncongruence of stance and positioning of

extremities—indicates association, nonassociation, or dissociation of group members.

Inclusiveness—Noninclusiveness

Whenever a group is meeting, especially if others are present who are not at that moment engaged in the group activity, the group members tend to define or delimit their immediate group by the placement of their bodies or extremities. When they are standing or have freedom to move furniture, they tend to form a circle. If they are located in a line, the members at each end turn inward and extend an arm or a leg across the open space as if to limit access in or out of the group. This effect we call "bookending." In American groups, it is not unusual for males to sit or stand on the flanks of a seated group; if a number of men are present, those of the highest status usually assume the end positions.

Very often the members of a group act as though there were reason to prevent or discourage certain subgroups from forming or to keep certain participants apart. This is seen in situations in which particular dyads—for example, pairs that might engage in courtship or flirtation, taboo relationships, or arguments—might interfere with other purposes of the group. The access of such members to each other is limited by the body placement and posture of a third participant, who may stand with a part of his body placed between the two who are to be kept separated. In a seated posture, someone may extend a leg or prop it up on a piece of furniture in order to form a barrier. Blocking of this type is also carried out in the following manner: The person on each side of the member to be controlled crosses his legs in such a way as to box in the center person.

It is often noted in established groups that the participants will place their chairs or bodies in such a way as to limit access of a newcomer to those members of the group who are of the opposite sex. For example, in a seminar room, several rows of male staff members are likely to be found between a male visitor and the women members of the group. . . .

A final instance of barrier behavior is seen whenever people are placed more closely together than is customary in the reciprocals of their culture. For any given culture, there are fixed physical distances for each type of relationship at which members subjectively experience comfort. American males standing in a one-to-one relationship position themselves about two feet apart. Southeastern European Jewish and Latin males stand closer. Under usual small-group conditions, two males will not sit side by side with their bodies touching. Where tighter spacing is forced upon group members, barrier behavior will appear. For example, two males crammed together on a sofa will turn their bodies slightly away from each other, cross their legs away from each other, and/or put their adjacent arms over the sides of their faces. Men and women seated in a close face-to-face proximity in other than intimate situations will cross their arms and/or legs and lean backward away from each other.

The reader can easily test the lawfulness of physical interpersonal space by "moving in" on a fellow group member and observing the barrier behavior that occurs.

Vis-à-vis or Parallel Bodily Orientations

In the simplest group, one consisting of two people, there are two basic ways in which the participants can orient their bodies to each other. They can face each other in a structure that I call vis-à-vis, or they may sit side by side, facing the same direction and oriented in common to some third party, task, or object—a relationship that I call parallelism.

Where three people are engaged with one another, there is a striking tendency for two of the three to sit in parallel body orientation, with both vis-à-vis the third person. In groups of four, it is common to see two sets of parallel body orientations vis-à-vis each other. In larger groups one commonly sees an individual dissociate himself in body orientation from the others and relate in vis-à-vis position to the camera, the observer of the group, or some activity outside the group. When it is inconvenient for participants to turn their entire bodies they orient their heads and extremities into these configurations.

When people show a postural orientation vis-à-vis each other, particular types of social interaction usually occur between them. Lexically, they engage in conversation or courtship or instructing or arguing. The common reciprocals of vis-à-vis postural orientation are teacher-student, doctor-patient, and lover-lover. Characteristically these activities are commonly thought of as involving an exchange of information or feeling: teaching, informing, nurturing, treating, courting, conversing, quarreling, and so on. In contrast, the parallel orientation characteristically involves activities in which two or more members engage mutually toward some third party or object. For example, two people sitting or standing side by side may support each other in an argument with a third. They may share in reading, writing, building, enjoying a painting, watching television, or telling a story.

The difference between these two types of activities can be abstracted as follows: In the vis-à-vis orientation the participants must *interact* with each other. Each must alternately contribute some part in a program if the program is to continue. The activities are those of interchange and conversation. Such a human relationship I will call *reciprocal*.

In contrast, the activities carried out in a parallel orientation are those which do not *require* more than one person. They are activities which can be and often are conducted by a single person. For example, when two people in parallel postures listen to another person they are participating in a shared action that could be carried out by a single listener. A similar situation obtains in the joint telling of a joke—as when a man and wife sit side by side telling a story to some third party. Only one person is necessary to tell a story, and, in a sense, members of a shared parallel orientation act as if they were a single person. . . .

These basic body orientations rarely involve the entire body of each participant. Instead, individuals in a group tend to split their body attention, orienting the upper half of the body in one direction and the lower half in another. By this mechanism, an individual in a group of three is likely to be vis-à-vis the second party in upper body orientation and vis-à-vis the third party in lower body orientation. These mixed configurations give the appearance of maintaining group stability by including all members in both vis-à-vis and parallel postural orientations. The vis-à-vis and parallel orientations with splitting are illustrated in Fig. 4.

CONGRUENCE—NONCONGRUENCE

Members of a group often hold their heads and extremities in the same position. For example, two or more of the people in a small group may sit with their legs crossed at the knee, their arms folded

Figure 4   Basic body orientations in a psychotherapy group, with splitting.

over their chests, and their heads cocked to the right. Their body positionings, therefore, are direct carbon copies of each other. It is also possible, however, that they will hold their extremities and heads in homologous rather than identical positions, so that they sit or stand in mirror-imaged postural relationship. Both the direct and mirror-imaged postures which are shown in Fig. 5 are subtypes of what I have called congruent postures.

Congruent body postures may occur in either a vis-à-vis or a parallel postural orientation.

Since an individual in a given culture can sit in only a limited number of postures, one immediately wonders whether postural congruence is purely coincidental. But even a very few continued observations of a group quickly end any theory of coincidence. Two, four, even six people often sit in postural congruence. When one member of a congruent set shifts posture, the others often quickly follow suit, so that the congruence is maintained through repeated changes of body positioning. In a group of three or more, it is common for two basic configurations of position to be used, with one subgroup maintaining congruence in one kind of positioning and another subgroup maintaining congruence in another. If one *listens* to such a group and examines what it is doing, one often finds that two points of view or approaches to an issue are being debated or advocated. Even in cases where opposing or alternate issues have not yet been formulated, one can notice that often one postural set is maintained by those on one side of the table, another by those on the opposite side of the table.

Old friends or colleagues who have long-term ties sometimes shift into postural congruence at times when they are temporarily arguing or taking opposing sides, as if to indicate the ultimate continuity of their relationship. In family psychotherapy one child often maintains postural congruence with one parent, while the other children do so with the other parent. In such cases one finds

Direct   *Mirror-Imaged*

Figure 5   Congruent postural relations.

that the clinical material indicates sharp ideational or affective divisions of the family into these two subgroups.

Just as there is a tendency to split postural orientation, so there is a tendency to split postural congruence. A person may maintain postural congruence with one person in his upper body, and with another in his lower body. In a large group, where two quite different sets of postural positioning are used, one may see the leader or moderator of the group using such splitting to maintain partial body congruence with both subgroups. In individual psychotherapy in which a patient, therapist, and observer are involved, therapist and patient may show such splitting, being congruent with each other in one half of their bodies and congruent with the research observer in the other half.

In a general way congruence in posture indicates similarity in views or roles in the group. There is, however, evidence of another significance of congruence or noncongruence—indication of status. When some member of an alliance differs markedly in social status from the others, he may maintain a posture quite unlike that of the others. When the basic activities of a vis-à-vis orientation involve relations of equality or peer relations, the postures are often congruent. In doctor-patient, parent-child, or teacher-student reciprocals, where it is important to indicate different status, congruence is less likely to occur. In situations where congruence is absent, there are often other evidences of nonassociation. The posturally noncongruent member might look out of the window, fail to look at the others, refrain from conversation, or simply give indications of being lost in his own thoughts.

CONCLUSION

According to the level of behavior, postures indicate the beginnings and endings of units of communicative behavior, the ways in which participants are related to each other, and the steps in a program. Although research has so far only sketched broad outlines of communicative behavior, it is already possible to use this information in clinical practice and everyday life. The briefest glance at postural configurations has great value in identifying the participants' location in a flow of social events and the nature of their relationships.

20

COMMUNICATIVE SILENCES: FORMS AND FUNCTIONS

Thomas J. Bruneau

Abstract

The nature of silence is discussed in an imposition of mind, as an
interdependent signification ground for speech signs, as a relationship
to mental time (as opposed to artificial time), and as it relates to
sensation, perception and metaphorical movement. Three major
forms of silence are defined: Psycholinguistic Silence, of which there
are two subtypes, designated Fast-time silence and Slow-time
silence; Interactive Silence; and Sociocultural Silence. The three major
forms are then briefly described as they relate to some important
human communication functions. In the absence of empirical
evidence, a number of hypotheses are offered.

Reprinted by permission of the International Communication Association
from "Communicative Silences: Forms and Functions" by Thomas J.
Bruneau in *Journal of Communication* 23:1 (1973):17–46.

THE GENERAL NATURE AND FORM OF SILENCE

Silence does not exist in the physical absolute—notions to the contrary are mythical. John Cage said it simply: "there is no such thing as absolute silence, something is always happening that makes a sound." (9) Silence, then, appears to be both a *concept* and an actual *process* of mind. Only man appears to have the ability to achieve silence; animals must tolerate sounds when awake. Silence appears to be a concept and process of mind which is imposed by each mind on itself and on the minds of others. This imposition appears to be sometimes an automatic, signalic functioning and, sometimes, a willed, mediated, symbolic imposition for the purpose of comparing mind with information input. This imposition appears necessary to mind, speech, and, especially, sanity. Man's mental imposition of silence upon his own mind appears to be a variable function—there appear to be degrees of intensity, duration, and frequency of silence, as well as levels of communicative functioning associated with imposed silence. Absolute silence, then, is impossible: even when not speaking aloud, man carries on a continuous interior monologue (74:431). As Thoreau observed: "It takes a man to make a room silent."[1] (18:350)

A major misconception preventing intellectual focus on silence is the common, basic assumption that silence is completely other than speech, its foreign opposite, its antagonist. An extreme, contrasting misconception is that speech *is* silence and silence *is* speech—that it is futile to distinquish them. Some modern theology, mysticism, philosophy, drama, and film are suggestive of the latter misconception (71).

Silence is to speech as the white of this paper is to this print. Physiologically, silence appears to be the mirror image of the shape of discernable sound for each person. Speech signs, created by necessity or will, appear to be mentally imposed *figures* on mentally imposed *grounds* of silence. Mind creates both. Sontag has clearly defined this interdependence: "Silence never ceases to imply its opposite and depend on its presence . . . so one must acknowledge a surrounding environment of sound or language in order to recognize silence . . . any given silence has its identity as a stretch of time being perforated by sound." (71:11) The entire system of spoken language would fail without man's ability to both tolerate and create sign sequences of silence-sound-silence units. In other words, significations of speech signs are possible because of their interdependence with imposed silence. It follows, then, that significations of various loci, intensities, durations, and frequencies of imposed silences are possible because of their interdependence with speech.

There appears, however, to be more signification in silence than in speech. This will be apparent in our discussion of different forms of silence. We have only just begun to discover significations in silence because Western cultures, especially American, are just beginning to conceptualize them. The rapid growth of focus on non-verbal communication should eventually lead into an intensive interest in silence.

Silence lends clarity to speech by destroying continuity. We must destroy continuity (which is insured by psychological memory) by going to the end of each emotion or thought (71:23). One point should be made here in passing. Destruction of continuity by imposing mental silence may not just be a simple matter of insuring psychological memory; it may allow the very existence and functioning of memory, as well as suggest its character. This topic will be discussed further under the heading of "Psycholinguistic Silence."

Much of the manner in which we have studied language function has denied the functioning of silences. We have attached our inquiry to the figures, comparing figure with figure, unit with unit, almost completely oblivious to the ground. Rate of speech, for instance, has been traditionally viewed as some ratio of speech units to artificial units of man-made time for the purpose of statistical comparison. It will be one of the positions of this essay that man frequently makes his own kind of time when he thinks. Much of the incongruence he faces may result from his own violations of his mental and somatic, natural time. A more realistic ratio of rate of speech, and one more related to mind-time (discussed below), would consist of elements of pauses and hesitations in proportion to judged difficulty level of verbal language.

Indeed, many other statistical notions of language may be related to imposed silences: "Zipf's law can be derived from simple assumptions that do not strain one's credulity . . . without appeal to least cost, maximal information, or any branch of the calculus of variations. The law is a simple consequence of those intermittent silences which we imagine to exist between successive words." (55) Miller, perhaps, should have said, "those intermittent silences which we *impose* between successive words."[2]

Repetition which is undifferentiated may approach and eventually equal ambiguous forms of silence. Both silence and repetition, to a certain point, seem to elicit a questioning uncertainty. It may be the case that this point is reached, using silent pauses or repetition, when decoder inferences about intended meaning take place or when mental information—comparing or certainty-testing occur in the decoder.

Continuous repetition seems to equal silence because, as Malisoff claims: "It is fatal to thought [or speech] altogether to make all things one. One is no better than nothing," (43:8) Both lengthy repetition and lengthy silence during expected communication seem to give each man an opportunity to inquire into his own uncertainty, unknowns, and his intolerances. Less extreme repetition often approaches the nature of silence as a process for some communicative purposes. Often, undifferentiated repetition is similar in communicative function to undifferentiated silence. For instance, it may be more than coincidence that recent protest is often marked by serious silence or repetitious chanting. Both can be interpreted easily as ambiguous and undifferentiated.[3]

To compare speech to an undefined, ambiguous nothingness or to assert silence as totally opposite speech in symbolic functioning is to reject the nature of speech. For instance, Wittgenstein's notion that, what we cannot speak about we must consign to silence (75:151) is such a rejection. This rejection seems to advocate that, symbolically, silence is nothing. The very contrast Wittgenstein makes concerning speech and silence seems to contradict one of his own basic, logical premises—that both elements of any comparison must be defined. He does not define silence. He was, then, comparing something with a vague, ambiguous nothing. Silence can only be defined by language, for as Anshen attests, it is impossible to interpret an unknown quantity by itself (1:10). It also seems ambiguous to *not* define silence and then use it as a contrast to a major language function such as rhetoric as in one recent essay (66).

It is almost absurd to persist in the hope that silence can eventually be defined by comparing it to itself. The art and philosophy of nothing to which silence seems invariably associated presently (12, 20, 35, 37, 39, 43, 49, 50, 57, 58, 60, 67, 70, 71, 72, 74, 75) ends in one simple conclusion: "Our time is noisy with appeals for silence . . . one recognizes the imperative of silence, but goes on speaking anyway. Discovering that one has nothing to say, one seeks a way to say *that*." (71:42).

Just as silence appears to be a concept and imposition of mind, so too is time. Artistically, aesthetically, and metaphorically, silence has often been associated with "slow-time." It is well known that different cultures, societal groupings and, perhaps, individuals hold different conceptions concerning time-count. Metaphysically and mystically silence has often been associated with the actual cessation of time—a floating, spatial reality which, carried to its negative extreme, ends in an undifferentiated, continuous /m:/ against a white everything. As Picard states: "If silence is so preponderant in time that time is completely absorbed by it, then time stands still." There is then nothing but silence: the silence of eternity." (64) It appears, then, that in *this* world at least, man's concept of time may very well be related concomitantly to man's concept of silence. Picard relates the two nicely: "Time is accompanied by silence, determined by silence . . . Time is expanded by silence." (63, 64:124) This expansion will be referred to as "Psycholinguistic slow-time silence." Sensation, perception, and metaphor are also highly related to silence and slow-time. These processes, like mind-time, may not correspond to mechanistic, artificial time.

Highly sensory events appear to be experienced in slow-time and/or silence for most persons. This appears to be the case regardless of sensory modality. These moments of wide eyes and fallen jaw are often followed by clamorous confirmation and expressive consensus seeking. Moments of high sensation, whether pleasant or unpleasant, seem almost to demand silence and absence of cognitive control. These moments may occur in only a matter of a mechanistic second or much longer. Slow motion film experiences, especially those involving graceful movements, seem to facilitate slow-time sensation as well as heightened aesthetic states. Breaking silence at these moments is often an aggravation to one experiencing slow-time. Many places of artistic display, such as music halls, art galleries and museums are places where diverse communication norms for maintaining silences or allowing speech seem to permit sensation. Empathetic silent response to the sensation of others appears to be a very strong response. The observation of another experiencing painful or pleasurable sensation most often demands silent witness.[4]

One's perceptual processing appears to be slowed and expanded as one slows or expands time by imposing silence. It is postulated here, that each individual's mind-time (and consequent awareness) during decoding of experience is a function of the intensity, duration, and frequency of his own imposed silence. It is also postulated here, that this function is highly related to each individual's ability to create his own silence and is also, of course, related to the intensity, duration, and frequency of the sensory input. One's basic percept acquisition and form, then, may very well be related to one's ability to control his own silences. Attentive silence can be demanded by others and this is very often the case, especially for young children. The proper instruction of children may very well be—in many instances—a matter of helping them control their own mental silences while the helpers control their own. Excellent literature defies conscious awareness of artificial, fast-time; a reader utilizing his own control of silence can almost suspend time.[5]

Encoder and decoder manipulation and imposition of silence appears to be the medium of metaphorical movement. Scott and others have implied that silence is the basis for metaphoric extension (66:155). Mazzo, in his interpretation of silence as movement in the works of St. Augustine, states: "Movement from words to silence, from signs to realities, is the fundamental presupposition of Augustinean allegorical exegesis. . . . Thus true rhetoric culminates in silence in which the mind is in immediate contact with reality." (49:181–87) Apparently referring to the same notion, Long advocated a new approach to silence, a silence of being: "The 'silence of being' refers to a *mode* of existence where silence does not refer to absence, but rather to the manner in which reality has its existence." (37:149)

Imposed slow-time silence appears to increase in intensity, duration, and frequency as non-verbal and verbal information increasingly denotes concrete, immediate reality. Imposing slow-time silences appears to create the very possibility for metaphoric movement. It is suggested here that metaphoric movement is *spatial* and organizational in mind. It is also proposed that slow-time, metaphoric movement occurs as a process of *making* slow-time in order to move through levels of verbally associated, affective experience in memory. This process appears to be similar to that of psycholinguistic, slow-time silence discussed more fully below. However, psycholinguistic, slow-time silences seem to operate on a different system of memory organization than metaphoric silence.

There appear to be three major forms of silence. The three forms of silence and some of their major functions have been suggested above. An attempt is made to further clarify these functions in the following sections of this essay.

PSYCHOLINGUISTIC SILENCE

Psycholinguistic silences are necessary and variable impositions of slow-time on the temporal sequence of speech. These impositions appear to be created by both encoders and decoders of speech. Encoders seem to impose discontinuity to reduce their own uncertainty by creating both signalic and symbolic hesitations to aid their own encoding processes. This is sometimes done consciously by experienced speakers to aid decoders. In addition, it is suggested here that decoders impose discontinuity to reduce uncertainty by creating mind-time (slow-time silence) for the decoding process. Hesitations are forms of silence. Hesitations can be either syntactic or semantic pauses (unfilled pause). Hesitations can also take the form of non-lexical intrusive sounds (such as the "uh" often referred to as filled pause); sentence corrections; word changes; repeats; phonemic or syllabic stutters; omissions of parts of words; sentence incompletions (5:360–61); and syllabic lengthening before junctures (48). A review of over forty reports of research focusing on hesitation, pause, and juncture in spoken discourse leads to some of the theoretical positions taken in this essay.

Research Evidence: Encoding

The research of Blankenship and Kay (5), De Vito (13:169–184; 14:14–17), Goldman-Eisler (21, 22, 23, 24, 25, 26, 27, 28, 30), Hawkins (29), Howell (32), Lay and Paivio (36), Lounsbury (38), Maclay and Osgood (40), McGuigan (52), and Martin (44, 45, 46, 47, 48) is especially pertinent to an understanding of psycholinguistic silences. Some plausible hypotheses concerning slowing speech during encoding are suggested by this research: (1) various types of hesitation in temporal sequencing of speech appear to be points at which grammatical, syntactical, and semantic decision-making or planning takes place; (2) two major and separate cognitive functions seem to occur during hesitations, (depending on the location and type of hesitation)—grammatical, syntactic decision-making and lexical or semantic decision-making; (3) various types of hesitation may be related to transitional probabilities of various speech units following these hesitations: (4) the length and type of hesitation may be related to verbal thought complexity—longer hesitations being a function of high cognitive complexity; (5) the length and type of hesitation may be related to successful task solutions; (6) encoder hesitations may be related to source credibility and attitude change; and (7) encoder hesitations may be related to encoder anxiety and stuttering.

The literature is theoretically less substantial concerning slowing time during the decoding of speech. As a listener variable, silences have yet to be empirically studied seriously. The research related to inner speech, however, appears to have much in common with many positions taken here. Perhaps the most important link was suggested by McGuigan in his review of the research regarding

covert or silent speech during language tasks: "Silent performance
of language tasks suggests that the covert oral response facilitates
the reception of external lanuage stimuli and the internal
processing of that information." (42) If we consider covert speech
as an aspect of *making* slow-time during decoding, the McGuigan
statement becomes significantly related to the theoretical positions
taken in this portion of the essay.

Research Evidence: Decoding

Ford examined children's imitation of sentences varying in pause
and intonation and suggested that pauses placed within grammatical
phrases were facilitating because they allowed subjects to take
advantage of grammatical structure sooner and, hence, make
predictions about what was going to be presented (19). Lounsbury
(38) hypothesized that units of speaker encoding (especially
those bounded by facultative pause points), often correspond to
units of decoding and that oft-repeated unit combinations of
encoding, approach coincidence with those of decoding. The
Lounsbury hypotheses, however, are advanced within the context
of statistical uncertainty as a function of encoding units indicated
by statistical transition probabilities rather than mind-time
slowing. Transitional probabilities and mind-time slowing may be
highly related when transitional probabilities are viewed as
speech-thought processes of decoders. Maclay and Osgood have
suggested that, "Presumably the hesitations that slow the speaker
at points of uncertainty also permit the listener to catch up, as
well as serving to stress the less predictable items. . . . it is also
possible that natural-appearing pauses and other hesitation
phenomena influence the listener's connotative judgment of the
speaker, e.g., of the speaker's 'sincerity.'" (50:43)

The notion of "natural appearing" pauses in encoder-decoder,
mind-time congruence is very interesting. McCrosky and Mehrley
found that excessive vocalized pauses and repetitions restricted
the amount of listener attitude change and decreased speaker
credibility (51). However, McCroskey and Mehrley seemed
to view hesitation phenomena of pause and repetition as
"unnecessary nonfluencies." Martin and Strange suggest that,
because pauses are sometimes informative, and sometimes not, it
seems plausible that listeners do not ordinarily "hear" them
during speech decoding (47). Goldman-Eisler had subjects read
aloud a manuscript written by someone else and found that
subjects seemed to hesitate where the original writers hesitated
and that: "Those who think alike appear to behave alike in the

matter of making pauses." (26:98) However, Goldman-Eisler
has not seriously considered the effect of manuscript punctuation
on hesitation or slowing. Italics, periods, question marks, dashes,
and exclamations may be important in this regard.

Implications

It is the contention here that there are two forms of imposed
psycholinguistic silence for decoding speech. *Fast-time silences*
are those imposed mental silences closely associated with the
temporal-horizontal sequencing of speech in mind. Fast-time
silences vary in mind-time, but are relatively low in intensity and
duration of mind-time. They are, however, high in frequency.
Their duration is usually less than two seconds of mechanical time.
Fast-time silences appear to be related to short duration
syntactical and grammatical hesitations or slowings when speech
is being decoded. These decoder silences appear to be signalic,
automatic processes. Some encoder hesitations, according to
Goldman-Eisler, may be related to response set and to reticular
blockage (28:79). It appears that most decoder impositions of
fast-time silence on encoder messages are a function of response
habituation or reticular blockage.

Slow-time silences are those imposed mental silences closely
associated with the semantic (and metaphorical) processes of
decoding speech. These silences are more symbolic than signalic.
It is suggested that slow-time silences relate to organizational,
categorical, and spatial movement through levels of experience
and levels of memory. The major hypotheses are that depth of
experience, complexity of storage, and difficulty of retrieval are
concomitantly related to intensity and duration of imposed slow-
time silence. Memory is viewed not only as storage of fixated
or engrammed verbal nominals or verbal objectifications; it is
also viewed as the qualified movements through vertical, spatial,
patterns of mental space. In other words, slow-time silence allows
for mind-time expansion and vertical, spatial movement. But, the
movement is often not completely vertical; some horizontal
movement or horizontal looping may take place within some
vertical levels during slow-time expansion.

This movement in slow-time as suggested previously, appears
to be a willed function which differs between individuals. Each
individual decoder may have the power to create his own
intensity, duration, and frequency of those slow-times he chooses
to accept. This seems to be especially the case with slow-time
silences an individual finds incongruent with his own systems of

mind, with his attitudinal response sets, or with his conceptions which disagree with the imposed slow-time silence of an encoder. There are, of course, many motives and forces which influence a decoder to impose silence upon his own mind. An encoder can, then, stimulate slow-time by managing speech-silence-speech units in a multitude of ways. He can also, of course, attempt to facilitate or inhibit the decoder's use of slow-time. Each decoder may have a certain learned ability for imposing slow-time. This level of ability may relate to an adult decoder's habitual level of tolerance for ambiguity. This ability level may also relate to an adult's rejection of thoughts and mind-time expansions which are different from his own. Goldman-Eisler seemed to be referring to this ability as the "capacity of organisms for delaying speech action." (28:76) This delaying action appears to be a matter of *how* individuals tolerate either sameness or difference.

Some slow-time hesitations of decoders appear to be automatic and habitual. Some appear to be semi-lexical, having both syntactic and semantic characteristics. It is perhaps impossible to rigidly differentiate all fast-time and slow-time silences—and perhaps unrealistic. In other words, we are referring here to a process model which varies dynamically in functioning. Some expansions, especially those where encoders and decoders are open to each other's mind-time requirements, appear to relate to what many refer to as "good, worthwhile communication."[6]

INTERACTIVE SILENCES

Interactive silences are pausal interruptions in dialogue, conversation, discussion, debate, etc. They can be related to affective, interpersonal relationships between people as well as to the exchange of information and/or problem solving. Psycholinguistic silences, of course, are constantly being utilized in interpersonal and small group communication. But many interactive silences are often longer than psycholinguistic, slow-time silences. However, psycholinguistic, slow-time silences are often difficult to distinguish from interactive silences—especially when two or more persons utilize slow-time silences similarly to share cognitions and solve problems symbolically together. Interactive silences differ from psycholinguistic silence mainly in each participant's conscious recognition of the degree and manner in which he is expected to participate in communicative exchange. Often decoders utilizing slow-time silence are not allowed by social convention to participate interactively with the encoder. The generalized silence of decoders in these cases is not subject to much change and cannot be considered to be a dynamic, interactive silence. Interactive silences between persons appear to be highly variable. They are highly bound to the nature of the message sharing process and especially to communicative situations and circumstances. Within interactive silences, many cognitive and affective decisions, inferences, and judgments occur. Interactive silences seem to be most appropriate to interpersonal status relationships.

Decision-making

The most basic form of decision made in interactive silence is the question of who will take the burden of speech. Within this particular silence, a larger number of other decisions often occur: decisions concerning initiating or terminating speech burden; speaker certification and listener recognition of the completion of thought, (or speech); questioning of the meaning of previous speech by all participants, (including the person giving up the burden); decisions about clarification or qualification of recent or past participant messages; non-verbal jockeying to gain the burden of speech; and many other decisions. Most of these decisions often appear to be moves by participants to prevent interactive silences from becoming too long. It appears that if silences become too long, interpersonal relationships are strained, uncertain, and perhaps threatened or beyond repair.

Many persons have asked the question, why have I blabbed? Perhaps, Huxley has answered this somewhat: "To refrain from idle talk is hard; to quiet the gibberings of memory and imagination is much harder; hardest of all is to still the voices of craving and aversion within the will." (33:218) The point being made here is that, within interactive silences, each member of a dyad or small group usually makes decisions to speak or remain silent. These decisions also appear to be a function of the interactive context, as a function of each member's concept of self. Kahn concurs with this viewpoint: "Silence, a nonengaged state of rest, offers the possibility of choosing what to do first or next. . . . Non-speaking gives man the power to enclose or disclose himself. He is free to make himself known or not, and this is, in the Existentialist sense, an active attitude." (35:204–5)

Studies of interactive silences and especially patterns of these silences in small group, problem-solving processes, could reveal some interesting results and implications. Throughout the literature on silence is a recurrent theme: decision-making and resolution transpire in moments of silence. There appears to be little, if any, evidence to question this notion in small-group literature. Therefore, an important additional hypothesis is in order: the successful reduction of uncertainty in knowledge states or the discovery of transformational rules for solving a defined small group problem are related to the loci, duration, and frequency of group silences. It is also hypothesized here that group problem solving is related to the intensity, duration, and frequency of *slow-time*, psycholinguistic silences of each individual in such groups.

Drawing Inferences

Lengthy interactive silences appear to allow each participant a chance to make inferences and judgments about the many possible meanings of a message (including the meaning of the silences). Lengthy interactive silences may also allow time for inferences and judgments about the character, motives, and personality of other participants. Long silences in interactive situations may promote informality too fast—making it necessary for cautious persons to halt the informality movement in their own mind by making small talk in order to keep from getting too close. Silence seems to promote movement toward interpersonal closeness. Perhaps some of the most awkward moments in interpersonal relations are experienced during interactive silences. The embarrassment which often occurs during greetings and partings between acquaintances attempting to establish a more permanent relationship is frequently punctured by interactive silences.

The most interpersonal battles take place in interactive silences—stronger than the simplicity of swearing. The silent lack of acknowledgment during a greeting by one or both participants who have been acquaintances or friends can be a strong form of attack.[7] The relentless torment which the ever-silent character, in Bergman's film, *Persona*, brings to bear on the ever-talking character, Alma, seems to give us direction for understanding silence as a form of interpersonal battle (3, 70). As Sontag claims, silence can become: "a virtually inviolable position of strength over the burden of talking." (71:17)

Exerting Control

Silence as interaction can be not only a means of commanding decoder attention, it can function as a means by which persons can acquire interpersonal attention from each other. For instance, one who usually talks to others frequently, upon maintaining silence in the face of those others, can draw inquiry. One's silence can create an ambiguous void in an interpersonal relationship— allowing others to either project inference or question their previous judgments about the relationship and thereby establish a new relationship. One who desires no relationships can manage his silences, of course, so that no relationship ever develops. Silence used as attention-getting can be used to create in others a questioning of their habitual manner of interpersonal conduct.

The character of authority-subordinate relationships appears to be discernible in interactive silences. The initial burden of speech is often the burden of a subordinate. This burden often presses toward respectful silence, depending on the strength of authority management of silence. The use of initial silencing strategy by the subordinate appears to help assert or reassert interpersonal and group power. This seems to occur as the subordinate moves toward longer and more frequent silences, whereupon authoritative silencing behaviors (if any were used) decrease and level off. There appears to be a "hushing," a movement to the whisper in the face of perceived and/or actual authoritative silencing power. The whisper may be a clear mark of response to perceived authority in certain situations—as well as a mark of respect where important messages are exchanged. The whisper seems to be related to situational context and occasion. The silences of place, object, and event will be discussed further under the heading of "Socio-cultural silence."

Non-person treatment is often characterized best as interactive use of silence or global interactive silences which are used by many persons unintentionally or unconsciously. Much of non-person treatment appears to be done out-of-awareness because of communication habits or styles. The form and process of status attribution seems to gain its greatest clarity and direction as a result of interactive silences. Some of the most powerful insults are dealt subordinates by persons in authority (or fighting for authority) in many organizational, social, and political hierarchies. Some of these silent insults are meant with constructive intent, some with destructive intent—both with and without awareness of intent. Many of these insults are imagined.

Norm violators are often treated with interactive silences following perceived violation. The Amish punishment by "shunning" is a case in point. Authority-subordinate relationships appear to gain clarity at these moments. Persons witnessing norm violations often expect silencing movement by authority or attempt to achieve this movement themselves. Silencing in the absence of authority is usually accomplished by maintaining *silence*.

Reacting to Diversity

Prejudice seems to be highly related to initial and, often, sustained global, interactive silences. Interactive silences, however, are shared. If they do indicate prejudice, it may be difficult to determine which interactants are prejudiced. It seems safe to assume a generalized silence in the face of diversity—especially when charges and counter-charges about prejudice could occur.

Physical diversity or divergence is often approached in silence by persons who are uncertain about acting appropriately in the face of physical diversity. Frequently, persons seem to have a generalized, habitual response set to reject difference. Persons who have a generalized habitual response set to reject physical diversity may also generalize this response to the rejection of psychological or verbal diversity. Fat persons, dwarfs, very tall persons, crippled persons with mobility problems, blind persons, persons with pronounced speech or hearing disorders, etc., have known nervous silences toward them. Differences in appearance, such as perceived ugliness, dress, and color of skin, when different than the situational norm, seem to be greeted by initial silences. The strength of these silences seems to depend on the uniqueness of the difference to the observer.

The stranger, or person who is viewed as strange, in most situations, has a great disadvantage. He often has the burden of breaking silence and imposing more certainty (or speech) to develop interpersonal relationships. But the stranger appears to have an advantage, too, if he can control his own interactive silences for some necessary reason. There appears to be curiosity toward strangers who are initially silent. Strangers who manage their silences well at these times can manage their silences in such a manner that they take only a small portion of the burden of speech in establishing relationships with others. In this manner, the stranger does not define his place in the social or political order too soon. But initial silence by a stranger should not be too strong or too lengthy—where others come to feel uncomfortable or insulted. It may be, too, that persons who desire certainty in their relationship with a new-comer to some sociopolitical order, will make inquiry by breaking silence first. All of this delicate manuevering is often buffered by get-acquainted parties or meetings for newcomers. Frequently however, a newcomer can be placed in the awkward position of subordination by being asked to immediately take the burden of speech—especially by being asked to *give* one. A speech by a newcomer is expected to be appropriate to the already established order of which he usually knows little. Some of these situations are handled so badly that the newcomer can only walk away mumbling, "I sure would have liked to see their faces had I said that."

Silence as reaction to verbal or psychological diversity in dyads or small groups is commonplace. Reaction to creative expression, innovation, new ideas, etc., is often an initially silent, motionless response. Many persons have witnessed what seemed like a sea of blank faces turn slowly towards them upon their making an unusual or unexpected statement. The very same reaction seems to follow an "inappropriate" statement—one of sensitive emotional expression, one which violates standardized communication norms, or a statement which questions authority. For instance, nothing can bring a grave silence to an entire high school classroom like a calm but firm student voice from the back of the room saying to an over-structured, whisper-producing teacher, "I believe that statement is in error." There appears to be a fine line between creative expression and "inappropriate expression." It is most unfortunate that many teachers and guidance persons are not conscious that such fine distinctions can be made. It is even more unfortunate that in most schools, even at present, most teachers seem much more adept at the silencing or silent conditioning of students than practicing utilization of their own silences as positive instructional and/or learning tools. This same condition appears to be the plight of many small groups involved in the process of solving problems or learning in other settings.

Reacting to Intensity of Emotion

Violent expression of various emotional states as a result of dissonance, insult, or repression is often met by the interactive silences of observers. This seems to result mainly because it is unexpected. When it is expected, strategies are employed to buffer it, prevent it, ignore it, or retreat from it. Deep emotion need not be expressed by outburst. Often, deep emotional states are expressed in silence. Intense grief, sorrow, and great disappointment are quiet states—words are difficult to find. Ritualized communications seem to find forms for allowing expression in such situations. Ritual in these situations appears to be very important because it offers some semblance of reality to persons too deep in ambiguous, mental silences. Perhaps one of the greatest insults is for friends not to at least attempt to show concern for a person in deep sorrowful or disappointing silence. Deep vengeance, jealousy and resentment can also be very silent—

before expressive eruption. Guilt, shame, and periods of penance are often silent conditions for both those experiencing them and those observing the judged wrong-doer. The deepest fears and most intense joys are wordless—or undifferentiated, repetitive sounds. In short: Silence is the language of all strong passions: love, anger, surprise, fear (18:350).

Interpersonal embarrassment is often an exercise in manipulating interactive silences. When someone becomes embarrassed, the actual recognition of one's own embarrassment seems to occur at a point of hesitation or silence—followed by efforts to reduce the embarrassment. Laughter, for instance, seems to quickly reduce many forms of embarrassment—laughter can be a blessing or an affront depending on the disposition of the embarrassed person. However, a lengthy silence by others toward one's embarrassment can be devastatingly uncomfortable. Laughter may very well function to *prevent* silence. Silence can increase embarrassment. The fear of losing one's place while giving a speech, of saying something which brings embarrassment, or most other reasons for fear of speaking seem to relate to a very strong fear in Western culture—fear of silence.

Basso's conclusions about silence in Western Apache culture may establish some bases upon which to associate many interactive silences in the West: 1. In Western Apache culture, the absence of verbal communication is associated with situations in which the status of focal participants is ambiguous. 2. Under these conditions, fixed role expectations lose their applicability and the illusion of predictability in social interaction is lost. 3. Keeping silent among the Western Apache is a response to uncertainty and unpredictability in social relations (2:22). At the same time silence can also imply almost absolute certainty for some participants. Most persons have also witnessed the righteous indignation of persons refraining from speech who are also silently resolute and convinced in their belief.

Maintaining or Altering Interpersonal Distance

Global interactive silence may also be a means of coping with new surroundings in a new group: when punctuated by long silences, words mean more. The quiet person who eventually and unexpectedly speaks up in a group seems to intuitively know this. Words almost become palpable when one talks less; one begins feeling more fully one's physical presence in a given space (71:20).

Interactive silence may be associated with movement in interpersonal distance. It may be hypothesized that as physical distance between persons decreases, (regardless of level of intimacy), interactive silences will increase in duration and frequency and psycholingustic slow-time silences will increase in intensity. This appears to be highly probable and somewhat obvious if one recalls his experience in elevators and crowded buses. However, the testing of these hypotheses with varying lengths of clock time, at varying physical distances, may provide some content and prescriptions for interpersonal training or guidance. A most interesting finding would be one relating to how such silences are broken at various distances. It may be hypothesized also that as interpersonal distance between persons begins to decrease in duration and frequency—and slow-time silences will tend to increase. The testing of these hypotheses could be vital for those group leaders or interpersonal trainers who wish participants to talk honestly about themselves or about sensitive topics but are dismayed by the lack of participant interaction. The use of leader silences in small groups is extremely powerful and must be used with great caution. Much needs to be learned about how interactive silences operate in interpersonal disclosure and climate. Merton seems to be speaking to this matter: "Compassion and respect enables us to know the solitude (silence, as used here) of another by finding him in the intimacy of our own interior solitude." (53:245) Lengthy group silences seem to bring about tension—a need to escape from togetherness. As a small group variable, silence has not received much, if any, manipulation in the non-therapeutic small group literature. Its potential as a variable relating to already judged important small group variables is enormous. It is not the purpose here to fully review the psycho-therapeutic use of silence in individual and group therapy. However, some of the theorizing from this literature may have important implications for interpersonal and small group therapy and instruction—as well as reveal some of the research potential in interactive silences.

Some hypotheses which are supported in the psychotherapeutic research literature are: (1) silences may allow a patient to bypass seemingly insurmountable resistance, enabling the patient to recoup and integrate psychic forces, and also, enhance the therapeutic alliance (10, 31); (2) longer patient silences in therapy may be an indication of progress in therapy and indicative of success (11); (3) silences appear to be longer at high anxious phases of psychiatric interviews than at low anxious phases (42); (4) silences may aid child patients by creating a field for attitudinal relearning (54); (5) the analyst's silence may be the most important catalyst for free association (62); and (6) individual and group silences, while having both positive and negative functions in the therapeutic process, may also indicate limited intellectual capacities, low comprehension, or constitutional or neurotic flatness (68). All of these hypotheses suggest studies of the functions of interactive silence in other interpersonal and small group communication.

SOCIO-CULTURAL SILENCES

Socio-cultural silences are those related to the characteristic manner in which entire social and cultural orders refrain from speech and manipulate both psycholinguistic and interactive silences. Socio-cultural silences may define cultural patterns of communication much better than what is said. Hymes and Basso have expressed this notion clearly: "An adequate ethnography of communication should not confine itself exclusively to the analysis of choice within verbal repertoires. It should also . . . specify those conditions under which the members of the society regularly decide to refrain from verbal behavior altogether." (2:15) Some of what will be discussed under this type of silence is viewed as concurrent support for some of the positions taken under the topic of interactive silences.

Western Cultural Silence

Western culture is characteristically noisy with sounds and speech—moments of silence and solitude are becoming rare, especially in the United States. Many Americans are so unconscious of silence that they are at a total loss of words to talk about it. Eastern culture seems to be characteristically silent—both general and lengthy interactive silences are common. Oliver, in the only substantial study of Eastern rhetoric, has observed that silence is a major focal point of Asian rhetoric: "In the ancient Orient . . . silence was valued rather than feared . . . silence in Asia has commonly been entirely acceptable, whereas in the West silence has generally been considered socially disagreeable." (61:264) Oliver also suggests: "There must also be serious consideration of the Asian recognition of the varied communicative functions of silence." (61:3) In short, there seems to be much conscious awareness of a multitude of meanings of silence in many Eastern and some Western sub-cultures (2, 15, 17, 20, 34, 43, 58, 59, 60, 73).

One major characteristic of most Western cultural silence (and the main illustrative example in this section of the essay), seems to relate to conceptions of man-made authority and conceptions of highest authority or God. Much of what was discussed previously concerning authority-subordinate relationships and use of interactive silences seems to relate to the functioning of socio-cultural silence.

Silencing by Authority

Global socio-cultural authority refers to the manner in which men relate to a generalized man-made authority. It may also relate to the use of silence for worship, reverence, and respectful acceptance. Silence, as it relates to authority conception, may also relate to the speech of blasphemy, icon-smashing tendencies, and bitter rejection. Religious rituals in many Christian orders, regardless of the conception of highest authority, are replete with movement toward silence. This movement appears to be controlled by dogma, communication norms, faith, and sometimes, by actual authority figures or perceived connection of these figures with highest authority. The statement, "Be silent, for so are the Gods," seems to summarize highest authority perceptions in Western culture. Entire systems of religious dogma seem to be built on either the control of silence as worship or the repetitive, chanting denial of silence. Silence required by dogma in ritual and ceremony can be a form of restraint from the speaking of contrary dogma—as well as a means to affirm or reaffirm dogma for the faithful. One does not penetrate his own silences easily when they are structured within various rituals and ceremonies. Perhaps the portions of dogma most subject to deep slow-time, psycholinguistic silences, but sheltered by ceremony and ritual, are those portions of dogma which are most uncertain and ambiguous. Ambiguous and uncertain dogma may also concern topics which are feared most.

To understand the impact of silencing as a form of socio-cultural conception of authority, one need only examine and trace through American history the effect of massive silencing and censoring strategies by both church and state in puritan America. Puritan America is an excellent example of a *1984* society. Expression of diversity, however slight, against the church or state authority was often met by gags, pranks, ridiculously brutal public silent penance, ear-lopping, branding, tongue tortures, etc. (15). These silencing strategies appeared to be a product of both *socio-political* conceptions of hierarchical ordering of authority as well as conceptions of the nature of highest authority or God. It is the position here that much of the manner in which cultures manage silence relates to cultural conceptions of God and life-hereafter. The conceptions of authority in Puritan America appear to be very much present today—but they appear to be highly unconscious, out-of-awareness, habitual forms of global authority and habitual communicative style. Socio-cultural conceptions of highest authority appear to transfer unconsciously into the uses of certain interactive, socio-political silences in organizational hierarchies of many cultures—especially Western cultures.

As has been implied, conceptions of authority are often conceptions of what can or what cannot be said; when one should appropriately maintain silent restraint, or the manner in which utterance appropriately breaks silence. Thus, silence appears to function in hierarchical orders of status attribution, of maintenance, and of change as witnessed in the communication norms characterized by interactive silences—as well as of habitual, global silences.

Silence is used to show respect (or disrespect) for a socio-political position or station. For instance, when teachers, clergy, doctors, lawyers, judges, and many others in authoritative positions enter rooms, a characteristic hush falls upon persons in that room. The silence speaks, saying, "We recognize and acknowledge your position by our silence." Often, certain roles are protected by rules or obligatory norms imposed on persons to aid the established order. Hence, teachers operate in some schools with discpline codes, doctors operate with noise regulations preventing noise inside and outside hospitals, clergy are protected by unstated moral codes, and judges can enforce silence by issuing contempt of court charges. Silence can also protect power by aggravating those seeking to destroy or discredit persons in power. This can be done by forcing subordinates into awkward positions whereby they exhibit behaviors detrimental to their own cause—because their frustration is aggravated by silent response to their efforts. Silence as absence of response to or lack of recognition of subordinates may very well be the main source of protection of power in socio-political orders where physical restraint has lost repute. Silent protest, however, may be a powerful means of neutralizing the power of protective silence—at appropriate moments. Much political power, then, appears to be derived and, even more, maintained by the manner in which silence is used.[8]

Silence can be used as a very successful strategy against violent expression and ignorance. Persons in many authoritative positions often ignore subordinates by silence or absence of response in interaction and globally, to counteract being ignored. Silence by authority is often a means to protect persons in authoritative positions for many reasons, e.g., for saving time, for preventing extraneous activity, and preserving privacy and solitude.

Silence can also be used by authority to require subordinates to do work, to think for themselves, or to create independence in those who cling to dependency relationships. These positive uses of silence by authority, for instance, are well known to persons expert at directing independent study or thought. The silence of creative authority can set up a creative force of silence which can allow dependent but potentially creative persons a chance to work hard to overcome that force. A person fighting such a force, not only seems to solve many problems of intellectual curiosity, but begins to start understanding some of his inaccurate inferences about authority-subordinate reationships. Most persons in positions of authority, however, do not seem to know about silence as a creative force. It does not seem reasonable that one manages a creative force of authority by silencing subordinates to build authoritative ego, by rigidly protecting position, or by destroying independence drives and self-reliance in subordinates. Nor does it seem reasonable that one builds a creative force if subordinate effort is never acknowledged. An angry subordinate who works very hard to protest inaccurate assumptions or smash icons against rigid authority, gains only a short satisfaction upon self-realization of success. Then the realization occurs to the subordinate that he must fill the void with his own creation. Rigid authority has not usually prepared such a person for this void, and the person retreats to rejection. The creative uses of interactive and generalized silences by authorities and subordinates require slow-time. The possibility for achieving slow-time appears to be rejected in the face of rigid, certain, and rapidly presented structurings of uncertain belief. It appears to be also rejected in the face of the cloaking of personal belief and value in multi-connotative wording, over-qualified and safe "objective" language, and disavowal of one's own viewpoint. In short, too much concern for encoding structure in language appears to prevent slow-time silence by decoders. One need not think in response to certainty structurings or, on the other hand, boring and lengthy ambiguity. Planned ambiguity, however, can be a powerful tool to be used in conjunction with the management of silences by those in teaching or guidance positions.

Authority conceptions held by many parents seem to transfer to their use of silencing behaviors toward their own children.

Children can easily become "non-persons," in effect, by silencing. This process may to be taking place presently on a national level in this country. The Hippie movement in this country has been effectively silenced. The youth protest movement has been effectively silenced. The reader may think that this has little to do with cultural uses of silence. However, the songs of youth listened to by millions of young people in this country's air waves are filled more than ever with the themes of loneliness, isolation, despair, and rejection of the present socio-political orders. Some of these songs are songs containing intensely deep, deep silences for millions of young listeners. Many of these silences may be too deep. The songs talk of death, eternity, complete oneness in friendship, quick escape, and, giving up the fight. These motifs appear to be the result of both silencing strategies of the general culture as well as the influence of drugs which alienate and isolate while temporarily creating the illusion of togetherness.

Places of Silence

There are many places, objects, and events to which silence is the expected response. Churches, courtrooms, schools, libraries, hospitals, funeral homes, battle sites, insane asylums, and prisons, for instance, are often places of silence. Not only are some of these places of silence, but often their icons elicit silence, e.g., tombs, testimonial landmarks (to persons or causes), and statues. Thus, places and their objects help to elicit silence for the purpose of maintaining norms and popular belief. Some of the most unusual public and private objects and events elicit silence. These silences should be the focus of much future research. Places and their objects can perpetuate socio-political ideologies and practice. This is really nothing new. Yet seldom, if ever, has silence been examined as medium of propaganda.

Silence in Rhetorical Control

Silence appears to be a major source of rhetorical control. This seems to be especially the case at ceremonial public events. One can stand in silent reverence (or silent protest) during the playing of national anthems or during flag raisings or lowerings. Taps forces silence at military remembrance occasions. Silence is almost required during prayer and testimony to the dead. Breaking silence on these occasions is viewed as a strong form of anti-social behavior. The person who breaks silence at such occasions may very well be socially ostracized, physically removed, or even

injured. Silence appears, then, to be a strong rhetorical strategy
to preserve socio-political ideology.

SUMMARY

It has been the intention of this four part essay to draw attention
to some misconceptions about the nature of silence and to define
three major forms of silence as well as discuss some of their
corresponding communicative functions. An attempt has
been made to establish a basic theoretical framework concerning
the relationships of silence to such processes as sensation,
perception, mentation, social interaction, and cultural
communication. Numerous hypotheses and postulates were
offered to provide direction for further thought and research.
Silence as a communicative function is complex and profound.
Our conceptions of time, based almost exclusively on clock time,
may be preventing us from inquiring into the meaning of silence.
Ganguly seems to summarize the need for a new direction:
"Silence characterizes the periphery of understanding: language
promises security and freedom. . . . However, language cannot
provide these goods, but silence can and does provide them." (20)

Notes

¹ Silence is not the same as solitude. Silence is to speech as solitude
is to society and social relations. Solitude promotes longer mental
silences, but it is not silence. Solitude is simply a refrain from social
relations and a preservation of privacy.

² Anshen has implied a similar notion: "The rest, the absence of
audible motion, is itself the object of the time-count and plays its role on
the same level as the audible sound." (1:7)

³ Stein may have been speaking to this point: "Into this void
[silence] each man projects his own significance." (74:423)

⁴ As John Donne once demanded: "For God's sake! Hold your tongue
and let me love." (16:735)

⁵ A common suggestion in sensory deprivation literature (though
seldom the direct focus of such literature) is the notion that persons in
silent isolation lose conception of artificial, mechanistic time [6, 69, 76,
77, 78]. Some quantitative evidence to the point suggests that persons
significantly underestimate clock time in silent isolation (56). The
literature also suggests that persons placed in silent isolation are driven
to seek sequential stimuli or some form of time-count. Whether this drive
is a function of fear of isolation or simply a conditioned response as a
result of past experience with artificial, mechanical time has not yet been
determined. The premise is that imposed silence is concomitantly related
to alteration of mind-time. This relationship will be discussed further.

⁶ Blackmur states the most basic position taken here: "Meaning is what silence does when it gets into words." (4:152) Within the many interactions between fast-time silences on the mind-time temporal axis and the slow-time silences on the mind-time spatial axis, there may be a process which supplies the elusive nexus between what is considered to be speech and what is considered to be verbal thought. The nexus, it is suggested, lies at the various and varying *intercepts* of fast-time and slow-time silences. The intercepts may provide the necessary resistance between mind-time and mind-space. Discovering this process may be facilitated by rejecting some of our habitual ways of utilizing clock time and rejecting some of our habitual ways of thinking about the processes of encoding and decoding.

⁷ You hesitate to stab me with a word, and know not Silence is the sharper sword," wrote Robert U. Johnson (8:1824). According to Pascal, silence is the greatest persecution (7:527).

⁸ The recent declaration of martial law by Philippines' President Marcos is an excellent, large scale example of the use of silence as control for the purpose of consolidating political power.

References

1. Anshen, Ruth N. "Language as Idea." In Ruth N. Anshen (ed.), *Language: An Enquiry into Its Meaning and Function*, vol. 8 (New York: Harper & Row, 1957), pp. 3–17.
2. Basso, Keith H. "To Give Up on Words: Silence in Western Apache Culture." *Southwestern Journal of Anthropology* **26**, (1970):213–230.
3. Bergman, Ingmar. *Persona*, (A film).
4. Blackmur, R. P. "The Language of Silence." In Ruth N. Anshen (ed.), *Language: An Enquiry into Its Meaning and Function, vol.* 8 (New York: Harper & Row, 1957), pp. 134–52.
5. Blankenship, J., and Kay, C. "Hesitation Phenomena in English Speech: A Study in Distribution." *Word* **20**, (1964):360–72.
6. Brown, Bobby R. "Effects of Social Isolation on Oral Communication." Master's thesis, Pennsylvania State University, 1964.
7. Brussell, Eugene E. *Dictionary of Quotable Definitions* (Englewood Cliffs, N.J.: Prentice-Hall, 1970).
8. Burton, Stevenson. *The Home Book of Quotations: Classical and Modern*, 9th ed. (New York: Dodd, Mead, 1964).
9. Cage, John. *Silence; Lectures and Writings* (Middletown, Conn.: Wesleyan University Press, 1961).
10. Calogeras, Roy C. "Silence as a Technical Parameter in Psycho-Analysis." *International Journal of Psycho-Analysis* **48**, (1967):538–543.

11. Cook, John J. "Silence in Psychotherapy." *Journal of Counseling Psychology* **11**, (1964):42–46.
12. De Mott, Benjamin. "Dirty Words?" *Hudson Review* **18**, (1965):31–44.
13. De Vito, Joseph A. *The Psychology of Speech and Language: An Introduction to Psycholinguistics* (New York: Random House, 1970).
14. De Vito, Joseph A. *Psycholinguistics: The Bobbs-Merrill Studies in Communication Disorders* (New York: Bobbs-Merrill, 1971).
15. Earle, Alice Morse. *Curious Punishments of Bygone Days* (New York: MacMillan, 1896).
16. Esar, Evan. *20,000 Quips and Quotes* (Garden City, N.Y.: Doubleday, 1968).
17. Fabun, Don. "The Silent Languages." In Joseph A. De Vito (ed.), *Communication: Concepts and Processes* (Englewood Cliffs, N.J.: Prentice-Hall, 1971), pp. 127–33.
18. Flesch, Rudolf (ed.). *The New Book of Unusual Quotations* (New York: Harper & Row, 1957).
19. Ford, Boyce L. "Children's Imitation of Sentences Which Vary in Pause and Intonation." *Dissertation Abstracts International* **31**, (1970):3727.
20. Ganguly, S. N. "Culture, Communication and Silence." *Philosophy and Phenomenological Research* **29**, (1968):182–200).
21. Goldman-Eisler, Frieda. "Individual Differences between Interviewees and Their Effect on Interviewee's Conversational Behavior." *Journal of Mental Science* **98**, (1952):660–71.
22. Goldman-Eisler, Frieda. "Speech Analysis and Mental Processes." *Language and Speech* **1**, (1958):59–75.
23. Goldman-Eisler, Frieda. "Speech Production and the Predictability of Words in Context." *Quarterly Journal of Experimental Psychology* **10**, (1958):96–106.
24. Goldman-Eisler, Frieda. "The Predictability of Words in Context and the Length of Pauses in Speech." *Language and Speech* **1**, (1958):226–231.
25. Goldman-Eisler, Frieda. "A Comparative Study of Hesitation Phenomena." *Language and Speech* **4**, (1961):18–26.
26. Goldman-Eisler, Frieda. "The Predictability of Words in Context and the Length of Pauses in Speech." *Journal of Communication* **11**, (1961):95–99.
27. Goldman-Eisler, Frieda. "Sequential Temporal Patterns and Cognitive Processes in Speech." *Acta Neurologica Psychiatrica Belgica* **67**, (1967):811–851.

28. Goldman-Eisler, Frieda. *Psycholinguistics: Experiments in Spontaneous Speech* (London: Academic Press, 1968).
29. Hawkins, P. R. "The Syntactic Location of Hesitation Pauses." *Language and Speech* 14, (1971):277–288.
30. Henderson, Alan, Goldman-Eisler, F., and Skarbek, Andrew. "The Common Value of Pausing Time in Spontaneous Speech." *Quarterly Journal of Experimental Psychology* 17, (1965):343–345.
31. Horanyi, B. "Uber das Schweigen als Heilmittel" ("Concerning Silences as a Therapeutic Medium"). *Zietschrift fur Psycholotherapie und Medizinische Psychologie* 9:155–157. Abstract, E. Schwerin, *Psychological Abstracts* 34, (1960):438.
32. Howell, Richard W., and Vetter, Harold J. "Hesitation in the Production of Speech." *Journal of General Psychology* (1969): 261–276.
33. Huxley, Aldous. "Silence." In *The Perennial Philosophy* (New York: Harper & Row, 1945), pp. 216–219.
34. Hymes, Dell. "Introduction: Toward Ethnographies of Communication." *American Anthropologist*. Special Publication (edited by J. J. Gumpers and D. Hymes), 66:1–34, no. 6, pt. 2.
35. Kahn, Ernst. "Functions of Silence in Life and Literature." *Contemporary Review* 194, (1958):204–206.
36. Lay, Clarry, and Paivio, Allan. "The Effects of Task Difficulty and Anxiety on Hesitations in Speech." *Canadian Journal of Behavioural Sciences* 1, (1969):25–37.
37. Long, Charles H. "Silence and Signification; A Note on Religion and Modernity." In Joseph M. Kitagawa and Charles H. Hong (eds.), *Myths and Symbols: Studies in Honor of Mircca Eliade* (University of Chicago Press, 1969), pp. 141–150.
38. Lounsbury, F. "Pausal, Juncture, and Hesitation Phenomena." In C. E. Osgood and T. A. Sebeok (eds.), *Psycholinguistics: A Survey of Theory and Research* (University of Indiana Press, 1965), pp. 98–101.
39. Love, Glen A. "*Winesburg, Ohio* and the Rhetoric of Silence." *American Literature* 40, (1968): 38–57.
40. Maclay H., and Osgood, C. E. "Hesitation Phenomena in Spontaneous English Speech." *Word* 15, (1959):19–44.
41. Maeterlinck, Maurice. "Silence." *The American Magazine* 132, (1941):152.
42. Mahl, G. "Disturbances and Silences in the Patient's Speech in Psychotherapy." *Journal of Abnormal and Social Psychology* 53, (1956):1–15.

43. Malisoff, William M. "Cratylus or an Essay on Silence (Not Illustrated)." *Philosophy of Science* **11**, (1944):3–8.
44. Martin, James G., and Strange, Winifred. "The Perception of Hesitation in Spontaneous Speech." *Perception and Psychophysics* **3**, (1968):427–438.
45. Martin, James G. "Two Psychological Mechanisms Specified by Hesitation in Spontaneous Speech." *Proceedings of the Annual Convention of the American Psychological Association* **3**, (1968):17–18.
46. Martin, J. G. "Hesitations in the Speaker's Production and Listener's Reproduction of Utterances." *Journal of Verbal Learning and Behavior* **6**, (1967):903–909.
47. Martin, J. G., and Strange, W. "Determinants of Hesitations in Spontaneous Speech." *Journal of Experimental Psychology* **76**, (1968):474–479.
48. Martin, James G.. "On Judging Pauses in Spontaneous Speech." *Journal of Verbal Learning and Verbal Ability* **9**, (1970):75–78.
49. Mazzeo, Joseph A. "St. Augustine's Rhetoric of Silence." *Journal of the History of Ideas* **23**, (1962):175–196.
50. McCormick, C. A. "Sound and Silence in Montale's 'Ossi Di Seppia'." *Modern Language Review* **62**, (1967):633–641.
51. McCroskey, J. C., and Mehrley, R. S. "The Effect of Disorganization on Attitude Change and Source Credibility." *Speech Monographs* **36**, (1969): 13–21.
52. McGuigan, F. J. "Covert Oral Behavior During the Silent Performance of Language Tasks." *Psychological Bulletin* **74**, (1970):309–326.
53. Merton, Thomas. "The Inward Solitude." In *No Man Is an Island*. (New York: Harcourt Brace Jovanovich, 1955), pp. 244–53.
54. Miller, B. M. "Communication with a Non-verbal Child." *American Journal of Psychoanalysis* **20**, (1960):79–82.
55. Miller, George A. "Some Effects of Intermittent Silence." *American Journal of Psychology* **70**, (1957):311–314.
56. Mitchell, Mildred B. "Time Disorientation and Estimation in Isolation." *USAF, ASD Technical Report*, No. 62277, 1962.
57. Moreno, Janice S. "Silence in the Poetry of Leopoldo Lugones." *Hispania* **46**, (1963):760–763.
58. Morris, Charles W. "Mysticism and Its Language." In Ruth N. Anshen (ed.), *Language: an Enquiry into Its Meaning and Function*, vol. 8 (New York: Harper & Row, 1957), pp. 179–87.
59. Mowrer Priscilla. "Notes on Navajo Silence Behavior." Master's thesis, University of Arizona, 1970.

60. Nikhilananda, Swami. "Aum: The Word of Words." In Ruth
    N. Anshen (ed.), *Language: an Enquiry into Its Meaning and
    Function*, vol. 8 (New York: Harper & Row, 1957), pp.
    80–85.
61. Oliver, Robert T. *Communication and Culture in Ancient
    India and China* (Syracuse University Press, 1971).
62. Paramo-Ortega, Raul. "Einige Bemerkungen uber das
    Schweigen des Analytikers" ("Several Observations Concerning
    the Silence of Analysts"). *Jahrbuch fur Psychologie, Psycho-
    therapie und Medizinische Anthropologie* **15**, (1967):
    247–252. In *Psychological Abstracts*, trans. B. A. Stanton **45**,
    (1971):255.
63. Pattison, E. M. "The Experience of Dying." *American Journal
    of Psychotherapy* **21**, (1967):32–43.
64. Picard, Max. *The World of Silence*, trans. Stanley Goodman
    (Chicago: Henry Regnery Co., 1952).
65. Picard Max. "Time and Silence." In Eric Larrabee and Rolf
    Meyersohn (eds.), *Mass Leisure* (Glencoe, Ill.: The Free
    Press, 1958), pp. 122–124.
66. Scott, Robert L. "Rhetoric and Silence." *Western Speech* **36**,
    (1972):146–158.
67. Seigel, Jerrold E. "Ideals of Eloquence and Silence in
    Petrarch." *Journal of the History of Ideas* **26**, (1965):147–174.
68. Slavson, S. R. "The Phenomenology and Dynamics of Silence
    in Psychotherapy Groups." *International Journal of Group
    Psychotherapy* **16**, (1966):395–404.
69. Smith, S., and Lewty, W. "Perceptual Isolation Using a Silent
    Room." *Lancet* **2**, (1958):342–345.
70. Sontag, Susan. "Bergman's Persona." In *Styles of Radical Will*
    (New York: Farrar, Straus, and Giroux, 1966), pp. 121–145.
71. Sontag, Susan. "The Aesthetics of Silence." In *Styles of
    Radical Will* (New York: Farrar, Straus, and Giroux, 1966),
    pp. 3–34.
72. Sontag, Susan. "Thinking Against Oneself: Reflections on
    Cioran." In *Styles of Radical Will* (New York: Farrar, Straus,
    and Giroux, 1966), pp. 74–95.
73. Stark, Freya. "On Silence." *Holiday* **38**, (Decmber 1965):12.
74. Stein, Karen F. "Metaphysical Silence in Absurd Drama."
    Modern Drama **13**, (1971):423–431.
75. Wittgenstein, Ludwig. *Tractatus Logico-Philosophicus*, trans.
    D. F. Pears and B. F. McGuinness (London: Routledge and
    Kegan Paul, 1961).
76. Zubek, John P., Sansom, W., and Prysiaznuik, A. "Intellectual
    Changes During Prolonged Perceptual Isolation (Darkness

and Silence)." *Canadian Journal of Psychology* **14**, (1960):
233–243.

77. Zubek, John P., Sansom, W., and Goving, J. "Perceptual
Changes after Prolonged Sensory Isolation (Darkness and
Silence)." *Canadian Journal of Psychologie* **15**, (1961):83–100.

78. Zubek, John P. (ed.). *Sensory Deprivation: Fifteen Years of
Research* (New York: Appleton-Century-Crofts, 1969).

79. Zuk, G. H. "On Silence and Babbling in Family Psychotherapy
with Schizophrenics." *Confinia Psychiatrica* **8**, (1965):49–56.

Part IV
THE INTERSUBJECTIVITY OF UNDERSTANDING

The first three parts of this book were designed to provide background useful in approaching the complex problems of communication and human understanding. We have seen that human information unfolds through complex patterns of sensory activity: silent information (the absence of body sounds), kinetic information (physical contact), auditory information (body sounds and vocal sounds), verbal information (content), and visual information (images). Each person translates a given configuration of human information into characteristic and novel forms. It is this very uniqueness of coding style that determines the potential for understanding others.

The essays in this section are based on two premises. One is that the potential for understanding human messages is defined by the degree to which the various participants first understand themselves. As Abraham Maslow states, "what you are not, you cannot perceive or understand. It cannot communicate itself to you." It is a mistake to suppose that anyone can stand beyond his or her own frame of reference, or understand things foreign to experience. The second premise is that communication requires the extension of one's own perspective to that of another in order for common ground and mutual understanding to be established. Within these broad limitations understanding becomes *intersubjective*. The prefiix *inter* suggests a correspondence *between* interactants and *subjective* conveys a sense of the integration that takes place between emotional involvement and objective reality-testing. In "Understanding Ourselves" Michael Polanyi extends the framework of intersubjective understanding to include explicit knowledge and implicit knowledge. *Explicit knowledge* is conscious, reflective awareness of one's place or position in the world; *tacit knowledge* is unformulated, incomplete discovery existing at the periphery or below the surface of awareness. Polanyi considers tacit knowledge the foundation of what we genuinely understand about ourselves. We expand our knowledge of the world by becoming more sensitive to the limits of our explicit, articulate understanding. It is this unexpressed, perhaps inexpressible (tacit) awareness of what we explicitly understand that provides the foundation of personal knowledge.

The distinction between understanding and awareness of one's understanding is critical to the concept of intersubjective understanding. One person could understand the perspective or stand of another either with or without the other's awareness of what is known about them. The same distinction applies to what the other knows about oneself. Intersubjective understanding creates interesting differences between the level of what is explicitly understood and what is tacitly known. Person A understands more about his or her own private experience than person B can ever hope to know; at the same time person B may well know more about certain aspects of the actual behavior of person A than person A will know. For example, person A has direct access to the facial expressions of person B, but not to his or her own. Another example is the sound of the voice; presumably the experience of one's own voice differs from what an observer experiences. These differences in what people observe and understand imply that human beings need contact with one another because of the inequities in their explicit and tacit knowledge.

Differences in levels of understanding become the focal points of interest in the model of "Interaction and Interexperience in Dyads" by R. D. Laing, H. Phillipson, and A. R. Lee. Their premise is that one person can understand another's behavior only indirectly

through his or her own experiential field. The concept of
interexperience consists of a common situation in which the
behavior of person A is filtered through the perceptual biases of
person B and vice versa. Experience depends on perception, and
perception depends in turn on interpretation. This distinction
between behavior and experience creates a tension between what
we perceive (or experience) as the behavior of another and
what they experience of their own behavior. Intersubjective
understanding depends on the complex interplay between what is
perceived by each party, the degree of overlap in those respective
perspectives (agreements), plus whatever degree of mutual
understanding exists in the various interpretations of a given
message. When interactants become aware of the differences and
similarities in their respective positions, a state of realization
exists. In short, the intersubjectivity of person A and B is a
function of A's view of A, B's view of A, A's view of B, and B's
view of B, plus each party's indirect view of the other.

Such a configuration helps to explain why Albert Schutz
insists in "Intersubjectivity and Understanding" that a
common communicative environment can not exist apart
from the "intentional interconnections of our conscious lives." It
is important to recognize that such interconnections do not cancel
out or neutralize the private world of each person, that core of
privacy that belongs to a particular person and to that person
alone. Rather, the uniqueness of experience continues in the
face-to-face environment, but it is altered by the immediate
context of what Schutz terms a "vivid presence," a state of
interconnection in which the interactants have the opportunity
to "grow old together"—meaning that two distinct streams of
consciousness become intersubjectively related to a given range
of simultaneous activities that unfold over space and time. The
unfolding sense of presence that is common to the respective
participants confers a sense of "we," a state of relatedness in which
the respective parties form a bond of "reciprocal witness" to
whatever takes place within a commonly shared, uniquely defined
symbolic environment.

The ideal conditions for intersubjective understanding are
satisfied through participation in what Martin Buber calls the
"Elements of the Interhuman." Beyond conversational ritual there
is a domain of meaning located "neither in one of the two partners
nor in both together, but only in their dialogue itself, in this
'between' which they live together." In living together, or growing
old together, long enough to get beyond the appearances of what
each one "wishes to seem," the focus of understanding shifts away

from what is spoken to the one who speaks, away from the content of the message to the relation between the "messengers." Buber equates this ideal state with the absence of pretense of persons who communicate themselves to one another "as what they are" and who also regard the other as they are, essentially different, unique. In the relation of "I" and "Thou," differences are confronted, not dismissed; each participant stands his or her own ground while granting, as equally legitimate, the stance assumed by the other. Buber concludes that intersubjective understanding has the potential to be confirmational; the life of dialogue validates and sanctions the personal knowledge of those who are fully present to one another.

21

UNDERSTANDING OURSELVES

Michael Polanyi

Man's capacity to think is his most outstanding attribute. Whoever
speaks of man will therefore have to speak at some stage of human
knowledge. This is a troublesome prospect. For the task·seems to
be without end: as soon as we had completed one such study,
our subject matter would have been extended by this very
achievement. We should have now to study the study that we
had just completed, since it, too, would be a work of man. And
so we should have to go on reflecting ever again on our last
reflections, in an endless and futile endeavour to comprise
completely the works of man.

This difficulty may appear far-fetched, but it is, in fact,
profoundly characteristic both of the nature of man and of the
nature of human knowledge. Man must try for ever to discover

Reprinted by permission of The University of Chicago Press from *The
Study of Man* by Michael Polanyi, 1959, pp. 11–39. © 1959 by The
University of Chicago Press.

knowledge that will stand up by itself, objectively, but the moment he reflects on his own knowledge he catches himself red-handed in the act of upholding his knowledge. He finds himself asserting it to be true, and this asserting and believing is an action which makes an addition to the world on which his knowledge bears. So every time we acquire knowledge we enlarge the world, the world of man, by something that is not yet incorporated in the object of the knowledge we hold, and in this sense a comprehensive knowledge of man must appear impossible.

The significance which I attribute to this logical oddity will become apparent in the solution suggested for it. Its solution seems to lie in the fact that human knowledge is of two kinds. What is usually described as knowledge, as set out in written words or maps, or mathematical formulae, is only one kind of knowledge; while unformulated knowledge, such as we have of something we are in the act of doing, is another form of knowledge. If we call the first kind explicit knowledge, and the second, tacit knowledge, we may say that *we always know tacitly that we are holding our explicit knowledge to be true*. If, therefore, we are satisfied to hold a part of our knowledge tacitly, the vain pursuit of reflecting ever again on our own reflections no longer arises. The question is whether we *can* be satisfied with this. Tacit knowing appears to be a doing of our own, lacking the public, objective, character of explicit knowledge. It may appear therefore to lack the essential quality of knowledge.

This objection cannot be lightly overruled; but I believe it to be mistaken. I deny that any participation of the knower in the shaping of knowledge must invalidate knowledge, though I admit that it impairs its objectivity.

. . . I shall try to transmit this conviction to you or at least to familiarize you with this view—for all I have to say may not convince you—by showing that tacit knowing is in fact the dominant principle of all knowledge, and that its rejection would, therefore, automatically involve the rejection of any knowledge whatever. I shall begin by demonstrating that the personal contribution by which the knower shapes his own knowledge manifestly predominates both at the *lowest levels* of knowing and in the *loftiest achievements* of the human intelligence; after which I shall extend my demonstration to the *intermediate zone* forming the bulk of human knowledge, where the decisive role of the tacit coefficient is not so easily recognizable.

I shall speak therefore first of the most primitive forms of human knowing, at which we arrive by descending to those forms of intelligence which man shares with the animals: the kind of intelligence that is situated behind the barrier of language. Animals have no speech, and all the towering superiority of man over the animals is due almost entirely to man's gift of speech. Babies and infants up to the age of eighteen months or so are mentally not much superior to chimpanzees of the same age; only when they start learning to speak do they rapidly out-distance and leave far behind their simian contemporaries. Even adults show no distinctly greater intelligence than animals so long as their minds work unaided by language. In the absence of linguistic clues man sees things, hears things, feels things, moves about, explores his surroundings and gets to know his way about, very much as animals do.

In order to bring out the logical characteristics of such tacit knowledge we must compare it with the articulate knowledge possessed by man. We see then in the first place that, obviously, the kind of knowledge which we share with the animals is incomparably poorer than that of an educated man, or indeed of any normally brought up human being. But while this richness of explicit knowledge is admittedly related to its distinctive logical characteristics, it is not itself a logical property. The essential *logical* difference between the two kinds of knowledge lies in the fact that we can critically reflect on something explicitly stated, in a way in which we cannot reflect on our tacit awareness of an experience.

To make this difference apparent, let me compare an instance of tacit knowledge with a knowledge of the *same subject* given in explicit form. I have mentioned that men can look round and explore their surroundings tacitly and that this propensity is also well developed in animals. It is known from studies of rats running a maze. A great connoisseur of rat behaviour, E. C. Tolman, has written that a rat gets to know its way about a maze as if it had acquired a mental map of it. And observations on human subjects suggest that a man, however intelligent, is no better at maze-running than a rat, unless assisted by notes, whether these are remembered verbally or sketched out in a drawing. But of course a man *can* make such notes or have them made for him. He may be provided with a detailed map of a region through which he is passing. The advantage of a map is obvious, both for the information which it conveys and for the more important reason that is is much easier to trace an itinerary on a map than to plan it without a map. But there is also a new risk involved in travelling by a map: namely that the map may be mistaken. And this is where critical reflection comes in. The peculiar risk that we take in relying on any explicitly

formulated knowledge is matched by a peculiar opportunity
offered by explicit knowledge for reflecting on it critically. We
can check the information embodied in a map, for example, by
reading it at some place that we can directly survey and compare
the map with the landmarks in front of us.

Such critical examination of the map is possible for two
reasons. First, because a map is a thing external to us and not
something we are ourselves doing or shaping, and second, because
even though it is merely an external object, it can yet speak to us.
It tells us something to which we can listen. It does that equally,
whether we have drawn up the map ourselves or bought it in a
shop, but for the moment it is the former case that we are
interested in, namely when the map is in fact a statement of our
own. In reading such an utterance we are playing back to
ourselves something we have said before so that we may listen
to it in a critical manner. A critical process of this kind may go
on for hours and indeed for weeks and months. I may go
through the manuscript of a whole book and examine the same
text sentence by sentence any number of times.

Obviously, nothing quite like this can take place on the
pre-articulate level. I can test the kind of mental map I possess
of a familiar region only in action, that is, by actually using it as
my guide. If I then lose my way, I can correct my ideas
accordingly. There is no other way of improving inarticulate
knowledge. I can see a thing only in one way at a time, and if
I am doubtful of what I see, all I can do is to look again and
perhaps see things differently then. Inarticulate intelligence can
only grope its way by plunging from one view of things into
another. Knowledge acquired and held in this manner may
therefore be called *a-critical*.

We can enlarge and greatly deepen this contrast between
tacit and articulate knowledge by extending it to the way in
which knowledge is acquired. Remember how a map is drawn up
by triangulation. Starting from a set of systematically collected
observations, we proceed according to strict rules applied to these
data. Only explicitly formulated knowledge can be thus derived
from specificable premises according to clear rules of inference.
And it is the most important function of critical thought to test
such explicit processes of inference, by rehearsing their chain
of reasoning in search of some weak link.

The contrast between the two domains should now be sharp
enough. Pre-verbal knowledge appears as a small lighted area
surrounded by immense darkness, a small patch illuminated by
accepting a-critically the unreasoned conclusions of our senses;

while man's articulate knowledge represents a panorama of the
whole universe established under the control of critical reflection.

. . . I-[have]-shown that purely tacit operations of the mind
are processes of understanding; I will go further now by
suggesting that the understanding of words and other symbols
is also a tacit process. Words can convey information, a series of
algebraic symbols can constitute a mathematical deduction, a
map can set out the topography of a region; but neither words
nor symbols nor maps can be said to communicate an understanding
of themselves. Though such statements will be made in a form
which best induces an understanding of their message, the sender
of the message will always have to rely for the comprehension
of his message on the intelligence of the person addressed. Only by
virtue of this act of comprehension, of this tacit contribution of
his own, can the receiving person be said to acquire knowledge
when he is presented with a statement.

This holds, of course, also at the point from which a statement
is issued. We utter a statement with the intention of saying
something. Though this intention may not include an anticipation
of all that will be said—since a message may develop further
as it is put into words—we always know approximately what we
mean to say a little before we say it. This is true even for
purely mechanical computations, on which we blindly rely for
uttering a statement; for we know in advance what we are doing,
in trusting such an operation to speak on our behalf.

I have now expanded the function of understanding into
that of knowing what we *intend*, what we *mean*, or what we *do*.
To this we may add now that nothing that is said, written or
printed, can ever mean anything in itself: for it is only a *person*
who utters something—or who listens to it or reads it—who can
mean something *by* it. All these semantic functions are the tacit
operations of a person. . . .

Our whole articulate equipment turns out to be merely
a tool-box, a supremely effective instrument for deploying our
inarticulate faculties. And we need not hesitate then to conclude
that the tacit personal coefficient of knowledge predominates
also in the domain of explicit knowledge and represents therefore
at all levels man's ultimate faculty for acquiring and holding
knowledge. . . .

We have seen that when we understand or mean something,
when we reorganize our understanding or when we confront
a statement with the facts to which it refers, we exercise
our tacit powers in search of a better intellectual control of the
matter in hand. We seek to clarify, verify or lend precision

to something said or experienced. We move away from a position that is felt to be somewhat problematic to another position which we find more satisfying. *And this is how we eventually come to hold a piece of knowledge to be true.* Here is the tacit doing of our own of which I spoke at the beginning, the unavoidable act of personal participation in our explicit knowledge of things: an act of which we can be aware merely in an unreflecting manner. And this situation appears now no longer as a logical oddity. For we have seen that the kind of tacit powers by which we commit ourselves to any particular statement operate in various elaborate forms throughout the realm of human knowledge, and that it is this personal coefficient alone which endows our explicit statements with meaning and conviction. All human knowledge is now seen to be shaped and sustained by the inarticulate mental faculties which we share with the animals.

This view entails a decisive change in our ideal of knowledge. The participation of the knower in shaping his knowledge, which had hitherto been tolerated only as a flaw— a shortcoming to be eliminated from perfect knowledge—is now recognized as the true guide and master of our cognitive powers. We acknowledge now that our powers of knowing operate widely without causing us to utter any explicit statements; and that even when they do issue in an utterance, this is used merely as an instrument for enlarging the range of the tacit answers that originated it.

22

INTERACTION AND INTEREXPERIENCE IN DYADS

R. D. Laing, H. Phillipson, and A. R. Lee

In a science of persons, we state as axiomatic that:

1. behaviour is a function of experience;
2. both experience and behaviour are always in relation to some one or something other than self.

The very simplest schema for the understanding of the behaviour of one person has to include at least two persons and a common situation. And this schema must include not only the interaction of the two, but their interexperience.

Reprinted from R. D. Laing, H. Phillipson, A. R. Lee, *Interpersonal Perception*, pp. 9–34. Copyright © by R. D. Laing, H. Phillipson, A. R. Lee. Used by permission of the authors and Springer Publishing Company, Inc., New York.

Thus:

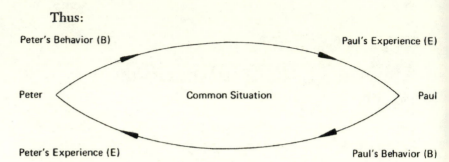

In terms of this schema, Peter's behaviour towards Paul is in part a function of Peter's experiences of Paul. Peter's experience of Paul is in part a function of Paul's behaviour towards Peter. Paul's behaviour towards Peter is in turn partly a function of his experience of Peter, which in turn is in part a function of Paul's behaviour towards him. Thus, the behaviour of Peter towards Paul, and of Paul towards Peter, cannot be subsumed under an exclusively inter*behavioural* schema (much less any *intra*personal schema) if Peter and Paul are axiomatic persons. For, if Peter and Paul are persons, the behaviour of each towards the other is mediated by the *experience* by each of the other, just as the experience of each is mediated by the behaviour of each.

The transformation of Paul's behaviour into Peter's experience entails all the constitutional and culturally-conditioned learned structures of perception that contribute to the ways Peter construes his world. Much of this learning has never been open to reflective awareness. To a much greater extent than most of us realize, and any of us wish to believe, we have been "programmed" like computing machines to handle incoming data according to prescribed instructions. Often this has been accompanied by meta-instructions against being aware that we are being thus instructed. This is an additional factor in the frequently great difficulty that many people have in opening their own "programming" to their own conscious reflection.

If each of us carries around a set of criteria by which we judge certain acts as loving and tender or hating and brutal, what may be a loving act to one person may be a hating act to another. For example, one woman may be delighted if her suitor uses a "caveman approach" with her; another woman may think of him as repugnant for just the same behaviour. The woman who sees the caveman approach as loving may in turn interpret a more subtle approach as "weak," whereas the woman who is repelled by a caveman approach may see the more subtle approach as "sensitive." Thus behaviour even of itself does not directly lead to experience. It must be perceived and interpreted according to some set of criteria. Although these intervening variables are not for the most part explicitly focused upon in this book, this does not mean that we are relegating them to a place of secondary significance in a comprehensive theory of interpersonal systems.

In order for the other's behaviour to become part of self's experience, self must perceive it. The very act of perception entails interpretation. The human being learns how to structure his perceptions, particuarly within his family, as a subsystem interplaying with its own contextual subculture, related institutions and overall larger culture. Let us take, for example, a situation in which a husband begins to cry. The behaviour is crying. This behaviour must now be experienced by his wife. It cannot be experienced without being interpreted. The interpretation will vary greatly from person to person, from culture to culture. For Jill, a man crying is inevitably to be interpreted as a sign of weakness. For Jane, a man crying will be interpreted as a sign of sensitivity. Each will react to a greater or lesser extent according to a preconceived interpretive model which she may or not be aware of. At its simplest level, Jill may have been taught by her father that a man never cries, that only a sissy does. Jane may have been taught by her father that a man can show emotion and that he is a better man for having done so. Frequently such intermediary steps (regulative schemata) that contribute to the determination of the experience are lost to awareness. Jill simply experiences her husband as weak; Jane simply experiences hers as sensitive. Neither is clear why. They might even find it difficult to describe the kinds of behaviour which have led them to their conclusions. Yet we must not simply attribute these interpretations to phantasy, as this term is often employed as a form of crypto-invalidation.

Our experience of another entails a particular interpretation of his behaviour. To feel loved is to perceive and interpret, that is, to experience, the actions of the other as loving. The alteration of my experience of my behaviour to your experience of my behaviour—there's the rub.

> I act in a way that is *cautious* to me, but *cowardly* to you.
> You act in a way that is *courageous* to you, but *foolhardy* to
>   me.
> She sees herself as *vivacious*, but he sees her as *superficial*.
> He sees himself as *friendly*, she sees him as *seductive*.
> She sees herself as *reserved*, he sees her as *haughty and aloof*.
> He sees himself as *gallant*, she sees him as *phoney*.

She sees herself as *feminine,* he sees her as *helpless and dependent.*

He sees himself as *masculine,* she sees him as *overbearing and dominating.*

Experience in all cases entails the perception of the act *and* the interpretation of it. Within the issue of perception is the issue of selection and reception. From the many things that we see and hear of the other we select a few to remember. Acts highly significant to us may be trivial to others. We happen not to have been paying attention at that moment; we missed what to the other was his most significant gesture or statement. But, even if the acts selected for interpretation are the same, even if each individual perceives these acts as the same act, the interpretation of the identical act may be very different. She winks at him in friendly complicity, and he sees it as seductive. The act is the same, the interpretation and hence the experience of it disjunctive. She refuses to kiss him goodnight out of "self-respect," but he sees it as rejection of him, and so on.

A child who is told by his mother to wear a sweater may resent her as coddling him, but to her it may seem to be simply a mark of natural concern.

In one society to burp after a good meal is good manners; in another it is uncouth. Thus, even though the piece of behaviour under consideration may be agreed upon, the interpretation of this behaviour may be diametrically disagreed upon.

What leads to diametrically opposed interpretations? In general, we can say interpretations are based on our past learning, particularly within our family (i.e., with our parents, siblings and relatives) but also in the larger society in which we travel.

Secondly, the act itself is interpreted according to the context in which it is found. Thus, for example, the refusal of a goodnight kiss after one date may seem to be perfectly normal for both parties, but after six months' dating a refusal would seem more significant to each of them. Also a refusal after a previous acceptance will seem more significant.

What happens when two people do not agree on the meaning to be assigned a particular act? A very complicated process ensues. If communication is optimum, they *understand* that they differ on the interpretation of the act, and also *realize that they both understand* that they differ in its interpretation. Once this is established they may get into a struggle over whether or not to change the act under consideration in the future. This struggle may take various forms:

Threat—Do this or else.
Coaxing—Please do this.
Bribery—If you do this I will do that in return.
Persuasion—I believe it is a good idea for you to do this
    because, etc.

However, often in human affairs where there is a disagreement
there is also a *misunderstanding* and *failure of realization of
misunderstanding*. This may be deliberate, i.e., a simple attempt
to ignore the other person's point of view, or it may be an
unwitting overlooking of the opposing viewpoint. In either case
a disruption of communication occurs. It seems to us that, *for
the first time*, our notation makes it possible to characterize and
pinpoint the levels and pattern of disruption of this kind.

Thus, in the schema on page 346, E and B are categories of
variables, each interposed or intervening between the direct
impact of B on B and E on E. There is no naked contiguity, as it
were, in interpersonal behaviour, between the behaviour of the
one person and the behaviour of the other, although much of
human behaviour (including the behaviour of psychologists)
can be seen as a unilateral or bilateral attempt to eliminate E
from the transaction. Similarly in this schema it is presumed
that there is no direct contiguity or actual conflux of one person's
experience with the other. The one person's experience is presumed
always to be mediated to the other through the intervening
category of the *behaviour* (including verbal) of the one person,
which in turn has to be perceived and interpreted in order to be
experienced by the other. This means that, for the purpose of
this enquiry, neither behaviour that is the direct consequence of
physical behavioural impact (as when one billiard ball hits another)
nor experience in the one person generated directly through the
experience of another (as in possible cases of extrasensory
perception) is regarded as personal.

Now, we know that to different extents in different people
and circumstances Peter's view of himself is related to what Peter
thinks Paul thinks of him; that is, to Peter's metaperspective and
meta-identity. If what Peter thinks Paul thinks of him is not
what Peter wants to have thought of him, Peter has, in principle,
as a means of controlling the condition that controls him, the
option of acting upon Paul to change Paul, or of acting upon his
own experience of Paul to change his experience of Paul. By
acting on Paul, Peter may intend to act upon Paul's experience
of Peter, or he may intend merely to act on Paul's action. If, for
instance, he says "Shut up", this injunction may say in effect:

"I don't care what you feel about me, just keep it to yourself."

That is, any act may be primarily addressed to the other or to myself, but if perceived it must affect both. If directed to the other, the immediate goal may be to effect change in the other, or to prevent change in the other. Similarly, if directed to self, the immediate aim may be to effect change in self, or to prevent change in self. But in dyadic relationships, any action on the other has effects on me, and any action on self affects the other. I may so act as to induce the other to experience me in a particular way. A great deal of human action has as its goal the induction of particular experiences in the other of oneself. I wish to be seen by the other as generous, or tough, or fair-minded. However, I may or may not know what it is that I have to do to induce the other to interpret my action and experience me as I desire, whether generous or tough or fair-minded. His criteria for making these evaluations may be diametrically opposed to my criteria, and this I may not be aware of. Thus a passively resistant person (e.g., a Gandhi) may seem to one person to be tough, whereas to another he may seem to be weak.

Further, the other may wittingly or unwittingly be set to interpret every possible action of mine as indicating a preconceived hypothesis (e.g., that I am hurtful). For example, at a conjoint therapy session a wife interpreted her husband's absence as proof that "he wished to hurt her." When he showed up late she quite calmly assumed that he had finally decided to *come* "in order to hurt her." This is a particularly difficult bind if at the same time the person implies that there is a right course of action that the other just hasn't found. In such a situation the covert operative set is that no matter what he does he intends to hurt, whereas the overt implication is that if he did not intend to hurt he would be doing the right thing.

I therefore tend to select others for whom I can be the other that I wish to be, so that I may then reappropriate the sort of meta-identity I want. This requires that I find another who agrees with my criteria. But such strategems may entail a remarkable alienation. My centre of gravity may become *the other I am to the other*. In such circumstances, in order to achieve the identity that I wish, through being the desired other for the other, the other must be malleable by me, or pervious to me. I must select carefully those others with whom I shall have to interact, acting towards them in such a way that I will be able to be to them what I want to be. I shall be in a serious dilemma, however, if I cannot make the other person regard me as that other that I wish to be for him. I may wish to be a mother to someone who is also wanting to be a mother, or to be generous to someone who insists on seeing me as mean, and so on. Alternatively, under those circumstances I may in desperation adopt the strategy of acting upon my *own* experience of the other, so that in a sense I render my meta-identity independent of the other.

Let us consider this latter strategy in more detail. We see it in one form of self's action on self, namely, Peter's action on his own experience of Paul, under the name of projection. Projection is a form of action directed at one's own experience of the other. It is called a "mental mechanism." This is a very misleading term, since it is neither mental nor mechanical. It is an action whose intentional object is one's own experience of the other. It is to the credit of psychoanalysis that it has brought to light actions of this kind.

Projection is clearly a most important stratagem and may function in different ways in an interpersonal system, but in every case it is one of a class of *actions whose primary object is not the other's experience of me, but my experience of the other*. Secondarily, of course, it must also affect the other's experience of me. For example, when the paranoid individual "projects," he may experience the other as hurting him and not helping him. This in turn forces the other to experience the paranoid as a person who sees him (o) as a hurtful person.

We said above that part of the theoretical problem constantly facing us is that we find it easier to think of each person in a dyad separately, or one at a time, rather than together. This is true, for instance, in terms of the theory of projection. There are a number of different aspects and versions of the concept of projection, not all rendered explicit.

We have already suggested that projection is one way of acting on the other by, paradoxically, not acting directly on him as a real person, but on one's experience of him. But if I convey to the other how I experience him I am certainly influencing him. Indeed, one of the most effective ways to affect the other's experience of me is to tell him how I experience him. Every flatterer knows that, all things being equal, one tends to like someone by whom one is liked. If I am ugly, I am not ugly only in my eyes, I see myself in the looking-glass of your eyes as ugly too. You are the witness of my ugliness. In fact, insofar as ugliness is relative, if you and everyone else saw me as beautiful, I might be ugly no more. If I cannot induce you to see me as I wish, I may act on my experience of you rather than your experience of me. I can invent your experience of me. Many projections, of course, are the apparently compulsive inventions of persons who see themselves as ugly, and wish to extrude this perception from their own self-self relation. At any rate, this is a commonly ascribed motive for projection. All projection involves a simultaneous negation of what projection replaces.

In Zarathustra, the ugliest man abolishes God because he cannot stand an eternal witness to his ugliness, and replaces him with nothing.

Projection refers to a mode of experiencing the other in which one experiences one's outer world in terms of one's inner world. Another way of putting this is that one experiences the perceptual world in terms of one's phantasy system, without realizing that one is doing this. One may seek to make the world actually embody one's phantasy, but this is another story, and projection can occur without so doing.

Pure projection tells us nothing about the other. Projection refers only to one area of the dyadic interaction, namely, the way you act on your own experience of me, or the way I act on my own experience of you, although it will, we know, be influenced by, and will influence, the other areas, since your way of experiencing me interrelates with the way I act towards you, and so on. The way Peter acts towards Paul will have something to do with the way Paul experiences Peter, and with the way Paul, for his part, now acts towards Peter. Unfortunately, there is no systematic theory to guide us here, and a paucity of empirical data. We have no language even to describe various things that can happen in other parts of the dyadic circuit when projection occurs in one section. For instance, how does Paul react to his realization that Peter's experience of Paul is largely projection, and to his realization that Peter's actions are not addressed to the Paul that Paul takes himself to be, but to a Paul who is largely Peter's invention? One way to ease the situation is for Paul systematically to discover the data upon which Peter is constructing him into a person he does not recognize. This is more exacting than to assume that Peter is purely inventing his view of Paul. By this tactic, it becomes Paul's job to discover the criteria by which Peter is coming to his discordant conclusions. These are inevitably there, but they may be hidden or so strange, even to Peter, let alone to Paul, that they are neglected, ignored, or considered insignificant; that is, invalidated in one way or another.

For example, a husband and wife, after eight years of marriage, described one of their first fights. This occurred on the second night of their honeymoon. They were both sitting at a bar in a hotel when the wife struck up a conversation with a

couple sitting next to them. To her dismay her husband refused
to join the conversation, remained aloof, gloomy and antagonistic
both to her and the other couple. Perceiving his mood, she
became angry at him for producing an awkward social situation
and making her feel "out on a limb." Tempers rose, and they
ended in a bitter fight in which each accused the other of being
inconsiderate. This was the extent of their report of the incident.
Eight years later, however, we were able to tease out some of
the additional factors involved. When asked why she had struck
up the conversation with the other couple, the wife replied:
"Well, I had never had a conversation with another couple as a
wife before. Previous to this I had always been a 'girl friend'
or 'fiancée' or ' daughter' or 'sister.' I thought of the honeymoon as
a fine time to try out my new role as a wife, to have a conversation
as a wife with my husband at my side. I had never had a husband
before, either." She thus carried into the situation her expectancy
that the honeymoon would be an opportunity to begin to socialize
as a couple with other couples. She looked forward to this eagerly
and joyfully. By contrast, her husband had a completely differing
view of the honeymoon. When questioned about his aloofness
during the conversation he said: "Of course I was aloof. The
honeymoon to me was a time to get away from everyone—a time
when two people could learn to take advantage of a golden
opportunity to ignore the rest of the world and simply explore
each other. I wanted us to be sufficient unto ourselves. To me,
everyone else in the world was a complication, a burden and an
interference. When my wife struck up that conversation with the
other couple I felt it as a direct insult. She was telling me in
effect that I was not man enough for her, that I was insufficient
to fill her demands. She made me feel inadequate and angry."

Eight years later they were able to laugh at the situation.
He could say, "If I had only known how you felt it would have
made a great difference." The crucial point is that each interpreted
the other's action as inconsiderate and even deliberately insulting.
These attributions of inconsiderateness and insult and maliciousness
were based on hidden discrepant value systems and discrepant
expectations based on these value systems.

Peter's concrete experience of Paul is a unity of the given
and the constructed: a synthesis of his own (Peter's) interpretations
of his perceptions based on his expectations and his (Peter's)
phantasy (projection), and of the distal stimulus that originates
from "Paul." The resultant fusion of projection-perception is the
phenomenal Paul as experienced by Peter. Thus Paul-for-Peter is

neither a total invention nor a pure perception of Peter's nor a simple duplication of Paul's view of Paul. Paul as actually experienced by Peter will be compounded of perception, interpretation and phantasy. One might speak of a perception coefficient, according to the degree to which perception prevails over projection, or projection over perception. Also, one might speak of a coefficient of mismatching or disjunctive interpretive systems. Now Peter's actions towards Paul may follow from Peter's experience of Paul that is largely projective (has a high phantasy-coefficient) or from mismatched interpretive systems. Peter's experience and consequent actions are likely to be disjunctive with Paul's view of Paul, and with Paul's view of Peter's view of Paul. It is likely that if Peter's view of Paul is very disjunctive with Paul's view of Paul, whether itself highly phantasized or not, then Peter's actions will be addressed to a Paul that Paul does not recognize. Paul may register that Peter treats him with more or less deference than Paul expects, or is too familiar, or is too distant, or is too frightened of him, or not sufficiently so. Paul may find that Peter acts not towards the Paul that Paul takes himself to be, but as a mother, a father, a son, a daughter, a brother, a sister, etc.

All this suggests that Peter cannot perceive himself as Peter if he does not perceive Paul as Paul. If the coefficient of phantasy or of mismatched expectancy systems rises in Peter's experience of Paul, one expects that Peter's view of himself will become correspondingly mismatched between his self-identity, meta-identity, and Paul's view of Peter, and Paul's view of Peter's meta-identity (not as yet trying to exhaust the different disjunctions) and that this will express itself in the increasingly "strange" way, that, in Paul's eyes, Peter acts towards Paul. It is not necessary to repeat this whole state of affairs, *mutatis mutandis*, exchanging Peter for Paul and Paul for Peter.

What we have to try to understand is how Peter's mismatched interpretations and phantasization[1] of his experience of Peter and Paul effects Paul, and how Paul's experiences of Paul and Peter in turn affect Peter's tendency to experience projectively and to act accordingly.

One might suppose that the easiest part of the circuit to become phantasized by Peter might be what was going on inside Paul, for here there is the minimum of validation available to Peter, except from the testimony of Paul.

Thus, Peter says, "I think you are unhappy inside."

Paul says, "No I'm not."

Peter may, however, attempt to validate his attribution about

Paul's relation to Paul by watching the actions of Paul. He may say, "If *I* acted in that way I would be unhappy," or, "When mother acted that way she was unhappy." He may have nothing that he can "put his finger on," but "senses" that Paul is unhappy. He may be correctly reconstructing Paul's experience by succeeding in synthesizing many cues from Paul's behaviour, or he may be "wrong" to construe Paul's behaviour in his own terms (Peter's) rather than Paul's, or he may put inside Paul unhappiness that he is trying not to feel inside himself. It is not easy to discover criteria of validity here, because Peter may actually make Paul unhappy by "going on" about it. Let us suppose, however, that Peter's view of Paul is disjunctive with Paul's view of Paul over the issue of Paul's relation to Paul. Is Paul unhappy? Peter, wittingly or unwittingly, may register from witting to unwitting cues from Paul's behavior that Paul is unhappy. Paul may be seeking to deny his unhappiness. On the other hand, Peter may be attributing to Paul what he is denying himself. Furthermore, Peter may seek to avoid feeling unhappy himself by *trying to make Paul unhappy*. One of his ways of doing this may be to tell Paul that he or Paul is unhappy. Let us suppose he does the latter. Paul may accuse Peter of trying to make him unhappy by telling him he is. Very likely, Peter will repudiate this attribution in favour, perhaps, of one of the order, "I am only trying to help you."

Sometimes, what appears to be projection is really a complicated mismatching of expectations, i.e., the interpretation that p gives to o's not fulfilling his expectation. Thus, if Peter, becomes upset about something, Paul may hope to help him by remaining calm and detached. However, Peter may feel that this is just the wrong thing for Paul to be doing when he is upset. His feeling may be that a really friendly, helpful person would be upset with him. If Paul does not know this and Peter does not communicate it, Peter may assume that Paul is deliberately staying aloof to hurt him. Paul may then conclude that Peter is "projecting" angry feelings onto him. This, then, is a situation where projection is attributed by Paul to Peter, but it has not actually occurred. This commonly happens in analytical therapy when the analyst (Paul) assumes that a detached mirrorlike attitude is the most helpful stance he can adopt towards the patient (Peter). However, the patient may feel that only an open self-disclosing person could be of help, and if he goes on to interpret the analyst's stance as not only unhelpful in effect but unhelpful in intention, then the analyst may in turn counter-attribute "projection" to the patient. A vicious circle of mismatched interpretations, expectancies, experiences, attributions and counter-attributions is now in play.

It starts to whirl something like this:

Peter:

1. I am upset.
2. Paul is acting very calm and dispassionate.

3. If Paul cared about me and wanted to help he would get involved and show some emotion also.
4. Paul knows that this upsets me.
5. If Paul knows that his behaviour upsets me, he must be intending to hurt me.
6. He must be cruel, sadistic. Maybe he gets pleasure out of it, etc.

Paul:

1. Peter is upset.
2. I'll try to help him by remaining calm and just listening.
3. He is getting even more upset. I must be even more calm.

4. He is accusing me of hurting him.
5. I'm really trying to help.

6. He must be projecting.

Attributions of this kind, based on a virtually inextricable mix of mismatched expectations and phantasy and perception, are the very stuff of interhuman reality. One has, for instance, to enter into this realm in order to understand how one person's attributions about others may begin to be particularly disturbing and disjunctive to the others, and come to be repeatedly invalidated by them, so that he may begin to be subject to the global attribution of being mad (Laing, 1961, 1964, 1965).

However, even all-round conjunctions—between Peter's view of Peter and Paul's view of Peter, Peter's view of Paul and Paul's view of Paul, Peter's view of Paul's view of Paul and Paul's view of Peter's view of Paul's view of Paul, Peter's view of Paul's view of Peter and Paul's view of Peter's view of Paul—do not validate a perceptive circle. They achieve all-round "reliability" but not "validity." They "validate", equally readily a *phantasy circle*. These whirling phantasy circles, we suggest, are as destructive to relationships, individual (or international), as are hurricanes to material reality.

To summarize so far. Through my behaviour I can act upon three areas of the other: on his experience of me; on his experience of himself; and upon his behaviour. In addition, I cannot act on the other himself directly, but I can act on my own *experience* of him.

Note

[1] The concept of phantasy as a mode of experience in a social system is developed by Laing elsewhere (1961, 1966).

References

Laing, R. D. *The Self and Others* (London: Tavistock, 1961).

Laing, R. D., and Esterson, A. *Sanity, Madness, and the Family* (New York: Basic Books, 1969).

Laing, R. D. "Mystification, Confusion and Conflict," in I. BoszormenyiNagy, and James L. Framo (eds.), *Intensive Family Therapy: Theoretical and Practical Aspects* (New York: Harper and Row, 1965).

Laing, R. D. "Family and Individual Structure," in P. Lomas, *Psychoanalytic Approaches to the Family* (London: Hogarth Press, 1966).

23

INTERSUBJECTIVITY AND UNDERSTANDING

Alfred Schutz

Intersubjectivity

If we retain the natural attitude as men among other men, the existence of others is no more questionable to us than the existence of an outer world. We are simply born into a world of others, and as long as we stick to the natural attitude we have no doubt that intelligent fellow-men do exist. . . .

Fellow Men Taken for Granted

The world of my daily life is by no means my private world but is from the outset an inter-subjective one, shared with my fellow

Reprinted by permission of The University of Chicago Press from *On Phenomenology and Social Relations* by Alfred Schutz, 1970, pp. 163–199. © 1970 by The University of Chicago Press.

men, experienced and interpreted by others: in brief, it is a
world common to all of us. The unique biographical situation in
which I find myself within the world at any moment of my
existence is only to a very small extent of my own making. I find
myself always within an historically given world which, as a
world of nature as well as a sociocultural world, had existed
before my birth and which will continue to exist after my death.
This means that this world is not only mine but also my fellow
men's environment; moreover, these fellow men are elements of
my own situation, as I am of theirs. Acting upon the others and
acted upon by them, I know of this mutual relationship, and this
knowledge also implies that they, the others, experience the
common world in a way substantially similar to mine. They, too,
find themselves in a unique biographical situation within a world
which is, like mine, structured in terms of actual and potential
reach, grouped around their actual Here and Now as the center in
the same dimensions and directions of space and time, an
historically given world of nature, society, and culture, etc. . . .
Man takes for granted the bodily existence of fellow men, their
conscious life, the possibility of intercommunication, and the
historical giveness of social organization and culture, just as he
takes for granted the world of nature into which he was born. . . .

The Communicative Common Environment

To be related to a common environment and to be united with
the Other in a community of persons—these two propositions
are inseparable. We could not be persons for others, even not for
ourselves, if we could not find with the others a common
environment as the counterpart of the intentional
interconnectedness of our conscious lives. This common
environment is established by comprehension, which in turn,
is founded upon the fact that the subjects reciprocally motivate
one another in their spiritual activities. . . . The persons
participating in the communicative environment are given one
to the other not as objects but as counter-subjects as consociates
in a societal community of persons. Sociality is constituted by
communicative acts in which the I turns to the others,
apprehending them as persons who turn to him, and both know
of this fact. . . . This leads to the fact that within the common
environment any subject has his particular subjective environment,
his private world, originally given to him and to him alone. He
perceives the same object as his partner but with adumbrations
dependent upon his particular Here and his phenomenal Now. . . .

General Thesis of the Alter Ego

Now let us go back again to the naïve attitude of daily life in which we live in our acts directed toward their objects. Among those objects which we experience in the vivid present are other people's behavior and thoughts. In listening to a lecturer, for instance, we seem to participate immediately in the development of his stream of thought. But —and this point is obviously a decisive one—our attitude in doing so is quite different from that we adopt in turning to our own stream of thought by reflection. We catch the other's thought in its vivid presence and not *modo preterito;* that is, we catch it as a "Now" and not as a "Just now." The other's speech and our listening are experienced as a vivid simultaneity. Now he starts a new sentence, he attaches word to word; we do not know how the sentence will end, and before its end we are uncertain what it means. The next sentence joins the first, paragraph follows paragraph; now he has expressed a thought and passes to another, and the whole is a lecture among other lectures and so on. It depends on circumstances how far we want to follow the development of his thought. But as long as we do so we participate in the immediate present of the other's thought.

The fact that I can grasp the other's stream of thought, and this means the subjectivity of the alter ego in its vivid present,[1] whereas I cannot grasp my own self but by way of reflection in its past, leads us to a definition of the alter ego: the alter ego is that subjective stream of thought which can be experienced in its vivid present. In order to bring it into view we do not have to stop fictitiously the other's stream of thought nor need we transform its 'Nows" into "Just Nows." It is simultaneous with our own stream of consciousness, we share together the same vivid present—in one word: we grow old together. The alter ego therefore is that stream of consciousness whose activities I can seize in their present by my own simultaneous activities.

This experience of the other's stream of consciousness in vivid simultaneity I propose to call the *general thesis of the alter ego's existence.* It implies that this stream of thought which is not mine shows the same fundamental structure as my own consciousness. This means that the other is like me, capable of acting and thinking; that his stream of thoughts show the same through and through connectedness as mine; that analogous to my own life of consciousness his shows the same time-structure, together with the specific experiences of retentions, reflections, protentions, anticipations, connected therewith and its phenomena of memory and attention, of kernel and horizon of the thought, and all the modifications thereof. It means, furthermore, that the other can live, as I do, either in his acts and thoughts, directed toward their objects or turn to his own acting and thinking; that he can experience his own Self only *modo praeterito*, but that he may look at my stream of consciousness in a vivid present; that, consequently, he has the genuine experience of growing old with me as I know that I do with him. . . .

Let us now state in summary which of our interpretive acts referring to another self are interpretations of our own experience. There is first the interpretation that the observed person is really a human being and not an image of some kind. The observer establishes this solely by interpretation of his own perceptions of the other's body. Second, there is the interpretation of all the external phases of action, that is, of all bodily movements and their effects. Here, as well, the observer is engaging in interpretation of his own perceptions, just as when he is watching the flight of a bird or the stirring of a branch in the wind. In order to understand what is occurring, he is appealing solely to his own past experience, not to what is going on in the mind of the observed person.[2] Finally, the same thing may be said of the perception of all the other person's expressive movements and all the signs which he uses, provided that one is here referring to the general and objective meaning of such manifestations and not their occasional and subjective meaning.

But, of course, by "understanding the other person" much more is meant, as a rule. This additional something, which is really the only strict meaning of the term, involves grasping what is really going on in the other person's mind, grasping those things of which the external manifestations are mere indications. To be sure, interpretation of such external indications and signs in terms of interpretation of one's own experiences must come first. But the interpretater will not be satisfied with this. He knows perfectly well from the total context of his own experience that, corresponding to the outer objective and public meaning which he has just deciphered, there is this other, inner, subjective meaning. He asks, then, "What is that woodcutter really thinking about? What is he up to? What does all this chopping mean to to him?" Or, in another case, "What does this person mean by speaking to me in this manner, at this particular moment? For the sake of what does he do this (what is his in-order-to motive)? What circumstance does he give as the reason for it (that is, what is his genuine because-motive)? What does the choice of these words indicate?" Questions like these point to the other person's *own* meaning-contexts, to the complex way in which his own lived experiences have been constituted. . . .

Reciprocity of Perspectives

In the natural attitude of common-sense thinking of daily life I take it for granted that intelligent fellow men exist. This implies that the objects of the world are, as a matter of principle, accessible to their knowledge, namely, either known to them or knowable by them. This I know and take for granted beyond question. But I know also and take for granted that, strictly speaking, the "same" object must mean something different to me and to any of my fellow men. This is so because

(i) I, being "here," am at another distance from and experience other aspects as being typical of the objects than he, who is "there." For the same reason, certain objects are out of my reach (of my seeing, hearing, my manipulatory sphere, etc.) but within his and vice versa.

(ii) My and my fellow man's biographically determined situations, and therewith my and his purpose at hand and my and his system of relevances originating in such purposes, must needs differ, at least to a certain extent.

Common sense thinking overcomes the differences in individual perspectives resulting from these factors by two basic idealizations:

(i) The idealization of the interchangeability of the standpoints: I take it for granted—and assume my fellow man does the same—that if I change places with him so that his "here" becomes mine, I would be at the same distance from things and see them in the same typicality as he actually does moreover, the same things would be in my reach which are actually in his. All this vice versa.

(ii) The idealization of the congruency of the system of relevances: Until counter-evidence I take it for granted—and assume my fellowman does the same—that the differences in perspectives originating in my and his unique biographical situations are irrelevant for the purpose at hand of either of us and that he and I, that "We," assume that both of us have selected and interpreted the actually or potentially common objects and their features in an identical manner or at least an "empirically identical" manner, namely, sufficient for all practical purposes.

It is obvious that both idealizations, that of the interchangeability of the standpoints and that of the congruency of relevances—both together constituting the *general thesis of recipocal perspective*—are typifying constructs of objects of thought which supersede the thought objects of my and my fellow man's private experience. By the operation of these constructs of common-sense thinking it is assumed that the sector of the world taken for granted by me is also taken for granted by you, my individual fellow man, even more that it is taken for granted by "Us," but this "We" does not merely include you and me but "everyone who belongs to us," namely everyone whose system of relevances is substantially (sufficiently) in conformity with yours and mine. Thus, the general thesis of reciporcal perspectives leads to the apprehension of objects and their aspects actually known by me and potentially known by you as everyone's knowledge. Such knowledge is conceived to be objective and anonymous, namely detached from and independent of my fellow man's definition of the situation, my and his unique biographical circumstances and the actual and potential purposes at hand therein involved.

The terms "objects" and "aspect of objects" have to be interpreted in the broadest possible sense as objects of knowledge taken for granted.

Notes

[1] It is not necessary to refer to an example of social interrelationship bound to the medium of speech. Whoever has played a game of tennis, performed chamber music, or made love has caught the other in his immediate vivid present.

[2] Of course, all such interpretations presume acceptance of the General Thesis of the Alter Ego, according to which the external object is understood to be animated, that is, to be the body of another self.

24

ELEMENTS OF THE INTERHUMAN[1]

Martin Buber

THE SOCIAL AND THE INTERHUMAN

It is usual to ascribe what takes place between men to the social realm, thereby blurring a basically important line of division between two essentially different areas of human life. I myself, when I began nearly fifty years ago to find by own bearings in the knowledge of society, making use of the then unknown concept of the interhuman,[2] made the same error. From that time it became increasingly clear to me that we have to do here with a separate category of our existence, even a separate dimension, to use a mathematical term, and one with which we are so familiar that its peculiarity has hitherto almost escaped us. Yet insight into its

peculiarity is extremely important not only for our thinking, but
also for our living.

We may speak of social phenomena wherever the life of a
number of men, lived with one another, bound up together, brings
in its train shared experiences and reactions. But to be thus bound
up together means only that each individual existence is enclosed
and contained in a group existence. It does not mean that between
one member and another of the group there exists any kind of
personal relation. They do feel that they belong together in a
way that is, so to speak, fundamentally different from every
possible belonging together with someone outside the group. And
there do arise, especially in the life or smaller groups, contacts
which frequently favour the birth of individual relations, but, on
the other hand, frequently make it more difficult. In no case,
however, does membership in a group necessarily involve an
existential relation between one member and another. It is true
that there have been groups in history which included highly
intensive and intimate relations between two of their members—
as, for instance, in the homosexual relations among the Japanese
Samurai or among Doric warriors—and these were countenanced
for the sake of the stricter cohesion of the group. But in general
it must be said that the leading elements in groups, especially in
the latter course of human history, have rather been inclined to
suppress the personal relation in favour of the purely collective
element. Where this latter element reigns alone or is predominant,
men feel themselves to be carried by the collectivity, which lifts
them out of loneliness and fear of the world and lostness. When
this happens—and for modern man it is an essential happening—
the life between person and person seems to retreat more and
more before the advance of the collective. The collective aims at
holding in check the inclination to personal life. It is as though
those who are bound together in groups should in the main be
concerned only with the work of the group and should turn to the
personal partners, who are tolerated by the group, only in
secondary meetings.

The difference between the two realms became very palpable
to me on one occasion when I had joined the procession through
a large town of a movement to which I did not belong. I did it
out of sympathy for the tragic development which I sensed was at
hand in the destiny of a friend who was one of the leaders of the
movement. While the procession was forming, I conversed with
him and with another, a goodhearted "wild man," who also had the
mark of death upon him. At that moment I still felt that the two
men really were there, over against me, each of them a man near

to me, near even in what was most remote from me; so different
from me that my soul continually suffered from this difference, yet
by virtue of this very difference confronting me with authentic
being. Then the formations started off, and after a short time I was
lifted out of all confrontation, drawn into the procession, falling in
with its aimless step; and it was obviously the very same for the
two with whom I had just exchanged human words. After a while
we passed a café where I had been sitting the previous day with a
musician whom I knew only slightly. The very moment we passed
it the door opened, the musician stood on the threshold, saw me,
apparently saw me alone, and waved to me. Straightway it seemed
to me as though I were taken out of the procession and of the
presence of my marching friends, and set there, confronting the
musician. I forgot that I was walking along with the same step:
I felt that I was standing over there by the man who had called
out to me, and without a word, with a smile of understanding, was
answering him. When consciousness of the facts returned to me,
the procession, with my companions and myself at its head, had
left the café behind.

The realm of the interhuman goes far beyond that of
sympathy. Such simple happenings can be part of it as, for
instance, when two strangers exchange glances in a crowded
streetcar, at once to sink back again into the convenient state of
wishing to know nothing about each other. But also every casual
encounter between opponents belongs to this realm, when it
affects the opponent's attitude—that is, when something, however
imperceptible, happens between the two, no matter whether it is
marked at the time by any feeling or not. The only thing that
matters is that for each of the two men the other happens as the
particular other, that each becomes aware of the other and is thus
related to him in such a way that he does not regard and use
him as his object, but as his partner in a living event, even if it is
no more than a boxing match. It is well known that some
existentialists assert that the basic factor between men is that
one is an object for the other. But so far as this is actually the
case, the special reality of the interhuman, the fact of the contact,
has been largely eliminated. It cannot indeed be entirely
eliminated. As a crude example, take two men who are observing
one another. The essential thing is not that the one makes the
other his object, but the fact that he is not fully able to do so and
the reason for his failure. We have in common with all existing
beings that we can be made objects of observation. But it is my
privilege as man that by the hidden activity of my being I can
establish an impassable barrier to objectification. Only in
partnership can my being be perceived as an existing whole.

The sociologist may object to any separation of the social and the interhuman on the ground that society is actually built upon human relations, and the theory of these relations is therefore to be regarded as the very foundation of sociology. But here an ambiguity in the concept "relation" becomes evident. We speak, for instance, of a comradely relation between two men in their work, and do not merely mean what happens between them as comrades, but also a lasting disposition which is actualized in those happenings and which even includes purely psychological events such as the recollection of the absent comrade. But by the sphere of the interhuman I mean solely actual happenings between men, whether wholly mutual or tending to grow into mutual relations. For the participation of both partners is in principle indispensable. The sphere of the interhuman is one in which a person is confronted by the other. We call its unfolding the dialogical.

In accordance with this it is basically erroneous to try to understand the interhuman phenomena as psychological. When two men converse together, the psychological is certainly an important part of the situation, as each listens and each prepares to speak. Yet this is only the hidden accompaniment to the conversation itself, the phonetic event fraught with meaning, whose meaning is to be found neither in one of the two partners nor in both together, but only in their dialogue itself, in this "between" which they live together.

BEING AND SEEMING

The essential problem of the sphere of the interhuman is the duality of being and seeming.

Although it is a familiar fact that men are often troubled about the impression they make on others, this has been much more discussed in moral philosophy than in anthropology. Yet this is one of the most important subjects for anthropological study.

We may distinguish between two different types of human existence. The one proceeds from what one really is, the other from what one wishes to seem. In general, the two are found mixed together. There have probably been few men who were entirely independent of the impression they made on others, while there has scarcely existed one who was exclusively determined by the impression made by him. We must be content to distinguish between men in whose essential attitude the one or the other predominates.

This distinction is most powerfully at work, as its nature indicates, in the interhuman realm—that is, in men's personal dealings with one another.

Take as the simplest and yet quite clear example the situation in which two persons look at one another—the first belonging to the first type, the second to the second. The one who lives from his being looks at the other just as one looks at someone with whom he has personal dealings. His look is "spontaneous," "without reserve"; of course he is not uninfluenced by the desire to make himself understood by the other, but he is uninfluenced by any thought of the idea of himself which he can or should awaken in the person whom he is looking at. His opposite is different. Since he is concerned with the image which his appearance, and especially his look or glance, produces in the other, he "makes" this look. With the help of the capacity, in greater or lesser degree peculiar to man, to make a definite element of his being appear in his look, he produces a look which is meant to have, and often enough does have, the effect of a spontaneous utterance—not only the utterance of a physical event supposed to be taking place at that very moment, but also, as it were, the reflection of a personal life of such-and-such a kind.

This must, however, be carefully distinguished from another area of seeming whose ontological legitimacy cannot be doubted. I mean the realm of "genuine seeming," where a lad, for instance, imitates his heroic model and while he is doing so is seized by the actuality of heroism, or a man plays the part of a destiny and conjures up authentic destiny. In this situation there is nothing false; the imitation is genuine imitation and the part played is genuine; the mask, too, is a mask and no deceit. But where the semblance originates from the lie and is permeated by it, the interhuman is threatened in its very existence. It is not that someone utters a lie, falsifies some account. The lie I mean does not take place in relation to particular facts, but in relation to existence itself, and it attacks interhuman existence as such. There are times when a man, to satisfy some stale conceit, forfeits the great chance of a true happening between I and Thou.

Let us now imagine two men, whose life is dominated by appearance, sitting and talking together. Call them Peter and Paul. Let us list the different configurations which are involved. First, there is Peter as he wishes to appear to Paul, and Paul as he wishes to appear to Peter. Then there is Peter as he really appears to Paul, that is, Paul's image of Peter, which in general does not in the least coincide with what Peter wishes Paul to see; and similarly there is the reverse situation. Further, there is Peter as he appears to himself, and Paul as he appears to himself. Lastly, there are the bodily Peter and the bodily Paul. Two living beings and six ghostly appearances, which mingle in many ways in the conversation between the two. Where is there room for any genuine interhuman life?

Whatever the meaning of the word "truth" may be in other realms, in the interhuman realm it means that men communicate themselves to one another as what they are. It does not depend on one saying to the other everything that occurs to him, but only on his letting no seeming creep in between himself and the other. It does not depend on one letting himself go before another, but on his granting to the man to whom he communicates himself a share in his being. This is a question of the authenticity of the interhuman, and where this is not to be found, neither is the human element itself authentic.

Therefore, as we begin to recognize the crisis of man as the crisis of what is between man and man, we must free the concept of uprightness from the thin moralistic tones which cling to it, and let it take its tone from the concept of bodily uprightness. If a presupposition of human life in primeval times is given in man's walking upright, the fulfillment of human life can only come through the soul's walking upright, through the great uprightness which is not tempted by any seeming because it has conquered all semblance.

But, one may ask, what if a man by his nature makes his life subservient to the images which he produces in others? Can he, in such a case, still become a man living from his being, can he escape from his nature?

The widespread tendency to live from the recurrent impression one makes instead of from the steadiness of one's being is not a "nature." It originates, in fact, on the other side of interhuman life itself, in men's dependence upon one another. It is no light thing to be confirmed in one's being by others, and seeming deceptively offers itself as a help in this. To yield to seeming is man's essential cowardice, to resist it in his essential courage. But this is not an inexorable state of affairs which is as it is and must so remain. One can struggle to come to oneself— that is, to come to confidence in being. One struggles, now more successfully, now less, but never in vain, even when one thinks he is defeated. One must at times pay dearly for life lived from the being; but it is never too dear. Yet is there not bad being, do weeds not grow everywhere? I have never known a young person who seemed to me irretrievably bad. Later indeed it becomes more and more difficult to penetrate the increasingly tough layer which has settled down on a man's being. Thus there arises the false perspective of the seemingly fixed "nature" which cannot be overcome. It is false; the foreground is deceitful; man as man can be redeemed.

Again we see Peter and Paul before us surrounded by the ghosts of the semblances. A ghost can be exorcized. Let us imagine that these two find it more and more repellent to be represented by ghosts. In each of them the will is stirred and strengthened to be confirmed in their being as what they really are and nothing else. We see the forces of real life at work as they drive out the ghosts, till the semblance vanishes and the depths of personal life call to one another.

PERSONAL MAKING PRESENT

By far the greater part of what is today called conversation among men would be more properly and precisely described as speechifying. In general, people do not really speak to one another, but each, although turned to the other, really speaks, to a fictitious court of appeal whose life consists of nothing but listening to him. Chekhov has given poetic expression to this state of affairs in *The Cherry Orchard*, where the only use the members of a family make of their being together is to talk past one another. But it is Sartre who has raised to a principle of existence what in Chekhov still appears as the deficiency of a person who is shut up in himself. Sartre regards the falls between the partners in a conversation as simply impassable. For him it is inevitable human destiny that a man has directly to do only with himself and his own affairs. The inner existence of the other is his own concern, not mine; there is no direct relation with the other, nor can there be. This is perhaps the clearest expression of the wretched fatalism of modern man, which regards degeneration as the unchangeable nature of *Homo sapiens* and the misfortune of having run into a blind alley as his primal fate, and which brands every thought of a breakthrough as reactionary romanticism. He who really knows how far our generation has lost the way of true freedom, of free giving between I and Thou, must himself, by virtue of the demand implicit in every great knowledge of his kind, practise directness—even if he were the only man on earth who did it—and not depart from it until scoffers are struck with fear, and hear in his voice the voice of their own suppressed longing.

The chief presupposition for the rise of genuine dialogue is that each should regard his partner as the very one he is. I become aware of him, aware that he is different, essentially different from myself, in the definite, unique way which is peculiar

to him, and I accept whom I thus see, so that in full earnest I can
direct what I say to him as the person he is. Perhaps from time
to time I must offer strict opposition to his view about the subject
of our conversation. But I accept this person, the personal bearer
of a conviction, in his definite being out of which his conviction
has grown—even though I must try to show, bit by bit, the
wrongness of this very conviction, I affirm the person I struggle
with: I struggle with him as his partner, I confirm him as creature
and as creation. I confirm him who is opposed to me as him who
is over against me. It is true that it now depends on the other
whether genuine dialogue, mutuality in speech arises between us.
But if I thus give to the other who confronts me his legitimate
standing as a man with whom I am ready to enter into dialogue,
then I may trust him and suppose him to be also ready to deal
with me as his partner.

But what does it mean to be "aware" of a man in the exact
sense in which I use the word? To be aware of a thing or a
being means, in quite general terms, to experience it as a whole
and yet at the same time without reduction or abstraction, in all
its concreteness. But a man, although he exists as a living being
among living beings and even as a thing among things, is
nevertheless something categorically different from all things and
all beings. A man cannot really be grasped except on the basis
of the gift of the spirit which belongs to man alone among all
things, the spirit as sharing decisively in the personal life of the
living man, that is, the spirit which determines the person. To
be aware of a man, therefore, means in particular to perceive
his wholeness as a person determined by the spirit; it means to
perceive the dynamic centre which stamps his every utterance,
action, and attitude with the recognizable sign of uniqueness.
Such an awareness is impossible, however, if and so long as the
other is the separated object of my contemplation or even
observation, for this wholeness and its centre do not let themselves
be known to contemplation or observation. It is only possible
when I step into an elemental relation with the other, that is,
when he becomes present to me. Hence I designate awareness in
this special sense as "personal making present".

The perception of one's fellow man as a whole, as a unity,
and as unique—even if his wholeness, unity, and uniqueness are
only partly developed, as is usually the case—is opposed in our
time by almost everything that is commonly understood as
specifically modern. In our time there predominates an analytical,
reductive, and deriving look between man and man. This look is
analytical, or rather pseudo analytical, since it treats the whole
being as put together and therefore able to be taken apart—not

only the so-called unconscious which is accessible to relative objectification, but also the psychic stream itself, which can never, in fact, be grasped as an object. This look is a reductive one because it tries to contract the manifold person, who is nourished by the micro cosmic richness of the possible, to some schematically surveyable and recurrent structures. And this look is a deriving one because it supposes it can grasp what a man has become, or even is becoming, in genetic formulae, and it thinks that even the dynamic central principle of the individual in this becoming can be represented by a general concept. An effort is being made today radically to destroy the mystery between man and man. The personal life, the ever near mystery, once the source of the stillest enthusiasms, is levelled down.

What I have just said is not an attack on the analytical method of the human sciences, a method which is indispensable wherever it furthers knowledge of a phenomenon without impairing the essentially different knowledge of its uniqueness that transcends the valid circle of the method. The science of man that makes use of the analytical method must accordingly always keep in view the boundary of such a contemplation, which stretches like a horizon around it. This duty makes the transposition of the method into life dubious; for it is excessively difficult to see where the boundary is in life.

If we want to do today's work and prepare tomorrow's with clear sight, then we must develop in ourselves and in the next generation a gift which lives in man's inwardness as a Cinderella, one day to be a princess. Some call it intuition, but that is not a wholly unambiguous concept. I prefer the name "imagining the real," for in its essential being this gift is not a looking at the other, but a bold swinging—demanding the most intensive stirring of one's being—into the life of the other. This is the nature of all genuine imagining, only that here the realm of my action is not the all-possible, but the particular real person who confronts me, whom I can attempt to make present to myself just in this way, and not otherwise, in his wholeness, unity, and uniqueness, and with his dynamic centre which realizes all these things ever anew.

Let it be said again that all this can only take place in a living partnership, that is, when I stand in a common situation with the other and expose myself vitally to his share in the situation as really his share. It is true that my basic attitude can remain unanswered, and the dialogue can die in seed. But if mutuality stirs, then the interhuman blossoms into genuine dialogue.

IMPOSITION AND UNFOLDING

I have referred to two things which impede the growth of life between man: the invasion of seeming, and the inadequacy of perception. We are now faced with a third, plainer than the others, and in this critical hour more powerful and more dangerous than ever.

There are two basic ways of affecting men in their views and their attitude to life. In the first a man tries to impose himself, his opinion and his attitude, on the other in such a way that the latter feels the psychical result of the action to be his own insight, which has only been freed by the influence. In the second basic way of affecting others, a man wishes to find and to further in the soul of the other the disposition toward what he has recognized in himself as the right. Because it is the right, it must also be alive in the microcosm of the other, as one possibility. The other need only be opened out in this potentiality of his; moreover, this opening out takes place not essentially by teaching, but by meeting, by existential communication between someone that is in actual being and someone that is in a process of becoming. The first way has been most powerfully developed in the realm of propaganda, the second in that of education.

The propagandist I have in mind, who imposes himself, is not in the least concerned with the person whom he desires to influence, as a person; various individual qualities are of importance only in so far as he can exploit them to win the other and must get to know them for this purpose. In his difference to everything personal the propagandist goes a substantial distance beyond the party for which he works. For the party, persons in their difference are of significance because each can be used according to his special qualities in a particular function. It is true that the personal is considered only in respect of the specific use to which it can be put, but within these limits it is recognized in practice. To propaganda as such, on the other hand, individual qualities are rather looked on as a burden, for propaganda is concerned simply with *more*—more members, more adherents, an increasing extent of support. Political methods, where they rule in an extreme form, as here, simply mean winning power over the other by depersonalizing him. This kind of propaganda enters upon different relations with force; it supplements it or replaces it, according to the need or the prospects, but it is in the last analysis nothing but sublimated violence, which has become imperceptible as such. It places

men's souls under a pressure which allows the illusion of
autonomy. Political methods at their height mean the effective
abolition of the human factor.

The educator whom I have in mind lives in a world of
individuals, a certain number of whom are always at any one time
committed to his care. He sees each of these individuals as in a
position to become a unique, single person, and thus the bearer
of a special task of existence which can be fulfilled through him
and through him alone. He sees every personal life as engaged
in such a process of actualization, and he knows from his own
experience that the forces making for actualization are all the time
involved in a microcosmic struggle with counterforces. He has
come to see himself as a helper of the actualizing forces. He
knows these forces; they have shaped and they still shape him.
Now he puts this person shaped by them at their disposal for a
new struggle and a new work. He cannot wish to impose himself,
for he believes in the effect of the actualizing forces, that is, he
believes that in every man what is right is established in a single
and uniquely personal way. No other way may be imposed on a
man, but another way, that of the educator, may and must
unfold what is right, as in this case it struggles for achievement,
and help it to develop.

The propagandist, who imposes himself, does not really
believe even in his own cause, for he does not trust it to attain
its effect of its own power without his special methods, whose
symbols are the loudspeaker and the television advertisement.
The educator who unfolds what is there believes in the primal
power which has scattered itself, and still scatters itself, in all
human beings in order that it may grow up in each man in the
special form of that man. He is confident that this growth needs
at each moment only that help which is given in meeting, and
that he is called to supply that help.

I have illustrated the character of the two basic attitudes and
their relation to one another by means of two extremely
antithetical examples. But wherever men have dealings with one
another, one or the other attitude is to be found in more or less
degree.

These two principles of imposing oneself on someone and
heping someone to unfold should not be confused with concepts
such as arrogance and humility. A man can be arrogant without
wishing to impose himself on others, and it is not enough to be
humble in order to help another unfold. Arrogance and humility
are dispositions of the soul, psychological facts with a moral
accent, while imposition and helping to unfold are events between

men, anthropological facts which point to an ontology, the ontology of the interhuman.

In the moral realm Kant expressed the essential principle that one's fellow man must never be thought of and treated merely as a means, but always at the same time as an independent end. The principle is expressed as on "ought," which is sustained by the idea of human dignity. My point of view, which is near to Kant's in its essential features, has another source and goal. It is concerned with the presuppositions of the interhuman. Man exists anthropologically not in his isolation, but in the completeness of the relation between man and man; what humanity is can be properly grasped only in vital reciprocity. For the proper existence of the interhuman it is necessary, as I have shown, that the semblance not intervene to spoil the relation of personal being to personal being. It is further necessary, as I have also shown, that each one means and makes present the other in his personal being. That neither should wish to impose himself on the other is the third basic presupposition of the interhuman. These presuppositions do not include the demand that one should influence the other in his unfolding; this is, however, an element that is suited to lead to a higher stage of the interhuman.

That there resides in every man the possibility of attaining authentic human existence in the special way peculiar to him can be grasped in the Aristotelian image of entelechy, innate self-realization; but one must note that it is an entelechy of the work of creation. It would be mistaken to speak here of individuation alone. Individuation is only the indispensable personal stamp of all realization of human existence. The self as such is not ultimately the essential, but the meaning of human existence given in creation again and again fulfills itself as self. The help that men give each other in becoming a self leads the life between men to its height. The dynamic glory of the being of man is first bodily present in the relation between two men each of whom in meaning the other also means the highest to which this person is called, and serves the self-realization of this human life as one true to creation without wishing to impose on the other anything of his own realization.

GENUINE DIALOGUE

We must now summarize and clarify the marks of genuine dialogue.

In genuine dialogue the turning to the partner takes place in all truth, that is, it is a turning of the being. Every speaker "means" the partner or partners to whom he turns as this personal

existence. To "mean" someone in this connection is at the same
time to exercise that degree of making present which is possible
to the speaker at that moment. The experiencing senses and the
imagining of the real which completes the findings of the senses
work together to make the other present as a whole and as a unique
being, as the person that he is. But the speaker does not merely
perceive the one who is present to him in this way; he receives
him as his partner, and that means that he confirms this other
being, so far as it is for him to confirm. The true turning of his
person to the other include this confirmation, this acceptance. Of
course, such a confirmation does not mean approval: but no matter
in what I am against the other, by accepting him as my partner
in genuine dialogue I have affirmed him as a person.

Further, if genuine dialogue is to arise, everyone who takes
part in it must bring himself into it. And that also means that he
must be willing on each occasion to say what is really in his mind
about the subject of the conversation. And that means further
that on each occasion he makes the contribution of his spirit
without reduction and without shifting his ground. Even men of
great integrity are under the illusion that they are not bound to
say everything "they have to say." But in the great faithfulness
which is the climate of genuine dialogue, what I have to say at
any one time already has in me the character of something that
wishes to be uttered, and I must not keep it back, keep it in myself.
It bears for me the unmistakable sign which indicates that it
belongs to the common life of the word. Where the dialogical
word genuinely exists, it must be given its right by keeping nothing
back. To keep nothing back is the exact opposite of unreserved
speech. Everything depends on the legitimacy of "what I have to
say." And of course I must also be intent to raise into an inner
word and then into a spoken word what I have to say at this
moment but do not yet possess as speech. To speak is both nature
and work, something that grows and something that is made, and
where it appears dialogically, in the climate of great faithfulness,
it has to fulfill ever anew the unity of the two.

Associated with this is that overcoming of semblance to which
I have referred. In the atmosphere of genuine dialogue, he who is
ruled by the thought of his own effect as the speaker of what he
has to speak, has a destructive effect. If instead of what has to be
said, I try to bring attention to my *I*, I have irrevocably miscarried
what I had to say; it enters the dialogue as a failure, and the
dialogue is a failure. Because genuine dialogue is an ontological
sphere which is constituted by the authenticity of being, every
invasion of semblance must damage it.

But where the dialogue is fulfilled in its being, between partners who have turned to one another in truth, who express themselves without reserve and are free of the desire for semblance, there is brought into being a memorable common fruitfulness which is to be found nowhere else. At such times, at each such time, the word arises in a substantial way between men who have been seized in their depths and opened out by the dynamic of an elemental togetherness. The interhuman opens out what otherwise remains unopened.

This phenomenon is indeed well known in dialogue between two persons; but I have also sometimes experienced it in a dialogue in which several have taken part.

About Easter of 1914 there met a group consisting of representatives of several European nations for a three-day discussion that was intended to be preliminary to further talks.[3] We wanted to discuss together how the catastrophe, which we all believed was imminent, could be avoided. Without our having agreed beforehand on any sort of modalities for our talk, all the presuppositions of genuine dialogue were fulfilled. From the first hour immediacy reigned between all of us, some of whom had just got to know one another; everyone spoke with an unheard-of unreserve, and clearly not a single one of the participants was in bondage to semblance. In respect of its purpose the meeting must be described as a failure (though even now in my heart it is still not a certainty that it had to be a failure); the irony of the situation was that we arranged the final discussion for the middle of August, and in the course of events the group was soon broken up. Nevertheless, in the time that followed, not one of the participants doubted that he shared in a triumph of the interhuman.

One more point must be noted. Of course it is not necessary for all who are joined in a genuine dialogue actually to speak; those who keep silent can on occasion be especially important. But each must be determined not to withdraw when the course of the conversation makes it proper for him to say what he has to say. No one, of course, can know in advance what it is that he has to say; genuine dialogue cannot be arranged beforehand. It has indeed its basic order in itself from the beginning, but nothing can be determined, the course is of the spirit, and some discover what they have to say only when they catch the call of the spirit

But it is also a matter of course that all the participants, without exception, must be of such nature that they are capable of satisfying the presuppositions of genuine dialogue and are ready to do so. The genuineness of the dialogue is called in question as soon as even a small number of those present are felt by themselves and by the others as not being expected to take any active part. Such a state of affairs can lead to very serious problems.

I had a friend whom I account one of the most considerable men of our age. He was a master of conversation, and he loved it: his genuineness as a speaker was evident. But once it happened that he was sitting with two friends and with the three wives, and a conversation arose in which by its nature the women were clearly not joining, although their presence in fact had a great influence. The conversation among the men soon developed into a duel between two of them (I was the third). The other "duelist," also a friend of mine, was of a noble nature; he too was a man of true conversation, but given more to objective fairness than to the play of the intellect, and a stranger to any controversy. The friend whom I have called a master of conversation did not speak with his usual composure and strength, but he scintillated, he fought, he triumphed. The dialogue was destroyed.

Notes

[1] Translated by Ronald Gregor Smith.

[2] "Das Zwischenmenschliche." See my Introduction to Werner Sombart, *Das Proletariat*, vol. 1 in *Die Gesellschaft: Sammlung sozialpsychologischer Monographion*, ed. by Martin Buber (1st ed.; Frankfurt am Main: Rütten & Loening 1906).

[3] I have set down elsewhere an episode from this meeting. See my essay "Dialogue" in *Between Man and Man*, especially pp. 4–6.

Part V
THE
ENVIRONMENT
OF
COMMUNICATION

One fundamental tenet of communication asserts that
communication must be interpreted only in its proper context.
Ordinarily we think of context in physical terms—location,
occasion, seating arrangement, background, atmosphere, mood,
and other aspects of our immediate physical surroundings. Yet we
all know that persons engaged in communication share far more
than common physical context. There is a social context; persons
who live in a given setting also share patterns of behavior, common
ideas and expectations, tastes and values, social conventions, and
comparable ways of looking at reality. What links all of these and
countless other commonalities of experience is nothing less than a
common cultural context. Within each culture is found a web of
subcultures bound by shared habits, work, friendship, resources,
and affiliations.

The essays in this section afford multiple perspectives
on the significance of environment on communication. In

Communication: The Flow of Information" Daniel Katz and
Robert Kahn examine the pervasive impact of institutions on the
structure of communication. All organizations require the use
of many different types of channels and networks. Yet the very
idea of a social system implies ". . . a selectivity of channels and
communicative acts—a mandate to avoid some and utilize others."
Contrary to the prevailing stereotype, the decision to "open all
channels of information" does not itself assure efficiency in
organizational activity: a full and free flow of information solves
some problems and creates others. More important than the sheer
number of available channels is the way given channels are used
within the larger context of what Katz and Kahn term the "coding
activity" of organizations.

Environments differ greatly in the device used to channel and
direct the flow of information. The study of communication until
quite recently has been approached in the manner of a telephone
repairman assigned to correct a faulty telephone line. His goal is to
restore efficiency, to locate and repair the fault, to minimize
distortion and noise. Conceived in such mechanistic terms, a
channel makes communication possible without altering it. Even
more misleading is the tendency to regard the influence of channels
in passive or neutral terms. Marshall McLuhan, probably more than
any other person, has been responsible for advancing a radically
different view of the role of the environment in communicative
experience. In his landmark essay "The Medium Is the Message,"
McLuhan shows why the meaning of message content cannot be
understood apart from the impact of the medium itself. What he
says about the technical media—that they shape and control
what we associate as the content of messages—holds for any
channel, particularly those used in face-to-face encounters.

The mass media complicate the flow of information from
person to person in two major ways. One is by negation. Attention
to one medium often rules out exposure to any other. For example,
the frequency of contact between neighbors has much to do with
the average number of hours spent watching TV. Yet media often
define the flow of information by making many different channels
available at once. To return to the instance of TV viewing and
neighborly conversation, it is quite probable that old acquaintances
will be renewed soon after the word is out that someone bought
the latest in color TV just in time for the Superbowl.

The last three essays examine the influence of culture on the
fabric of interaction between people and institutions. Culture may
be regarded as the most intrusive and general environmental
context for communication. In "Intercultural Communication"

Edward Hall and William Whyte examine the impact of culture on a diverse range of social behaviors: styles and patterns of talk, interpretations of language, semantic considerations, modes of expression, norms of physical contact, variation in scheduling and timing of social contacts, reactions to physical settings, and interpretations of social class and role.

In 'Adumbration as a Feature of Intercultural Communication," Hall analyzes some of the profound consequences of adumbration on what might be termed the metacommunication or subtext of messages. Adumbration consists of any sign or cue which "enables organisms to engage in the mutual exchange and evaluation of covert information or what each can expect from the other . . . [and] foreshadow what organisms will do, perform corrective functions, and help set the direction a given communication will take, as well as the actions resulting from it."

The final essay examines a major controversy over language. When we consider the enormous range of factors that shape what people say and do when in the presence of others, the line of influence becomes less direct and more anonymous as we shift our focus increasingly away from the immediate physical environment. Question: Where does the line of human influence stop? Some claim the ultimate boundary of human awareness extends to the outer limits of one's culture; others insist that culture shapes experience, but not to the extent of denying our participation in certain primitive forms of human expressions that have universal meaning across all cultures. Peter Farb considers the dual claims that culture limits language and that the limits of language "mean the limits of my world." The Sapir-Whorf Hypothesis contends that language provides the basic categories used to make sense out of our experience of the world. Farb traces the evidence and concludes that language creates boundaries but not necessarily a prison. Language makes it easier for us to experience certain meanings, but it does not prevent us from finding other ways of conveying our sense of the way things are.

25

COMMUNICATION: THE FLOW OF INFORMATION

Daniel Katz and Robert L. Kahn

The world we live in is basically a world of people. Most of
our actions toward others and their actions toward us are
communicative acts in whole or in part, whether or not they
reach verbal expression. This is as true of behavior in organizations
as in other contexts. We have said that human organizations are
informational as well as energic systems, and that every
organization must take in and utilize information. The intake
and distribution of information are also energic processes, of course;
acts of sending and receiving information demand energy for their
accomplishment. Their energic demands, however, are negligible
in comparison with their significance and implications as symbolic
acts—as acts of communication and control.

When one walks from a factory to the adjoining head-house or office, the contrast is conspicuous. One goes from noise to quiet, from heavy electrical cables and steam pipes to slim telephone lines, from a machine-dominated to a people-dominated envivronment. One goes, in short, from a sector of the organization in which energic exchange is primary and information exchange secondary, to a sector where the priorities are reversed. The closer one gets to the organizational center of control and decision-making, the more pronounced is the emphasis on information exchange.

In this sense, communication—the exchange of information and the transmission of meaning—is the very essence of a social system or an organization. The input of physical energy is dependent upon information about it, and the input of human energy is made possible through communicative acts. Similarly the transformation of energy (the accomplishment of work) depends upon communication between people in each organizational subsystem and upon communication between subsystems. The product exported carries meaning as it meets needs and wants, and its use is further influenced by the advertising or public relations material about it. The amount of support which an organization receives from its social environment is also affected by the information which elite groups and wider publics have acquired about its goals, activities, and accomplishments.

Communication is thus a social process of the broadest relevance in the functioning of any group, organization, or society. It is possible to subsume under it such forms of social interaction as the exertion of influence, cooperation, social contagion or imitation, and leadership. We shall consider communication in this broad sense, with emphasis upon the structural aspects of the information process in organizations, but with attention also to the motivational basis for transmitting and receiving messages.

It is a common assumption that many of our problems, individual and social, are the result of inadequate and faulty communication. As Newcomb (1947) points out, autistic hostility decreases communication and in turn decreased communication enhances autistic hostility. If we can only increase the flow of information, we are told, we can solve these problems. This assumption is found in our doctrine of universal education. It is fundamental in most campaigns of public relations and public enlightenment. Our democratic institutions, with their concern for freedom of speech and assembly, their rejection of censorship, and their acceptance of the principle of equal time for the arguments of opposing political parties, have extended the notion

of competition in the market place to a free market for ideas. Truth
will prevail if there is ready access to all the relevant information.

The glorification of a full and free information flow is a
healthy step forward in intraorganizational problems as well as in
the relations of an organization to the larger social system. It is,
however, a gross oversimplification. Communication may reveal
problems as well as eliminate them. A conflict in values, for
example, may go unnoticed until communication is attempted.
Communication may also have the effect, intended or unintended,
of obscuring and confusing existing problems. The vogue enjoyed
by the word *image* in recent years reflects in part an unattractive
preoccupation with communication as a means of changing the
perception of things without the expense and inconvenience of
changing the things themselves. The television commercials, with
their incessant and spurious assertion of new products and properties
are the worst of numberless examples. In short, the advocacy of
communication needs to be qualified with respect to the kind of
information relevant to the solution of given problems and with
respect to the nature of the communication process between
individuals, between groups, and between subsystems.

Communication needs to be seen not as a process occurring
between any sender of messages and any potential recipient, but
in relation to the social system in which it occurs and the particular
function it performs in that system. General principles of
communcation as a social-psychological process are fine; they set
the limits within which we must operate. But they need to be
supplemented by an analysis of the social system, so that they can
be applied correctly to given situations.

The discovery of the crucial role of communication led to an
enthusiastic advocacy of increased information as the solution to
many organizational problems. More and better communication
(especially, more) was the slogan. Information to rank-and-file
employees about company goals and policies was the doctrine;
the means too often were stylized programs and house
organs homogenized by the Flesch formula for basic English.
Communication up the line to give top echelons a more accurate
picture of the lower levels was a complementary emphasis.

SOCIAL SYSTEMS AS RESTRICTED COMMUNICATION NETWORKS

Though there were and are good outcomes of this simplistic
approach, there are also weak, negligible, and negative outcomes.
The blanket emphasis upon more communication fails to take into

account the functioning of an organization as a social system and the specific needs of the subsystems.

In the first place, as Thelen (1960b) points out, an organized state of affairs, a social system, implies the restriction of communication among its members. If we take an unorganized group, say 60, people milling around at random in a large room, the number of potential channels of communication is $n(n-1)/2$ or 1770. If, however, they are organized into a network of twelve combinations of five such that each person on a five-man team has one clearly defined role and is interdependent with four other people, the number of channels within the work group is reduced to *ten* in a completely interdependent condition or to *four* in a serial dependent position.

Without going into such complexities as task-relevant communication, the major point is clear. To move from an unorganized state to an organized state requires the introduction of constraints and restrictions to reduce diffuse and random communication to channels appropriate for the accomplishment of organizational objectives. It may require also the introduction of incentives to use those channels and use them appropriately, rather than leave them silent or use them for organizationally irrelevant purposes. Organizational development sometimes demands the creation of new communication channels. The very nature of a social system, however, implies a selectivity of channels and communicative acts—a mandate to avoid some and to utilize others.

In terms of information theory, unrestricted communication produces noise in the system. Without patterning, without pauses, without precision, there is sound but there is no music. Without structure, without spacing, without specifications, there is a Babel of tongues but there is no meaning.

The same basic problem of selectivity in communications can be considered in terms of Ashby's (1952) conceptual model. Thelen (1960a) summarizes the Ashby contribution in these terms.

> *Any living system* is an infinitely complex association of subsystems. The complex suprasystem has all the properties of a subsystem plus communication across the boundaries of subsystems. Ashby's brilliant treatment (1952) shows that stability of the suprasystem would take infinitely long to achieve if there were "full and rich communication" among the subsystems (because in effect all the variables of all the subsystems would have to be satisfied at once—a most unlikely event). If communication among subsystems is restricted or if they are temporarily isolated, then each subsystem achieves its own stability with minimum interference by the changing environment of other systems seeking *their* stability. With restricted communication, success can accumulate (from successive trials, for example),

whereas in the single suprasystem, success is all-or-none. . . . Thus the way an overall system moves toward its equilibrium depends very much on the functional connectedness of its parts. Adapatation of the whole system makes use of two conditions: Enough connectedness that operation of one subsystem can activate another so that the contributions of all can contribute to the whole; and enough separation of subsystems that some specialization of function is possible and such that "equilibrium" can be approached in the system as a whole. But no complex suprasystem would ever have equilibrium in all its subsystems at the same time. Each subsystem has the "power of veto" over equilibria in other subsystems, and under a variety of conditions one subsystem can dominate another.

Our loosely organized political system reflects the system requirements of restriction of full and free communication. Chaos in national decision-making is avoided by the device of the two-party system. Instead of representing in clear fashion in Congress all the factional groups and subsystems within the nation, we go through a quadrennial process of successive agreements within the major parties, culminating in the nomination of a presidential candidate by each of them. This is in effect a restriction and channeling of the communication process. Once candidates are selected, the factional groups within each party tend to unite behind one ticket, and the amount of communication to the candidates is restricted. The rank-and-file voter neither communicates up the line nor receives much in the way of communication down the line except for the projected image of the candidate and the general image of the party.

In fact, the average voter is woefully ignorant of the stand of his party on most political issues. On 16 major issues of the 1956 presidential election, the proportion of people who had an opinion, knew what the government was doing, and saw some difference between the parties never exceeded 36 percent and for some issues was as low as 18 percent (Campbell et al., 1960). This is one price we pay for the organization distance between the voters and political leaders. Nevertheless, the two-party system has the advantage of overall political stability and facilitation of national decision-making. If all interested groups and ideological factions had their own parties and their own representatives in Congress, we would have more complete communication between the people and their elected leaders but we would have terrific problems of attaining system stability. We would have many possibilities of veto by coalition of minority groups, of legislative stalemates, and of national indecision. Some European countries with multiple-party systems, with more communication, and perhaps better-informed electorates have had such problems.

THE CODING PROCESS

Individuals, groups, and organizations share a general characteristic which must be recognized as a major determinant of communication: The coding process. Any system which is the recipient of information, whether it be an individual or an organization, has a characteristic coding process, a limited set of coding categories to which it assimilates the information received. The nature of the system imposes omission, selection, refinement, elaboration, distortion, and transformation upon the incoming communications. Just as the human eye selects and transforms light waves to which it is attuned to give perceptions of color and objects, so too does any system convert stimulation according to its own properties. It has been demonstrated that human beings bring with them into most situations sets of categories for judging the facts before them. Walter Lippmann (1922) called attention to the coding process years ago in the following famous passages. Even then he was merely putting into dramatic form what had been recognized by the ancient philosophers.

> For the most part we do not first see, and then define, we define first and then see. In the great blooming, buzzing confusion of the outer world, we pick out what our culture has already defined for us, and we tend to perceive that which we have picked out in the form stereotyped for us by our culture. (p. 31)
>
> What matters is the character of the stereotypes and the gullibility and which we employ them. And these in the end depend upon those inclusive patterns which constitute our philosophy of life. If in that philosophy we assume that the world is codified according to a code we possess, we are likely to make our reports of what is going on describe a world run by our code. (p. 90)
>
> Most of us would deal with affairs through a rather haphazard and shifting assortment of stereotypes, if a comparatively few men in each generation were not constantly engaged in arranging, standardizing, and improving them into logical systems, known as the Laws of Political Economy, the Principles of Politics, and the like. (pp. 104–105)

Organizations, too, have their own coding systems which determine the amount and type of information they receive from the external world and the transformation of it according to their own systemic properties. The most general limitation is that the position people occupy in organizational space will determine their perception and interpretation of incoming information and their search for additional information. In other words, the structure and functions of a given subsystem will be reflected in the frame of reference and way of thinking of the role incumbents of that sector of organizational space.

All members of an organization are affected by the fact that they occupy a common organizational space in contrast to those who are not members. By passing the boundary and becoming a functional member of the organization, the person takes on some of the coding system of the organization since he accepts some of its norms and values, absorbs some of its subculture, and develops shared expectations and values with other members. The boundary condition is thus responsible for the dilemma that the person within the system cannot perceive things and communicate about them in the same way that an outsider would. If a person is within a system, he sees its operations differently than if he were on the outside looking in. It is extremely difficult to occupy different positions in social space without a resulting differential perception. Where boundary conditions are fluid and organizational members are very loosely confined within the system (as with people sent abroad to live among foreign nationals for some governmental agency) there will be limited tours of duty, alternation between foreign and domestic service, and careful debriefing sessions to insure that life outside the physical boundaries of the country has not imparted too much of the point of view of the outsider.

THE PROBLEM OF TRANSLATION ACROSS SUBSYSTEM BOUNDARIES

Within an organization there are problems of clear communication across subsystems. The messages emanating in one part of the organization need translation if they are to be fully effective in other parts. . . . Earlier . . ., reference was made to Parsons' (1960) specific application of this principle to the chain of command. Instead of a unitary chain from the top to the bottom of an organization, Parsons pointed out that there are significant breaks between the institutional and managerial levels and again between the managerial and technical levels. Communications, then, must be transmitted in general enough terms to permit modification within each of these levels. The same type of translation problem occurs between any pair of substructures having their own functions and their own coding schema. Without adequate translation across subsystem boundaries, communications can add to the noise in the system.

References

Ashby, W. R. *Design for a Brain* (New York: Wiley, 1952).

Campbell, A., Converse, P. E., Miller, W. E., and Stokes, D. E. *The American Voter* (New York: Wiley, 1960).

Lippmann, W. *Public Opinion* (New York: Harcourt Brace Jovanovich, 1922).

Newcomb, T. M. "Autistic Hostility and Social Reality." *Human Relations* 1, (1948):69–86.

Parsons, T. *Structure and Process in Modern Societies* (New York: Free Press, 1960).

Thelen, H. A. "Exploration of a Growth Model for Psychic, Biological, and Social Systems." Mimeographed paper, 1960(a).

Thelen, H. A. Personal communication to authors, 1960(b).

26

THE MEDIUM IS THE MESSAGE

Marshall McLuhan

In a culture like ours, long accustomed to splitting and dividing all things as a means of control, it is sometimes a bit of a shock to be reminded that, in operational and practical fact, the medium is the message. This is merely to say that the personal and social consequences of any medium—that is, of any extension of ourselves—result from the new scale that is introduced into our affairs by each extension of ourselves, or by any new technology. Thus, with automation, for example, the new patterns of human association tend to eliminate jobs, it is true. That is the negative result. Positively, automation creates roles for people, which is to say depth of involvement in their work and human association that our preceding mechanical technology had destroyed. Many people would be disposed to say that it was not the machine, but what one did with the machine, that was its meaning or message. In terms of the ways in which the machine altered our relations to one another and to ourselves, it mattered not in the least whether it turned out cornflakes or Cadillacs. The restructuring of human work and association was shaped by the techniques of fragmentation that is the essence of machine technology. The essence of automation technology is the opposite. It is integral and decentralist in depth, just as the machine was fragmentary, centralist, and superficial in its patterning of human relationships.

The instance of the electric light may prove illuminating in this connection. The electric light is pure information. It is a medium without a message, as it were, unless it is used to spell out some verbal ad or name. This fact, characteristic of all media, means that the "content" of any medium is always another medium. The content of writing is speech, just as the written word is the content of print, and print is the content of the telegraph. If it is asked, "What is the content of speech?" it is necessary to say, "It is an actual process of thought, which is in itself nonverbal." An abstract painting represents direct manifestation of creative thought processes as they might appear in computer designs. What we are considering here, however, are the psychic and social consequences of the designs or patterns as they amplify or accelerate existing processes. For the "message" of any medium or technology is the change of scale or pace or pattern that it introduces into human affairs. The railway did not introduce movement or transportation or wheel or road into human society, but is accelerated and enlarged the scale of previous human functions, creating totally new kinds of cities and new kinds of work and leisure. This happened whether the railway functioned in a tropical or a northern environment, and is quite independent of the freight or content of the railway medium. The airplane, on the other hand, by accelerating the rate of transportation, tends to dissolve the railway form of city, politics, and association, quite independently of what the airplane is used for.

Let us return to the electric light. Whether the light is being used for brain surgery or night baseball is a matter of indifference. It could be argued that these activities are in some way the "content" of the electric light, since they could not exist without the electric light. This fact merely underlines the point that "the medium is the message" because it is the medium that shapes and controls the scale and form of human association and action.

The content or uses of such media are as diverse as they are ineffectual in shaping the form of human association. Indeed, it is only too typical that the "content" of any medium blinds us to the character of the medium. It is only today that industries have become aware of the various kinds of business in which they are engaged. When IBM discovered that it was not in the business of making office equipment or business machines, but that it was in the business of processing information, then it began to navigate with clear vision. The General Electric Company makes a considerable portion of its profits from electric light bulbs and lighting systems. It has not yet discovered that, quite as much as A.T.&T., it is in the business of moving information.

The electric light escapes attention as a communication medium just because it has no "content." And this makes it an invaluable instance of how people fail to study media at all. For it is not till the electric light is used to spell out some brand name that it is noticed as a medium. Then it is not the light but the "content" (or what is really another medium) that is noticed. The message of the electric light is like the message of electric power in industry, totally radical, pervasive, and decentralized. For electric light and power are separate from their uses, yet they eliminate time and space factors in human association exactly as do radio, telegraph, telephone, and TV, creating involvement in depth.

A fairly complete handbook for studying the extensions of man could be made up from selections from Shakespeare. Some might quibble about whether or not he was referring to TV in these familiar lines from *Romeo and Juliet:*

> But soft! what light through yonder window breaks?
> It speaks, and yet says nothing.

In *Othello,* which, as much as *King Lear,* is concerned with the torment of people transformed by illusions, there are these lines that bespeak Shakespeare's intuition of the transforming powers of new media:

> Is there not charms
> By which the property of youth and maidhood
> May be abus'd? Have you not read Roderigo,
> Of some such thing?

In Shakespeare's *Troilus and Cressida,* which is almost completely devoted to both a psychic and social study of communication, Shakespeare states his awareness that true social and political navigation depend upon anticipating the consequences of innovation:

> The providence that's in a watchful state
> Knows almost every grain of Plutus' gold,
> Finds bottom in the uncomprehensive deeps,
> Keeps place with thought, and almost like the gods
> Does thoughts unveil in their dumb cradles.

The increasing awareness of the action of media, quite independently of their "content" or programming, was indicated in the annoyed and anonymous stanza:

> In Modern thought, (if not in fact)
> Nothing is that doesn't act,
> So that is reckoned wisdom which
> Describes the scratch but not the itch.

The same kind of total, configurational awareness that reveals why the medium is socially the message has occurred in the most recent and radical medical theories. In his *Stress of Life*, Hans Selye tells of the dismay of a research colleague on hearing of Selye's theory:

> When he saw me thus launched on yet another enraptured description of what I had observed in animals treated with this or that impure, toxic material, he looked at me with desperately sad eyes and said in obvious despair: "But Selye, try to realize what you are doing before it is too late! You have now decided to spend your entire life studying the pharmacology of dirt!"
>
> (Hans Selye, *The Stress of Life*)

As Selye deals with the total environmental situation in his "stress" theory of disease, so the latest approach to media study considers not only the "content" but the medium and the cultural matrix within which the particular medium operates. The older unawareness of the psychic and social effects of media can be illustrated from almost any of the conventional pronouncements.

In accepting an honorary degree from the University of Notre Dame a few years ago, General David Sarnoff made this statement: "We are too prone to make technological instruments the scapegoats for the sins of those who wield them. The products of modern science are not in themselves good or bad; it is the way they are used that determines their value." That is the voice of the current somnambulism. Suppose we were to say, "Apple pie is in itself neither good nor bad; it is the way it is used that determines its value." Or, "The smallpox virus is in itself neither

good nor bad; it is the way it is used that determines its value."
Again, "Firearms are in themselves neither good nor bad; it is
the way they are used that determines their value." That is, if
the slugs reach the right people firearms are good. If the TV
tube fires the right ammunition at the right people it is good. I
am not being perverse. There is simply nothing in the Sarnoff
statement that will bear scrutiny, for it ignores the nature of the
medium, of any and all media, in the true Narcissus style of
one hypnotized by the amputation and extension of his own being
in a new technical form. General Sarnoff went on to explain his
attitude to the technology of print, saying that it was true that
print caused much trash to circulate, but it had also disseminated
the Bible and the thoughts of seers and philosophers. It has
never occurred to General Sarnoff that any technology could do
anything but *add* itself on to what we already are.

Such economists as Robert Theobald, W. W. Restow, and
John Kenneth Galbraith have been explaining for years how
it is that "classical economics" cannot explain change or growth.
And the paradox of mechanization is that although it is itself
the cause of maximal growth and change, the principle of
mechanization excludes the very possibility of growth or the
understanding of change. For mechanization is achieved by
fragmentation of any process and by putting the fragmented parts
in a series. Yet, as David Hume showed in the eighteenth
century, there is no principle of causality in a mere sequence.
That one thing follows another accounts for nothing. Nothing
follows from following, except change. So the greatest of all
reversals occurred with electricity, that ended sequence by making
things instant. With instant speed the causes of things began to
emerge to awareness again, as they had not done with things in
sequence and in concatenation accordingly. Instead of asking
which came first, the chicken or the egg, it suddenly seemed
that a chicken was an egg's idea for getting more eggs.

Just before an airplane breaks the sound barrier, sound
waves become visible on the wings of the plane. The sudden
visibility of sound just as sound ends is an apt instance of that
great pattern of being that reveals new and opposite forms just as
the earlier forms reach their peak performance. Mechanization
was never so vividly fragmented or sequential as in the birth of
the movies, the moment that translated us beyond mechanism
into the world of growth and organic interrelation. The movie, by
sheer speeding up the mechanical, carried us from the world of
sequence and connections into the world of creative configuration
and structure. The message of the movie medium is that of

transition from lineal connection to configurations. It is the transition that produced the now quite correct observation: "If it works, it's obsolete." When electric speed further takes over from mechanical movie sequences, then the lines of force in structures and in media become loud and clear. We return to the inclusive form of the icon.

To a highly literate and mechanized culture the movie appeared as a world of triumphant illusions and dreams that money could buy. It was at this moment of the movie that cubism occurred, and it has been described by E. H. Gombrich (*Art and Illusion*) as "the most radical attempt to stamp out ambiguity and to enforce one reading of the picture—that of a man-made construction, a colored canvas." For cubism substitutes all facets of an object simultaneously for the "point of view" or facet of perspective illusion. Instead of the specialized illusion of the third dimension on canvas, cubism sets up an interplay of planes and contradiction or dramatic conflict of patterns, lights, textures that "drives home the message" by involvement. This is held by many to be an exercise in painting, not in illusion.

In other words, cubism, by giving the inside and outside, the top, bottom, back, and front and the rest, in two dimensions drops the illusion of perspective in favor of instant sensory awareness of the whole. Cubism, by seizing on instant total awareness, suddenly announced that *the medium is the message*. Is it not evident that the moment that sequence yields to the simultaneous, one is in the world of the structure and of configuraion? Is that not what has happened in physics as in painting, poetry, and in communication? Specialized segments of attention have shifted to total field, and we can now say, "The medium is the message" quite naturally. Before the electric speed and total field, it was not obvious that the medium is the message. The message, it seemed, was the "content," as people used to ask what a painting was *about*. Yet they never thought to ask what a melody was about, nor what a house or a dress was about. In such matters, people retained some sense of the whole pattern, of form and function as a unity. But in the electric age this integral idea of structure and configuration has become so prevalent that educational theory has taken up the matter. Instead of working with specialized "problems" in arithmetic, the structural approach now follows the lines of force in the field of number and has small children meditating about number theory and "sets."

Cardinal Newman said of Napoleon, "He understood the grammar of gunpower." Napoleon had paid some attention to other media as well, especially the semaphore telegraph that

gave him a great advantage over his enemies. He is on record
for saying that "Three hostile newspapers are more to be feared
than a thousand bayonets."

Alexis de Tocqueville was the first to master the grammar of
print and typography. He was thus able to read off the message of
coming change in France and America as if he were reading aloud
from a text that had been handed to him. In fact, the nineteenth
century in France and in America was such an open book to de
Tocqueville because he had learned the grammar of print. So he,
also, knew when that grammar did not apply. He was asked
why he did not write a book on England, since he knew and
admired England. He replied:

> One would have to have an unusual degree of philosophical folly to
> believe oneself able to judge England in six months. A year always
> seemed to me too short a time in which to appreciate the United
> States properly, and it is much easier to acquire clear and precise
> notions about the American Union than about Great Britain. In
> America all laws derive in a sense from the same line of thought.
> The whole of society, so to speak, is founded upon a single fact,
> everything springs from a simple principle. One could compare
> America to a forest pierced by a multitude of straight roads all
> converging on the same point. One has only to find the center and
> everything is revealed at a glance. But in England the paths run
> criss-cross, and it is only by travelling down each one of them that
> one can build up a picture of the whole.

De Tocqueville, in earlier work on the French Revolution, had
explained how it was the printed word that, achieving cultural
saturation in the eighteenth century, had homogenized the French
nation. Frenchmen were the same kind of people from north to
south. The typographic principles of uniformity; continuity, and
lineality had overlaid the complexities of ancient feudal and oral
society. The Revolution was carried out by the new literati and
lawyers.

In England, however, such was the power of the ancient oral
traditions of common law, backed by the medieval institution of
Parliament, that no uniformity or continuity of the new visual print
culture could take complete hold. The result was that the most
important event in English history has never taken place; namely,
the English Revolution on the lines of the French Revolution.
The American Revolution had no medieval legal institutions to
discard or to root out, apart from monarchy. And many have held
that the American Presidency has become very much more personal
and monarchical than any European monarch ever could be.

De Tocqueville's contrast between England and America is clearly based on the fact of typography and of print culture creating uniformity and continuity. England, he says, has rejected this principle and clung to the dynamic or oral common-law tradition. Hence the discontinuity and unpredictable quality of English culture. The grammer of print cannot help to construe the message of oral and nonwritten culture and institutions. The English aristocracy was properly classified as barbarian by Matthew Arnold because its power and status had nothing to do with literacy or with the cultural forms of typography. Said the Duke of Gloucester to Edward Gibbon upon the publication of his *Decline and Fall:* "Another damned fat book, eh, Mr. Gibbons? Scribble, scribble, scribble, eh, Mr. Gibbon?" De Tocqueville was a highly literate aristocrat who was quite able to be detached from the values and assumptions of typography. That is why he alone understood the grammar of typography. And it is only on those terms, standing aside from any structure or medium, that its principles and lines of force can be discerned. For any medium has the power of imposing its own assumption on the unwary. Prediction and control consist in avoiding this subliminal state of Narcissus trance. But the greatest aid to this end is simply in knowing that the spell can occur immediately upon contact, as in the first bars of a melody.

A Passage to India by E. M. Forster is a dramatic study of the inability of oral and intuitive oriental culture to meet with the rational, visual European patterns of experience. "Rational," of course, has for the West long meant "uniform and continuous and sequential." In other words, we have confused reason with literacy, and rationalism with a single technology. Thus in the electric age man seems to the conventional West to become irrational. In Forster's novel the moment of truth and dislocation from the typographic trance of the West comes in the Marabar Caves. Adela Quested's reasoning powers cannot cope with the total inclusive field of resonance that is India. After the Caves: "Life went on as usual, but had no consequences, that is to say, sounds did not echo nor thought develop. Everything seemed cut off at its root and therefore infected with illusion."

A Passage to India (the phrase is from Whitman, who saw America headed Eastward) is a parable of Western man in the electric age, and is only incidentally related to Europe or the Orient. The ultimate conflict between sight and sound, between written and oral kinds of perception and organization of existence is upon us. Since understanding stops action, as Nietzsche observed, we can moderate the fierceness of this conflict by understanding the media that extend us and raise these wars within and without us.

Detribalization by literacy and its traumatic effects on tribal man is the theme of a book by the psychiatrist J. C. Carothers, *The African Mind in Health and Disease* (World Health Organization, Geneva, 1953). Much of his material appeared in an article in *Psychiatry* magazine, November 1959: "The Culture, Psychiatry, and the Written Word." Again, it is electric speed that has revealed the lines of force operating from Western technology in the remotest areas of bush, savannah, and desert. One example is the Bedouin with his battery raido on board the camel. Submerging natives with floods of concepts for which nothing has prepared them is the normal action of all of our technology. But with electric media Western man himself experiences exactly the same inundation as the remote native. We are no more prepared to encounter radio and TV in our literate milieu than the native of Ghana is able to cope with the literacy that takes him out of his collective tribal world and beaches him in individual isolation. We are as numb in our new electric world as the native involved in our literate and mechanical culture.

Electric speed mingles the cultures of prehistory with the dregs of industrial marketeers, the nonliterate with the semiliterate and the postliterate. Mental breakdown of varying degrees is the very common result of uprooting and inundation with new information and endless new patterns of information. Wyndham Lewis made this a theme of his group of novels called *The Human Age*. The first of these, *The Childermass*, is concerned precisely with accelerated media change as a kind of massacre of the innocents. In our own world as we become more aware of the effects of technology on psychic formation and manifestation, we are losing all confidence in our right to assign guilt. Ancient prehistoric societies regard violent crime as pathetic. The killer is regarded as we do a cancer victim. "How terrible it must be to feel like that," they say. J. M. Synge took up this idea very effectively in his *Playboy of the Western World*.

If the criminal appears as a noncomformist who is unable to meet the demand of technology that we behave in uniform and continuous patterns, literate man is quite inclined to see others who cannot conform as somewhat pathetic. Especially the child, the cripple, the woman, and the colored person appear in a world of visual and typographic technology as victims of injustice. On the other hand, in a culture that assigns roles instead of jobs to people—the dwarf, the skew, the child create their own spaces.

They are not expected to fit into some uniform and repeatable niche that is not their size anyway. Consider the phrase "It's a man's world." As a quantitative observation endlessly repeated from within a homogenized culture, this phrase refers to the men in such a culture who have to be homogenized Dagwoods in order to belong at all. It is in our I.Q. testing that we have produced the greatest flood of misbegotten standards. Unaware of our typographical cultural bias, our testers assume that uniform and continuous habits are a sign of intelligence, thus eliminating the ear man and the tactile man.

C. P. Snow, reviewing a book of A. L. Rowse (*The New York Times Book Review*, December 24, 1961, on *Appeasement* and the road to Munich, decribes the top level of British brains and experience in the 1930s. "Their I.Q.'s were much higher than usual among political bosses. Why were they such a disaster?" The view of Rowse, Snow approves: "They would not listen to warnings because they did not wish to hear." Being anti-Red made it impossible for them to read the message of Hitler. But their failure was as nothing compared to our present one. The American stake in literacy as a technology or uniformity applied to every level of education, government, industry, and social life is totally threatened by the electric technology. The threat of Stalin or Hitler was external. The electric technology is within the gates, and we are numb, deaf, blind, and mute about its encounter with the Gutenberg technology, on and through which the American way of life was formed. It is, however, not time to suggest strategies when the threat has not even been acknowledged to exist. I am in the position of Louis Pasteur telling doctors that their greatest enemy was quite invisible, and quite unrecognized by them. Our conventional response to all media, namely that it is how they are used that counts, is the numb stance of the technological idiot. For the "content" of a medium is like the juicy piece of meat carried by the burglar to distract the watchdog of the mind. The effect of the medium is made strong and intense just because it is given another medium as "content." The content of a movie is a novel or a play or an opera. The effect of the movie form is not related to its program content. The "content" of writing or print is speech, but the reader is almost entirely unaware either of print or of speech.

Arnold Tonybee is innocent of any understanding of media as they have shaped history, but he is full of examples that the student of media can use. At one moment he can seriously suggest that adult education, such as the Workers Educational Assoication in Britain, is a useful counterforce to the popular press. Tonybee

considers that although all of the oriental societies have in
our time accepted the industrial technology and its political
consequences: "On the cultural plane, however, there is no
uniform corresponding tendency." (Somervell, I, 267) This is like
the voice of the literate man, floundering in a milieu of ads, who
boasts, "Personally, I pay no attention to ads." The spiritual and
cultural reservations that the oriental peoples may have toward our
technology will avail them not at all. The effects of technology
do not occur at the level of opinions or concepts, but alter sense
ratios or patterns of perception steadily and without any resistance.
The serious artist is the only person able to encounter technology
with impunity, just because he is an expert aware of the changes
in sense perception.

The operation of the money medium in seventeenth-century
Japan had effects not unlike the operation of typography in the
West. The penetration of the money economy, wrote G. B. Sansom
(in *Japan*, Cresset Press, London, 1931) "caused a slow but
irresistible revolution, culminating in the break-down of feudal
government and the resumption of intercourse with foreign
countries after more than two hundred years of seclusion." Money
has reorganized the sense life of peoples just because it is an
extension of our sense lives. This change does not depend upon
approval or disapproval of those living in the society.

Arnold Tonybee made one approach to the transforming
power of media in his concept of "etherialization," which he holds
to be the principle of progressive simplification and efficienecy in
any organization or technology. Typically, he is ignoring the *effect*
of the challenge of these forms upon the response of our senses.
He imagines that it is the response of our opinions that is relevant
to the effect of media and technology in society, a "point of view"
that is plainly the result of the typographic spell. For the man
in a literate and homogenized society ceases to be sensitive to the
diverse and discontinuous life of forms. He acquires the illusion of
third dimension and the "private point of view" as part of his
Narcissus fixation, and is quite shut off from Blake's awareness or
that of the Psalmist, that we become what we behold.

Today when we want to get our bearings in our own culture,
and have need to stand aside from the bias and pressure exerted by
any technical form of human expression, we have only to visit a
society where that particular form has not been felt, or a historical
period in which it was unknown. Professor Wilbur Schramm made
such a tactical move in studying *Television in the Lives of Our
Children*. He found areas where TV had not penetrated at all and
ran some tests. Since he had made no study of the peculiar nature

of the TV image, his tests were of "content" preferences, viewing time, and vocabulary counts. In a word, his approach to the problem was a literary one, albeit unconsciously so. Consequently, he had nothing to report. Had his methods been employed in 1500 A.D. to discover the effects of the printed book in the lives of children or adults, he could have found out nothing of the changes in human and social psychology resulting from typography. Print created individualism and nationalism in the sixteenth century. Program and "content" analysis offer no clues to the magic of these media or to their subliminal charge.

Leonard Doob, in his report *Communication in Africa,* tells of one African who took great pains to listen each evening to the BBC news, even though he could understand nothing of it. Just to be in the presence of those sounds at 7 P.M. each day was important for him. His attitude to speech was like ours to melody—the resonant intonation was meaning enough. In the seventeenth century our ancestors still shared this native's attitude to the forms of media, as is plain in the following sentiment of the Frenchman Bernard Lam expressed in *The Art of Speaking* (London, 1969):

> 'Tis an effect of the Wisdom of God, who created Man to be happy, that whatever is useful to his conversation (way of life) is agreeable to him . . . because all victual that conduces to nourishment is relishable, whereas other things that cannot be assimilated and be turned into our substance are insipid. A Discourse cannot be pleasant to the Hearer that is not easie to the Speaker; nor can it be easily pronounced unless it be heard with delight.

Here is an equilibrium theory of human diet and expression such as even now we are only striving to work out again for media after centuries of fragmentation and specialism.

Pope Pius XII was deeply concerned that there be serious study of the media today. On February 17, 1950, he said:

> It is not an exaggeration to say that the future of modern society and the stability of its inner life depend in large part on the maintenance of an equilibrium between the strength of the techniques of communication and the capacity of the individual's own reaction.

Failure in this respect has for centuries been typical and total for mankind. Subliminal and docile acceptance of media impact has made them prisons without walls for their human users. As A. J. Liebling remarked in his book *The Press,* a man is not free if he cannot see where he is going, even if he has a gun to help him get there. For each of the media is also a powerful weapon with which to clobber other media and other groups. The result is that the present age has been one of multiple civil wars that are not limited to the world of art and entertainment. In *War and Human Progress*, Professor J. U. Nef declared: "The total wars of our time have been the result of a series of intellectual mistakes. . . ."

If the formative power in the media are the media themselves, that raises a host of large matters that can only be mentioned here, although they deserve volumes. Namely, that technological media are staples or natural resources, exactly as are coal and cotton and oil. Anybody will concede that society whose economy is dependent upon one or two major staples like cotton, or grain, or lumber, or fish, or cattle is going to have some obvious social patterns of organization as a result. Stress on a few major staples creates extreme instability in the economy but great endurance in the population. The pathos and humor of the American South are embedded in such an economy of limited staples. For a society configured by reliance on a few commodities accepts them as a social bond quite as much as the metropolis does the press. Cotton and oil, like radio and TV, become "fixed charges" on the entire psychic life of the community. And this pervasive fact creates the unique cultural flavor of any society. It pays through the nose and all its other senses for each staple that shapes its life.

That our human senses, of which all media are extensions, are also fixed charges on our personal energies, and that they also configure the awareness and experience of each one of us, may be perceived in another connection mentioned by the psychologist C. G. Jung:

> Every Roman was surrounded by slaves. The slave and his psychology flooded ancient Italy, and every Roman became inwardly, and of course unwittingly, a slave. Because living constantly in the atmosphere of slaves, he became infected through the unconscious with their psychology. No one can shield himself from such an influence (*Contributions to Analytical Psychology*, London, 1928).

27

INTERCULTURAL COMMUNICATION

Edward T. Hall and William Foote Whyte

How can anthropological knowledge help the man of action in dealing with people of another culture? We shall seek to answer that question by examining the process of intercultural communication.

Anthropologists have long claimed that a knowledge of culture is valuable to the administrator. More and more people in business and government are willing to take this claim seriously, but they ask that we put culture to them in terms they can understand and act upon.

When the layman thinks of culture, he is likely to think in terms of (1) the way people dress, (2) the beliefs they hold, and (3) the customs they practice—with an accent upon the esoteric. Without undertaking any comprehensive definition, we can

Reproduced by the permission of the Society for Applied Anthropology from *Human Organization* 19 (1):5–12. 1960. Footnotes are omitted.

concede that all three are aspects of culture, and yet point out that they do not get us very far, either theoretically or practically.

Dress is misleading, if we assume that differences in dress indicate differences in belief and behavior. If that were the case, then we should expect to find people dressed like ourselves to be thinking and acting like ourselves. While there are still peoples wearing "colorful" apparel quite different from ours, we find in many industrializing societies that the people with whom we deal dress much as we do—and yet think and act quite differently.

Knowledge of beliefs may leave us up in the air because the connections between beliefs and behavior are seldom obvious. In the case of religious beliefs, we may know, for example, that the Mohammedan must pray to Allah a certain number of times a day and that therefore the working day must provide for praying time. This is important, to be sure, but the point is so obvious that it is unlikely to be overlooked by anyone. The administrator must also grasp the less dramatic aspects of everyday behavior, and here a knowledge of beliefs is a very imperfect guide.

Customs provide more guidance, providing we do not limit ourselves to the esoteric and also search for the pattern of behavior into which a given custom fits. The anthropologist, in dealing with customary behavior, is not content with identifying individual items. To him, these items are not miscellaneous. They have meaning only as they are fitted together into a pattern.

But even assuming that the pattern can be communicated to the administrator, there is still something important lacking. The pattern shows how the people act—when among themselves. The administrator is not directly concerned with that situation. Whatever background information he has, he needs to interpret to himself how the people act *in relation to himself*. He is dealing with a cross-cultural situation. The link between the two cultures is provided by acts of communication between the administrator, representing one culture, and people representing another. If communication is effective, then understanding grows with collaborative action. If communication is faulty, then no book knowledge of culture can assure effective action.

This is not to devalue the knowledge of culture that can be provided by the anthropologist. It is only to suggest that the point of implementation of the knowledge must be in the communication process. Let us therefore examine the process of intercultural communication. By so doing we can accomplish two things: (a) Broaden knowledge of ourselves by revealing some of our own unconscious communicative acts: (b) clear away heretofore almost insurmountable obstacles to understanding in the cross-cultural process. We also learn that communication, as it is used here, goes far beyond words and includes many other acts upon which judgments are based of what is transpiring and from which we draw conclusions as to what has occurred in the past.

Culture affects communication in various ways. It determines the time and timing of interpersonal events, the places where it is appropriate to discuss particular topics, the physical distance separating one speaker from another, the tone of voice that is appropriate to the subject matter. Culture, in this sense, delineates the amount and type of physical contact, if any, which convention permits or demands, and the intensity of emotion which goes with it. Culture includes the relationship of *what is said to what is meant*—as when "no" means "maybe" and "tomorrow" means "never." Culture, too, determines whether a given matter—say, a business contract—should be initially discussed between two persons or hacked out in a day-long conference which includes four or five senior officials from each side, with perhaps an assist from the little man who brings in the coffee.

These are important matters which the businessman who hopes to trade abroad ignores at his peril. They are also elusive, for every man takes his own culture for granted. Even a well-informed national of another country is hard put to explain why, in his own land, the custom is thus-and-so rather than so-and-thus; as hard put, indeed, as you would probably be if asked what is the "rule" which governs the precise time in a relationship that you begin using another man's first name. One "just knows." In other words, you do not know and cannot explain satisfactorily because you learn this sort of thing unconsciously in your upbringing, in your culture, and you take such knowledge for granted. Yet the impact of culture on communication can be observed and the lessons taught.

Since the most obvious form of communication is by language, we will first consider words, meanings, voice tones, emotions, and physical contact; then take up, in turn, the cultural impact of time, place, and social class relations on business situations in various lands. Finally, we will suggest what the individual administrator may do to increase his effectiveness abroad, and what students of culture may do to advance this application of anthropology.

BEYOND LANGUAGE

Americans are often accused of not being very good at language, or at least not very much interested in learning foreign languages.

There is little evidence that any people are inherently "better" at languages than any other, given the opportunity and incentive to learn. The West and Central European who has since childhood been in daily contact with two or three languages learns to speak them all, and frequently to read and write them as well. Under similar conditions, American children do the same. Indeed, a not uncommon sight on the backroads of Western Europe is a mute, red-faced American military family lost on a Sunday drive while the youngest child, barely able to lisp his own English, leans from the window to interpret the directions of some gnarled farmer whose dialect is largely unintelligible to most of his own countrymen.

We should not underestimate the damage our lack of language facility as a nation has done to our relations all over the world. Obviously, if you cannot speak a man's language, you are terribly handicapped in communicating with him.

But languages can be learned and yet most, if not all, of the disabling errors described in this article could still be made. Vocabulary, grammar, even verbal facility are not enough. Unless a man understands the subtle cues that are implicit in language, tone, gestures, and expression, he will not only consistently misinterpret what is said to him, but he may offend irretrievably without knowing how or why.

DO THEY MEAN WHAT THEY SAY?

Can't you believe what a man says? We all recognize that the basic honesty of the speaker is involved. What we often fail to recognize, however, is that the question involves cultural influences that have nothing to do with the honesty or dependability of the individual.

In the United States we put a premium on direct expression. The "good" American is supposed to say what he means and to mean what he says. If, on important matters, we discover that someone spoke deviously or evasively, we would be inclined to regard him thereafter as unreliable if not out-and-out dishonest.

In some other cultures, the words and their meanings do not have such a direct connection. People may be more concerned with the emotional context of the situation than with the meaning of particular words. This leads them to give an agreeable and pleasant answer to a question when a literal, factual answer might be unpleasant or embarrassing.

This situation is not unknown in our culture, of course. How many times have you muttered your delighted appreciation for a boring evening? We term this simple politeness and understand each other perfectly.

On the other hand, analogous "polite" behavior on a matter of factory production would be incomprehensible. An American businessman would be most unlikely to question another businessman's word if he were technically qualified and said that his plant could produce 1,000 gross of widgets a month. We are "taught" that it is none of our business to inquire too deeply into the details of his production system. This would be prying and might be considered an attempt to steal his operational plans.

Yet this cultural pattern has trapped many an American into believing that when a Japanese manufacturer answered a direct question with the reply that he could produce 1,000 gross of widgets, he meant what he said. If the American had been escorted through the factory and saw quite clearly that its capacity was, at the most, perhaps 500 gross of widgets per month, he would be likely to say to himself:

> Well, this fellow probably has a brother-in-law who has a factory who can make up the difference. He isn't telling the whole story because he's afraid I might try to make a better deal with the brother-in-law. Besides, what business is it of mine, so long as he meets the schedule?

The cables begin to burn after the American returns home and only 500 gross of widgets arrive each month.

What the American did not know was that in Japanese culture one avoids the direct questions unless the questioner is absolutely certain that the answer will not embarrass the Japanese businessman in any way whatsoever. In Japan for one to admit being unable to perform a given operation or measure up to a given standard means a bitter loss of face. Given a foreigner who is so stupid, ignorant, or insensitive as to ask an embarrassing question, the Japanese is likely to choose what appears to him the lesser of two evils.

Americans caught in this cross-cultural communications trap are apt to feel doubly deceived because the Japanese manufacturer may well be an established and respected member of the business community.

EXCITABLE PEOPLE?

Man communicates not by words alone. His tone of voice, his facial expressions, his gestures all contribute to the infinitely varied calculus of meaning. But the confusion of tongues is more than matched by the confusion of gesture and other culture cues. One man's nod is another man's negative. Each culture has its own rich array of meaningful signs, symbols, gestures, emotional connotations, historical references, traditional responses and—equally significant—pointed silences. These have been built up over the millennia as (who can say?) snarls, growls, and love murmurs gathered meaning and dignity with long use, to end up perhaps as the worn coinage of trite expression.

Consider the Anglo-Saxon tradition of preserving one's calm. The American is taught by his culture to suppress his feelings. He is conditioned to regard emotion as generally bad (except in weak women who can't help themselves) and a stern self-control as good. The more important a matter, the more solemn and outwardly dispassionate he is likely to be. A cool head, granite visage, dispassionate logic—it is no accident that the Western story hero consistently displays these characteristics.

In the Middle East it is otherwise. From childhood, the Arab is permitted, even encouraged, to express his feelings without inhibition. Grown men can weep, shout, gesture expressively and violently, jump up and down—and be admired as sincere.

The modulated, controlled Anglo-Saxon is likely to be regarded with suspicion—he must be hiding something, practicing to deceive.

The exuberant and emotional Arab is likely to disturb the Anglo-Saxon, cause him to writhe inwardly with embarrassment—for isn't this childish behavior? And aren't things getting rather out of hand?

Then, again, there is the matter of how loudly one should talk.

In the Arab world, in discussions among equals, the men attain a decibel level that would be considered aggressive, objectionable, and obnoxious in the United States. Loudness connotes strength and sincerity among Arabs; a soft tone implies weakness, deviousness. This is so "right" in the Arab culture that several Arabs have told us they discounted anything heard over the "Voice of America" because the signal was so weak!

Personal status modulates voice tone, however, even in Arab society. The Saudi Arab shows respect to his superior—to a shiek, say—by lowering his voice and mumbling. The affluent American may also be addressed in this fashion, making almost impossible an already difficult situation. Since in the American culture one unconsciously "asks" another to raise his voice by raising one's own, the American speaks louder. This lowers the Arab's tone more and increases the mumble. This triggers a shouting response in the American—which cues the Arab into a frightened "I'm not being respectful enough" tone well below audibility.

They are not likely to part with much respect for each other.

TO TOUCH OR NOT TO TOUCH?

How much physical contact should appropriately accompany social or business conversation?

In the United States we discourage physical contact, particularly between adult males. The most common physical contact is the handshake and, compared to Europeans, we use it sparingly.

The handshake is the most detached and impersonal form of greeting or farewell in Latin America. Somewhat more friendly is the left hand placed on another man's shoulder during a handshake. Definitely more intimate and warm is the "*doble abrazo*" in which two men embrace by placing their arms around each other's shoulders.

These are not difficult conventions to live with, particularly since the North American can easily permit the Latin American to take the initiative in any form of contact more intimate than the handshake. Far more difficult for the North American to learn to live with comfortably are the less stylized forms of physical contact such as the hand on one's arm during conversation. To the North American this is edging toward what in his culture is an uncomfortable something—possibly sexual—which inhibits his own communication.

Yet there are cultures which restrict physical contact for more than we do. An American at a cocktail party in Java tripped over the invisible cultural ropes which mark the boundaries of acceptable behavior. He was seeking to develop a business relationship with a prominent Javanese and seemed to be doing very well. Yet, when the cocktail party ended, so apparently did a promising beginning. For the North American spent nearly six months trying to arrange a second meeting. He finally learned, through pitying intermediaries, that at the cocktail party he had momentarily placed his arm on the shoulder of the Javanese—and in the presence of other people. Humiliating! Almost unpardonable in traditional Javanese etiquette.

In this particular case, the unwitting breach was mended by a graceful apology. It is worth noting, however, that a truly cordial business relationship never did develop.

THE FIVE DIMENSIONS OF TIME

If we peel away a few layers of cultural clothing, we begin to reach almost totally unconscious reactions. Our ideas of time, for example, are deeply instilled in us when we are children. If they are contradicted by another's behavior, we react with anger, not knowing exactly why. For the businessman, five important temporal concepts are: Appointment time, discussion time, acquaintance time, visiting time, and time schedules.

Anyone who has traveled abroad or dealt at all extensively with non-Americans learns that punctuality is variously interpreted. It is one thing to recognize this with the mind; to adjust to a different kind of *appointment time* is quite another.

In Latin America, you should expect to spend hours waiting in outer offices. If you bring your American interpretation of what constitutes punctuality to a Latin American office, you will fray your temper and elevate your blood pressure. For a 45-minute wait is not unusual—nor more unusual than a five-minute wait would be in the United States. No insult is intended, no arbitrary pecking order is being established. If, in the United States, you would not be outraged by a five-minute wait, you should not be outraged by the Latin-American's 45-minute delay in seeing you. The time pie is differently cut, that's all

Further, the Latin American doesn't usually schedule individual appointments to the exclusion of other appointments. The informal clock of his upbringing ticks more slowly and he rather enjoys seeing several people on different matters at the same time. The three-ring circus atmosphere which results, if interpreted in the American's scale of time and propriety, seems to signal him to go away, to tell him that he is not being properly treated, to indicate that his dignity is under attack. Not so. The clock on the wall may look the same but it tells a different sort of time.

The cultural error may be compounded by a further miscalculation. In the United States, a consistently tardy man is likely to be considered undependable, and by our cultural clock this is a reasonable conclusion. For you to judge a Latin American by your scale of time values is to risk a major error.

Suppose you have waited 45 minutes and there is a man in his office, by some miracle alone in the room with you. Do you now get down to business and stop "wasting time"?

If you are not forewarned by experience or a friendly advisor, you may try to do this. And it would usually be a mistake. For, in the American culture, *discussion* is a means to an end: The

deal. You try to make your point quickly, efficiently, neatly.
If your purpose is to arrange some major affairs, your instinct
is probably to settle the major issues first, leave the details for
later, possibly for the technical people to work out.

For the Latin American, the discussion is a part of the spice
of life. Just as he tends not to be overly concerned about reserving
you your specific segment of time, he tends not as rigidly to
separate business from nonbusiness. He runs it all together and
wants to make something of a social event out of what you, in your
culture, regard as strictly business.

The Latin American is not alone in this. The Greek
businessman, partly for the same and partly for different reasons,
does not lean toward the "hit-and-run" school of business
behavior, either. The Greek businessman adds to the social
element, however, a feeling about what length of discussion
time constitutes good faith. In America, we show good faith by
ignoring the details. "Let's agree on the main points. The details
will take care of themselves."

Not so the Greek. He signifies good will and good faith by
what may seem to you an interminable discussion which includes
every conceivable detail. Otherwise, you see, he cannot help
but feel that the other man might by trying to pull the wool over
his eyes. Our habit, in what we feel to be our relaxed and friendly
way, of postponing details until later, smacks the Greek between
the eyes as a maneuver to flank him. Even if you can somehow
convince him that this is not the case, the meeting must still go on
a certain indefinite—but, by our standards, long—time or he
will feel disquieted.

The American desire to get down to business and on with
other things works to our disadvantage in other parts of the
world, too; and not only in business. The head of a large,
successful Japanese firm commented: "You Americans have a
terrible weakness. We Japanese know about it and exploit it
every chance we get. You are impatient. We have learned that
if we just make you wait long enough, you'll agree to anything."

Whether this is literally true or not, the Japanese executive
singled out a trait of American culture which most of us share
and which, one may assume from the newspapers, the Russians
have not overlooked, either.

By acquaintance time we mean how long you must know
a man before you are willing to do business with him.

In the United States, if we know that a salesman represents
a well-known, reputable company, and if we need his product,
he may walk away from the first meeting with an order in his

pocket. A few minutes conversation to decide matters of price, delivery, payment, model of product—nothing more is involved. In Central America, local custom does not permit a salesman to land in town, call on the customer and walk away with an order, no matter how badly your prospect wants and needs your product. It is traditional there that you must see your man at least three times before you can discuss the nature of your business.

Does this mean that the South American businessman does not recognize the merits of one product over another? Of course it doesn't. It is just that the weight of tradition presses him to do business within a circle of friends. If a product he needs is not available within his circle, he does not go outside it so much as he enlarges the circle itself to include a new friend who can supply the want. Apart from his cultural need to "feel right" about a new relationship, there is the logic of his business system. One of the realities of his life is that it is dangerous to enter into business with someone over whom you have no more than formal, legal "control." In the past decades, his legal system has not always been as firm as ours and he has learned through experience that he needs the sanctions implicit in the informal system of friendship.

Visiting time involves the question of who sets the time for a visit. George Coelho, a social psychologist from India, gives an illustrative case. A U.S. businessman received this invitation from an Indian businessman: "Won't you and your family come and see us? Come anytime." Several weeks later, the Indian repeated the invitation in the same words. Each time the American replied that he would certainly like to drop in—but he never did. The reason is obvious in terms of our culture. Here "come any time" is just an expression of friendliness. You are not really expected to show up unless your host proposes a specific time. In India, on the contrary, the words are meant literally— that the host is putting himself at the disposal of his guest and really expects him to come. It is the essence of politeness to leave it to the guest to set a time at his convenience. If the guest never comes, the Indian naturally assumes that he does not want to come. Such a misunderstanding can lead to a serious rift between men who are trying to do business with each other.

Time schedules present Americans with another problem in many parts of the world. Without schedules, deadlines, priorities, and time-tables, we tend to feel that our country could not run at all. Not only are they essential to getting work done, but they also play an important role in the informal communication process. Deadlines indicate priorities and priorities signal the relative importance of people and the processes they control. These are all so much a part of our lives that a day hardly passes without some reference to them. "I have to be there by 6:30." "If I don't have these plans out by 5:00 they'll be useless." "I told J. B. I'd be finished by noon tomorrow and now he tells me to drop everything and get hot on the McDermott account. What do I do now?"

In our system, there are severe penalties for not completing work on time and important rewards for holding to schedules. One's integrity and reputation are at stake.

You can imagine the fundamental conflicts that arise when we attempt to do business with people who are just as strongly oriented away from time schedules as we are toward them.

The Middle Eastern peoples are a case in point. Not only is our idea of time schedules no part of Arab life but the mere mention of a deadine to an Arab is like waving a red flag in front of a bull. In his culture, your emphasis on a deadline has the emotional effect on him that his backing you into a corner and threatening you with a club would have on you.

One effect of this conflict of unconscious habit patterns is that hundreds of American-owned radio sets are lying on the shelves of Arab radio repair shops, untouched. The Americans made the serious cross-cultural error of asking to have the repair completed by a certain time.

How do you cope with this? How does the Arab get another Arab to do anything? Every culture has its own ways of bringing pressure to get resuts. The usual Arab way is one which Americans avoid as "bad manners." It is needling.

An Arab businessman whose car broke down explained it this way:

> First, I go to the garage and tell the mechanic what is wrong with my car. I wouldn't want to give him the idea that I didn't know. After that, I leave the car and walk around the block. When I come back to the garage, I ask him if he has started to work yet. On my way home from lunch I stop in and ask him how things are going. When I go back to the office I stop by again. In the evening I return and peer over his shoulder for a while. If I didn't keep this up, he'd be off working on someone else's car.

If you haven't been needled by an Arab, you just haven't been needled.

A PLACE FOR EVERYTHING

We say that there is a time and place for everything, but compared to other countries and cultures we give very little emphasis to place distinctions. Business is almost a universal value with us; it can be discussed almost anywhere, except perhaps in church. One can even talk business on the church steps going to and from the service. Politics is only slightly more restricted in the places appropriate for its discussion.

In other parts of the world, there are decided place restrictions on the discussion of business and politics. The American who is not conscious of the unwritten laws will offend if he abides by his own rather than by the local rules.

In India, you should not talk business when visiting a man's home. If you do, you prejudice your chances of ever working out a satisfactory business relationship.

In Latin America, although university students take an active interest in politics, tradition decrees that a politician should avoid political subjects when speaking on university grounds. A Latin American politician commented to anthropologist Allan Holmberg that neither he nor his fellow politicians would have dared attempt a political speech on the grounds of the University of San Marcos in Peru—as did Vice President Nixon.

To complicate matters further, the student body of San Marcos, anticipating the visit, had voted that Mr. Nixon would not be welcome. The University Rector had issued no invitation, presumably because he expected what did, in fact, happen.

As a final touch, Mr. Nixon's interpreter was a man in full military uniform. In Latin American countries, some of which had recently overthrown military dictators, the symbolism of the military uniform could hardly contribute to a cordial atmosphere. Latin Americans need no reminder that the United States is a great military power.

Mr. Nixon's efforts were planned in the best traditions of our own culture: He hoped to improve relations through a direct, frank, and face-to-face discussion with students—the future leaders of their country. Unfortunately, this approach did not fit in at all with the culture of the host country. Of course, elements hostile to the United States did their best to capitalize upon this cross-cultural misunderstanding. However, even Latin Americans friendly to us, while admiring the Vice President's courage, found themselves acutely embarrassed by the behavior of their people and ours in the ensuing difficulties.

BEING COMFORTABLE IN SPACE

Like time and place, differing ideas of space hide traps for the uninformed. Without realizing it, almost any person raised in the United States is likely to give an unintended snub to a Latin

American simply in the way we handle space relationships, particularly during conversations.

In North America, the "proper" distance to stand when talking to another adult male you do not know well is about two feet, at least in a formal business conversation. (Naturally at a cocktail party, the distance shrinks, but anything under eight to ten inches is likely to provoke an apology or an attempt to back up.)

To a Latin American, with his cultural traditions and habits, a distance of two feet seems to him approximately what five feet would to us. To him we seem distant and cold; to us, he gives an impression of pushiness.

As soon as a Latin American moves close enough for him to feel comfortable, we feel uncomfortable and edge back. We once observed a conversation between a Latin and a North American which began at one end of a 40-foot hall. At intervals we noticed them again, finally at the other end of the hall. This rather amusing displacement had been accomplished by an almost continual series of small backward steps on the part of the American, trying unconsciously to reach a comfortable talking distance, and an equal closing of the gap by the Latin American as he attempted to reach his accustomed conversation space.

Americans in their offices in Latin America tend to keep native acquaintances at our distance—not the Latin American's distance—by taking up a position behind a desk or typewriter. The barricade approach to communication is practiced even by old hands in Latin America who are completely unaware of its cultural significance. They know only that they are comfortable without realizing that the distance and equipment unconsciously make the Latin American uncomfortable.

HOW CLASS CHANNELS COMMUNICATION

We would be mistaken to regard the communication patterns which we observe around the world as no more than a miscellaneous collection of customs. The communication pattern of a given society is part of its total culture pattern and can only be understood in that context.

We cannot undertake here to relate many examples of communication behavior to the underlying culture of the country. For the businessman, it might be useful to mention the difficulties in the relationship between social levels and the problem of information feedback from lower to higher levels in industrial organizations abroad.

There is in Latin America a pattern of human relations and union-management relations quite different from that with which we are familiar in the United States. Everett Hagen of MIT has noted the heavier emphasis upon line authority and the lesser development of staff organizations in Latin American plants when compared with North American counterparts. To a much greater extent than in the United States, the government becomes involved in the handling of all kinds of labor problems.

These differences seem to be clearly related to the culture and social organization of Latin American. We find there that society has been much more rigidly stratified than it has with us. As a corollary, we find a greater emphasis upon authority in family and the community.

This emphasis upon status and class distinction makes it very difficult for people of different status levels to express themselves freely and frankly in discussion and argument. In the past, the pattern has been for the man of lower status to express deference to his superior in any face-to-face contact. This is so even when everyone knows that the subordinate dislikes the superior. The culture of Latin America places a great premium upon keeping personal relations harmonious on the surface.

In the United States, we feel that it is not only desirable but natural to speak up to your superior, to tell the brass exactly what you think, even when you disagree with him. Of course, we do not always do this, but we think that we should, and we feel guilty if we fail to speak our minds frankly. When workers in our factories first get elected to local union office, they may find themselves quite self-conscious about speaking up to the brass and arguing grievances. Many of them, however, quickly learn to do it and enjoy the experience. American culture emphasizes the thrashing-out of differences in face-to-face contacts. It deemphasizes the importance of status. As a result, we have built institutions for handling industrial disputes on the basis of the local situation, and we rely on direct discussion by the parties immediately involved.

In Latin America, where it is exceedingly difficult for people to express their differences face-to-face and where status differences and authority are much more strongly emphasized than here, the workers tend to look to a third party—the government—to take care of their problems. Though the workers have great difficulty in thrashing out their problems with management, they find no difficulty in telling government representatives their problems. And it is to their government that they look for an authority to settle their grievances with management.

Status and class also decide whether business will be done on an individual or a group basis.

In the United States, we are growing more and more accustomed to working as members of large organizations. Despite this, we still assume that there is no need to send a delegation to do a job that one capable man might well handle.

In some other parts of the world, the individual cannot expect to gain the respect necessary to accomplish this purpose, no matter how capable he is, unless he brings along an appropriate number of associates.

In the United States, we would rarely think it necessary or proper to call on a customer in a group. He might well be antagonized by the hard sell. In Japan—as an example—the importance of the occasion and of the man is measured by whom he takes along.

This practice goes far down in the business and government hierarchies. Even a university professor is likely to bring one or two retainers along on academic business. Otherwise people might think that he was a nobody and that his affairs were of little moment.

Even when a group is involved in the U.S., the head man is the spokesman and sets the tone. This is not always the case in Japan. Two young Japanese once requested an older American widely respected in Tokyo to accompany them so that they could "stand on his face." He was not expected to enter into the negotiation; his function was simply to be present as an indication that their intentions were serious.

ADJUSTMENT GOES BOTH WAYS

One need not have devoted his life to a study of various cultures to see that none of them is static. All are constantly changing and one element of change is the very fact that U.S. enterprise enters a foreign field. This is inevitable and may be constructive if we know how to utilize our knowledge. The problem is for us to be aware of our impact and to learn how to induce changes skillfully.

Rather than try to answer the general question of how two cultures interact, we will consider the key problem of personnel selection and development in two particular intercultural situations, both in Latin cultures.

One U.S. company had totally different experiences with

"Smith" and "Jones" in the handling of its labor relations. The local union leaders were bitterly hostile to Smith, whereas they could not praise Jones enough. These were puzzling reactions to higher management. Smith seemed a fair-minded and understanding man; it was difficult to fathom how anyone could be bitter against him. At the same time, Jones did not appear to be currying favor by his generosity in giving away the firm's assets. To management, he seemed to be just as firm a negotiator as Smith.

The explanation was found in the two men's communication characteristics. When the union leaders came in to negotiate with Smith, he would let them state their case fully and freely—without interruption, but also without comment. When they had finished, he would say, "I'm sorry. We can't do it." He would follow this blunt statement with a brief and entirely cogent explanation of his reasons for refusal. If the union leaders persisted in their arguments, Smith would paraphrase his first statement, calmly and succincitly. In either case, the discussion was over in a few minutes. The union leaders would storm out of Smith's office complaining bitterly about the cold and heartless man with whom they had to deal.

Jones handled the situation differently. His final conclusion was the same as Smith's—but he would state it only after two or three hours of discussion. Furthermore, Jones participated actively in these discussions, questioning the union leaders for more information, relating the case in question to previous cases, philosophizing about labor relations and human rights and exchanging stories about work experience. When the discussion came to an end, the union leaders would leave the office, commenting on how warmhearted and understanding he was, and how confident they were that he would help them when it was possible for him to do so. They actually seemed more satisfied with a negative decision from Jones than they did with a hard-won concession with Smith.

This was clearly a case where the personality of Jones happened to match certain discernible requirements of the Latin American culture. It was happenstance in this case that Jones worked out and Smith did not, for by American standards both were top-flight men. Since a talent for the kind of negotiation that the Latin American considers graceful and acceptable can hardly be developed in a grown man (or perhaps even in a young one), the basic problem is one of personnel selection in terms of the culture where the candidate is to work.

The second case is more complicated because it involves much deeper intercultural adjustments. The management of the

parent U.S. company concerned had learned—as have the directors
of most large firms with good-sized installations overseas—that
one cannot afford to have all of the top and middle-management
positions manned by North Americans. It is necessary to advance
nationals up the overseas-management ladder as rapidly as their
abilities permit. So the nationals have to learn not only the technical
aspects of their jobs but also how to function at higher levels
in the organization.

Latin culture emphasizes authority in the home, church,
and community. Within the organization this produces a built-in
hesitancy about speaking up to one's superiors. The initiative, the
acceptance of responsibility which we value in our organizations
had to be stimulated. How could it be done?

We observed one management man who had done a
remarkable job of building up these very qualities in his general
foremen and foremen. To begin with, he stimulated informal
contacts between himself and these men through social events to
which the men and their wives came. He saw to it that his senior
North American assistants and their wives were also present.
Knowing the language, he mixed freely with all. At the plant, he
circulated about, dropped in not to inspect or check up, but to
joke and to break down the great barrier that existed in the local
traditions between authority and the subordinates.

Next, he developed a pattern of three-level meetings. At the
top, he himself, the superintendents, and the general formen,
and foremen. Then the general foremen, foremen, and workers.

At the top level meeting, the American management chief
set the pattern of encouraging his subordinates to challenge his own
ideas, to come up with original thoughts. When his superintendents
(also North Americans) disagreed with him, he made it clear that
they were to state their objections fully. At first, the general
foreman looked surprised and uneasy. They noted, however, that
the senior men who argued with the boss were encouraged and
praised. Timorously, with great hesitation, they began to add their
own suggestions. As time went on, they more and more accepted
the new convention and pitched in without inhibition.

28

ADUMBRATION AS A FEATURE OF INTERCULTURAL COMMUNICATION

Edward T. Hall

More than two decades of observing Americans working with other cultures lead me to believe that the majority fall into two groups. One group—mostly professional linguists and anthropologists— is convinced that it is a waste of time to send a man abroad until he is thoroughly conversant with the language and culture on all levels. The other group, appalled by the cost of implementing such a policy and drawing from naïve experience, sees language and culture only as screens that have to be penetrated in order to find the *real* man or people underneath. This second group believes that there is a dichotomy between man and his language-culture and also that good will is the primary material needed to pave the road to understanding.

Intuitively, the specialist in intercultural communications has

Reprinted by permission of the American Anthropological Association from *American Anthropologist* 66 (6, Pt. 2), (1964).

known for a long time that neither of these positions is appropriate as a matter of policy. There are many times when all the good will in the world would not reach the mind of, say, a Japanese. On the other hand, knowledge of the language and culture will not enable one to "get through" to the other fellow in every instance, even if he is a member of one's own culture.

Anyone who has lived and worked abroad knows that the overseas world is full of surprises, not all of them pleasant, which are due to accumulated slippage in reading subtle signs of which we are often unaware. The surprises that characterize life abroad, as well as at home, are due not so much to ignorance of overt culture as to changes or shifts in the signs that we read to penetrate peoples' facades, signs that tell us what's going on underneath. Goffman (1957, 1959) refers to this process as "going backstage." Ability to read these signs enables us to be "sensitive," to know how the other person is reacting to what we are saying and doing.

To do this, one must be able to read and interpret correctly what I have termed "adumbrations": those indications preceding or surrounding formal communications which enable organisms to engage in the mutual exchange and evaluation of covert information on what each can expect from the other. Adumbrations are the feedback mechanisms that enable us to steer a smooth course through life or to prepare for attack when combat cannot be avoided. They foreshadow what organisms will do, perform corrective functions, and help set the directions a given communication will take, as well as the actions resulting from it. As we shall see, absence of the adumbrative feature can have catastrophic consequences. In addition. adumbrations are often closely linked with territory, or personal space, occur on different levels, and have proxemic implications (Hall, 1955, 1959, 1963a, 1963b).

Most, if not all, of the conceptual models I have examined have implicit in them the concept that the events referred to occur at different levels in depth. Thinking in the fields of depth psychology, ethnography, and descriptive linguistics has from the very beginning been intermingled on the matter of levels. Freud made the original contribution. Since then, recognition of the need to distinguish between different analytic levels has become fairly widespread, owing to work of Boas (111), Linton (1936), Kluckhohn (1943), Sapir (1921, 1925, 1927), Sullivan (1947), and others.

Recently, there has been a shift to another dimension. Goffman's frontstage-backstage model implies a horizontal rather than a vertical dimension. Recent studies in ethology suggest that a temporal dimension should be added to our ever-growing inventory.

A LINGUISTIC MODEL FOR ANALYSIS OF CULTURE

In 1953, Trager and I introduced the notion that cultural events occur not on two but on three levels: the formal, the informal, and the technical. We described how these different levels function and can be identified. My own description (Hall, 1959) does not deviate in any significant degree from the joint version. However, I have come to feel that it was somewhat oversimplified and this I shall attempt to correct.

Originally, Trager and I had collected microtexts of references to time as they occurred in the context of conversations in natural settings. After a while (an informal reference) we noted that the items we were collecting were not at all of the same degree of specificity but were in fact quite different. This observation suggested a three-part classification that we later called formal, informal, and technical. Brief examples will suffice here: *Technical:* "Resolving time is 1 μ see"; *Formal:* "We always start services promptly at 11"; *Informal:* "I'll see you later." In English we have not only a word for time but an extensive formal vocabulary devoted to it. Whorf's description of linguistic events (see papers in Carroll, 1956) is based on *formal* differences between languages, and this is one reason why they are so difficult to grasp, a generalization which still holds. (On technical, formal, and informal, see Hall, 1959, ch. IV, for extended discussion.)

To use a spatial metaphor, the formal-informal-technical concept is like a river: The readily perceived main current is the technical, surrounded by the informal back eddies and quiet pools, all of which are contained in a formal channel. Like all analogies, this one has limitations, yet it did help in the organization of our data and in talking to outsiders about what we were doing. When we were developing it, we suggested (Hall and Trager, 1953; Hall, 1959) that a linguistic model was an excellent one for the analysis of culture; that, in fact, all culture could be viewed as communication and all cultural events could be analyzed with the methods of linguistics.

The linguistic model has served us well and will continue to do so, but it requires some broadening, as noted by several linguists (Hockett, 1958; Sebeok, 1962). The great strengths of linguistics are that it has distinguished between *etic* and *emic* events (Hymes, 1962; Greenberg, 1959a, 1959b) and has been able to handle greater and greater complexity. Descriptive linguistic models break down, however, when it is necessary to deal with feedback or teleology. The ability to handle the complexity necessary for discourse analysis has not proceeded with any degree of sophistication, with one exception (Joos, 1962).

Recent advances in isolating the relationship of biochemistry to the environment (Christian, 1961: Deevey, 1960), however, explain population control as the result of a series of interlocking and interdependent servomechanisms that conform to information theory principles as laid down by Wiener (1948), Shannon and Weaver (1949), Pierce (1956), and their followers. Gillard (1962) has shown how display behavior also fits this pattern and is also an important process in evolution. Hockett (1958) defined communication so generally as to comprise any event that triggers a response in another organism.

It would seem then that the time is ripe to take the first (even though faltering) steps towards the integration of linguistic models with the communication models of wider scope recently developed in the fields referred to above.

It is suggested that interpersonal communication occurs as a hierarchy of formally determined cybernetic responses. Two processes to which adumbrative behavior is particularly important are those beginning with the informal and becoming increasingly technical, in stages, whenever an inappropriate response is met on either side, and, conversely, those beginning with the technical, and becoming increasingly informal, as appropriate responses are met. Courtship and business negotiation offer many examples of such processes. When the parties know each other well and have enough in common, there is very little need for technical statements. The greater the distance (and the greater the investment), the more necessary it becomes to spell things out, even to the point of specifying which language version, say English or Spanish, of a contract will hold in case of litigation. In other words, the degree of explicit information content of a communication is a function of the degree to which the other party is already appropriately programmed. Less explicit means serve the ends of economy, and often avoid the commitment of organisms beyond a point of no return if things don't seem to be going well. On the other hand, some things can be accomplished only if the less explicit means can be successfully employed. Much interaction is under constraints like those set by the girl who wants to be kissed but not to be asked.

These same processes hold true to a lesser degree within a primarily technical sphere, such as conversations between

scientists on scientific topics, in the laboratory, as contrasted
to publication in a scientific journal.

All this represents a redefinition of the formal, the informal,
and the technical levels and is a first attempt to bring these
concepts into line with the general principles (but not the
details) of information theory.[1] This change in definition is made
possible by recognition of constant feedback in man and in
animals on every level from the biochemical to the international
(Hall, 1959).

IMPORTANCE OF ADUMBRATION
IN COMMUNICATION

This paper focuses on the informal adnumbrative process. It
advances the hypothesis that the formal or technical message
is more often understood than the informal, but, since the latter
influences the meaning of the former, there is always a paratixic
element (noise) present in any conversation and this element
becomes greater as cultural distance increases.

In essence, every communication appears to comprise three
interrelated parts or phases: A beginning phase, a peak phase,
and a terminating phase, analogous to a sine wave on an
oscilloscope. Muscians refer to the first and last as the attack
and decay phase of a musical note.

What happens in one phase apparently influences the other
two very considerably. That is, communications have an
adumbrative phase (the part that indicates what is coming),
the message itself, and a terminal or transition phase that signals
how things went or the nature of reply expected. It is my
hypothesis that the greatest confusion in intercultural
communication can often be traced to failures in catching the
true significance of the adumbrative and/or the terminal-transition
phase, while, as a general rule, the message itself is often
understood. Since the communication is taken as a whole in
which the parts are interrelated, however, distortion of or failure
to grasp the beginning or end can result in *total* distortion, or
what Sullivan (1947) called parataxic communication. (For
intracultural consequences as within a family, of contradiction
between the message and its context, including the temporal
phases dealt with here, see Bateson [1960, 1963] and cf. Ruesch
[1961, passim].)

I am going to dwell chiefly on nonverbal communication of
which there are many varieties (Hall, 1959; Hymes, 1962),
drawing chiefly on my work in time and space as communication.

One can begin with the setting which is a form of communication; changes in the setting foreshadow other changes. One might assume that we are talking about the cues, but this is not so. The cue is a short message of minimal redundancy in full awareness from A to B that indicates what A wants B to do. The adumbration, on the other hand, is a perceivable manifestation of A's feelings of which he may not even be aware: His tone of voice (paralinguistic behavior), facial expression, even his dress, posture, and handling of appointments "in time." While most of us are familiar with cues as a special type of communication, adumbrations are less well understood. They were first described under a different name by ecologists studying the behavior of other life forms (ranging from lizards to birds), courting, fighting, socializing, and caring for their young.

PRE-HUMAN ADUMBRATIVE BEHAVIOR

Adumbration can be observed in all vertebrates, although it is easier for man to recognize it in some forms than in others. Display is the principle vehicle of adumbration among animals. Gilliard (1962) lists four types of display: vocal, mechanical, mobile, and static-terrestrial. Most, if not all, bird calls can be classified as vocal display. Various mechanical means are also used to produce display by sound. The peacock's tail feathers rustle as he spreads them in display. The bowerbird snaps his bill, the gorilla thumps his chest (Schaller, 1963), and the rattlesnake vibrates his tail to produce a threatening buzz. Movement displays are varied; their most familiar form is the strutting of male pigeons, the neck-stretching and head-bobbing of the gulls. Almost anyone familiar with chickens will recognize the static-terrestrial posturing of the barnyard cock as a display.

Recently display has received more and more attention from the ethologist and the animal psychologist and is seen as an active agent in evolution. It also performs a number of extraordinarily important and vital functions, many of them associated with language in man. Correct interpretation of the significance of given displays is normally limited to within the species, sometimes to within genera.

Display behavior is not limited to a single act but is a sequence of events that combine in different ways with different results. Anyone who has observed gulls will have noted a good deal of posturing and head-bogging. Tinbergen (1954) gives an excellent description of the significance of this behavior, which appears so bizarre at first glance.

During the mating season, a male blackheaded gull lays
claim to a territory, a small plot of land that he defends against
his own kind, particularly other males. Whenever another gull
lands on his turf, the gull responds with a "long call" (vocal
display) and postures his body obliquely (static-terrestrial
display). This is the first in a series of "threat displays." During
the second step, the two gulls draw closer together, lean forward,
and often perform movements of the head and neck (movement
displays) that look as if they were choking each other. Then
they assume "upright posture" (static-terrestrial display). The
third step in the sequence is "head flogging." Performed by only
one of two males, it signals submission and serves to suppress
further aggression. During courtship, head flogging is performed
by *both* the male and the female to signal appeasement. This
three-step scene (approach, threat, appeasement) is played over
and over again until the two gulls apparently get to know each
other (are mutually programed) and learn that in this instance
both can be counted on to end the aggressive exchange sequence
by giving the appeasement display. *Repetition* and the ability to
recognize individuals are important elements in communication
sequences such as these.

In still another context, male sea lizards on the Galapagos
Islands, defending their territories during mating, engage in
mutual display and nobody gets hurt. The ethologist
Eibl-Eibesfeldt (1961), recognizing and wishing to test the
function of display in suppressing aggression, put male sea lizards
in other lizards' territories, thereby short-circuiting the normal
display sequence. As soon as this happened, terrible fighting
broke out.[2]

Those who have studied display are generally agreed that
it performs several important communicative functions both
within a species and between species. It reduces the amount
of actual combat and limits serious fighting to interspecies.
During courtship it synchronizes the behavior of the sexes, gets
attention, suppresses nonsexual responses, and releases the
submissive posture in the female. On the other hand, lack of
participation in a given display pattern isolates even closely
related species from each other, thus acting as an evolutionary
force in the maintenance of reproductive isolation.

In encounters between species, ability to interpret correctly
at least part of the display sequence is of critical importance.
Hediger (1955), the animal psychologist, has stressed the
necessity for men to be able to identify the adumbration behavior
of other species. Pandas, bears, and snakes are dangerous to man

because it is difficult to know how they are feeling from moment to moment.[3]

The hypothesis can be advanced that: *Unless the adumbrative sequence is known, two species or societies or two individuals cannot interact in any way towards each other except in a parataxic manner and with ultimate aggression.* Within species, short-circuiting the adumberative sequence leads to serious fighting.[4]

THE ADUMBRATIVE FUNCTION IN MAN

As we have seen, some of the functions of adumbration are: to protect organisms (including man) from becoming over-committed, to give them some control over their encounters with others, to protect egos, and to provide an automatic buffer or means of transition from one segment of a communication sequence to another; adumbration may also serve to establish intimacy. In many cultures, there are intermediaries who act in an adumbrative role, relative to the focal messages of a relationship. They may serve as buffers to save face and prevent over-commitment, on the one hand, to establish the necessary or desired closeness on the other. In our own culture, time, space, and materials communicate on many levels including the adumbrative level.

The examples I shall use are drawn from my studies of proxemics, the human use of microspace (Hall, 1963a, 1963b). There are three different types of microspace (Hall, 1963a, 1963b): fixed-feature space (including the setting); semifixed-feature space (components that are part of the setting and can be moved); and dynamic space (man's informal repertoire for handling space). The desirability of choosing a proper setting for a communication is so well known that there would be no need to mention it, if it were not for the fact the choice of setting differs from culture to culture, often for the same act.

This is one reason why Americans in foreign lands who become ill often suffer from anxiety as soon as they go to the doctor. Sivadon (ms.) has stressed the importance, even for the indigenous population, of recognizing the adumbrative side of the setting. He states that hospital waiting rooms and doctors' offices should emphasize the familiar and be as free as possible of the unknown, such as glass cases full of chromium instruments which are familiar to the physician but not to the patient.

In the international political arena, adumbrative space has proved to be significant indeed. All other things being equal, and given a willingness to negotiate in the first place, there is little adumbrative significance for Americans regarding the choice of the place of a negotiation. Our approach is to get on with negotiations and "not hold up the show." Allowing the other party to choose or move a negotiation site, once it has been established, signifies only that we intend to be "reasonable." However, when the American negotiators readily agreed to move the setting of the Korean truce negotiations from the Swedish peace ship in Seoul harbor to Panmunjom, the Chinese Communists apparently assumed that this represented an "appeasement" display. As most Americans will remember, it took a while to disabuse them of this misconception.

In the international business context, there are numerous examples of how familiarity with the differences in the adumbrative significance of the setting helped negotiations, while ignorance hindered them. Some of our more adept American firms have learned that they do better if they create settings with design features which enable their Latin American counterparts to progress, like Tinbergen's gulls, through known stages in the business courtship. One very successful Wall Street executive specializing in Latin America chooses a club that features dark, oak-paneled walls, heavy, leather-covered chairs, high ceilings, and stained-glass windows, a setting that is impressive and at the same time "simpatico" to his clients. A little settee with a low table in front permits the necessary closeness to begin a relationship. As many American business men have discovered, the home is *not* the setting that a Latin American chooses to consummate a business deal. The home is for the family and not for business.

In Japan, business men often take the preliminary steps in a negotiation on the golf course. As one oil executive put it, "We soon learned, from the number of golf games involved, how to compute the size of the contract we were going to negotiate."

Some of the most familiar instances of adumbrations in which the feelings are at variance with the overt behavior pattern are those having to do with where people stand and sit in relation to each other and whether they touch each other. There is, first of all, a large group in which touching is important, even with strangers. An equally numerous group of people avoids touching. Those who are not used to being approached closely are made uncomfortable by the laying-on of hands and take it as preliminary to either a fight or a sexual "pass."

Stated this way, there seems to be nothing mysterious about adumbrative communication and, *in fact, the idea is deceptively simple*. My hypothesis is that the specific technical communication on the overt level is seldom seriously misinterpreted, even in cross-cultural contexts, if the adumbrative part is read correctly. What is most often misinterpreted is the adumbration. In some instances, this can be serious enough to prevent the real communication from ever emerging or even to result in a fight.

In the course of this discussion, nothing has been said about transitions or juncture phenomena in transcultural encounters, mostly because virtually nothing is known about it. Our own version of Western culture seems to emphasize the build-up or attack phase and to pay little attention to the equivalent of terminal junctures and transitions. Yet I recall numerous instances when I was forced to look back on a sequence of events that seemed to be going on because of an ending that appeared abrupt. In most instances it was impossible to judge whether things went well or badly until someone familiar with the local dialect of behavior could be consulted.

SUMMARY

In this article there has been no attempt to be definitive, and only broad outlines have been sketched. In summary, the view seems to be gaining currency that communication occurs simultaneously on several levels in depth, as well as proceeding sequentially according to quite rigid but unstated rules. How a given communication sequence develops can be seen as a function of the strength of motivations of the two parties, their knowledge of the system, and how they respond to each other's adumbrations. All communication in this sense can be viewed as a discourse, even though different styles (Joos, 1962) are used, while ability to participate in the discourse is a function of programing.

In the display sequences of animals, we find simple models of behavior that may have relevance to man within cultures and across cultures. The study of animal behavior is relevant because man does not experience as much difficulty with speech (even if the language is different) as he does with these older, more primitive, and possibly more basic communications which are currently in the early stages of examination. In the larger sense, display is seen to perform important functions in evolution and in population control which may also be of some relevance to man.

Notes

[1] See also Sebeok (1962) for integration of ethological data with information theory; Reusch and Kees (1956) use an information theory model but not a linguistic one as a point of departure.

[2] For a more detailed treatment of display, the reader is referred to Hinde and Tinbergen (1958).

[3] It is also a distortion, or absence, of normal adumbrative functions that makes the assaultive psychotic so dangerous. Personnel treating such patients are in constant danger until they learn to pick up the subtle signs that foretell impending aggression.

[4] One of the consequences of overcrowding may be that there is not enough room for proper display.

References

Boas, Franz. "Introduction." In F. Boas (ed.), *Handbook of American Indian Languages, Bulletin of the Bureau of American Ethnology*, 1911, **40**, part I, Washington, D.C.

Bateson, G. "Minimal Requirements for a Theory of Schizophrenia." *A.M.A. Archives of General Psychiatry* 2, (1960):477–491.

Bateson, G. "Exchange of Information about Patterns of Human Behavior." In W. Fields and W. Abbott (eds.), *Information Storage and Neural Control* (Springfield, Ill.: Thomas, 1963), pp. 1–12.

Carroll, John B. *Language, Thought and Reality. Selected Writings of Benjamin Lee Whorf* (New York: Wiley, 1956).

Christian, John J. "Phenomena Associated with Population Density." *Proceedings National Academy of Sciences* **47**, (1961): 428–449.

Deevey, E. S. "The Hare and the Haruspex: A Cautionary Tale." *American Scientist* **48**, (1960):415.

Eibl-Eibesfeldt, I., "The Fighting Behavior of Animals." *Scientific American* **207**, (1961): 112–122.

Gilliard, E. "On the Breeding Behavior of the Cock-of-the-Rock (*aves, rupicola rupicola*)." *Bulletin of the American Museum of Natural History* **124**, (1962):article 2.

Gilliard, E. "The Evolution of Bowerbirds." *Scientific American* **209**, (1963):38–46.

Goffman, E. "Alienation from Interaction." *Human Relations* **10**, (1957):47–60.

Goffman, E. *The Presentation of Self in Everyday Life* (Garden City, N.Y.: Doubleday, 1959).

Greenberg, J. "Language and Evolution." In Betty Meggers (ed.), *Evolution and Anthropoloy* (Washington, D.C.: The Anthropological Society of Washington, 1959a).

Greenberg, J. "Current Trends in Linguistics." *Science* **130**, (1959b):1165–1170.

Hall, E. T. "The Anthropology of Manners." *Scientific American* **192**, (1955):85–89.

Hall, E. T. *The Silent Language* (Garden City, N.Y.: Doubleday, 1959).

Hall, E. T. "Proxemics—the Study of Man's Spatial Relations." In Iago Gladston (ed.), *Man's Image in Medicine and Anthropology* (New York: International Universities Press, 1963a).

Hall, E. T. "A System for the Notation of Proxemic Behavior." *American Anthropologist* 65, (1963b):1003–1026.

Hall, E. T., and Trager, G. L. *The Analysis of Culture* (Washington, D.C.: American Council of Learned Societies, 1953).

Hediger, H. *Studies of the Psychology and Behavior of Captive Animals in Zoos and Circuses* (London: Buttersworths Scientific Publications, 1955).

Hinde, R., and Tinbergen, N. "The Comparative Study of Species' Specific Behavior." In Anne Roe and G. G. Simpson (eds.), *Behavior and Evolution* (New Haven, Conn.: Yale University Press, 1958).

Hockett, C. F. *A Course in Modern Linguistics* (New York: Macmillan, 1958).

Hymes, D. "The Ethnography of Speaking." In T. G. Gladwin and W. C. Sturtevant (eds.), *Anthropology and Human Behavior* (Washington, D.C.: The Anthropological Society of Washington, 1962), pp. 15–53.

Joos, M. *The Five Clocks*, Supplement to *International Journal of American Linguistics* 28, (1962):part V.

Kluckhohn, C. "Covert Culture and Administrative Problems." *American Anthropologist* 45, (1943):213–227.

Linton, R. *The Study of Man* (New York: Appleton-Century-Crofts, 1936).

Pierce, T. *Electrons, Waves, and Messages* (New York: Hanover House, 1956).

Ruesch, J. *Therapeutic Communication* (New York: Norton, 1961).

Ruesch, J., and Kees, W. *Nonverbal Communication* (Berkeley and Los Angeles: University of California Press, 1956).

Sapir, Edward. *Language* (New York: Harcourt Brace Jovanovich, 1921).

Sapir, Edward, "Sound Patterns in Language." *Language* 1, (1925):37–51.

Sapir, Edward. "The Unconscious Patterning of Behavior in Society." In E. S. Dummer (ed.), *The Unconscious: A Symposium* (New York, 1927).

Schaller, G. B. *The Mountain Gorilla* (Chicago: University of Chicago Press, 1963).

Sebeok, T. A. "Coding in the Evolution of Signaling Behavior." *Behavioral Science* 7, (1962):430–442.

Shannon, C. A., and Weaver, W. *The Mathematical Theory of Communication* (Urbana: University of Illinois Press, 1949).

Sivadon, P. "Techniques of Sociotherapy." Ms.

Sullivan, H. S. *Conceptions of Modern Psychiatry* (Washington, D.C.: William Alanson White Foundation, 1947).

Tinbergen, N. "The Origins and Evolution of Courtship and Threat Display." In A. C. Hardy, T. S. Huxley, and E. B. Ford (eds.), *Evolution as a Process* (London: Allen & Unwin, 1954).

Wiener, N. *Cybernetics* (New York: Wiley, 1948).

29

MAN AT THE MERCY
OF LANGUAGE

Peter Farb

Every human being is creative both in putting together novel
statements and in employing them in various speech situations.
Yet no one is free to employ his innate capacity in any way he
wishes. Indeed, freedom of speech does not exist anywhere,
for every community on earth forbids the use of certain sounds,
words, and sentences in various speech situations. In the
American speech community, for example, the habitual liar faces
social sanctions—and criminal punishment should he lie under
oath. Speakers are not allowed to misrepresent what they are
selling, to defame other people in public, to maliciously shout
"Fire!" in a crowded movie theater, or to utter obscenities on
the telephone. In addition, less obvious constraints upon freedom
of speech may exist. They may be the structures of languages

Reprinted by permission of Alfred A. Knopf from *Word Play* by Peter
Farb, 1974.

themselves—and they may restrict the speaker as rigidly as do the community's social sanctions.

Every moment of the day the world bombards the human speaker with information and experiences. It clamors for his attention, claws at his senses, intrudes into his thoughts. Only a very small portion of this total experience is language—yet the speaker must use this small portion to report on all the experiences that exist or ever existed in the totality of the world since time began. Try to think about the stars, a grasshopper, love or hate, pain, anything at all—and it must be done in terms of language. There is no other way; thinking is language spoken to oneself. Until language has made sense of experience, that experience is meaningless.

This inseparableness of everything in the world from language has intrigued modern thinkers, most notably Ludwig Wittgenstein, of Cambridge University, who was possibly this century's most influential philosopher. He stated the problem very directly "The limits of my language mean the limits of my world." Wittgenstein offered pessimistic answers to questions about the ability of language to reveal the world. He claimed that language limited his capacity to express certain ideas and opinions; nevertheless, he did manage to say a great deal about topics he felt were inexpressible. By the time of his death in 1951, Wittgenstein had arrived at a more positive view of language. If its limits—that is, the precise point at which sense becomes nonsense—could somehow be defined, then speakers would not attempt to express the inexpressible. Therefore, said Wittgenstein, do not put too great a burden upon language. Learn its limitations and try to accommodate yourself to them, for language offers all the reality you can ever hope to know.

For tens, and perhaps hundreds, of thousands of years, people regarded language as a holy instrument that let them look out upon the world in wonder and fear and joy. "In the beginning was the Word" is the reassuring first line of the Gospel According to St. John. Only in the last few decades have people suspected that their window on the world has a glass that gives a distorted view. Language no longer is certain to open up new sights to the imagination; rather, it is thought by some to obscure the vision of reality. The French philosopher Jean-Paul Sartre, who has often written about what he calls today's "crisis of language," has stated: "Things are divorced from their names. They are there, grotesque, headstrong, gigantic, and it seems ridiculous to . . . say anything at all about them; I am in the midst of things, nameless things." Indeed, in this century many of the foundation "things" of civilization—God, truth, fact, humanity, freedom, good and evil—have become nameless and have lost their traditional reference points. An entire generation has grown up that distrusts language's ability to express a true picture of reality and that relies upon the empty intercalations of *like, you know, I mean.* The world has grown inarticulate at the very time that an unprecedented number of words flood the media. The output has burgeoned, but speakers have retreated into the worn paths of stock phrases. A statistical study of telephone speech showed that a vocabuary of only 737 words was used in 96 per cent of such conversations. Apparently people speak more, yet say less.

Exaggerated anxieties about language's ability to express reality result in the pathology of "logophobia" (literally, "fear of words"). Logophobia has found popular expression in recent decades in the movement known as General Semantics. Two books with this point of view have had a wide readership—Stuart Chase's *Tyranny of Words* and S. I. Hayakawa's *Language in Action*—and both derive their ideas largely from the writings of a Polish count. Alfred Korzybski (1879-1950) was an engineer, an officer in the Russian army, an official at the League of Nations, and a researcher into mental illness after he migrated to the United States. The key element in his theory about language was: "The map does not represent all of the territory." That is, no matter how much detail a cartographer puts into a drawing of a map, it can never represent all of the ridges, slopes, valleys, and hillocks in a territory. Korzybski similarly believed that language can no more say everything about an event than the map can show everything in a territory. *The grass is green* cannot be a true utterance because it is incomplete. What kind of grass? Where is it growing? What shade of green is meant?

Korzybski felt that speakers could nevertheless emancipate themselves from the tyranny of language by changing their orientation. They must imitate mathematics as a way to state precise relationships between things; they must avoid abstractions; they must be wary of the troublesome word *is* because it often implies an identification that does not exist in reality. Freedom from language's distortions would be achieved by rigorously rating all statements to determine whether speakers could back them up. And no longer would general words that expressed categories be acceptabe. A *cow* would not be just a cow, but a particular kind of animal, with certain characteristics, named "Elsie" or "Bossie."

Almost all linguists reject Korzybski's theories on the basis of their logophobia and their inadequate solutions. Nevertheless, he did isolate a logical contradiction: Language is supposed to communicate experience, yet by its very nature it is incapable of doing so. A moment's thought reveals how ill-equipped language is to render a true account of an experience. Picture an autumn scene with a single leaf close up: it's color scarlet and edged with burnished gold, the spaces between the veins eaten out by insects in a filigree pattern, the edges gracefully curled, the different textures of the upper and lower surfaces, the intense light of Indian summer falling on the leaf. And this leaf which I have scarcely begun to describe is only one out of the countless millions that surround a stroller in the autumn woods, each unique in its color and shape, the way it catches the light and flutters in the breeze.

How can language possibly render such an experience? The obvious fact is that it cannot—and few people would want it to, for such detail would bog down language in a morass of trivial observations. People do not demand that language describe an entire experience, even if it could. No one confuses speech about a leaf with a real leaf any more than people confuse a painting of a leaf with a leaf. The function of language is not to duplicate reality, but to recall it, comment upon it, and make predictions about it. A much more significant limitation upon language is that each language can comment upon experience only in its own way. Some languages of interior New Guinea, for example, are severely hampered in conveying even leaf color because they lack a convenient terminology to describe colors other than black and white.

Since human beings are both with the same senses and approximately the same degree of intelligence, they should be able to report equally well whatever they experience. But different languages make such equality difficult to achieve. Imagine two forest rangers, one a white speaker of Standard English and the other an Indian speaker of Navaho, riding together on inspection in Arizona. They notice a broken wire fence. When they return to their station, the English-speaking ranger reports *A fence is broken*. He is satisfied that he has perceived the situation well and has reported it conscientiously. The Navaho, though, would consider such a report vague and perhaps even meaningless. His report of the same experience would be much different in Navaho—simply because his language demands it of him.

First of all, a Navaho speaker must clarify whether the "fence" is animate or inanimate; after all, the "fence" might refer to the slang for a receiver of stolen goods or to a fence lizard. The verb the Navaho speaker selects from several alternatives will indicate that the fence was long, thin, and constructed of many strands, thereby presumably wire (the English-speaking ranger's report failed to mention whether the fence was wood, wire, or chain link). The Navaho language then demands that a speaker report with precision upon the act of breaking; the Indian ranger must choose between two different verbs that tell whether the fence was broken by a human act or by some nonhuman agency such as a windstorm. Finally, the verb must indicate the present status of the fence, whether it is stationary or is, perhaps, being whipped by the wind. The Navaho's report would translate something like this: "A fence (which belongs to a particular category of inanimate things, constructed of long and thin material composed of many strands) is (moved to a position, after which it is now at rest) broken (by nonhumans, in a certain way)." The Navaho's report takes about as long to utter as the English-speaking ranger's, but it makes numerous distinctions that it never occurred to the white ranger to make, simply because the English language does not oblige him to make them.

Each language encourages its speakers to tell certain things and to ignore other things. *The women bake a cake* is an acceptable English sentence. Speakers of many other languages, though, would regard it as inadequate and would demand more specific information, such as whether exactly two women or more than two women did the baking, and whether the women are nearby or distant. Some languages would force their speakers to select a word for "cake" that tells whether the cake is round or rectangular and whether or not the cake is visible to the listener at the time of speaking. Many languages are not as concerned as English that the tense of the verb tell whether the cake was baked in the past, is being baked now, or will be baked in the future—although some languages make even finer distinctions of tense than English does. Several American Indian languages of the Pacific Northwest divide the English past tense into recent past, remote past, and mythological past.

The way people talk about the color spectrum, and even perceive it, varies from one speech community to another, although all human eyes see the same colors because colors have their own reality in the physical world. Color consists of visible wavelengths which blend imperceptibly into one another. No sharp breaks in the spectrum separate one color from another, such as orange from red. But when speakers in most European communities look at a rainbow, they imagine they see six sharp bands of color: red, orange, yellow, green, blue, and purple.

Chopping the continuous spectrum of the rainbow into color categories in this way is an arbitrary division made by European speech communities. People elsewhere in the world, who speak languages unrelated to European ones, have their own ways of partitioning the color spectrum. The Shona of Rhodesia and the Bassa of Liberia, for example, have fewer color categories than speakers of European languages, and they also break up the spectrum at different points, as the diagrams show:

English

red	orange	yellow	green	blue	purple

Shona

cipsuka	cicena	citema	cipsuka

Bassa

ziza	hui

The Shona speaker divides the spectrum into three portions, which it pronounces approximately as *cipsuka, cicena,* and *citema* (cipsuka appears twice because it refers to colors at both the red end and the purple end of the spectrum). Of course, the Shona speaker is able to perceive and to describe other colors— in the same way that a speaker of English knows that *light orangish* yellow is a variant of yellow—but the Shona's basic divisions represent the portions of the spectrum for which his language has convenient labels.

Charts obtainable at paint stores provide samples of hundreds of colors to help homeowners select the exact ones they want. An English speaker who glances quickly at one of these charts recognizes certain colors and can name them immediately as *yellow, green,* and so forth. Other colors require a moment of hesitation before the speaker finally decides that a particular hue falls into the category of, let us say, *green* rather than *yellow.* Still other colors demand not only considerable thought but also a hyphenated compromise, such as *greenish-yellow.* Finally, the English-speaker finds himself totally unable to name many colors by any of the categories available to him; he is forced to make up his own term or to use a comparison, such as *It looks like the color of swamp water.* The ease with which verbal labels can be attached to colors is known as "codability." The color that a speaker of English unhesitatingly describes as *green* has high codability for him, and it also evokes a quick response from speakers of his language, who immediately know what hues fall into that category. Similarly, when a Shona says *citema*, a high-codability color, other members of his speech community immediately know that he refers to "greenish-blue." In contrast, the color that a speaker describes as *like swamp water* has low codability, which means that other speakers cannot be certain exactly what color is intended.

Some linguists have found in color codability a fruitful way to experiment with the relationships between thought and language. In one such experiment, people who served as test subjects were shown a large selection of plastic squares, each colored differently. Usually, when someone sees a color, his mind stores it for a mere few moments and he can identify the color again only if he sees it almost immediately. If a delay occurs, the stored image is no longer a reliable guide because it has become faint and distorted. Yet when the squares were hidden from sight even for several minutes, the test subjects could pick out again certain colors— the high-codability ones for which the English language has convenient labels like *red, blue, yellow*, and so on. Subjects were able to remember the high-codability colors because they had simply attached common English-language words to them. In other words, they stored colors in their minds not as colors but as verbal labels for them. Even though the images had completely faded from their memories after a few moments, the subjects still remembered the verbal labels they had given the colors—and they were therefore able to identify the plastic squares again. The human being's ability to encode experience in this way is not limited to color. Similar experiments have been performed with other experiences, such as the recognition of facial expression, and the results have been the same.

Experiments like these have shown that at least one aspect of human thought—memory—is strongly influenced by language. That is not the same thing, however, as proving that man is at the mercy of his language. The convenient labels that a speech community gives to certain colors are a great aid in remembering them, but the absence of such labels does not prohibt a community from talking about the low-codability colors. When people develop a need for an expanded color vocabulary—as have artists, decorators, and fashion designers—they simply invent one. Witness the recent plethora of colors for decorating the home: *riviera blue, alpine green, lime frost, birch gray*, and so forth.

Nevertheless, the colors that a speaker "sees" often depend very much upon the language he speaks, because each language offers its own high-codability color terms. Recently, two anthropologists at the University of California, Brent Berlin and Paul Kay, have attempted to show that speech communities follow an evolutionary path in the basic color terms they offer their speakers. For example, several New Guinea tribes have in their vocabularies only two basic color words, which translate roughly as "black" (or "dark") and "white" or ("light"). A greater number of languages in widely separated areas of the world possess three color terms—and the startling fact is that they usually retain words for "black" and "white" and add the same third color, "red." The languages that have four color terms retain "black," "white," and "red"—and almost always add either "green" or "yellow." Languages with five color terms add the "green" or the "yellow" that was missed at the fourth level, with the result that nearly all such languages have words for "black" or ("dark"), "white" or ("light"), "red," "green," and "yellow," and for no other colors. Languages with six terms add a word for "blue," and those with seven terms add a word for "brown."

The completely unanticipated inference of this study is that the languages of the world, regardless of their grammars, follow an evolutionary sequence, at least so far as color terms go. A language usually does not have a word that means "brown" unless it already has the six earlier color words. A language rarely has "blue" in its vocabulary unless it already has words for both "green" and "yellow." (English, and most western European languages, Russian, Japanese, and several others add four additional color terms—"gray," "pink," "orange," and "purple"—but these languages do not do so until they already offer the seven previous color terms.) Berlin and Kay believe that a language, at any given point in time, can be assigned to only one stage of basic color terms and apparently must have passed through the prior stages in the appropriate sequence. Such regularity on the part of unrelated languages in adding color terms is astonishing, and no one has as yet offered a suitable explanation for it.

Berlin and Kay have also correlated this sequence with the general complexity of the cultures in which the languages are spoken. Languages with only the two color terms "black" and "white" are spoken in cultures at a very simple level of technology—and the only languages known to have all eleven terms are spoken in cultures with a long history of complexity. Between these two extremes are the languages of such peoples as the Tiv of Africa with three terms, the Homeric Greeks and Ibo of Africa with four terms, the Bushmen of Africa and the Eskimos of North America with five, and the Mandarin Chinese as well as the Hausa and

Nupe of Africa with six. Of course, it is understandable that cultures have more need to talk about different colors as they grow more complex. Small bands of New Guinea hunters need to evaluate the darkness of shadows which might conceal enemies or animal prey; complex European cultures need additional terms to talk about color-coded electrical circuits. Ever since Berlin and Kay put forth in 1969 their startling analysis of the basic color terms in ninety-eight languages, their findings have been under attack, primarily on the basis of questioned methodology and ethnocentric bias. But their general conclusions have also been defended by other researchers. Apparently Berlin and Kay have isolated some general truths about how people around the world talk about color and the possible evolutionary implications of language—even though neither they nor anyone else has been able to offer a suitable explanation for why languages seem to add words for colors to their vocabularies in such an orderly sequence.

Nor is the way in which a speech community rounds off its numbers haphazard; rather it is explainable as an interplay between language and culture. Americans and Englishmen have traditionally expressed excellence in sports by certain round numbers—the 4-minute mile, the 7-foot high jump, the 70-foot shot put, the .300 baseball batting average. Once a speech community has established a general range of goals of excellence that are within the realm of possibility, the exact number chosen has little to do with the objective reality of measurable goals. Instead, the community chooses an exact goal that makes sense to it linguistically in terms of the measure it uses and the way it rounds off numbers. That is why Americans and Englishmen never talk about the 3 7/8-minute mile or the 69-foot shot put.

The American-British target for the 100-yard dash is 9 seconds, but the French speech community, which uses the metric system, expresses the target as 100 meters in 10 seconds. Simple arithmetic shows that the two goals do not refer to equal distances covered in comparable amounts of time. Allowing for 10 seconds of running time, the metric race would mean covering 109.36 yards and the American-British race would mean covering 111.1 yards. Obviously, the French goal for excellence speaks about a different real distance than the American or English—simply because a Frenchman rounds off his numbers for distances and for time in a different way than English-speaking peoples do. When speakers thus round off numbers to make them manageable, they give preference to those numbers that their speech community regards as significant. Americans see nothing wrong with rounding off numbers to 4 because they are familiar with that number for measurement, as in 4 ounces in a quarter pound or 4 quarts in a gallon. A Frenchman, however, would not regard such a number as round at all; because of his familiarity with the decimal system, he would round off to 5.

A speech community's method of rounding off its numbers often bears no relation to the real situation, and it may actually work against the best interests of the community. Fishing laws in some states specify, for example, that a half a dozen trout larger than 10 inches may be caught in a day. Research by fish-management specialists might instead indicate that trout would thrive better if fishermen took 7 (not half a dozen) trout larger than 10½ (not 10) inches—but Americans round off to 6 and 10, not to 7 and 10½. The ideal speed for a stretch of highway, as scientifically determined by engineers, might be 57 miles per hour—but that number will be rounded off to a too-slow 55 or a too-fast 60 because it is customary for highway speeds to be based on the decimal system. Only one justification exists for the use of imprecise rounded numbers. The speech community has decreed that the linguistic ease of inexact combinations is preferable to the linguistic complexilty of precise numbers.

That the way speakers round off numbers is often a linguistic convenience is clearly seen by comparing English with other languages. The ancient Greeks rounded off to 60 and 360 for their high numbers; and the old Germanic languages of northern Europe used 120 to mean "many." Most of the Indian tribes in primeval California based their numbers on multiples of 5 and 10. However, at least half a dozen tribes found great significance in the number 4, no doubt because it expressed the cardinal directions. Others emphasized the number 6, which probably represented the four directions plus the above-ground and below-ground worlds. The Yuki of northern California were unique in counting in multiples of 8 and in rounding off high numbers at 64.

A misunderstanding about the way Chinese speakers round off their numbers has led many Europeans to state glibly that "in China you're a year old when you're born." That is because most European systems of stating one's age are different from the Chinese. In English, a speaker usually states his age as his most recent birthday followed by the measure *years old*. Exceptions are young children who often place their age between birthdays, as in *I'm three and a half years old*, and parents who usually express the age of infants in months and weeks. Chinese also use a round number followed by the measure *swei* in place of the English measure *years old*. Confusion has resulted because *swei* is not exactly equivalent to the English measure but rather is closer in meaning to "the number of years during all or part of which one has been alive." In the case of newborn infants, they have, according to the *swei* measure, already lived for "part" of a year—and therefore their age is *yi swei*, which English translators usually render erroneously as "one year old" instead of as "part of one year."

Each language also encourages certain kinds of place names and makes difficult the formation of others. *Golden Gate* is a typical English place name, a noun (*Gate*) modified by an adjective (*Golden*)—but *Gately Gold* is an improbable construction in English and no place is likely to bear such a name. The importance of a language's structure in determining place names was pointed out by the anthropologist Franz Boas when he compared terms used by the Kwakiutl Indians and the Eskimos. The Kwakiutl are a seafaring people of British Columbia, Canada, whose survival is based solely on what they can wrest from the Pacific Ocean and the nearby rivers. So it is no wonder that their place names rarely celebrate history or myth but instead are descriptive in order to give practical benefits in navigation and in food-gathering, such as Island at the Foot of the Mountains, Mouth of the River, Having Wind, Place for Stopping, and so on. The Kwakiutl language makes it easy to form descriptive names because suffixes can be conveniently added to stem words. For example, a Kwakiutl speaker can discriminate among a great number of different kinds of islands—Island at the Point, Island in the Middle, and so on—simply by adding the suffixes for "at the point" and "in the middle" to the stem word for "island."

The nearby Eskimos also base their culture on the sea, and so they might be expected to name places in a similar way. But they do not—because the structure of their language makes it very difficult to do so. What are suffixes in Kwakiutl are in Eskimo the very words to which suffixes are added. Eskimos cannot create the name Island at the Point because in their language "at the point" is not a suffix but a stem word to which other words are added. To describe a place as Island at the Point, the Eskimo speaker would have to put together a circumlocution much too complicated for everyday use. Furthermore, the Eskimo language offers its speakers only a limited number of suffixes to attach to stem words, whereas Kwakiutl offers a great many. The result is that Kwakiutl possesses an extraordinarily rich and poetic catalogue of place names—such as Birch Trees at the Mouth of the River and Receptacle of the North Wind, names that make one's heart yearn to visit the places they identify—whereas the Eskimo list is considerably shorter and much less metaphorical.

Eskimos do not differ significantly from Kwakiutls in intelligence, imagination, the ability to asbstract, or other mental capacities. Solely because of the structure of his language, the Eskimo fisherman is unable to talk easily about a place the Kwakiutl names Birch Trees at the Mouth of the River. If an Eskimo has no easy way to talk about a clump of birches at the mouth of a river, will he therefore be less alert to perceive that kind of a place? And is it possible that language, instead of clarifying reality, forces the Eskimo to think about the world in ways different from speakers of Kwakiutl or other languages?

Such a connection between language and thought is rooted in common-sense beliefs, but no one gave much attention to the matter before Wilhelm von Humboldt, the nineteenth-century German philologist and diplomat. He stated that the structure of a language expresses the inner life of its speakers: "Man lives with the world about him, principally, indeed exclusively, as language presents it." In this century, the case for a close relationship between language and reality was stated by Edward Sapir:

> Human beings do not live in the objective world alone, nor alone in the world of social activity as ordinarily understood, but are very much at the mercy of the particular language which has become the medium for their society. . . . The fact of the matter is that the "real world" is to a large extent built up on the language habits of the group. No two languages are ever sufficiently similar to be considered as representing the same social reality. The worlds in which different societies live are distinct worlds, not merely the same world with different labels attached.

About 1932 one of Sapir's students at Yale, Benjamin Lee Whorf drew on Sapir's ideas and began an intensive study of the language of the Hopi Indians of Arizona. Whorf's brilliant analysis of Hopi placed common sense beliefs about language and thought on a scientific basis—and it also seemed to support the view that man is a prisoner of his language. Whorf concluded that language "is not merely a reproducing instrument for voicing ideas but rather is itself the shaper of ideas. . . . We dissect nature along lines laid down by our native languages."

Whorf emphasized grammar—rather than vocabulary, which had previously intrigued scholars—as an indicator of the way a language can direct a speaker into certain habits of thought. The Eskimo speaker, for example, possesses a large and precise vocabulary to make exacting distinctions between the kinds and conditions of seals, such as "young spotted seal," "swimming male ribbon seal," and so on. But such an extensive vocabulary has less to do with the structure of the Eskimo language than with the fact that seals are important for the survival of its speakers. The Eskimo would find equally strange the distinctions that the English vocabulary makes about horses—*hare, stallion, pony, paint, appaloosa,* and so forth. And both Eskimos and Americans would be bewildered by the seventeen terms for cattle among the Masai of Africa, the twenty terms for rice among the Ifugeo of the Philippines, or the thousands of Arabic words associated with camels.

Instead of vocabulary, Whorf concentrated on the differences in structure between Hopi and the European languages—and also on what he believed were associated differences in the ways speakers of these languages viewed the world. In his analysis of plurality, for example, he noted that English uses a plural form for both *five men* and *five days.* Men and days are both nouns, but they are otherwise quite different. A speaker can see with his own eyes a group of five men, but he cannot perceive five days through any of his senses. To visualize what a day looks like, the speaker of English has to conjure up some sort of abstract picture, such as a circle, and then imagine a group of five such circles. The Hopi has no such problem. He does not rely on his imagination to provide him with plurals that cannot be detected by his senses. He would never use a cyclic noun—one that refers to "days," "years," or other units of time—in the same way that he would use an aggregate noun ("men"). His language is more precise, and he has a separate category altogether for cycles. For him, cycles do not have plurals but rather duration, and so the Hopi equivalent for the English *He stayed five days* is "He stayed until the sixth day."

Nor does the Hopi language possess tenses, which in most European languages stand time in a row as distinct units of past, present, and future. A speaker of English expresses an event that is happening in the present as *He runs* or *He is running,* but the speaker of Hopi can select from a much wider choice of present tenses, depending upon his knowledge, or lack of it, about the validity of the statement he is making: "I know that he is running at this very moment." "I know that he is running, at this moment even though I cannot see him." "I remember that I saw him running and I presume he is still running." "I am told that he is running.'"

A further contrast between the two languages concerns duration and intensity. English employs such words as *long, short,* and *slow* for duration and *much, large,* and *high* for intensity. Speakers of English, accustomed to this usage, overlook the fact that these words refer to size, shape, number, or motion— that is, they are really metaphors for space. Such a situation is quite ridiculous because duration and intensity are not spatial. Yet speakers of English unconsciously use these metaphors for space in even the simplest utterances—such as *He* SLOWLY *grasped the* POINT *of the* LONG *story* or *The* LEVEL *of the assignment was* TOO HIGH *and so the student considered it* A LOT OF *nonsense.* The Hopi language is equally striking in its avoidance of metaphors of imaginary space for qualities that are nonspatial.

After his painstaking analysis of such differences between Hopi and European languages, Whorf asked the question that was central to his research. Do the Hopi and European cultures confirm the fact that their languages conceptualize reality in different ways? And his answer was that they do. Whereas European cultures are organized in terms of space and time, the Hopi culture, Whorf believed, emphasizes events. To speakers of European languages, time is a commodity that occurs between fixed points and can be measured. Time is said to be *wasted* or *saved;* an army fighting a rear-guard action tries to *buy* time; a television station *sells* time to an advertiser. People in the European tradition keep diaries, records, accounts, and histories; their economic systems emphasize wages paid for the amount of time worked, rent for the time a dwelling is occupied, interest for the time money is loaned.

Hopi culture has none of these beliefs about time, but instead thinks of it in terms of events. Plant a seed—and it will grow. The span of time the growing takes is not the important thing, but rather the way in which the event of growth follows the event of planting. The Hopi is concerned that the sequence of events in the construction of a building be in the correct order, not that it takes a certain amount of time to complete the job. That is why the building of a Hopi house, adobe brick by adobe brick, may go on for years. Whorf's comparison of Hopi and European languages and cultures—considerably more involved than the summary I have presented—convinced him that the contrasting world views of their speakers resulted from contrasts in their languages. He concluded that, linguistically speaking, no human being is born free; his mind was made up for him from the day he was born by the language of his speech community. Whorf questioned people's ability to be objective, and he threw into doubt the rationality of everyday utterances. He suggested that all their lives English speakers have been tricked by their language into thinking along certain channels—and it is small consolation to know that the Hopi has also been tricked, but in a different way.

Whorf's theories about the relationship between culture and language have been greeted enthusiastically by some scholars and attacked or treated warily by others. The weakness of the Sapir-Whorf Hypothesis, as it has come to be known, the impossibility of generalizing about entire cultures and then attributing these generalizations to the languages spoken. The absence of clocks, calendars, and written histories obviously gave the Hopis a different view of time than that found among speakers of European languages. But such an observation is not the same thing as proving that these cultural differencs were caused by the differences between Hopi and European grammars. In fact, an interest in time-reckoning is not characteristic solely of European cultures but can be found among speakers of languages as different as Egyptian, Chinese, and Maya. And, on the other hand, thousands of unrelated speech communities share with the Hopis a lack of concern about keeping track of time. To attempt to explain cultural differences and similarities as a significant result of the languages spoken is to leave numerous facts about culture unexplained. The great religions, of the world—Judaism, Christianity, Hinduism, and Mohammedanism—have flourished among diverse peoples who speak languages with sharply different grammars. Mohammedanism, for example, has been accepted by speakers of languages with grammars as completely different as those of the Hamito-Semitic, Turkish, Indo-Iranian, Tibeto-Burman, and Malayo-Polynesian families. And the reverse is true as well. Cultures as diverse as the Aztec Empire of Mexico and the Ute hunting bands of the Great Basin spoke very closely related tongues.

Nevertheless, attempts have been made to prove the Sapir-Whorf Hypothesis, such as one experiment which used as test subjects bilingual Japanese women, living in San Francisco, who had married American servicemen. The women spoke English to their husbands, children, and neighbors, and in most everyday speech situations; they spoke Japanese whenever they came together to gossip, reminisce, and discuss the news from home. Each Japanese woman thus inhabited two language worlds—and according to the predictions of the hypothesis, the women should think differently in each of these worlds. The experiment consisted of two visits to each woman by a bilingual Japanese interviewer. During the first interview he chatted with them only in Japanese; during the second he carried on the same discussion and asked the same questions in English. The results were quite unremarkable;

they showed that the attitudes of each woman differed markedly, depending upon whether she spoke Japanese or English. Here, for example, is the way the same woman completed the same sentences at the two intervivews:

> "When my wishes conflict with my family's . . .
> . . . it is a time of great unhappiness," (Japanese)
> . . . I do what I want." (English)
> "Real friends should . . .
> . . . help each other." (Japanese)
> . . . be very frank." (English)

Clearly, major variables in the experiment had been eliminated— since the women were interviewed twice by the same person in the same location of their homes, and they discussed the same topics—with but one exception. And that sole exception was language. The drastic differences in attitudes of the women could be accounted for only by the language world each inhabited when she spoke.

The Sapir-Whorf Hypothesis also predicts that language makes its speakers intellectually lazy. They will categorize new experiences in the well-worn channels they have been used to since birth, even though these channels might appear foolish to an outsider. The language spoken by the Western Apaches of Arizona, for example, has long had its own channels for classifying the parts of the human body, a system which ignores certain distinctions made in other languages and which makes different ones of its own. Then, about 1930, a new cultural item, the automobile, was introduced into the Apache reservation. An automobile, surely, is different from a human body, yet the Apaches simply applied their existing classification for the human body to the automobile. The chart on the next page lists approximate pronunciations of the Apache words for the parts of the human body, the way they are categorized—and the way their meanings were extended to classify that new cultural item, the automobile.

Many linguists nowadays are wary of the Sapir-Whorf Hypothesis. Research that has attempted to confirm the hypothesis, such as the experiment with the Japanese women or the study of Apache terms for the automobile, is usually regarded as fascinating examples rather than as universal truths about the way speech communities view the world. Neither Whorf nor any of his followers has proven to everyone's satisfaction that differences between two speech communities in their capacity to understand external reality are based entirely or even overwhelmingly on differences in their languages. Whorf overemphasized one point (that languages differ in what can be said in them) at the expense of a greater truth (that they differ as to what is *relatively easy* to express in them). Languages, rather than causing cultural differences between speech communities, seem instead to reflect the different cultural concerns of their speakers. The history of language is not so much the story of people misled by their languages as it is the story of a successful struggle against the limitations built into all language systems. The Western Apache system for classifying the human body did not lock them into certain habitual patterns of thought that prevented them from understanding the automobile. In fact, the existence of these patterns may have aided the Apaches in making sense out of that new cultural item.

The true value of Whorf's theories is not the one he worked so painstakingly to demonstrate—that language tryannizes speakers by forcing them to think in certain ways. Rather, his work, emphasized something of even greater importance: the close alliance between language and the total culture of the speech community. No linguist today doubts that language and culture interpenetrate one another; nor does any linguist fail to pay due respect to Whorf for emphasizing this fact.

APACHE WORDS FOR PARTS OF THE HUMAN BODY AND THE AUTOMOBILE

EXTERNAL ANATOMY	HUMAN ANATOMICAL TERMS	EXTENDED AUTO MEANINGS
daw	"chin and jaw"	"front bumper"
wos	"shoulder"	"front fender"
gun	"hand and arm"	"front wheel"
kai	"thigh and buttocks"	"rear fender"
ze	"mouth"	"gas-pipe opening"
ke	"foot"	"rear wheel"
chun	"back"	"chassis"
inda	"eye"	"headlight"
FACE		
chee	"nose"	"hood"
ta	"forehead"	"auto top"
ENTRAILS		
tsaws	"vein"	"electrical wiring"
zik	"liver"	"battery"
pit	"stomach"	"gas tank"
chih	"intestine"	"radiator hose"
jih	"heart"	"distributor"
jisoleh	"lung"	"radiator"

Postscript

The subject of communication theory is not located within any particular niche, nook, or cranny of academic inquiry. In fact, critical considerations have no distinctive location or fixed boundaries. To study viable conceptions of human communication is to become an active participant in what transpires across the life span. Applied social knowledge qualifies as a vital enterprise. One may gain entrance as an astute observer of how other persons interact across a wide array of social contexts. One may decide to exit from the public sphere to reflect, see, and imagine how collective endeavors begin, change, or end in multiple ways that make things better or keep them from getting worse. The expansive generation of informed conceptions of human communication is best conceived as a busy intersection. Theory is directed toward a careful analysis of a rich confluence of people, places, and things. Human inquiry, therefore, is not constructed in the manner of a housing project, a gated community, or a seaside resort. What transpires when speaking subjects engage in shared activities is everyone's business because each participant and every observer have a personal stake in how things turn out.

Index